CHINA'S ECONOMIC MIRACLE

www.royalcollins.com

CHINA'S ECONOMIC MIRACLE

Experiences for Russia and the World

Sergei Glazyev

Translated by Zhang Zhen

RC

Books Beyond Boundaries

ROYAL COLLINS

China's Economic Miracle: Experiences for Russia and the World

Sergei Glazyev
Translated by Zhang Zhen

First published in 2024 by Royal Collins Publishing Group Inc.
Groupe Publication Royal Collins Inc.
550-555 boul. René-Lévesque O Montréal (Québec) H2Z1B1 Canada

ISBN: 978-1-4878-1217-1

To find out more about our publications, please visit www.royalcollins.com.

Contents

Section 5   The China-Russia Strategic Partnership as the Basis for a GEP and the Emergence of a New MHI

Abbreviations

ADBC	Agricultural Development Bank of China
AEI	American Enterprise Institute
AIIB	Asian Infrastructure Investment Bank
AIPV	American Indo-Pacific Vision Initiative
ASD	asteroid-space danger
ASEAN	Association of Southeast Asian Nations
ASYCUDA	Automated System for Customs Data Processing
B&R	Belt and Road
BRI	Belt and Road Initiative
BRICS	Brazil, Russia, India, China, and South Africa
CDB	China Development Bank
CEECs	Central and Eastern European countries
CPC	Communist Party of China
CMEA	Council for Mutual Economic Assistance
CPSU	Communist Party of the Soviet Union
CSTO	Collective Security Treaty Organization
DIC	defence industry complex
EAEU	Eurasian Economic Union

ECB	European Central Bank
EDB	Eurasian Development Bank
EU	European Union
FD	fiduciary money
FDI	Foreign Direct Investment
FRS	Federal Reserve System
G20	The Group of Twenty
GDP	gross domestic product
GEP	Greater Eurasian Partnership
GES	Global Economic Structure
GMO	genetically modified organism
IMF	International Monetary Fund
LED	light-emitting diode
NATO	North Atlantic Treaty Organization
NEP	New Economic Policy
NPC	National People's Congress
PBC	People's Bank of China
R&D	Research and Development
SCCA	systemic cycles of capital accumulation
SCO	Shanghai Cooperation Organization
SDR	Special Drawing Rights
SWIFT	Society for Worldwide Interbank Financial Telecommunication
TO	Technical Orders
TP	Technical Principles
UNCTAD	United Nations Conference on Trade and Development
USSR	Union of Soviet Socialist Republics
US	United States
WEM	world economic modes
WEO	World Economic Order

Introduction

C HINA'S ECONOMIC MIRACLE IS STILL TO BE INTERPRETED. IN THE WEST, IT has been ignored for a long time. Even after China overtook the United States in terms of gross domestic product (GDP) in purchasing power parity in 2014, the Western media still refers to the economy of China as "the second largest in the world." Fortunately for China, the American ruling elite has underestimated China's achievements throughout the years of China's unprecedented economic recovery, catching up with sanctions and the trade war against China too late. China has already become the undisputed economic leader of the 21st century. At the same time, the American ruling elite cannot reconcile themselves to the loss of the world leadership. To recognize that all their attempts to restrain the development of the PRC with trade wars, sanctions, and menacing shouts have no result—the PRC is consistently ahead of the United States in an increasing number of economic, scientific, technological, and social development indicators.

In their effort to sow confusion and destabilize the social and political situation in the PRC, the American intelligence services organized an act of provocation to infect the population of China with the coronavirus synthesized on their demand. However, the PRC leadership quickly coped with the threat, demonstrating to the world an example of an effective state sanitary and epidemiological, as well as information policy, while the United States was unable to adequately resist the epidemic. Without resorting to casuistry, let us operate with the most revealing figures: the number of recorded deaths as of May 2, 2022, is 5,092 in China and

993,733 in the United States, with a population of the latter 4.5 times less than in China. Given that China finished 2020 with a GDP growth of 2.3%, while the United States had a fall in GDP by the same 2.3%. This digital "mirror" clearly illustrates the comparative effectiveness of the state institutions of the United States and China—the leaders of the outdated outgoing and new progressive world economic structures, respectively. The Communist Party of China (CPC) was able to instantly mobilize the entire management system to level out pandemic shocks, while the American establishment was unable to cope with the equally complex phenomena. Moreover, irrespective of the party determining the dominant line in Washington—"donkeys" or "elephants"—hundreds of thousands of deaths of their own citizens and thrashing of the oversaturated with money economy become a derivative of their policy.

Even two years ago, anyone, including your humble servant, who pointed to the obvious artificial origin of the global infection, was almost ostracized, but now with the discovery of the network of American biological laboratories that worked, among other things with bat and birds' viruses, in Ukraine by the Russian military, no one doubts that COVID-19 and its variants were synthesized by the demand of the American government and intelligence services. The latter, obsessed with misanthropic and racist motives, have been organizing and funding research on the transmission of viruses from bats to humans for at least 20 years, editing its genome accordingly. And all this was done in the countries whose populations are genetically close to Russia and China. We became the first countries against which biological weapons were used. We were able to repel with honor this attack of the extravagant American ruling and financial elite, who live and act based on their invented exclusivity and with the aim of achieving world hegemony by any means.

And in other areas of ensuring national security, China successfully repels the attacks of the United States, which is powerless to restrain China's development. In response to the attempts to destabilize the social and political situation in the PRC through the "soft power" of information and cognitive technologies, the Chinese created their own social networks, fencing themselves off from the hostile information space on the Internet with the "Great Firewall of China." The cyberterrorism of American intelligence agencies is successfully fended off by Chinese specialists. In response to the sanctions against Chinese high-tech companies, the PRC leadership is rapidly developing its own science and technology base, declaring the achievement of self-sufficiency in this area as the most important priority of the current five-year period.

There is no doubt that the ambitious goal of making the PRC a leading scientific and technological power will be fulfilled in the same way as the previous strategic goals of overcoming poverty and ensuring the average, by world standards, the prosperity of the Chinese population was achieved. For half a century since Deng Xiaoping's reform and opening-up policy, China has made an unprecedented leap from deep backwardness to the world leader in terms of output volume and economic development. The population moved from huts to the best cities in the world in terms of the urban environment quality. Unpaved country roads have been replaced by high-speed rails and highways. From a predominantly agricultural country with prevailing manual labor, China has become a world leader in the field of intellectualization and robotization of production. The once illiterate population today, almost without exception, has a higher or vocational secondary education. And this amazing leap in the development of the world's largest country in terms of population occurred in just two generations.

I first visited China in 1991 and was shocked by the flow of cyclists moving through the wide streets of Beijing early in the morning heading to work. Next to my hotel, a large building that was literally surrounded by many workers day and night was under construction. In 1994, I was invited to the South of China. The Pudong territory was under development in Shanghai; in the countryside, the peasants were still moving by horse-drawn vehicles; in Shenzhen, the Huawei company, which assembled telephone exchanges, was located in a small building. Hong Kong skyscrapers could be seen far on the horizon against the backdrop of undeveloped grassy land. When Chinese comrades were telling us about the plans for the development of these territories, we were smiling and considered them naive dreamers and their stories—a dream. Twenty years later, when I arrived in China at the invitation of the government, I was shocked. The dream had come true right before our very eyes. Under the leadership of the CPC, the people of China performed a miracle. It is hard to believe if you do not see with your own eyes the largest, most technologically advanced, and most comfortable metropolis in the world that grew out of the Shanghai slums, if you do not visit the world's best gadget manufacturers in cozy Shenzhen, if you do not take the world's fastest trains, do not visit transforming buildings, do not see with your own eyes unmanned electric vehicles with solar panels, and do not personally experience the grandiose scale of modern Chinese industry.

The people of China enthusiastically support their government, drawing on their personal experience of improving the standard and quality of life. I had an opportunity to communicate with the Chinese of different generations. The older generation proudly talks about how hard they worked to create today's well-being. The middle generation is passionate about their work in business, science, and production, working from morning to night without days off, fulfilling their potential in creative activities. The younger generation is already full of dignity, indulging themselves with consumer goods and a critical attitude toward a completely comfortable reality. With the growth of the standard of living and life expectancy, there appear new demographic restrictions on economic growth, previously unknown in China: the aging of the population and the decline in the birth rate below sub-replacement fertility, which leads to a reduction and, consequently, a termination of the growth of the working-age population. The period of super-high growth rates of production is replaced by a phase of maturity, in which declining rates of economic growth are accompanied by an increase in its quality. The political leadership sets the tasks of improving the quality of the environment, increasing the comfort of urban life, and prioritizing the development of healthcare and education.

Today, the PRC provides more than half of the world's GDP growth, being the most powerful locomotive of global economic development. If the current trends continue, China will retain this leading role until the middle of this century. The management system created in China is becoming a role model in many countries. The grand project of the Belt and Road (B&R) implemented by the Chinese government involves dozens of countries in joint investments based on the principles of mutual benefit from the combination of competitive advantages while unconditionally respecting the principles of national sovereignty. The combined power of China's development institutions and the scale of their application to finance investment in the development of both Chinese and joint ventures far exceeds the investment mechanisms of international cooperation available to other countries. China is becoming a leader in the formation of the new international economic order. This happens due to a qualitatively more effective system for managing economic development, created by the Chinese leadership in comparison with the leaders of the last century—the US (United States) and the USSR (Union of Soviet Socialist Republics).

All "objective" explanations of high growth rates of the Chinese economy by its initial backwardness are no longer relevant and are only to some extent fair. Partially, they ignore the main thing—the creative approach of the Chinese leadership to building a new system of industrial relations, which, as the Chinese economy takes first place in the world, is becoming more and more self-sufficient and attractive. The Chinese themselves call their system socialist, while developing private enterprise and applying the mechanisms of market competition. The leaders of the CPC continue building socialism, avoiding ideological clichés. They prefer to formulate tasks in terms of national well-being, setting goals for overcoming poverty and creating a society of average prosperity, subsequently reaching the world's highest quality of life. At the same time, they try to avoid excessive social inequality by maintaining the labor basis for the national income distribution and orienting the institutions of economic regulation toward productive activities and long-term investments in productive forces development.

It is the progressiveness of the system of management created in the PRC that explains the economic miracle of China. A hundred years ago, a similar economic miracle began in the USSR, and the US created systems for managing economy development that were qualitatively superior in efficiency to the old capitalist economy organization of the colonial European empires. With completely opposite political forms, the systems for managing the economy development through large vertically integrated structures, the expanded reproduction of which was financed by the unlimited emission of fiduciary money (FD), were similar. The bipolar imperial world economic structure created on their basis ensured the development of the world economy until the collapse of the USSR, and after the collapse, the transition to a new world economic structure, the core of which was the PRC, began.

The hypothesis on which we base this book lies in the fact that long-term global economic development is cyclical and helical. It combines half-century-long waves of economic conjuncture discovered by N. D. Kondratieff[1] and secular systemic cycles of capital accumulation (SCCA) discovered by G. Arrighi,[2] which are based on life cycles of technological and world economic orders, respectively.

The use of the concept of "order" is intended to reflect the reproducing integrity of interrelated elements: industries connected by technological cooperation (technological order) and economic entities united by institutions (world economic order). The interconnection of elements predetermines their life cycles synchronization, at least in the phase of maturity and decline, as well as the intermittent nature of economic development, where numerous elements periodically change simultaneously, acquiring a spasmodic nature of technological (when technological orders change) and social (when world economic orders change) revolutions.

We define the technological order[3] as groups of technologically related industries aggregates that are distinguished in the technological structure of the economy, connected with each other by the same type of technological chains and forming reproducible integrity. Each order is a holistic and sustainable formation, within which a complete macro-production cycle is carried out, including extracting and getting primary resources, all stages of their processing, and manufacturing of a set of end products that satisfy the corresponding type of public consumption.

We have defined the world economic order as *a system of interrelated international and national institutions that ensure the reproduction of the economy and determine the mechanism of international economic relations.* The change of secular cycles of capital accumulation occurs as a result of the completion of the life cycle of the corresponding world economic order and the formation of a new one. They can also be defined as systems for managing the development of the economy with a typical structure of power and economic relations.

The processes of formation and change of technological and world economic orders can be interpreted in terms of the concepts of productive forces and relations of production applied in historical materialism. According to the classical definition, productive forces are the material factors and technologies necessary to transform raw materials into products (goods). Relations of production are relations that are formed between people in the process of production, exchange, distribution, and consumption of material goods. There is a deep internal connection between productive forces and relations of production, mediated by the systems of control of man-machine production and technological systems.[4]

The Marxist paradigm of history periodization was based on the idea of the interaction between productive forces and relations of production as a dialectical process of unfolding the contradiction between them. According to this idea, if the relations of production correspond to the nature of the productive forces, they contribute to the development of the latter and move them forward. However, at a certain stage, the productive forces outgrow the established relations of production, which turn into their fetters. There arises a *conflict* between the productive forces and relations of production. The conflict finds its expression in the aggravation of social and political contradictions and serves as the basis for a *social revolution* that destroys outdated relations of production and replaces them with new ones, giving scope for the development of productive forces.

According to K. Marx, "At a certain stage of development, the material productive forces of society come into conflict with the existing relations of production or—this merely expresses the same thing in legal terms—with the property relations within the framework of which they have operated hitherto. From forms of development of the productive forces, these relations turn into their fetters. Then, an era of social revolution begins. The changes in the economic foundation lead sooner or later to the transformation of the whole immense superstructure. In studying such transformations, it is always necessary to distinguish between the material transformation of the economic conditions of production, which can be determined with the precision of natural science, and the legal, political, religious, artistic, or philosophic—in short, ideological forms in which men become conscious of this conflict and fight it out. Just as one does not judge an individual by what he thinks about himself, so one cannot judge such a period of transformation by its consciousness, but, on the contrary, this consciousness must be explained from the contradictions of material life, from the conflict existing between the social forces of production and the relations of production. No social order is ever destroyed before all the productive forces it requires have been developed, and new superior relations of production never replace older ones before the material conditions for their existence have matured within the framework of the old society. Mankind thus inevitably sets itself only such tasks as it is able to solve, since closer examination will always show that the problem itself arises only when the material conditions for its solution are already present or at least in the course of formation. ..."[5]

In the underlying this book, the theory of long-term economic development as a process of periodic change in technological and world economic orders, technological and socio-political revolutions are distinguished. Technological revolutions reflect qualitative changes in the composition of the productive forces, while socio-political revolutions reflect the content of relations of production. They do not always coincide since the cycles of change in technological and world economic orders differ in their duration. The rigidity of the relations of production is significantly higher than the technological relations of productive forces and, as a result, the life cycle of the world economic order is much longer than the technological one. Two technological orders fit into one life cycle of the world economic order.[6] The once-in-a-century overlap of these two cyclical processes in the phase of crisis creates a dangerous resonance that leads to the destruction of the entire system of world economic and political relations. During such periods, there is a sharp destabilization of the system of international relations, as well as the destruction of the old and the formation of a new world order. The possibilities of socio-economic development based on the existing system of institutions and technologies are exhausted. The previously leading countries encounter insurmountable difficulties in maintaining the same rates of economic growth. The overaccumulation of capital in obsolete production and technological complexes plunges their economy into depression, and the existing system of institutions complicates the formation of new technological chains. Along with new institutions of production organization, they are making their way in other countries, striving to become the leaders of economic development.

The institutions of the leading country, which have a dominant influence on international norms governing the world market and international trade, economic and financial relations, are of key importance for the formation of the structure of power and business relations of each world economic order. Each such order has limits to its growth, determined by the accumulation of internal contradictions within the framework of the reproduction of its constituent institutions. The development of these contradictions continues until the destabilization of the system of international economic and political relations and has so far been resolved by world wars. The latter was organized and incited by the leading country losing its dominant position in the obsolete world economic order to strengthen control over the periphery of the world economy to strengthen its competitive advantages and weaken the positions of possible competitors. From among the latter, however, a new leader, who was the bearer of a more progressive system of institutions and industrial relations, always appeared. Until the last moment, the new leader evaded participation in the war to enter the final stage in the camp of the winners and seize global leadership.

The former leaders seek to maintain dominance in the world market by strengthening control over their geo-economic "periphery," including the methods of military and political coercion. As a rule, this entails world wars in which the obsolete leader wastes resources without achieving the desired effect. Having taken dominant positions, the potential new leader tries to take a wait-and-see attitude to preserve its productive forces and attract the minds, capitals, and treasures of the fighting countries fleeing the war. Increasing its capabilities, the new leader enters the world stage when the warring rivals are weakened enough to appropriate the fruits of victory. Simultaneously with the change of the world leader, the institutions of the new world economic order are expanding, ensuring the retention of the existing material and technical achievements and creating new opportunities for the development of the productive forces of society.

It is this transitional period, combining technological and social revolution, that is currently taking place. The imperial world economic order, whose destruction began with the collapse of the USSR, is fading into the past. At present, its second center, the US, which is the core of the American systemic cycle of capital accumulation, is being destroyed. The world economic system is moving to the Asian cycle of capital accumulation, which is based on an integral world economic order.[7]

The integral world economic order of the Asian century cycle of accumulation is characterized by a combination of institutions of state planning and market self-organization, state control over the main parameters of the economy reproduction and free enterprise system, and the ideology of the common good and private initiative. At the same time, the forms of political structure may differ fundamentally. The priority of public interests over private ones remains unchanged, which is expressed in strict mechanisms of personal responsibility of citizens for conscientious behavior, the precise performance of their duties, compliance with laws, and serving national goals.

The primacy of public interests over private ones is expressed in the institutional structure of economic regulation characteristic of the new world economic order. First of all, it is expressed in state control over the key parameters of capital reproduction through the mechanisms of planning, lending, subsidizing, pricing, and regulating the basic conditions of entrepreneurial activity. At the same time, the state does not so much give orders as it plays the role of a moderator, forming mechanisms for social partnership and interaction between the main social groups. Officials do not try to manage entrepreneurs but organize the joint work of the business, scientific, and engineering communities to form common development goals and develop methods for achieving them. Entrepreneurs, in turn, inscribe the motive of maximizing profits and enrichment into ethical norms that protect the interests of society. The use of businesses that are not profit-maximizing but have social value is expanding, such as the creation and development of non-profit organizations, incubators, and Islamic and Orthodox banking. Cash flows are managed with ethical standards in mind and restrictions placed on criminal and immoral activities financing. The mechanisms of state regulation of the economy also follow these principles.

The state ensures the provision of a long-term and cheap loan, and businessmen guarantee its goal-oriented application in specific investment projects to develop production. The state provides access to the infrastructure and services of natural monopolies at low prices, and enterprises are responsible for the production of competitive products. To improve the product quality, the state organizes and finances the necessary R&D (Research and Development), as well as staff education and training, and entrepreneurs implement innovations and invest in new technologies. The public-private partnership is subordinated to the public interests of economic development, improving national welfare and the quality of life. The ideology of international cooperation changes accordingly—the model of liberal globalization in the interests of the world financial oligarchy is replaced by the paradigm of sustainable development for the benefit of all mankind. The role and significance of money, around the accumulation of which in the hands of the ruling elite of the dominant states revolved all the secular cycles of capital accumulation, changes as well. In the new world economic order, money becomes a tool for ensuring the reproduction and development of the economy in the public interest.

Combining state planning and market self-organization, state control over money flow and private enterprise and integrating the interests of all social groups around the goal of improving public welfare, the PRC has demonstrated a record growth rate of investment and innovation activity and has been leading the world in economic growth for more than thirty years. Despite the five-fold increase in the volume of dollars over the past decade, the economy in the US continues to stagnate, while China combines the maximum levels of economy monetization, savings rates, and economic growth rates. Focused on maximizing current profits, the American financial oligarchy is clearly inferior in terms of efficiency in managing the development of the economy to the Chinese communists, who use market mechanisms to increase national welfare through increased production and investment.

China is a leader in the formation of a new world economic order, creatively using the experience of both Soviet socialism and Western capitalism. The Chinese communists were able to draw the right conclusions from the collapse of the rigidly centralized system of managing the socialist economy, having altered it to market mechanisms of self-organization. It is notable that centralized management was preserved in the financial sector, infrastructure, and basic industries, which created general conditions for the growth of the business sector. This gave the economy dynamism, and the managerial resources released from routine planning procedures were focused on strategic management and harmonization of various interests, ensuring the reproduction of the economy of social groups. Unlike the Soviet one, the Chinese system of economic management has learned to rebuild it technologically and institutionally, shutting down obsolete production in time, cutting off inefficient enterprises from resources, and helping the best workers master the latest technologies.

The Chinese approach to constructing a market economy is fundamentally different from the Russian one in its pragmatism and creative approach to reforms. They are based not on doctrinal patterns but on practical experience in managing the economy. Like engineers designing a new car, Chinese leaders consistently develop new relations of production by solving specific problems, conducting experiments, and selecting the best options. Patiently, step by step, they are building market socialism, constantly improving the system of public administration, and distinguishing only those institutions that work for the development of the economy and the improvement of public welfare. Preserving the achievements of socialism, the Chinese Communists include regulators of market relations in the system of public administration and supplement forms of state ownership with private and collective ones in such a way as to achieve an increase in the efficiency of the economy in the interests of the whole nation.

As already stated, the rapid economic growth of China, which continues during the global financial recession and the subsequent stagnation of the world economy, can be explained by the efficiency of managing the development of the national economic system. It combines strategic and indicative plans with targeted lending for investment projects and programs, on the one hand, and market competition in an open economy environment with selective state regulation, on the other. Strategic planning indicates promising areas of economic development based on long-term forecasts of scientific and technological progress and comprehension of the possibilities for the advanced development of the Chinese economy within the global framework. Indicative planning provides guidelines for the activities of state authorities at all levels to create conditions for increasing investment activity to expand production and improve the standards of living of the population. It also provides entrepreneurs with the opportunity to take advantage of these conditions. Market competition ensures efficiency, and targeted lending provides financing for the implementation of investment projects and the achievement of planned goals. State regulation stimulates business activity for expanded production and restrains its destructive manifestations (export of capital, financial pyramids, etc.). Openness enables the import of advanced technologies and the export of end products, encouraging entrepreneurs to increase their product competitiveness.

The core of the entire system of Chinese economy regulation is the comprehensive stimulation of investment and innovation activity. The key role is played by the public sector, which is based on the national banking system that generates credit for indicative plans for the growth of investment and production; transport and energy infrastructure whose development is prioritized in state plans; state corporations concentrating resources for the scientific and technological development of the economy as well as for the development and implementation of advanced technologies. The driving force of development is public investment, which is followed by an increase in private investment: entrepreneurs respond by increasing business activity to reduce risks and use public infrastructure. Later, with the growth of production, incomes, and savings of the population increased, creating an incremental cash flow for funding new investments. At the same time, the People's Bank of China (PBC) continues credit expansion through state banks and development institutions to meet the investment needs of modernization and expansion of production, as stated in the indicative plans of the government, provinces, cities, towns, and corporations. The financial investment platforms created for this purpose make it possible to reduce risks and ensure that the credit resources issued by the PBC are directed into the development of promising industries in accordance with government priorities.

The Chinese themselves call their system socialism while at the same time developing private entrepreneurship and using market competition. The CPC leadership continues building socialism, eschewing ideological clichés. They prefer to formulate tasks in terms of the national welfare, setting goals for poverty alleviation and the building of a moderately prosperous society, subsequently improving people's lives. They try to avoid excessive social inequality by maintaining the labor basis of the distribution of national income and orienting the institutions of economic regulation toward productive activity and long-term investments in the development of productive forces. This is a common feature of the countries that form the "core" of the new world economic order.

China's economic miracle is a vivid example of the embodiment of the theory of convergence of the capitalist and socialist systems—the antipodes of the previous world economic order. The dialectical synthesis of the opposing relations of production, based on the selection of constructive mechanisms for economic development, has given an astonishing result in the formation of a new world economic order.

The formation of a new world economic order entails the reform of the world economic order and international relations. The revival of social and economic development planning and state regulation of the main parameters of capital reproduction, pro-active industrial policy, and control over cross-border capital flows and currency control from a "menu" prohibited by Washington financial institutions is turning into generally accepted instruments of international economic relations. In contrast to the "Washington Consensus," a number of scientists started talking about the "Beijing Consensus," which is much more attractive for developing countries, where the majority of human population lives.[8] It is based on the principles of non-discrimination and mutual respect for the sovereignty and national interests of the cooperating states, focusing not on serving international capital but on raising national welfare. At the same time, a new regime for the protection of intellectual property rights and technology transfer may arise, new rules for international trade in energy and resources as well as for international migration are likely to be adopted, and new agreements to limit harmful emissions, etc. may be concluded.

The approach to international politics characteristic of the core countries of the new world economic order (refusal to interfere in internal affairs, refusal to military intervention, and trade embargoes) provides developing countries with a real alternative to the US-centric liberal globalization based on building equal and mutually beneficial relations.[9] Many of them are gradually drawn into the formation of an integral world economic order, building an effective system of international cooperation with its core countries. The center of world development is moving to Southeast Asia, which gives a number of researchers an opportunity to talk about the beginning of a new Asian century-old cycle of capital accumulation.[10]

That is the reason why the study of China's experience of economic development based on the principles of the new world economic order, which we have called integral, is of great importance for the whole world. While this book is written primarily for the Chinese reader, its observations and conclusions will be useful to policymakers in countries wishing to replicate China's economic miracle.

NOTES

1. N. D. Kondratieff, "On the Notion of Economic Statics, Dynamics and Fluctuations," 1989; N. D. Kondratieff, *Basic Problems of Economic Statics and Dynamics* (M.: Ekonomika); N. D. Kondratieff, *Large Cycles of Conjuncture and the Theory of Foreseeing. Selected Works* (M.: Ekonomika, 2002).

2. G. Arrighi, *The Long Twentieth Century: Money, Power and the Origins of Our Times* (London: Verso, 1994).

3. Scientific discovery "Regularity of Technological Orders Change in the Process of the World and National Economies Development" (registration certificate No. 65-S issued by the International Academy of Authors of Scientific Discoveries and Inventions).

4. N. A. Tsagolov, ed., *A Course of Political Economy*, 2 vols. (M.: Economika, 1973), 59.

5. K. Marx, "A Contribution to the Critique of Political Economy," in *K. Marx, F. Engels, Essays*, vol. 13 (Moscow: State Publishing House of Political Literature, 1961), 8.

6. A. Aivazov and V. Belikov, "Economic Foundations of the Civilizational Waves of Human Development," *Partnership of Civilizations*, no. 3–4 (2016).

7. G. Arrighi, *The Long Twentieth Century: Money, Power and the Origins of Our Time* (M.: Publishing House Territory of the Future, 2006).

8. J. C. Ramo, "The Beijing Consensus," The Foreign Policy Centre, 2004; "The Beijing Consensus: An Alternative Approach to Development," World Foresight Forum, The Hague, The Netherlands, 2011, Issue Brief No. 02.

9. J. C. Ramo, "The Beijing Consensus," London: The Foreign Policy Centre, 2004.

10. G. Arrighi, *The Long Twentieth Century: Money, Power and the Origins of Our Times*; A. Aivazov, "Periodic System of World Capitalist Development" *Almanac Development and Economics*, no. 2 (March 2012).

SECTION 1

The Origin of China's Economic Miracle

The first section analyses the tremendous breakthrough in the economic development of the PRC at the end of the last century when the basis for the modern Chinese economic miracle was formed. In this period, the economy of Russia and other post-Soviet republics plunged into chaos. The result of the "shock therapy" carried out by them, which laid in a sharp dismantling of all elements of the socialist economy with the expectation of the automatic inclusion of market mechanisms— was an economic collapse. Against this background, the rapid rise of the Chinese economy, which preserved the supporting structures of strategic planning, price regulation, and money circulation, as well as state ownership and socialist ideology in its regulation, looked like a real miracle. At the same time, as well as in the post-Soviet space, market reforms were carried out in the PRC. However, they were not slumping but manageable: while maintaining socialist institutions for regulating economic reproduction, market mechanisms of competition and pricing were gradually growing, directive planning was smoothly transformed into strategic one, and ministries were carefully transformed into corporations, supplemented by a network of private enterprises. Unlike the primitive and highly ideological "shock therapy" in the former Soviet republics and the simple absorption of the Eastern European socialist countries by transnational corporations, the reform of the Chinese economy was carried out in a controlled manner in an evolutionary and pragmatic way. This section analyses the fundamental differences between the transition to a market economy in the PRC and the USSR and compares its results.

CHAPTER 1

China's Economic Breakthrough in the Late 20th Century

1.1 Overall Performance

In the years since the founding of the PRC in 1949, and especially in the last 22 years (1979–2000), monumental changes have taken place in the Chinese economy. From an extremely backward, semi-feudal, semi-colonial country with a national economy destroyed by many years of wars, China has become one of the largest industrial and agrarian states in the world. After the economic recovery in 1952, for the period of 26 years (1953–1978), the national income production increased by more than 4.5 times, and in 22 years (1979–2000) of new reforms, by another 7.4 times. In terms of total GDP, when calculated at purchasing power parity, China became the world's second-largest economy after the US.

Except for the failed second Five-Year Plan (1958-1962) and three years (1967, 1968, 1976) of the "Cultural Revolution," when the production volume fell below the previous year's indicators,[1] all other years the Chinese economy grew, sometimes at a very high pace (see Table 1). The average annual growth rate of the national income in 1953–1978 was 6.9%, and the GDP growth rate in 1979–2000 was 9.5%. Subsequently, China demonstrated the highest economic growth rates in the world.

Table 1   China's GDP Annual Growth Rates in Five-Year Plans (as %)

Five-year plans, years	GGDP	Agriculture (1st area)	Industry and construction (2nd area)	Including Transportation, telecommunications, trade, and other services (3rd area)
1st, 1953–1957	8.9	3.7	19.4	9.7
2nd, 1958–1962	3.1	-5.9	1.0	-0.8
Recovery period, 1963–1965	4.7	11.5	21.0	6.9
3rd, 1966–1970	8.3	2.6	12.3	3.8
4th, 1971–1975	5.5	3.0	8.8	4.6
5th, 1976–1980	6.1	0.7	9.4	7.4
6th, 1981–1985	0.7	8.2	10.0	15.2
7th, 1986–1990	7.9	4.2	9.0	9.4
8th, 1991–1995	2.0	4.2	17.4	10.0
9th, 1996–2000	8.3	3.5	10.0	7.8

Source: China Statistical Yearbook (Beijing, 2000), 55; China Statistical Abstract (1999), 14–16; Economic Daily, March 1, 2001.

The factors of China's economic growth also include the following:[2]

(1) Labor supply (it is estimated that its potential is formed from the rural population) and extensive human resources

(2) Drop in unemployment and comparable labor costs

(3) Potential for women's employment

(4) Political development

(5) Effective leadership of the country and responsible approach of the CPC

(6) Sustained "reform and opening-up"

(7) Continuity of economic development and following its main phases (which, among others, include import substitution and export orientation)

(8) Foreign direct investment (FDI) and special economic zones

(9) Development of private entrepreneurship

(10) Energy supply and alternative energy sources

(11) Infrastructure investment

(12) Economic diversification

(13) Developing the sphere of education and improving its quality

(14) Continued implementation of the Going Global strategy

(15) Specific geopolitics

(16) Solving the problem of raw materials saturation

(17) Loyalty to traditions and preservation of core values

Meanwhile, from the data given in Table 2 and in Figure 1, it can be seen that in the last century, the PRC economy developed unevenly. Moreover, the amplitude of oscillations was large. In 1961, for example, the decline in the national income production amounted to 29.7%. In 1967 and 1968, the decline in rates compared with 1966 amounted to 24.2%.[3] After 1978, the Chinese economy did not experience such deep swings in growth rates. Nevertheless, accelerations and decelerations in the dynamics of growth continued. There are currently nine notable cyclical upswings and downswings in the PRC economy.

Such vigorous, albeit uneven, growth required the mobilization of vast natural, material, and financial resources, as well as the physical and moral effort of the vast majority of the population. Table 3 demonstrates indicators of investment activity that explain the high and sometimes very high rates of economic growth. The main source of accelerated growth is the high savings rate. From nine Five-Year Plans, it exceeded 30% in seven Five-Year Plans, and in the 8th Five-Year Plan, it almost reached 40%.[4]

Table 2   Economic Growth Cycles of the PRC as Exemplified by Growth Rate of
GDP Production

Cycles	Years	%	Cycles	Years	%
I	1953	14.0	VI	1977	7.8
	1954	5.8		1978	11.7
	1955	6.4		1979	7.6
	1956	14.1		1980	7.8
	1957	4.5		1981	5.2
II	1958	22.0	VII	1982	9.1
	1959	8.2		1983	10.9
	1960	−1.4		1984	15.2
	1961	−29.7		1985	13.5
	1962	−6.5		1986	8.8
III	1963	10.7	VIII	1987	11.6
	1964	16.5		1988	11.3
	1965	17.0		1989	4.1
	1966	17.0		1990	3.8
	1967	−7.2	IX	1991	9.2
	1968	−6.5		1992	14.2
	1969	19.3		1993	13.5
	1970	23.3		1994	12.6
IV	1971	7.0		1995	10.5
	1972	2.9		1996	9.6
V	1973	8.3		1997	8.8
	1974	1.1		1998	7.8
	1975	8.3		1999	7.1
	1976	−2.7		2000	8.0

Source: China Statistical Yearbook (1991), 34; *China Statistical Abstract* (2001), 21.

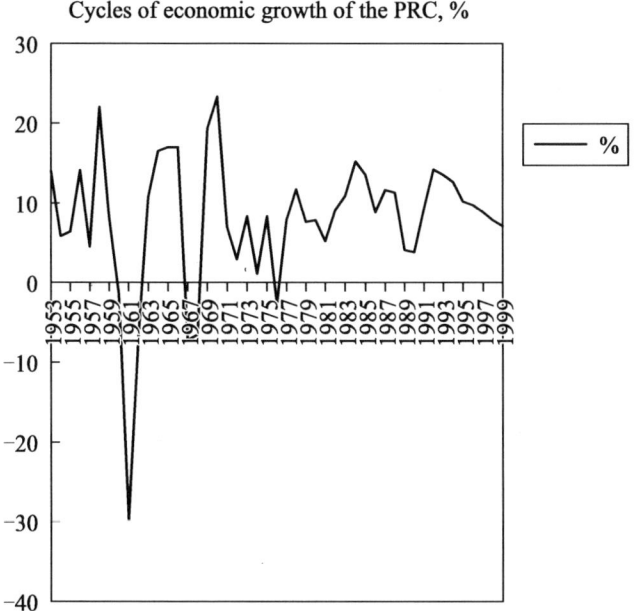

Figure 1   Dynamics of GDP Growth Rates

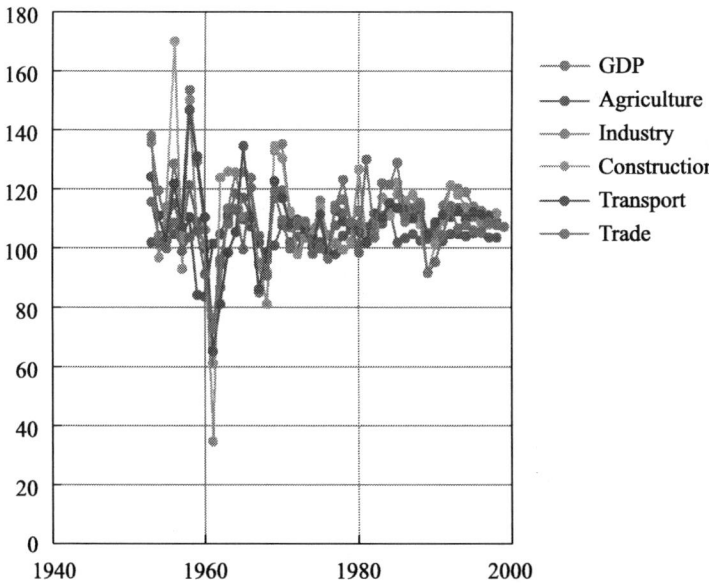

Figure 2   Dynamics of GDP and Key Industries of the National Economy's Growth Rates

Table 3   Average Annual Savings Rate, Average Annual Investment Growth Rates, and Average Annual GDP Growth Rates for Five-Year Plans (as %)

Five-year plans, years	Savings rate	Average annual	
		Investment growth rates	GDP growth rates
1st, 1953–1957	24.2	...	8.9
2nd, 1958–1962	30.8	...	–3.1
Recovery period, 1963–1965	22.7	...	14.7
3rd, 1966–1970	26.3	...	8.3
4th, 1971–1975	33.0	...	5.5
5th, 1976–1980	33.2	...	6.1
6th, 1981–1985	34.3	19.4	10.7
7th, 1986–1990	36.3	16.5	7.9
8th, 1991–1995	39.3	36.9	12.0
9th, 1996–2000	37.5	11.0	8.3

Source: *China Statistical Yearbook* (1991), 34; *China Statistical Yearbook* (1998), 67; *China Statistical Abstract* (1999), 14.

To achieve such a rapid and long-term economic recovery, appropriate organizational and economic systems and mechanisms for implementing the development plans established by the PRC leadership were necessary. The accumulation and investment system, as well as the accumulation and investment mechanism that allowed China to create modern productive forces, are the core ones.

In the early years of building socialism, China did not have the material and financial mechanisms to make an economic breakthrough. China did not have modern mechanical engineering, construction industry, heavy industry, as well as significant funds, engineering personnel, and workers. The situation was aggravated by the fact that after the formation of the PRC, the developed industrial countries declared a boycott of it. However, the Soviet Union, which played a decisive role in defeating the Japanese army of occupation and establishing the foundations of socialism in the PRC, supported China. This fact initiated the industrialization of China. Researchers distinguish three periods of development of the accumulation and investment complex in the PRC.

1.2 Mobilization Period of Economic Growth (1950–1978)

The first period covers 29 years (1950–1978). One hundred fifty-six modern plants supplied by the USSR and assembled with the help of Soviet specialists became the material and technical base of a fundamentally new investment complex in China. The training of qualified personnel in the PRC was organized with the active assistance of Soviet specialists. A large amount of scientific and technical documentation was handed over to the Chinese. At the same time, the foundations of the financial system necessary for the mobilization and concentration of financial resources were created in the PRC.

The Soviet-type model of centralized directive planning was taken as the basis for managing the development of the national economy in the process of PRC creation. The state, represented by the State Council, took a hard line of mastering the economic management, which was of a mobilization nature. This was manifested, firstly, in a rapid increase in the share of the national income distributed by means of the state budget; secondly, in the key role of the budget in investing in new construction; thirdly, in the huge scope of commodities subject to directive planned distribution; fourthly, in the wide introduction of rationing for the basic means of subsistence; fifthly, in direct deductions to the state budget for almost all net profits of enterprises; sixthly, in the centralized pricing for almost all means of production and consumer goods.

The following data demonstrate the speed of mastering economic management by the State Council of the People's Republic of China. As early as 1952, i.e., at the end of the recovery period, 30.3% of the produced national income was distributed through the state budget. During the years of the Great Leap Forward in 1960, this figure rose to 45.3% and declined in subsequent years. Shortly before the transition to market reforms in 1978, it was 38.2%.[5] All these years, the state budget remained the main source of investment. In 1953, it accounted for 83.5% of investment in fixed assets; in 1957, this figure rose to 91.7%. Then it decreased. Nevertheless, in 1978, the share of the budget in the investment of fixed assets was 77.7%.

In the first years of the PRC's existence, an industrial base for socialist economy development, which required a high-investment economy, was created. In 1950, it was 10%; in 1951, it was around 15%; in 1952, it was 21.4%. It remained stable (23%–25%) in 1953–1957. With the transition to the Great Leap Forward in the field of accumulation, maximalist attitudes such as: "save more, consume less" or "low incomes, low consumption, high accumulation rate" were promoted. In

1958–1960, the accumulation rate was 33.9%, 43.8%, and 39.6%, respectively. It significantly exceeded the possibilities of the material content of investments, which inevitably led to a decrease in the economic efficiency of capital investments in the national economy development. With the failure of the Great Leap Forward in 1962, the rate of accumulation fell to 10.4%. Its new rise began in 1965–1966 and continued into the 1970s.

One of the main challenges in the formation of the accumulation and investment complex was the search for the sources of accumulation and the formation of a specific mechanism for fund accumulation. In 1950, immediately after the proclamation of the PRC foundation, the State Council issued the National Tax Policy Implementation Rules. The document specified 14 taxes,[6] which, depending on their nature, were levied across the country: private, individual, state, industrial, trade, intermediary services taxes, etc. This system, with some adjustments, existed till 1958.[7]

The main sources of accumulation, especially in the early years, were the agricultural sector, state, private, and individual enterprises in all business areas. Funds (generally in kind) from villages were withdrawn mainly through the agricultural tax and procurement of agricultural products. At the same time, the state withdrew agricultural products even from the poorest farms. As a result, the state concentrated major food resources in its hands.

Such form of accumulation as the direct use of the labor of tens of millions of peasants for repairing and constructing irrigation facilities, roads, and other infrastructure facilities occupied an important place in this historical period in the countryside. In 1979, the total irrigated area was 45 million hectares, and 25 million of them were created after the establishment of the PRC.

Rapidly growing industry made an even greater contribution to real and financial accumulation. In 1958, the PRC simplified the tax system and reduced the number of taxes. Industrial enterprises were basically subject only to industrial and commercial tax.[8] Almost all net profit and depreciation costs were deducted from the budget.

Similar to the USSR, the system of centralized directive planning created in the PRC included state pricing for all basic consumer goods and means of production. The expanded economic reproduction was ensured by centralized rationing and resource allocation based on material balances by the public procurement system.

The inflation rate is an important indicator of a healthy financial system and the accumulation and investment complex. The dynamics of this indicator have always been the focus of attention of the PRC's top leaders throughout its history.

Galloping inflation, let alone hyperinflation, was considered the prime destroyers of economic growth and the reason for increased social tension. The most resolute struggle against the bursts of inflation began already in the 1950s–1970s. For the period of 29 years (1950–1978), the general retail prices index in cities increased by 61.8%, i.e., 1.7% per annum on average, and for food, there was an 86.7% increase or 2.2% per annum.[9] During this period, there were only two surges in prices— in 1951 by 14.4% and 11.1%, and in 1961 by 22.0% and 28.3%, respectively. Moreover, each increase in prices was followed by a decline in subsequent years. In total, for the period of eight years, prices increased from 2 to 5.8%; for the period of nine years, they were at the level of 100%–101.4%; and for another eight years, they were decreasing.[10]

The State Planning Commission, established in November 1952, has been the most important administrative and economic unit in managing the economy of the PRC. The State Planning Commission had an extensive network of planning units in provinces, counties, and districts. This structure permeated the whole society. The implementation of the resolutions of the CPC Central Committee and the government concerning the development of the national economy was ensured through the State Planning Commission. Its primary task was to translate the general guidelines set out in political documents into the language of figures. In the 1950s–1970s, the State Planning Commission determined which groups of products were subject to directive planning, set production and efficiency indicators for enterprises, assigned product suppliers and consumers, etc. The competence of the State Planning Commission included planning the activities and development of the accumulation and investment complex.

With the complication of economic ties, the independence of enterprises increased while the share of directive indicators decreased. However, it remained significant even under the condition of transition to the market economy, covering the most important types of products. In 1980, 837 types of means of production, including 256 types within the competence of the center, were subject to state distribution.[11] State distribution accounted for 74.3% of steel, 57.9% of coal, 80.9% of timber, etc. Card distribution covered all major consumer goods—grain, vegetable oil, meat, textiles, footwear, and other industrial commodities.

The principle of maximizing capital investments in production development was of key importance at all levels of economic management. It extended not only to resource mobilization but to their distribution and application as well. During the entire period of the economy industrialization in 1958–1978, there were the following priorities of the state investment policy: at the macroeconomic level—

maximization of productive accumulation to the detriment of non-productive accumulation; at the intersectoral level—to maximize accumulations in industry to the detriment of agriculture; at the sectoral level—to maximize savings in heavy industry which manufactures means of production to the detriment of the development of consumer goods production; at the intra-industry level—for the priority development of metallurgy as a basic sector of the economy.

As a result of the centralized economic industrialization by administrative methods, in the first 30 years of the PRC's existence, the foundations of the industrial complex were created, and its own engineering, scientific, technical, and managerial personnel, as well as qualified (advanced) detachments of the working class appeared. The efficiency of industrial enterprises' operations was very high. At the same time, the commodity-money balance of the economy was maintained.

During the 1st Five-Year Plan (1953–1957), the return on funds fluctuated within the range of 30.0%–34.6%, and the return on cost was 20.3%–24.5%. In subsequent years, this indicator decreased but remained high. In 1978 it was 24.8% and 24.5% respectively. The indicator of the ratio of net profit to funds demonstrated the same tendency. During the 1st Five-Year Plan, it fluctuated within 22.0%–23.9%, and during the 5th (1976–1980), it fluctuated within 11.4%–16.0%.[12]

The years of economic development under consideration, in essence, initiated a long period of primitive capital accumulation in the PRC, which was carried out in very difficult historical conditions, both domestic and international. The construction of the foundations of a modern for that period industrial complex, including the material basis of the accumulation and investment complex in the form of mechanical engineering, chemical, metallurgical, construction industries, etc., was of paramount significance in these years. For the period of 1953–1957, fixed assets in the country increased by 18.7 times in terms of initial cost, 19.2 times in residual value, and 28 and 29.7 times in state assets, respectively.

The increase in investment in fixed assets continued even during the Great Leap Forward. Despite the contemptuous disregard of monetary indicators, there was a continued growth of capital investments during this period. In 1958–1962, there was a 2.3 times increase in fixed production assets.[13] Although this disrupted the balance of economic growth, strong recovery rates followed each decline in growth rates. Thus, after a two-year decline in the national income production in 1967 and 1969 by 7.2 and 6.5%, respectively, this indicator increased, and in 1969, it amounted to 19.3% and 23.3% in 1970. Production increased.[14] In 1978, the PRC extracted 618 million tons of coal and 104.1 million tons of oil, produced

256.6 billion kWh of electricity, 65.2 million tons of cement, and 22.1 million tons of rolled products, smelted 31.8 million tons of steel, etc.

One of the achievements in the country was the construction of an extensive irrigation network by the peasants. Along with the intensification of chemicalization and the contribution of agronomy, the network doubled the grain harvest in the period of 1962–1979 (from 160 to 332 million tons).[15] Crop growth became the main condition for the survival of the extensive and rapidly growing Chinese population. During 1950–1978, China's population increased by 421 million people. The increase in the food facility created the necessary conditions for the development of economic activity and the growth of industrial production.

As the importance of scientific and technological progress grew and the structure of the economy became more complex, the efficiency of the centralized directive distribution system decreased, which was manifested in growing imbalances and slowing down economic development. These imbalances were acutely felt by the population. The general rationing of the means of subsistence was accompanied by a shortage of some goods with a surplus of others. Concentrating on increasing investment in the production development, the directive management system neglected the protection of the environment. The forced growth of industrial production led to high pollution and destruction of the environment. Massive pollution of rivers, lakes, and coastal shelves took place. During the first 30 years, 33.3 million hectares of arable land was withdrawn from agricultural turnover for constructing plants, factories, roads, dams, etc.[16] Some of them were restored by cultivating virgin land on the outskirts. However, in general, with a huge increase in population, land resources decreased. If in 1957 the area was 112 million hectares, then in 1978 it decreased to 99.4 million hectares.[17] Against the background of the accelerated growth in the means of production, incomes, and the level of consumption of the population, especially the rural one, stagnated for many years. To prevent social and political tension, a reorientation of the economy to meet the needs of the population was required.

1.3 Transition from the Mobilization Economy to the Socialist Market (1979–1995)

After the failed policy of the Great Leap Forward, the leading circles of the PRC understood that the solution to the national problems was possible only on the basis of economic development and recovery. At the same time, criticism of the excessive centralized management and the directive and planned management system was growing. The Great Leap Forward did not accelerate. On the contrary, it retarded the development of productive forces and preserved China's backwardness. The success of the market economy in industrialized countries was set as an example.

In these difficult conditions, in the first instance, it was necessary to harmonize public consciousness to give new guidelines to the party and state activists. Ordinary people needed brief and understandable ideological guidelines. Deng Xiaoping succeeded in this by abandoning the outdated dogmas of Marxism and Leninism and depoliticizing the system of national economy management. According to him, the plan and the market are the means of economic management. These categories are universal, not formational. The plan and the market as means of control are used both under capitalism and socialism. There are no antagonistic contradictions between the plan and the market.[18] Therefore, the best aspects of both should be used in the Chinese economy.

This approach was of great theoretical and practical significance. It formed the basis of the PRC's economic policy after 1978. Recognition of the necessity for active application of planned and market-based methods of management required reforming the system of planning and its transfer to commodity-money relations. At the same time, the ways for reforms were opened. The transition to market relations required the formation of other mechanisms for financing development, rather than those on which the economic system was previously based.

An evolutionary approach, based on Deng Xiaoping's well-known warning: "Cross the river by feeling the stones," was chosen for carrying out market reforms. You can't reform for the sake of reform. A threefold goal of reform has been made clear: to develop productive forces, enhance aggregate economic power, and improve people's lives.

The transition of the PRC from a planned economy to a "socialist market economy," or, more precisely, to a planned market economy, can be divided into three stages: from 1979 to 1983, from 1984 to 1991, and from 1992 to 1995. Each stage was distinguished by its reforms aimed at increasing the rate of economic growth.

1.3.1 The beginning of economic liberalization

The first attempt to introduce market mechanisms, including partial liberalization of pricing and other tools for economic regulation in 1979–1980, was accompanied by an increase in money creation by 26.3% and 28.3%,[19] respectively, and an increase in prices. In 1980, retail prices in cities increased by 8.1%.[20] In 1981, the experiment was terminated as unprepared. The next three years (1981–1983) were spent on vigorous preparations for a new stage of liberalization, which was associated with accelerated economic growth.

Market reforms were carried out in an evolutionary way. In 1979–1983, the transition of the economy to commodity-money and commercial relations was carried out under the guidance of the "planned economy, supplemented by market regulation." At the same time, the role of directive and administrative methods in planning was reduced, and indirect instruments of regulation were intensified. The course to replace directive planning with a strategic one, including monetary policy tools and indicative planning, was taken. The most radical liberalization affected agriculture, where decollectivization and the development of private forms of entrepreneurship and land use were carried out.

The transition to a mixed economy, combining central planning with market mechanisms, required a new system of economic activity regulation. Granting state enterprises greater economic independence, the transition to market principles of their financing, a rapid increase in the number and qualitative diversity of business entities, and attracting foreign investors to the country raised the issue of changing the economic mechanism based on the principles of strict state administrative and distribution management. Under the new conditions, the existing 12 taxes[21] and "transferring part of the profits to the state" were not able to ensure an increase in state budget revenues. Maintaining a balance in the state financial system required a fundamental change in the tax system.

The new tax system was implemented in two stages. In the first stage (1979–1983), along with the old system of raising funds for the budget, including the transfer of a part of the profits, new taxes were introduced and tested. In the second stage (1984–1991), the economy was transferred to the tax system for the formation of government budget revenues, which were replenished with new taxes from year to year. In the early 1990s, their number exceeded 30. State-owned enterprises were subject to nine taxes (in addition to specific ones), including tax on products, value-added tax, tax on trade, industrial and commercial tax, income tax, regulatory tax, payroll tax, bonus tax, and construction tax.[22] While reforming the tax system, the depreciation system, as well as the sources of financing and the mechanism for investing in fixed assets, was changed (Table 4).

Table 4   Changes in the Structure of Fixed Assets' Investment Sources in the PRC in 1957–1990 (as %)

Investment sources	1957	1978	1980	1985	1989	1990
State budget	88.6	62.2	44.7	16.0	8.3	8.7
Lending	...	1.7	11.7	20.1	7.3	19.6
Foreign investment	...	4.2	7.2	3.6	6.6	6.3
Enterprises and households' savings	11.4	31.9	36.5	60.3	56.9	52.3
Other sources	...	...	...	...	10.9	13.1

Source: China Statistical Yearbook (1991), 24.

For the period of 32 years (1958–1989), the share of the state budget in fixed assets investment decreased by 10.7 times and compared with 1978—by 7.5 times. The main subjects of accumulation and investment were enterprises, ministries, agencies, individuals, private and foreign entrepreneurs, as well as banks, which played an increasing role in investment lending. The role of foreign loans and investments by entrepreneurs from Hong Kong, Taiwan, and foreign investors rapidly increased. However, as can be seen from the data given in Table 5, the role of the public sector in economic growth investment remained significant.

A gradual decrease in the share of state-owned enterprises as a source of accumulation and investment in the national economy can be seen from the data given in Table 5. After the reduction in the share of state property (by 12.2%) in investments in 1981, this indicator subsequently fluctuated between 64%–66%. Thus, the role of the public sector in providing investment remained predominant. At the same time, the importance of another component of the basis of socialist capital accumulation, collective property, was increasing. The share of collective enterprises in investments fluctuated in different years by 10%–15%. At the very beginning of the reforms, the share of individual entrepreneurs in savings and investment soared (from 13.1% to 22.5%). It remained stable till the end of this period.

The transformation of the economic system of the PRC toward the creation of a mixed economy and the active use of commodity-money relations started gaining momentum after the Third Plenary Session of the 12th CPC Central Committee (October 1984).

Table 5   Changes in the Investment Sources Structure in the PRC by the Type of Ownership (as %)

Year	Property		
	State	Collective	Individual
1980	81.9	5.0	13.1
1981	69.5	12.0	18.6
1982	68.7	14.2	17.1
1983	66.6	10.9	22.5
1984	64.7	9.4	22.3
1985	66.1	12.9	21.0
1986	66.6	12.6	20.8
1987	64.6	14.4	21.0
1988	63.5	15.0	21.5
1989	63.7	12.9	23.4
1990	66.1	11.7	22.2

Source: *China Statistical Yearbook* (2001), 158.

The resolution of the plenum on the reform of the economic system explicitly aimed the executive authorities at the decisive introduction of market principles and the development of diversity and external openness as the most important ways to accelerate the pace of the national economy modernization and increase its power and production efficiency. However, the unchangeable conditions for an accelerated transition to the market remained the preservation of public property and its leading role, the preservation of a unified state financial, banking, and fiscal system, with their indispensable reform and adaptation to market conditions.

The general logic of the reforms was, firstly, in a drastic reduction in directive planning of mandatory indicators set by the center and granting of greater economic rights to local authorities and enterprises in matters of production, sales of products, wages, formation of funds, blue-collar and white-collar jobs; secondly, in narrowing the scope of centralized pricing and expanding the scope of market pricing; thirdly, in providing unprecedented opportunities through various benefits, including taxation, for the development of personal and private entrepreneurship; fourthly, in the further restructuring of financial, fiscal, investment and credit policies while maintaining a unified banking and financial system.

The measures taken were supposed to create conditions for the rapid transformation of enterprises into "real commodity producers" operating on the principles of self-government, self-sufficiency, self-financing, self-development, and self-control. The vigorous implementation of the decisions of the CPC Central Committee on the reform of the economic system was supposed to ensure the rapid development of the market principles in the economy. It could not but be accompanied by advanced monetization of the economy.

The monetization of the economy objectively entails an increase in the need for money as a universal means of binding all resources in a market economy. In the 1980s–1990s, the need for money in the PRC was desperate, which was determined, firstly, by the low degree of monetization of the semi-subsistence and subsistence economy in the pre-reform period; secondly, the extreme demand for expanding production and providing jobs and means of subsistence for a rapidly growing population; thirdly, the imperfection and lack of development of the monetary and price system, monetary and commodity circulation; fourthly, the current demand for production and construction. Pressure for money was exacerbated by the initial imbalance between the needs for the population's means of subsistence and the means of consumer goods production, on the one hand, and the weak production capabilities to satisfy them, on the other. An acute shortage of material resources and a low level of production in contrast to the needs of the population served as a prerequisite for deficit financing, which required an expansion of credit.

1.3.2 Transition from accelerating market reforms in the economy to its recovery (1984–1991)

Target-oriented use of credit was widely applied in 1984–1988 to accelerate market reforms and stimulate production growth (Table 6). Investment lending in the growth of fixed assets was prioritized. Investments annual growth rates in 1984–1988 fluctuated from 28.2% to 38%. Bank issue was the main source of investment resources financing, and targeted lending was the main channel. The average annual increase in loans to fixed assets in 1985–1990 was 30%. Lending to industrial enterprises was abundant. There was a 20% or more annual increase in the purchasing power of the population and the wage fund. To ensure the ongoing economic policy, targeted money emission was launched. In 1984, the amount of money in circulation immediately increased by 49.5%, and in a five-year period (1984–1988), their annual growth was 33.3%. Due to monetary financing in 1985–1986, the rate of investment in GDP reached 38.7% and 38.4%, respectively.

Table 6   Dynamics of GDP Growth, Investment in Fixed Assets and Prices in 1981–1990 (as %)

Year	Growth rates					
	Including					
	DDP	Total investments as a whole	State	Collective	Other types of property	Composite consumer price index in cities
1981	5.2	5.5	–10.5	150.4	49.8	2.4
1982	9.1	28.0	26.6	51.3	18.2	1.9
1983	0.9	16.2	12.6	–10.3	52.7	1.5
1984	5.2	28.2	24.5	52.7	27.1	2.8
1985	3.5	38.8	41.8	37.2	30.9	8.8
1986	8.8	22.7	23.7	19.6	21.3	6.0
1987	1.6	21.5	17.8	39.6	22.6	7.3
1988	1.3	25.4	23.3	30.1	28.4	18.5
1989	4.1	–7.2	–7.0	–19.9	1.0	17.8
1990	3.8	2.4	6.3	–7.1	–3.0	2.1

Source: China Statistical Yearbook (2001), 51, 158, 281.

The implementation of a targeted credit emission policy for the period of four to five years had a great stimulating effect on the economic situation in the PRC. An important result of the policy was an increase in the rate of economic development. In 1984–1988, the average annual GDP growth was 12.1%. Industry, construction, and the service sector demonstrated particularly high growth rates. A significant increase in coal mining, as well as production of electricity, iron, steel, cement, engineering products, and cultural and household appliances (receivers and TV sets, bicycles, etc.), lies behind these figures.

However, the great leap made in industry, construction, trade, and the service sector also had negative consequences. The weakening of state regulation in the distribution of material resources, money, and pricing against the backdrop of trade liberalization and the growing money supply was accompanied by economic imbalance. With easy access to cheap credit, tens of thousands of enterprises and regional authorities had excessive demands for resources, numerous of which quickly became scarce. There was a growing disproportion in the economy between the rapidly growing aggregate demand and the lagging aggregate supply, which affected the rise in prices (see Table 7). For the period of five years (1985–1989), the composite price index for industrial products increased by 71.0%, including for the metallurgical industry products by 77.0%, chemical industry products by 70.0%, engineering industry products by 63.3%, construction materials by 94.2%, and for timber industry products even by 146.7%. Food prices rose even faster. Rated grain and vegetable oil rose in price by 193.4% and 91.1%, respectively; the prices for fresh vegetables, fish, and livestock products that were regulated by the market rose by 120.0%, 166.8%, and 144.7%, respectively. This was an unprecedented rise in prices in the history of the PRC, which caused increased social and political tension in the country.[23]

One of the main factors of inflation was the rise in prices for agricultural products. In 1985–1989, despite the increasing chemicalization production in this sector, it could not reach the level of 1984. Only in 1989, due to the measures taken, it was possible to raise the gross grain harvest to the level of 1984 and to exceed it in 1990. But in those six years, China's population increased by 100 million people.

Inflationary processes started in industry as well. Despite market competition, there was an increase in the cost of industrial products and a decrease in its profitability. For the period of six years (1985–1990), the cost of a unit of industrial production increased by 152.3%. The return on assets and product profitability decreased accordingly. If the first indicator in 1984 was 24.2%, and the second was 31.0%, then in 1989, both indicators decreased to 17.2 and 18.3%, respectively, and in 1990 to 12.4 and 14.4%.

Both public finance and the finances of industries and enterprises were in a difficult situation. If the losses of state enterprises amounted to 2.6 billion yuan in 1984, then they reached 8.2 billion in 1988, 18.0 billion in 1989, and 34.9 billion in 1990. There were also many unprofitable enterprises requiring support among collective enterprises. State subsidies to enterprises grew like a snowball. In 1986, their total amount was 32,468 million yuan, and in 1989, already 59,888 million yuan. Every year, the burden of subsidies to food prices became more and more challenging for the state budget. In 1984, they amounted to 21,834 million yuan; in 1989, it was 37,340 million, and in 1990 was 38,080 million yuan. The total amount of subsidies to enterprises and subsidies to food prices in 1989 amounted to 33.6% of state budget expenditures. This must be added by assistance to the peasantry in the amount of 15.9 billion yuan in 1988 and 19.7 billion yuan in 1989. The share of expenditures for all these needs in 1989 was 40.3% of the expenditure part of the budget. With the transition to market pricing, the budget deficit started its conversion from a latent form to an open one and rapidly increased. In 1984, it was 4.45 billion yuan, 7.9 billion in 1988, 9.2 billion in 1989, and 13.9 billion yuan in 1990. However, these amounts so far constituted a modest share of its income and expenses.

Growing disproportions also covered the social sphere. As a result of the forced introduction of market relations in the economy, the property stratification of Chinese society accelerated. In the 7th Five-Year Plan, real wages increased only in 1986. In 1987, they remained at the level of the previous year; in 1988, they dropped by 0.8%, and in 1989 by 4.8%.[24] Social tension was growing.

The PRC leaders faced the question of either continuing the reforms at the same pace and with the same method or stopping, looking around, and putting the national economy in order. As fundamental pragmatists, the Chinese leaders chose the latter. In September 1988, the 3rd plenary session of the 13th CPC Central Committee was held. The current situation in the national economy was carefully analyzed, and the decision on a three-year transition to "recovery and streamlining" was approved. In compliance with the resolution, only in October 1988, the State Council adopted 15 acts aimed at streamlining the situation in the field of capital construction, finance, money, and commodity circulation, as well as eliminating the accumulated imbalances.

On March 15, 1989, a detailed resolution on the basic principles of policy in the field of the national economic structure was published. The core of the streamlining policy was the strengthening of centralized management of all sectors of the economy using a wide variety of measures, including economic, administrative, ideological, political, legal, and disciplinary ones. The resolution determined tough measures to reduce and restore order in capital construction, limit the growth rate of consumer demand, curb inflation, and improve monetary and commodity circulation, as well as finance.

From late 1988, the pace of investment growth started plummeting. In 1989, the total volume of investments of all types of ownership decreased, with disregard for inflation, in comparison with 1988 by 8%, and with regard to inflation, by no less than 25%. Although in 1990 the volume of investments increased by 7.5% compared to 1989, with disregard for price growth, and by 5% regarding it, it remained significantly lower than in 1988. Control over lending, the growth of household incomes, and the payroll fund were tightened. The growth of the money supply in circulation was reduced from 46.7% in 1988 to 9.8% in 1989 and to 12.8% in 1990.

Tough measures were taken in the field of pricing. In 1990, the increase in the composite consumer price index was reduced to 2.1%, including for food, from 23.0% in 1988 to 0.3%; for vegetables, from 31.7 to 0.4%; for meat, from 36.8 to 2.1%, etc. Compared with 1988, prices in the collective (free) markets in 1990 were lower by 5.7%. In general, a balance between aggregate demand and aggregate supply was achieved.

Two years of vigorous implementation of improving and streamlining the economy by the central authorities had a positive impact on the economy. These measures contributed to the strengthening of the economic system and the preservation of the reform policy. Nevertheless, the economic recovery was also accompanied by negative phenomena. Thus, the reduction in investment volume was the main reason for the reduction in capital construction. In 1990, compared with 1988, the number of new buildings decreased by 23,000. The completion of many construction projects was delayed. As a result, GDP growth in 1989 fell to 4.1% and in 1990 to 3.8%.[25] According to the metaphor of many economists, the transfer of an overheated economy into a more or less normal course of development took place in the "hard landing" mode.

Although in the process of recovery, it was generally possible to balance aggregate demand and aggregate supply, their structures, nevertheless, did not coincide. There was a surplus in production of some goods and a shortage in others, as well as deep disproportions between agriculture, the fuel and energy complex, and raw materials, on the one hand, and the national economy as a whole, and between light and heavy industry, on the other. Transport capacity, specifically rail, remained a bottleneck.

The inclusion of huge masses of young people of working age (about 90 million people) in economic activity under conditions of an acute shortage of productive capital ensured high rates of economic growth mainly due to extensive factors and low production efficiency, which, moreover, tended to decrease. The problem of employment was aggravated. The unprofitability of industry, the volume of subsidies in relation to the price level, and the budget deficit increased.

In the sphere of circulation, problems in the sale of many types of industrial products, including consumer products (bicycles, sewing machines, radio sets, TV sets, etc.) started aggravating, and excess in inventory reserves increased. Market conditions deteriorated. Demand even for such consumer products as grain, clothing, footwear, cotton fabrics, and construction materials declined.

Nevertheless, on the whole, during the two years of recovery and streamlining, the Chinese pragmatists managed to save their economy from chaos and restore its ratios. However, the fundamental problems of increasing economic efficiency were still far from being solved.

1.3.3 Consideration of the lessons of uneven development and adoption of a ten-year program (1991–2000)

The results of the PRC's economic development in 1984–1988 were subjected to rigorous and detailed analysis in scientific, political, and government circles. It was recognized that both low and very high rates of development are unacceptable for the Chinese economy. This vision was enshrined in the "Outline of the 10-Year Program and the 8th Five-Year Plan for National Economic and Social Development of the PRC," which were adopted in March 1991 at the *Fourth session* of the *7th* National People's Congress (*NPC*). Both the program (1991–2000) and the plan (1991–1995) were developed as a concrete embodiment of the second step of the economic strategy. They included a wide range of China's global issues. The 1990s in China passed under the sign of major transformations in the field of production, population, the interaction between society and nature, and the continuation and deepening of economic reforms.

Summarising the essence of the "Basic Provisions," it can be said that they were a program of deep modernization of the national economy, improving the quality of economic growth and production efficiency. One of the principal directions for the implementation of the tasks set both in the program and the plan was supposed to be economic restructuring, its reorientation to meet the needs of the population, whose structure was rapidly becoming more complex, as well as accelerating the renewal of production assets. For this purpose, the sectors of the national economy were ranked according to priorities. Agriculture came to the fore. Special emphasis was put on grain collection. Such basic industries as fuel, electricity, natural raw materials, transport, and irrigation were put in second place. Their development was envisaged in conjunction with the reconstruction and transfer of enterprises to a modern technical and technological level. It was planned to build new and increase the capacity of old hydroelectric power plants, state regional power plants, thermal power stations, and nuclear power plants, increase coal and oil production capacities, and build railways, highways, ports, airports, and communication lines. Plans for the modernization of enterprises of the machine-building and metallurgical complex were laid.

The rates and indicators of growth were determined both for the national economy as a whole and for individual sectors. According to the plan for the 8th Five-Year Plan approved by the NPC session and the program up to 2000, the average annual GDP growth rate was set at the level of 6%, including 3.5% for agriculture and 6.8% for industry. In 1991–1995 it was planned to increase GDP by 33.6% (an average of 6% per annum), agricultural production by 18.9% (3.5%), industry by 37.1% (6.5%), and services in the tertiary sector by 53.9% (9%). Moderate growth of only 5.7% per annum was planned for investment activity, including 2.1% for new construction in the public sector and 9.8% per annum for reconstruction (see Table 8).

The main task in the social sphere was to eliminate poverty and build "a moderately prosperous society" ("xiao kang"), i.e., in meeting the basic needs of the growing population for food, clothing, housing, fuel, household, and cultural goods, and for those able to work—with jobs.

The fundamental direction in the creation of a new economic system was the formation of a socialist planned-market management mechanism. The very understanding of planning, which was supposed to be implemented in two forms, directive and guiding, was revised. The 8th Five-Year Plan became the Five-Year Plan for achieving stable development and improving product quality and production efficiency.

1991 in China was held in line with the implementation of the 8th Five-Year Plan adopted by the NPC session. The results were very encouraging. The economy started growing again. In 1992, at the traditional March session of the NPC, the Premier of the State Council, Li Peng, the Chairman of the State Planning Commission, and the Minister of Finance made routine reports on the work of the government for the previous year and setting goals for the current economic year. In 1992, the GDP growth rate was planned at the level of 6%, investments by 8%, industrial products by 14.2%, and retail trade turnover by 13.2%. According to preliminary plans, the state budget was supposed to turn from deficit to deficit-free: it was planned to increase revenues by 9.2% and expenditures by 8.6%. Much attention in the reports was given to increasing production efficiency and product quality.

The third stage of economic growth in China began in the early 1990s. The CPC Central Committee, scientific institutes, and government agencies closely monitored and assessed the events unfolding in the Soviet Union. In January 1992, Deng Xiaoping visited the south of the country. Premier of the State Council Li Peng visited five provinces and regions of Northwest China (Shaanxi, Gansu, Qinghai, Ningxia, and Xinjiang), which were in immediate proximity to the Central Asian region, Kazakhstan, and the MPR. At meetings with provincial leaders, referring to the speeches of Deng Xiaoping, as well as the decisions of the Political Bureau of the CPC Central Committee, Li Peng said that a favorable situation had developed both in the world and in China, and this chance should not be missed. Therefore, the CPC Central Committee decided to accelerate the reforms implementation and the need for general growth of the national economy of the PRC. With regard to the northwestern provinces, Li Peng put forward the "Grand Western Development Program" and actively developed relations with the republics of Central Asia. By June 1992, a fundamental assessment of the current situation in the world and China was formulated in the upper echelons of the PRC power. In the press, it was presented in the following way: after the end of the Cold War, a favorable situation developed for China in the world, which was combined with a positive situation in China itself. Given the modern challenge, China received a "rare historical opportunity," which in no case should be missed.

The main conclusion to "cling to" the given historical chance, accelerate the course of reform and opening-up, as well as "bring the economy to a new level" was drawn from the situation. To solve this problem, it was recommended to use any useful management tools for Chinese economic development, regardless of its source: capitalist or socialist. The only criterion for the correctness of the decisions taken is increasing China's economic power. In this way, the theory of Pitirim Sorokin about the convergence of the socialist and capitalist economies, which was substantiated in the 1960s, foreseeing the emergence of an integral system that combines their best qualities and does not have the drawbacks of each, was practically confirmed.[26]

In line with making the most of the favorable opportunities to accelerate the implementation of the policy of reform and opening-up, the 14th National Congress of the CPC was held in October 1992. The idea of "acceleration" received massive support from the population and rapidly spread throughout the country. It was perceived especially frenetically in the eastern coastal provinces. The course to accelerate the policy of reform and openness put forward by Deng Xiaoping was dictated by the objective need to link the rapidly growing population with the necessity to create an appropriate number of jobs and sources of income. Since 1992, the third, most rapid stage of economic growth after 1978 began in the PRC.

In accordance with the experience of previous years, a new cycle of acceleration began with the money issuance for investment lending. During the 8th Five-Year Plan, 6163.8 billion yuan was allocated for these purposes, which in current prices was 3.1 times higher than the volume of investments in fixed assets in the previous five-year period. Compared with 1990, the volume of investment increased from 444.9 billion yuan to 1940 billion yuan in 1995, i.e., 4.36 times. Bank lending remained one of the main investment channels, and its volume increased by more than 2.9 times over the five-year period. The investment rate (the ratio of investment to GDP) rose to an incredibly high level. In 1993 it reached 43.4%, and 40.8% in 1994. This figure was even higher in metropolitan areas and some provinces. In 1993, this figure was 72.4% in Beijing, 49.0% in Shanghai, 53.0% in Jiangsu, 47.2% in Zhejiang, 49.5% in Shandong, and 48.0% in Guangdong.

The payroll fund over the period of the Five-Year Plan increased more than 2.7 times—from 295.1 billion yuan in 1990 to 810 billion yuan in 1995. A new round of money emission with an increase in all the main monetary aggregates (M0, M1, M2) began. In five years, the money supply in circulation (M0) increased from 264.4 billion yuan to 788.5 billion yuan, i.e., 3 times. Particularly large injections of new capital took place in 1992 (an increase in M0 by 42.6%) and in 1993 (by 50.0%). Super-high rates of capital injection into the economy took place in June 1992–June 1993. Thus, in January-June 1993, investments in fixed assets in the public sector increased by 69% compared to the corresponding period of the previous year. In some months, their growth reached 138%.

And yet again, Chinese reformers put to shame the dogmatists at the International Monetary Fund (IMF), who had imposed opposite, tight monetary policies on Russia and other post-Soviet states. Growth acceleration is impossible without intensive monetization of the economy. If in Russia, following the advice of the IMF, the monetary authorities pursued a policy of contracting the money supply, which resulted in the stagflation trap, in the PRC, cash replenishment was carried out to ensure expanded reproduction of the economy. The money "pumping" into the economy is carried out with the aim of inciting and stimulating the acceleration ("heating") of economic growth. With the correct management of the money supply for lending with the aim to increase the production of goods and investments in new technologies, inflation can be restrained by a timely increase in the supply of goods and services, as well as by reducing the costs of their production. Early 1992, with a new round of accelerating economic growth, was accompanied by the cash injection into the national economy, unprecedented even for the 7th Five-Year Plan (see Table 7).

Massive cash injections into the economy and partial satisfaction of the money hunger this time produced a great stimulating effect on the increase in the rate of economic growth. Over the five-year period, GDP production increased 3.1 times in current prices (from 1853.1 billion yuan in 1990 to 5773.3 billion yuan in 1995) and by 74.5% in comparable prices. In 1992–1993, GDP growth amounted to 14.2% and 13.5%, respectively. Its rates slightly decreased but were high in 1994 (12.6%) and in 1995 (10.2%). Based on statistics, during the 8th Five-Year Plan, China achieved the highest rate of economic development. The average annual GDP growth rate was 12.0% (Table 7).

Table 7   Main Indicators of Economic Growth in the PRC (1990–1995)

Indicators	1990	1991	1992	1993	1994	1995
Fixed assets investment* (previous year = 100.0)	102.4	123.9	144.4	161.8	130.4	117.5
Investment rate (investment-to-GDP ratio)	34.7	34.8	36.2	43.3	41.2	40.8
Fixed assets loans* (previous year = 100.0)	116.1	148.5	168.4	138.8	130.1	105.0
Payroll fund (previous year = 100.0)	112.7	112.6	118.5	124.8	135.2	121.7
Currency in circulation (M_0), billion yuan	264.4	317.8	433.6	586.5	728.9	788.5
Currency in circulation (M_0) (previous year = 100,0)	112.8	120.0	135.4	135.8	124.3	108.2

(Continued)

GDP** (previous year = 100.0)	103.8	109.2	114.2	113.5	112.6	110.2
Gross industrial output** (previous year = 100.0)	107.8	114.8	124.7	127.3	124.2	120.3
Energy extraction (previous year = 100.0)	102.2	100.9	102.3	99.8	106.6	104.4
Gross grain harvest (1990 = 100.0)	100.0	97.6	99.2	102.3	99.7	104.5
Composite consumer price index (previous year = 100.0)	102.1	102.9	105.4	113.2	121.7	114.8

Source: China Statistical Yearbook (1995), 32, 108, 199, 233, 347; *China Statistical Yearbook* (1998), 67, 187, 301; *China Statistical Abstract* (Beijing, 1996), 3, 8, 43, 74, 89.
Note: *in current prices, **in comparable prices.

Industry, primarily collective, township, and settlement, as well as rural ones, made the greatest contribution to the output growth. The industrial production growth was 24.7% in 1992, 27.3% in 1993, and 24.2% in 1994. It stimulated the development of the service sector. The key factors for the rapid production growth were capital investments in light industry with the use of available technologies and the influx of a growing workforce. The priority was still given to the mass production of consumer goods. As a result, in a matter of years, China became the world's largest manufacturer of bicycles, sewing machines, watches, televisions, radio equipment, etc., flooding its shops and markets with these products. Under conditions of overpopulation, great attention was paid to accelerating the development of trade, transport, communications, and services, whose annual growth rates fluctuated in the range of 6%–17%.

Agriculture, including crop production, as well as forestry, animal husbandry, and fishery, showed more even growth rates in the 8th Five-Year Plan, although its share in the GDP structure continued to decline. This primarily refers to crop production and specifically to grain, cotton, and oilseed production. During the 8th Five-Year Plan, the weather for agriculture was also favorable. The total grain production increased by almost 10% compared to the 7th Five-Year Plan. Notwithstanding large inflationary spikes and disruptions in trade, the food complex provided a huge population with basic food.

Table 8 Target Indicators for GDP, Industry, and Investment Growth for 1991–1995 and Their Actual Implementation

Indicators	Planned, as %	Actually implemented, as %	Ratio (Actually implemented to Planned), times
Average annual GDP growth rate	6.0	12.0	2.0
Total GDP growth for the five-year period	33.6	76.2	2.3
Average annual growth rate of industrial production	6.8	17.4	2.6
Industrial production growth for the five-year period	37.1	122.7	3.4
Average annual investment growth rate for the five-year period	5.7	36.9	6.5
Total investment growth	31.9	380.8	11.9

Source: "China's Economy on the Eve of the 21st Century (1991–2000)," Newsletter, no. 2 (M.: The Institute of the Far East of the RAS, 1997): 25; China Statistical Abstract (1999), 12–14, 42.

During the 8th Five-Year Plan, the PRC achieved the highest rates of economic growth in its history. The main target indicators were more than doubled: GDP growth rates by 2 times, GDP volume growth by 2.3 times, industrial production growth rates by 2.6 times, and its volume by 3.4 times (see Table 8). In terms of GDP volume, China significantly advanced among the largest countries in the world.

1.3.4 Regress and cooling the "overheated" economy

The policy of accelerated growth led to an increase in structural imbalances connected with the private producers' desire to relocate investment resources to high-turnover industries. The local authorities of some provinces aimed to fill the gap in investment resources by "surrogate" money creation and debt securities (mostly short-term) issuance. This decision inevitably undermined the country's monetary circulation system and threatened the emergence of "financial pyramids."

The first measures of growth regulation were taken by the government in the first quarter of 1993. In late June of 1993, the government adopted a detailed resolution, which provided for the termination of any actions that undermined the formation of centralized state monetary funds, the establishment of strict control over the money creation and debt securities issue, specifically in the regions; the complete separation of the PBC, state-owned banks, and commercial banks from nonbank financial institutions and other economic institutions; prohibition of the "grey market" government bond trading.

In the field of money management, the need to tighten the issuing policy, stop lending to nonbank financial institutions by the PBC, prevent violations of the annual credit plan, the need for strict control in credit provision, and the temporary cancellation of loan repayments was indicated. The interests of depositors were also considered. To save the population's deposits and enterprises from depreciation, the interest rate was increased in two stages. The status of the People's Bank in macroeconomic regulation was raised. The fiscal system management was strengthened. The attention was drawn to the necessity to strengthen control over the collection of taxes, to the inadmissibility of illegal exemption from taxes of enterprises and organizations, as well as to the weak effectiveness of control over public organizations and enterprises, whose incomes and consumer demand are growing rapidly. The issue of government bonds was temporarily suspended. Control over foreign exchange transactions was strengthened, and foreign currency circulation in the domestic market was strictly limited. Foreign exchange speculation was prosecuted. Investments in fixed assets were restricted, and the inclusion of new facilities in state construction projects was limited. Restraining measures were implemented in relation to price increases, especially prices for goods and services set by the state. At the same time, food and cash insurance funds were created to protect the population from rising prices.[27]

Disinflation measures were implemented through state structures, including the banking system, wholesale trade, and state-owned enterprises, and were partially successful. However, they did not include the private and liberalized sectors, where prices continued to rise. In 1994, the general retail price index rose to 21.7%, and in cities, consumer goods rose by 25%, including grain by 50.7%, vegetable oil by 61.3%, meat by 41.6%, and vegetables by 33.3%. In December 1994, the State Council issued an order to implement ten measures to suppress inflation. Pursuing these aims, in early 1995, the CPC Central Committee and the State Council activated all lower party and executive bodies related to the national economy management. A system to curb inflation and restore order in pricing was developed. As a result, the aggregate inflation index was brought down to 14.8% in 1995 and to 0.8% in 1997.

The acceleration of economic growth, which started in 1992, once again culminated in the application of strict macroeconomic regulation by the government with the use of a system of administrative measures that proved its effectiveness. Thus, the Chinese reformers once again put to shame the dogmatists from the IMF, who argued that the emission of money always entails a rise in prices, which cannot be stopped by any administrative methods. China's "economic miracle" is explained by an extremely effective system of managing economic development, which used all conceivable tools, both market and administrative. To accelerate economic growth, Chinese leaders increased targeted money creation and used administrative methods for macroeconomic stabilization. Economic regulation was highly selective and focused on achieving specific results in all management areas.

1.3.5 Transition from extensive to intensive growth

The acceleration and stabilization of the economy, which took place in 1992–1995, was accompanied by an extensive discussion in the scientific community. Chinese economists saw the reasons for the repeated surges and slowdowns in development in the fact that this growth was based, firstly, mainly on the setting up of small enterprises; secondly, on the gross growth of low efficient investments; thirdly, on wasteful expenditures of natural, human, and financial resources; and fourthly, on the pursuit of inflating cost indicators to the detriment of improving quality, upgrading and expanding product range.[28]

During several campaigns "for the general industrialization" of the country in 1984–1995, the spontaneous construction of many single-industry enterprises in the national economy led to numerous disproportions. One of the manifestations of these disproportions in the overpopulated country was the emergence of excess capacity, which was not used to its full potential. According to the data of the third industrial census conducted in 1995, the capacities and their use in some industries were as follows:[29]

Table 9   The Degree of Capacity Utilization and Product Sales by Main Types of Goods

Total types of goods		Capacity utilization rate, as %	Degree of product sales, as %
Units	%		
285	100.0	...	...
18	6.3	> 95	> 95
29	10.1	> 95	< 95
115	40.2	< 75	> 95
123	43.4	< 60	< 95

From the data given in Table 9, it follows that only the capacities to produce 18 types of goods in demand were used by 95% or more. For other types of goods, there were problems either with sales (29 types of goods), with the use of production capacities (115 types of goods), or simultaneously with the use of capacities and sales (123 types of goods). In general, production capacities were underused to varying degrees in the production of 238 (83.6%) types of goods. Major sales problems arose during the production of 152 (53.5%) types of goods. In late 1997, 754.5 billion yuan of unsold goods accumulated in China's warehouses, which accounted for 12% of all products intended for sale. The above-mentioned problems can be clearly illustrated with specific examples (see Table 10).

Disproportions caused by rapid economic growth were manifested both in price surges and in the overproduction of various types of industrial goods. From a country where demand had always exceeded supply for most manufactured goods, China turned into a country where supply exceeded demand. As a result, many enterprises had to reduce production, temporarily suspend it, or even shut down completely. The efficiency of industrial enterprises of all forms of ownership continued to fall, their unprofitability and the total amount of debt increased. Thus, the return on funds from 25.2% in 1980 fell to 12.2% in 1990 and to 8.29 in 1995.[30] It should be noted that the difference in the level of profitability indicators of state and non-state-owned enterprises is insignificant.

Table 10   Capacity Utilization Rate in Individual Industries

Type of goods	Unit of measure	Capacities	Production	Utilization rate, as %
Rolled steel	mln. tons	150	90	60
Cement	mln. tons	600	480	80
Sulphuric acid	thous. tons	800	560	69.6
Lacquer paints	thous. tons	4,325	2,106	48.7
Plastic	thous. tons	6,705	5,169	77.1
Tyre casings	mln. units	145.3	79.5	54.7
Tyres	mln. units	198.8	79.5	37.4
Printed fabrics	bln. meters	57.7	13.7	23.6
Industrial steam boilers	thous. tons of steam	146.6	124	8.5
Internal combustion engines	mln. kW	360.4	158.2	43.9
Machine tools	thous.	443	203	45.8
Petroleum plants	thous. units	145	26	17.9
Vehicles	thous. units	3,285	1,145.3	44.2
Buses	thous. units	519	337	64.9
Motorcycle	thous. units	14,896	8,254	55.4
Bicycles	mln. units	82	44.7	54.5
Color TV receivers	mln. units	44.7	20.6	46.1
Washing machines	mln. units	21.8	9.5	43.4
Refrigerators	mln. units	18.2	9.2	50.4
Photo cameras	mln. units	57.7	33.3	57.7
Microcomputers	thous. units	6,248	836	13.4

Source: Study on the Strategy of the 10th "Five-Year" Plan, vol. 1 (Beijing: China Population Press, 2000), 87–88.

The unprofitability of enterprises of all forms of ownership increased. During the 8th Five-Year Plan, it almost doubled and reached 88.3 billion yuan. State-owned enterprises accounted for 72.4% of the total losses. According to the official data, in 1997, among all industrial enterprises, 23.6% were unprofitable, including 39.2% among state-owned enterprises. The loss ratio was higher (41.0%) among medium-sized and large enterprises. The share of unprofitable enterprises among private and individual ones was 34.5%.

The negative consequences of rapid industrialization were the irrational use of natural resources and environmental degradation. In almost all areas of production, China consumed significantly more raw materials needed to produce a unit of output than in advanced industrial countries. The following results of surveys by Chinese specialists are indicative of the waste of material resources per unit of output. To produce a unit of output, the PRC spent 6–10 times more of the 12 most important natural resources (energy, metals, cement, cotton, etc.) than developed countries. Rice production uses 40% more water per hectare than in the United States. The beneficial effects of mineral fertilizers in China are used by 30%, while in developed countries, they are used by 50%.[31] On average, 417 grams of (standardized) coal were needed to produce 1 kWh in the PRC, which is 23%–30% higher than in the US, Germany, and the former USSR. Numerous similar examples could be cited from Chinese field studies. All of them bear records of the relatively backward state of the technical and process base of production in China.

An acute problem was the withdrawal of arable land from agricultural turnover. During the first 40 years of the PRC's existence, 40.7 million hectares of arable land were withdrawn from agricultural turnover. Despite the adopted laws, this process did not stop. Only in ten years (1986–1995) agriculture lost 6,984.2 thousand hectares of arable land.

The growing industry causes great harm by emissions of exhaust gases, water, and solid waste products. In 1995, 37,285 million tons of industrial wastewater were discharged into the water basin, and only 12 billion (33%) of it were treated. A total of 12,341 billion cubic meters of exhaust gases were emitted into the atmosphere, and only 63.9 billion of them were treated (52%). 644.7 million tons of solid industrial waste were dumped on the soil. As a result of such economic activities in the early 1990s, out of more than 1200 rivers and large tributaries, 850 (70%) were polluted. The shortage of fresh water, specifically in the north of the country, was growing rapidly. There was a shortage of water in half of the cities and towns.[32] For this reason, in the rainless years, enterprises stopped, and there was a decrease in harvest. In the north and northwest of the country, hundreds of thousands of hectares of land were of poor usability or unusable due to ongoing erosion and desertification, the groundwater horizon was rapidly decreasing, and the land reserves were drying up and deforming. An environmental crisis was a consequence of rapid economic growth on a relatively technologically backward base.

Such destructive and comprehensive processes of environmental degradation are based on the traditional inertial extensive reproduction, which had been formed in China for centuries under the pressure of massive population growth under conditions of limited natural resources (primarily land) for crop production and animal husbandry development. The production of means of subsistence was based primarily on manual labor with the use of primitive equipment. After the formation of the PRC, a modern industrial core was formed in the economy with the development of industrialization, but the inertial extensive type of production was dominating in non-industrialized sectors. The relationship of society with nature moved into a new stage of environmental degradation. The transfer of a massive and rapidly increasing human population to the industrial economy in China was accompanied by the massive and rapid destruction of natural resources.

With the rapid growth of the population and labor resources, manual labor and extensive types of reproduction expanded. Notwithstanding industrialization, up to half of the labor force was occupied by manual and low-skilled labor. The extensive type of expanded reproduction remained the main means of survival for the massive population.

By the mid-1990s, apart from the huge labor force, which was the main source of extensive types of reproduction, all other sources of extensive growth were either close to depletion (land, water) or used extremely wastefully (coal, oil, water, air, etc.). The wasteful nature of growth, low technical level, and dispersion of material and financial resources became the main obstacles to the creation of an efficient and high-tech economy. The conclusion of Chinese scientists was unequivocal: within the framework of the extensive type of expanded reproduction, in the next 15 years, China will not be able to continue the economic recovery that took place in 1979–1995. "Extensive economic growth cannot ensure continuous, high-speed, and healthy economic development," was the conclusion of Chinese economists.[33] This method of reproduction is not able to ensure sustainable economic development and the necessary efficiency of capital investments. Preparations for a new stage of economic growth based on scientific and technological progress and innovative development began. This required the advanced development of scientific and technical potential.

1.3.6 The beginning of a new turn in economic

The growing disproportions in the economic, social, and environmental spheres forced the Chinese policymakers and academic community to look for a way out not by repeating new "leaps" but by understanding the real situation and introducing fundamental changes to the growth strategy. The development of this concept began in the 1980s. These activities were intensified in the early 1990s in connection with the new acceleration that began at the discretion of Deng Xiaoping in 1992–1995 and the ensuing "overheating" of the economy, disproportions, inflation, and overproduction of goods in different industries.

The 9th Five-Year Plan (1996–2000) for the Economic and Social Development of the PRC and Long-Range Objectives to the Year 2010 (hereinafter referred to as the "Objectives 2010") became the answer to solving the emerging problems.[34] Two strategic transitions became the core of these Objectives: the transition from the "traditionally planned economy to the system of the socialist market economy" and the transition from the "extensive method of growth to the intensive one." The main thing is the transition to intensive development, which in fact means the reconstruction of a multi-level economy scattered over a vast area and raising it to a modern resource- and energy-saving, as well as scientific and technological level. During the 9th Five-Year Plan, it was planned to carry out a "soft landing" of the economy, i.e., its recovery after the "accelerations" undertaken in the 1980s and in the early 1990s, as well as to begin the transition to an intensive, resource-saving method of growth. In the field of economic relations, there were tasks to carry out deep reforms of state enterprises and create an "initial structure of modern enterprises," as well as an "initial structure of the socialist market economy system."

The 9th Five-Year Plan was extremely eventful. During the intense organizational activity of the government, the tasks set were fulfilled. The average annual GDP growth for five years was 8.3%; inflation was curbed. In 1996, it was reduced to 6.1% and 0.7% in 1997, and then prices began to decline: in 1998, the general retail price index decreased by 2.6%, 3% in 1999, and 1.5% in 2000.[35]

During the 9th Five-Year Plan, the PRC persistently advanced along the path of solving the main strategic task—the development of productive forces, advancing them to a higher scientific and technological level, and building up the overall economic power. Key industrial facilities were actively constructed, new capacities were introduced, and obsolete ones were reconstructed, hopelessly backward ones were discarded. In 1998, 117 key industrial facilities were under construction, and 18 of them were completed. In 1999, the number of key facilities was 102, including 36 under construction in the fuel and energy complex, 27 in transportation, three in metallurgy, five in petrochemistry, and 12 in the agricultural sector. The commissioning of new capacities can be judged by the scale of production growth. The electric power industry developed particularly fast. For the 22-year period (1979–2000), electricity generation increased 5.3 times, 2.2 times in the 1990s, 34.6% for the 9th Five-Year Plan, or by 348.6 billion kWh. Steel production increased by 5.3 times, 1.9 times, and 34.7%, respectively, and cement production increased by 9.2 times, 2.8 times, and 25.5%, respectively.

Based on the basic industries strengthening, the key industries developed at a high pace: mechanical engineering, electronics, petrochemistry, construction industry, automotive industry, and computer science, which determine the technical image of the national economy. Particular attention was paid to the aerospace industry and bioengineering.

Back in the 1980s, extensive material and technical facilities were created to produce industrial goods, the use of which made it possible to fill the shelves of shops and markets with popular consumer goods in a short time. At the new stage, the growth of permanent facilities construction was concentrated on the reconstruction and modernization of production capacities and accelerated introduction of the latest productive assets. The source of the new technology was both domestic developments and foreign technology purchased through import channels, obtained through state technology loans, and imported by foreign and Chinese investors from Taiwan, Hong Kong, and Macao. According to the third census of industrial production, in late 1995, in the township and city enterprises, which account for 70.1% of the equipment of the entire industry of the country, out of more than 3,200 main types of production equipment, 47.1% accounted for imported equipment and 52.9% for the domestic one.

The equipment renewal in industry substantially accelerated during the 9th Five-Year Plan. The main source of new equipment was domestic production based on modernized foreign models. The Chinese leaders skilfully applied all possible methods of catching up with development, including the improvement and replication of foreign models.

However, during the 9th Five-Year Plan, the investment rate was reduced, and its annual average amounted to 37.9%, with an average annual increase in investment in fixed assets of 10.3% compared to 36.9% during the 8th Five-Year Plan. For the period of five years, 13.889 billion yuan was invested in the national economy, i.e., almost 2.2 times more than during the 8th Five-Year Plan (6380.8 billion yuan). The public sector remained the main investor: in 1999, it accounted for 53.4% and 50.0% in 2000; the collective sector accounted for 14.0% and 14.5%, respectively; the individual sector accounted for 13.3% and 14.1%, and the private and foreign sectors accounted for 19.3% and 21.4% in the aggregate.[36] The overwhelming proportion (56.1%) of investment resources was directed to the development and reconstruction of material production, 15.0% to the construction of real estate objects, and 28.9% to other purposes. The data in Table 11 illustrates the application of various sources of investment resources for the construction of permanent facilities in 1996–2000.

Table 11   Structure of Investment Sources for the Construction of Permanent Facilities (as %)

Investment resources sources	1996	1997	1998	1999	2000
All investment resources	100.0	100.0	100.0	100.0	100.0
1. State budget	6.1	6.4	8.8	12.2	12.1
2. Bank lending	22.8	22.0	24.6	24.8	26.7
3. Government bond issue		0.8	1.2	2.0	1.2
4. Use of foreign capital	14.5	14.1	11.7	8.2	6.9
Direct investment		6.5	4.7	2.5	2.5
Foreign loan		5.4	5.2	...	...
5. Personal savings	44.1	46.5	42.9	42.2	42.8
Central offices		4.3	4.1	...	...
Provinces, autonomous regions		7.6	7.3	...	...
Districts		6.0	6.3	...	...
Counties		4.5	4.6	...	...
Enterprises and organizations		24.1	20.7	21.5	23.5
Stock issues		0.4	0.4	0.3	0.3
6. Other sources	11.2	10.2	10.8	10.6	10.1

Source: China Statistical Yearbook (1998), 192; *China Statistical Abstract* (1999), 45; *China Statistical Abstract* (2001), 53.

A powerful source of the productive forces development was the implementation of the opening up during the 8th and the 9th Five-Year Plans. Despite the decline in the rate of foreign trade turnover in 1998 and 1999 in connection with the financial crisis in Southeast Asia, for the period of five years, China imported equipment, raw materials, and goods worth $740.8 billion, which is 2.1 times more than during the 8th Five-Year Plan. Approximately 16% of this rapidly growing amount was spent on raw materials and energy resources, and import volume was increasing every year.[37] The remaining 84% of imports accounted for machinery and equipment for mechanical engineering, transport, chemical, and metallurgical industries products, as well as electronics. For a five-year period (1996–2000), the total amount of imported transport equipment and equipment for machine-building enterprises was $325.8 billion, and for all industrial goods was $661.7 billion.[38]

The second major channel for obtaining modern technology was state loans, which, as a rule, are taken to provide equipment for major new construction projects, such as the construction of the Beijing-Shanghai high-speed railway, the Sanxia (Three Gorges) hydroelectric complex, etc. The total amount of state borrowing in 1989–2000 amounted to $162.8 billion. For the five years of the 9th Five-Year Plan, the state's external debt increased by $55.9 billion.[39]

The third channel was the direct investment of the Chinese from Hong Kong, Taiwan, and Macao, as well as foreign investors from other countries. The entire amount of foreign capital raised in 1979–2000 amounted to $446.6 billion, including an increase of $213.5 billion during the 9th Five-Year Plan.[40]

The fourth channel was a growing scientific exchange, which was carried out in various forms: sending Chinese specialists and scientists to foreign research organizations or universities; students and graduate students to universities; purchasing scientific and technical equipment for laboratories, literature, and licenses; invitation of scientists and specialists to give lectures and work in the PRC.

The active renewal of fixed assets since the late 1990s was supplemented by the culling and shutdown of hopelessly backward and inefficient enterprises, which were also harmful to the environment. In 1999, numerous obsolete and pollution-intensive production facilities in various industries were decommissioned, and thousands of mines and dozens of polluting plants were shut down (Table 12).[41]

Similar operations to dispose of obsolete fixed assets were carried out in other industries, including the production of chemical fertilizers, pesticides, synthetic fibers, plastics, rubber, etc. As a rule, small and some medium-sized enterprises were subject to closure. These measures did not affect large enterprises which had enough resources for modernization.

Table 12   The Number of Outdated and Pollution-Intensive Production Facilities
Shut Down

Industries	Number of enterprises	Decommissioned capacities
Coal mining	31,000 mines	250 mln. tons
Petrochemistry	70 oil refineries	...
Metallurgy:		
blast furnace ironmaking	1,387 blast furnaces	9,750 thous. tons
steelmaking	...	18,290 thous. tons
Cement production	...	40,000 thous. tons
Glass	...	15,000 containers
Thermal power stations	...	3 mln. kW
Textile	...	9,060 thous. spindles

In some sectors, the closure of enterprises with an outdated technological base led to a decline in production. The closure of small enterprises particularly affected the fuel and energy complex. In terms of reference fuel in 2000 compared to 1996, the amount of primary energy decreased by 246.2 million tons, and coal mining by 399 million tons. Despite the growth in electricity production, the electricity consumption per employee in China remained low: less than 0.9 tons of reference fuel per person per year. This is 8–15 times less than in developed countries. In 1998, per capita electricity production in the United States was 12.7, in Canada was 19.2, in France was 8.9, in Japan was 8.6, and in Russia was 6 times more than in the PRC. Thus, China developed in the conditions of the most severe energy deficiency.

Focus on the intensification and acceleration of the technical development of the economy required further deepening of the economy's monetization. In the ruling and scientific circles of the PRC, the active use of money and the improvement of financial institutions are regarded not as an end in itself, but as a means of raising material production, and the real sector of the economy. One of the vital tasks in the field of finance and monetary circulation remained the creation of a favorable savings and investment environment in a country with low inflation. As already noted, the Chinese leaders considered the increase in the annual general price index to 10% as the maximum level of inflation. Economic, administrative, and political measures were used to solve this issue.

The main factor in the fight against inflation was the growth of material production, primarily the production of consumer goods. Such an unusual phenomenon as a decrease in prices for products of some industries with a 49% increase in GDP over five years, and money in circulation by 86.5%, is also explained by some overpricing in the previous five-year period, switching a part of the demand to services, a decline in the solvent demand and deformation of its structure, as well as strengthening of the national currency.

With the rise of inflation, a commensurately tight monetary and financial policy was implemented, in accordance with which investment rates and money emissions decreased, and control over the fiscal system, as well as the growth of the payroll fund and other types of income, was strengthened. As a result of the emergency measures adoption for the period of a year or two, the rate of price growth was brought down to a level significantly below 10% (Table 13).

Table 13   Prices Dynamics (as %)

Year				Including			
	General index	Consumer price index	Industrial product price index	Metallurgy products	Electricity	Chemical industry products	Petroleum products
1994	21.7	24.1	24.0*	57.7*	39.5	15.4	71.3*
1995	14.8	17.1	14.9	5.5	9.5	26.2	21.2
1996	6.1	8.3	2.9	–2.3	13.1	3.4	4.6
1997	0.8	2.8	–0.3	–2.7	14.0	–4.5	7.4
1998	–2.6	–0.8	–4.1	–6.9	5.5	–7.1	–7.0
1999	–3.0	–1.4	–2.4	–4.2	0.9	–3.5	9.6
2000	...	0.4	2.8	3.3	2.4	1.0	44.3

Source: China Statistical Yearbook (2000), 289, 305; *China Statistical Abstract* (2001), 87.
Note: * 1993.

Starting from 1997 to 1998, the reduction in the rate of price growth turned into an absolute decline. Devastating inflation turned into a new threat—a sharp aggravation of the problem of implementation and insufficient demand. The strengthening of the yuan and the increase in its weight were accompanied by a decrease in interest rates for deposits and loans. Bank interest rates have been reduced every year since 1996, and in some years, they were reduced several times.

Table 14   Change in Interest Rates (as %)

Periods	For deposits		Periods	For loans	
	11.07.1993	10.06.1999		11.07.1993	10.06.1999
3 months	6.66	1.98	...	...	...
6 months	9.0	2.16	6 months	9.0	5.58
1 year	10.98	2.25	up to 1 year	10.98	5.85
2 years	11.70	2.43	1–3 years	12.24	5.94
3 years	12.24	2.70	3–5 years	13.86	6.03
5 years	13.80	2.88	5 years and more	14.04	6.21
8 years and more	17.10	...	...	...	...

Source: *China Statistical Yearbook* (1994), 548–549; *China Statistical Yearbook* (2000), 642–643; *China Statistical Yearbook* (2001), 640–641.

Table 15   Deepening the Monetization of the Chinese Economy in 1996–2000

Year	M0 = currency in circulation	M1 = M0 + money in current accounts in commercial banks	M2 = M1 + money in saving accounts in banks + keeping foreign currency
1995, bln. Yuan,	788	2398	6075
M to GDP, %	13.5	41.0	105.8
2000, bln. Yuan	1,470	5,300	13,500
M to GDP, %	16.4	59.3	151.0
Average annual growth rates of M in 1996–2000, %	13.3	17.2	17.3
Increase in monetary aggregates in 2000 compared to 1995, %	86.5	221.0	222.2

Source: Institute of the Far Eastern Studies of the Russian Academy of Sciences, *China on the Path of Modernization and Reform, 1949–1999* (M.: Oriental Literature, 1999), 299; *Economic Daily*, March 1, 2001.

In 1998, for instance, interest rates were reduced 7 times.[42] The value of bank interest rates in 1993–1999 and their change can be seen from the data provided in

Table 14. The implementation of a commensurately tight monetary and financial policy was accompanied by a continued deepening of the economy monetization (Table 15).

The suppression of inflation, the strengthening of the yuan, and the reduction in prices (interest) for loans contributed to the improvement of finances, money circulation, and the creation of a favorable savings and investment climate in the country, which was a financial basis for economic growth.

With the development of multistructurality, as well as the expansion of the independence of enterprises and the decollectivization of the countryside, a huge number of small enterprises without sufficient financial capabilities for capital accumulation appeared. The functioning of more than 250 million independent economic entities required special measures to concentrate the investment resources necessary to modernize the economy based on a new technological order. Zeng Peiyan, Chairman of the National Committee for Planning and Development of the PRC, spoke about the instability of the foundations of the economic recovery at the NPC session in March 2001. The reason for this statement was the weakening of the accumulation and investment process, mainly in non-state structures, which threatened to reduce the rate of GDP growth during the 9th Five-Year Plan.

To avoid this, in 1998, the government made a transition from a "proportionately tight financial and monetary policy" to an "active financial policy," the core of which was the fact that the government issues a state loan with the expectation that, in addition to direct investment in the national economy, it would encourage local authorities to increase investment, and banks to grant additional loans. In 1998–2000, three long-term construction loans totaling 360 billion yuan were issued. This amount was supplemented by the investment of local authorities, departments, and enterprises. Banks provided an additional loan totaling 750 billion yuan.

In fact, China's monetary authorities switched to the modern technology of money creation against the growth of government obligations, practiced in the advanced capitalist countries that issue world reserve currencies. These funds were used to develop infrastructure, stimulate the scientific and technical reconstruction of enterprises, improve the quality and class of products, protect the environment, and fund universities, laboratories, and research institutes conducting research on infrastructure facilities. The targeted use of additional funds was subject to strict control. In case of violation of their use, the perpetrators were punished. According to the Minister of Finance Xiang Huaicheng, the transition to an active fiscal policy made it possible to raise the GDP growth rate in 1998 by 1.5%, in 1999 by 2%, and in 2000 by 1.7%. If the aforementioned measures had not been taken, then GDP growth in 1998 would have been 6.3% instead of 7.8%, 5.1% instead of 7.1% in 1999, and 6.3% instead of 8% in 2000.

The emission of money secured by government debt bonds made it possible to resort to an increase in government spending. During the 9th Five-Year Plan of the PRC, the state budget deficit increased from 53 billion in 1996 to 229.8 billion in 2000. It was mostly formed due to increasing subsidies for the development of depressed regions, as well as backbone industries and regions. In 1995, 247.1 billion yuan were transferred to the regions from the central budget; in 2000, this sum amounted to 466.8 billion, and in 2001 almost 520 billion. In 1996–1999, loss-making enterprises were subsidized 132.9 billion yuan, subsidies to prices amounted to 241.6 billion, and agricultural support exceeded 237 billion yuan. An important source of funds to cover the budget deficit during the 9th Five-Year Plan was the issue and placement of government debt bonds. The scale of their issue was also growing from year to year. In 1998, the total amount of bonds issued amounted to 389.1 billion yuan and 418 billion in 2000, and it was planned to increase their issue to 500.4 billion in 2001.

1.3.7 Transition to the 10th Five-Year Plan

Despite the rapid economic development and large-scale economic modernization, the PRC leaders were critical of its state, paying attention to the following issues:[43]

(1) Irrational structure of production, lack of coordination of regional development, poor quality of the entire economic system

(2) Low-efficient enterprises, high unprofitability, growing debts, and non-payments; the incompleteness of the modern enterprise's system creation

(3) Insufficiently high quality of products, small depth of its processing, small product range, and low product rating, resulting in its weak competitiveness in world markets

(4) A *large gap* in the level of development of science, technology, and education from the advanced world level; lack of close correlation between production, science, and education

(5) Increasing demographic pressure and growing scarcity of water, land, oil, gas, and other important raw materials; environmental difficulties in a number of regions of the country

(6) Imperfect system of the socialist market; chaotic nature of the economy and markets in some areas

(7) The growing differentiation in the incomes of the population, the slow growth in the incomes of the peasants working on the land

(8) Dangerous phenomena of corruption, theft of government property, decay, idleness, embezzlement, formalism, and bureaucracy, as well as the presence of socially unsettled areas

There were also problems with maintaining the planned pace of economic development.

The planning strategy for the 10th Five-Year Plan was aimed at solving these problems. The State Council draft plan of the "Outline for the 10th Five-Year Plan for National Economic and Social Development of the People's Republic of China"[44] (hereinafter referred to as the "Basic Provisions") was approved by the regular session of the NPC in March 2001.

As the main guideline of the "Basic Provisions," the principle of development was put forward as an iron law, which is logically determined by China's economic and social conditions, is put forward as the main course of development in the "Basic Provisions." Development is considered as the key to solving the fundamental problems that burden the national economy of the PRC. The text contains several indicators that were expected to be achieved in 2005. The average annual growth rate of GDP production was planned with a margin of 7%. Its volume was supposed to reach 12.5 trillion yuan in 2005, i.e., to increase by almost 40% compared to 2000. The structure of GDP would also change. As a result of lower growth rates, the share of agriculture decreased, the share of industry and the service sector slightly increased, and the employment rate in the manufacturing sectors changed (Table 16):[45]

A major part of the "Basic Provisions" is devoted to determining the conditions, factors, and objectives necessary for the implementation of the principle of development. The problems of streamlining the structure and raising material production to a new scientific and technical level are put to the fore. The requirement to stabilize the potential opportunities for growing grain crops was put forward in line with specific measures in agriculture.

Table 16   Sectoral Structure of the Economy

Year	Agriculture (I sector)	Industry, construction (II sector)	Transport, communication, trade, and other services (III sector)
GDP production by economic sectors (as %)			
1999	17.7	49.3	33.0
2005	13.0	51.0	36.0
Employment by industry sector (as %)			
1999	50.1	23.0	26.9
2005	44.0	23.0	33.0

For this purpose, it was proposed to preserve the existing arable area, expand seed farms, improve irrigation systems, increase the fertility of medium and low-yielding fields, streamline the placement of the created marketable grain storages, and increase the material and financial support for the main areas of food production. The tasks to increase the size of farm households are set.

Industry in the PRC was regarded as the backbone of the economy, as the main means of achieving the strategic goal of creating a modern state, as a source of scientific and technological reconstruction of the entire national economy, and maintaining high rates of economic growth. Metallurgy, machine tool building, instrument engineering, electronics, petrochemistry and chemistry, building materials production, automotive industry, aviation industry, and space industries were aimed at accelerated scientific and technological reconstruction, mastering high and fine technologies, and reducing the lag from developed countries. "Blind" (unauthorized, unplanned) and duplicated construction of industrial facilities was prohibited. Major projects were implemented in the development of the electric power industry. In addition to the already constructed Sanxia (Three Gorges), Xiaolangdi, and other hydroelectric power plants, it was planned to start the construction of eight more large hydroelectric power plants.

According to the plan, science and education were supposed to become the pioneers in the creation of modern China. Scientists were required to stay ahead and make every effort to achieve world-class advanced levels or to reduce the gap as much as possible in the leading fields of science in the shortest possible time and to break ahead in some areas. Advanced informatization and digitalization of the economy were considered as powerful incentives for its development. Financing for the fundamental sciences and the most important applied research was undertaken by the state. For this purpose, in 2005, it was planned to increase investments in the development of science from 0.6% of GDP in 1998 to 1.5% of GDP, which amounted to 188 billion yuan ($22.7 billion) in the prices of 1998, and 3.6 times exceeded similar investments made in 1998. Work on strengthening the connection between production, science, technology, and education was actively carried out. R&D centers and centers for implementation were rapidly created at large enterprises, factories-technical colleges, and research production zones were organized.

One of the main factors for stimulating economic growth was supposed to be the vigorous implementation of reforms in almost all activity areas. State enterprise reforms intensification and creation of a system of modern enterprises, which started in the 1990s, came to the fore. An enterprise, a company, or a corporation working for the market and meeting growing demand, which relies on scientific and technological progress as its driving force, were supposed to become leading economic entities. As a result, the level of industrial development, the quality of its products, and competitiveness in global markets were supposed to rise.

Expansion of the opening up and the development of trade, as well as scientific and technical ties, are considered as a powerful incentive for economic growth and scientific and technological progress. The PRC considered accession to the WTO as an objective necessity, which would make it possible to significantly expand sales markets for the growing domestic industry and increase the import of new equipment, modern technologies, advanced scientific achievements, and various raw materials and energy resources.

Despite quite radical periodical changes in the economic course, the Chinese leaders maintained and developed the financial and investment system of the state based on targeted money creation for the progressive expansion of crediting economic development. Even during periods of economic liberalization, the Chinese government, as it was in 1984–1988 and in 1992–1994, maintained control over the macroeconomic situation, taking timely anti-inflationary measures. With the threat of macroeconomic destabilization, the government resolutely started streamlining the economic system and suppressing inflation. Being extremely persistent in achieving strategic goals, the Chinese leaders did not persist when they saw that the implementation of their tactical decisions was challenging but timely scaled-down work. This gave rise to a wave-like, cyclical nature of economic dynamics while maintaining the general trend of economic growth outpacing other countries. Such an approach, which oriented economic transformations not to a pre-created political model, but to solving the key tasks of economic growth, ensured success in the economic development and reforms.

1.3.8 Monetization of the PRC's economy (1996–2000)

The key element of the reform and opening-up policy proclaimed and consistently pursued by Deng Xiaoping was the transfer of commodity exchange from a semi-natural to a commodity-money form and the commercialization of economic turnover. During the period of the transition and later, scientists, practitioners, and ordinary people found numerous challenges in this transition. Many of them are still relevant. But considering the achieved economic level and growth rates, it should be recognized that this transition was carried out at the highest professional level and with high civic responsibility for the future of the country. In contrast to the market reforms in the former CMEA (Council for Mutual Economic Assistance) member states, which were based on the ideological approach of "shock therapy," China did without a transformational recession and retained the gains of socialism both in the social sphere and in the economic development management.

At the turn of the 1970s and 1980s, imbalances in the Chinese economy reached a critical level. Although production, albeit unevenly, developed, the growth of the money supply was strictly restrained. In 1978, the amount of active money (M0) to GDP was only 6%. If we add current deposits in banks (M1), this ratio will rise to 26% and up to 32%, including long-term deposits, deposits in foreign currency, and fiduciary deposits (M2), which is 2.5–3 times lower than the needs of the functioning modern economy. Such a small amount of active money could not perform its most important functions of binding resources in the process of economic reproducing, as well as preserving and accumulating value. The lack of active money in circulation was compensated by the barter nature of commodity circulation and normalized administrative distribution. The development of production and capital accumulation were restrained.

By the late 1970s, in addition to purely economic reasons, numerous acute problems accumulated in the social field. Economic and social problems developed into political ones. During the years of the "Cultural Revolution," the already low real incomes of both the urban and rural populations decreased. To avoid the accumulation of huge masses of the unemployed population, a rapid expansion of the sphere of economic activity was required to involve young people of working age (16–17 million people per year) in production. The CPC leaders were faced with the need for an urgent reduction of socio-political tension. Monetary instruments to ensure expanded reproduction were required for economic development and the solution of social problems.

Deciding on the development of market mechanisms, the Chinese reformers abandoned the administrative-distributive "non-monetary" system for regulating commodities circulation and started intensive monetization of the economy. As a result, for the period of 17 years (1979–1995), M0 increased by 37.2 times, M1 increased by 25.3 times, and M2 increased by 52.4 times. The structure of the money supply and the ratio of monetary aggregates to GDP changed. In 2000, M0/GDP reached 16.6%, M1/GDP reached 60.3%, and M2/GDP reached 152.6%.

According to Table 17, in only two years (1985 and 1995), the growth rates of the money supply in circulation (M0) fell below the GDP growth rates. On average, the money supply growth was 2.4 times higher than the GDP growth rate.

It was an unprecedented monetary injection into the economy. The transition to a market economy from a chronically scarce and rigidly rationed economy with the unsatisfied needs of a massive population was fraught with their transformation into a *money* overhang, which, in the economy with short supply, started really threatening with an inflationary explosion. Therefore, the rapid monetary pumping was carried out under strict control. The money created was used by the state strictly for the intended purpose of binding available resources to finance investments and expanded economic reproduction.

During monetization, ways for the most efficient use of money creation to ensure economic growth were tested. In the first instance, the unprofitability of the agro-industrial complex was eliminated—purchase prices for agricultural products were increased. The decision on this was made at the Plenary Session of the 11th CPC Central Committee in December 1978. On average, in 1979, prices rose by 22.1%, including 30.1% for grains. The increase in prices for agricultural products continued in subsequent years. For the period of 17 years, they were increased by 5.3 times, including 7.1 times for grain and 6.3 times for cotton. This policy ensured the achievement of the following goals:

Table 17   The Process of the PRC's Economy Monetization

Year	GDP growth		M0 growth		M1 growth		M2 growth	
	Bln. RMB*	Previous year = 100.0**	Bln. RMB	Previous year = 100.0	Bln. RMB	Previous year = 100.0	Bln. RMB	Previous year = 100.0
1978	362.41	111.7	21.20	...	94.85	...	115.91	...
1979	403.82	107.6	22.70	126.3	117.71	124.1	145.81	125.8
1980	451.78	107.8	34.62	129.3	144.34	122.6	184.29	126.4
1981	486.03	106.2	39.63	114.5	171.08	118.5	223.45	121.2
1982	530.18	109.1	43.91	110.8	191.44	111.9	258.98	115.9
1983	595.74	112.4	52.98	120.7	218.25	114.0	307.50	118.7
1984	720.67	115.2	79.21	149.5	293.16	134.3	414.63	134.8
1985	898.91	113.5	98.00	112.4	334.09	114.0	519.89	126.4
1986	1,020.14	108.8	121.84	136.9	423.22	126.7	672.10	129.3
1987	1,195.45	111.6	145.46	119.4	571.46	135.0	834.97	124.2
1988	1,492.23	111.3	213.40	146.7	695.05	121.6	1,009.96	121.0
1989	1,691.78	104.1	234.40	109.8	734.71	105.7	1,194.96	118.3
1990	1,859.84	103.8	264.44	112.8	879.32	119.7	1,529.37	128.0
1991	2,166.25	109.2	317.78	120.0	1,086.66	123.6	1,943.99	127.1
1992	2,540.21	114.2	433.60	135.4	1,501.57	138.3	2,540.21	130.7
1993	3,456.05	113.5	586.47	135.8	1,869.49	117.5	3,150.10	124.0
1994	4,642.58	112.6	728.86	124.3	2,054.07	109.9	4,692.35	149.0
1995	5,765.00	110.2	788.50	108.2	2,398.00	116.7	6,075.00	129.5
1996	6,685.05	109.6	880.20	111.6	2,851.48	118.9	7,609.49	125.3
1997	7,314.27	108.8	1,017.76	115.6	3,482.68	122.1	9,099.53	119.6
1998	7,696.72	107.8	1,120.42	110.1	3,895.37	111.8	10,449.85	114.8
1999	8,057.94	107.1	1,345.55	120.1	4,583.72	117.7	11,989.79	114.7
2000	8,818.96	108.0	1,465.27	108.9	5,314.72	115.9	13,461.03	112.3

Source: China Statistical Yearbook (1988, 1993, 1996, 2001); *Economic Daily*, no. 12 (1996), 28.
Note: * in current prices, ** in comparable prices.

(1) The prices of agricultural products were equated to the costs of production and value.

(2) Production growth was stimulated by activating demand for money for means of production, primarily for mineral fertilizers, herbicides, irrigation water, etc.

(3) Marketability of agricultural production increased with its growth; the problem of providing food for the rapidly growing population of cities and developing industry with raw materials was solved.

(4) Cash incomes of peasants increased, which contributed to the growth of rural demand for industrial consumer goods.

Ultimately, the growth of agricultural production formed the basis for ensuring the reproduction of the population, the expansion of economic activity, and economic and cultural growth in the PRC. The increase in agricultural production ensured the balance of monetary circulation in the PRC.

The second direction of the money injection was an increase in the cash income of workers and employees, which was carried out through the following main channels:

(1) Increase in wages for civil servants and public sector workers (state apparatus, education, healthcare, science, culture, etc.)

(2) Carrying out a payroll reform with the creation of mechanisms for its increase

(3) Compensation of workers and employees' expenses in connection with increased food prices

(4) Subsidizing utility services

(5) Social sphere financing

The third massive flow of money supply was directed to the investment sphere, where the following most important tasks of economic growth were solved:

(1) Conducting a large-scale structural maneuver in the 1980s by redistributing financial and material resources in support of the mass production of industrial consumer goods (sewing machines, bicycles, watches, TV and radio sets, etc.)

(2) Implementation of major projects for the country's industrialization and expansion of economic activity for tens of millions of young people reaching the working age

(3) Modernization of industry, transport, telecommunications, and other industries on an advanced technological basis

(4)   Lending to increase the working capital of industrial enterprises, primarily state-owned ones

The fourth direction of the use of money creation was the financing of the army and military-industrial complex modernization.

And finally, the fifth direction of cash injections was the stimulation of foreign economic openness and lending to increase the export of goods and the import of technology.

Targeted management of the money creation made it possible to successfully implement strategic plans for accelerating economic development and raising social welfare, transferring the economy to the mode of commodity money and commercial circulation, accelerating investment growth rates and carrying out modernization, providing employment for the growing population, and increasing trade volumes.

Along with the growth of the money supply, the money incomes of the population increased rapidly. Over the 17-year period of reforms (1979–1995), the national payroll fund increased 14.2 times, including 13 times in the public sector and 11.8 times in the collective sector. The highest growth rates were during the 8th Five-Year Plan (1991–1995), when its absolute size increased by 2.7 times. Other sectors of the economy (private, state capitalist, and capitalist) rose quickly. Although their development started in 1978 from scratch, these sectors already accounted for 7.9% of the national payroll fund in 1995. For the period of 17 years, the average money wage increased almost 9 times, and during the 8th Five-Year Plan, it increased 2.57 times.

The process of income growth in the countryside proceeded just as intensively. For the period of 17 years, the net income of peasants in current prices increased 11.8 times, and during the 8th Five-Year Plan, it increased 2.3 times. As commodity-money relations reached the countryside, the commercialization of agriculture took place, and the foundations of the peasants' way of life were modernized.

Contrary to the postulates of the theory of market equilibrium and the dogmas of its vulgar version of monetarism, the broad monetary financing of government spending, investments in infrastructure development, loans to replenish working capital, and capital investment of industrial enterprises did not lead to inflationary. To prevent them, the targeted use of the issued money was ensured in addition to the main anti-inflationary measures for the purpose of the rapid increase in agricultural production, converting the defense and heavy industries toward the production of consumer goods, investing in the development of the textile, light, and food industries, as well as the transportation network. Thus, the increase in the money supply was neutralized by the advanced growth in the production of goods and services that were in demand. This made it possible to avoid inflation and, conversely, sometimes led to deflation due to the excess production of consumer goods.

The rapid reaction of agricultural production to credit expansion was specifically important. The following main sources and factors of agricultural resource growth should be noted:

(1) Relatively favorable natural and climatic conditions (temperate, warm-temperate, and subtropical climate in most of the country's territory, a long growing season, which allows growing two or even three crops a year in a vast territory, sufficient and abundant moistening in many agricultural areas)

(2) The presence of an extensive irrigation network, which currently covers more than half of arable land (48 million hectares)

(3) Intensive chemicalization of agriculture. In 1995, 241 kg of chemical fertilizers were applied per 1 ha of the cultivated area against 59 kg in 1978 (or 378 and 88 kg, respectively, per 1 ha of plow land)

(4) Widespread use of simple labor to expand the cultivation of agricultural products. If in 1952, 173 million people were employed in agriculture, and then this number reached 348 million in 1993, i.e., it doubled; over the years of reforms, the number of people employed in agriculture increased by 100 million people

(5) Maintaining the profitability of agricultural production and tax-sparing policy. As already noted, reforms in agriculture started with an increase in purchase prices for agricultural products. For the period of 11 years (1979–1990), the purchase prices for grain were raised 2.85 times, and for mineral fertilizers—2.76 times. Protectionist prices for grain were introduced, providing peasants with compensation for the cost of production and income. At the same time, the share of agricultural tax in tax revenues to the state (local) budget decreased

(6) Removal of various kinds of restrictions for peasant farms in agricultural product production.

Following the agro-industrial complex, the increase in lending to industrial consumer goods production also had an immediate effect. In a matter of years, the counters of shops and markets were literally glutted with bicycles, sewing and washing machines, TV sets, refrigerators, furniture, fabrics, shoes, etc. The lifestyle of the Chinese people changed.

The growth in the production and supply of consumer goods was crucial to preventing inflation. In addition to targeted lending to the growth in consumer goods production, the executive authorities controlled the increase in money incomes and pricing and resorted to taxing high incomes on a widescale basis. An important element of the stability of the Chinese economy and society until 1993 was the maintenance of a rationed (guaranteed) supply of the urban population with grain and vegetable oil at state prices.

Among anti-inflationary measures, an important place was given to stimulating household savings. In contrast to the period of the "Cultural Revolution," when the deposits of the population were stimulated by political and administrative methods, in the late 1970s, economic interest was put at the heart of the deposit business. This was done with the help of several levers: firstly, the state guaranteed the reliability of deposits; secondly, the production of consumer goods was constantly increasing, and the product range was expanding; thirdly, the coupon (normalized) system was eliminated, and a transition to free (except for grain and vegetable oil in cities) trade was made; fourthly, depositors were given an opportunity to freely dispose of their deposits, which was not allowed during the years of the "Cultural Revolution"; fifthly, the interest rate varied with the rate of inflation. For the period of four years (1990–1993), the interest rate was raised and lowered 5 times. The lowest rate was set in April 1991: for current deposits, it was 1.8% per annum, and for deposits for a period of 8 years or more, it was 10.8%; the highest rate was set in July 1993 (3.15% and 17.10% respectively) when consumer goods prices rose rapidly. This policy proved to be very effective, organically combined with the inherent Chinese tendency to thrift. For the period of 18 years (1979–1996), the total amount of household deposits increased 183 times. In 1996, the growth of household deposits amounted to almost 13.0% of GDP and 37.2% of investments in fixed assets.

The state conducted a gradual liberalization of pricing and a restrictive income policy, stimulating savings and using progressive taxation of personal income. The set of measures taken, which, on the one hand, provided for an increase in consumer goods production and, on the other hand, the regulation of incomes and prices, restrained the growth of the latter and made it possible to prevent an inflationary burst. Price liberalization started with luxury goods and non-essential consumer goods. At the same time, administrative regulation of prices for strategic goods, essential goods, and services continued. Much time and effort were devoted to the implementation of pricing policy and the formation of a macro-regulated pricing environment. In the 1980s, there were six "adjustments" and three "great liberations" of consumer prices in China. As a rule, prices for goods that were in abundance in the markets were released. At the same time, prices inevitably rose. According to the official data, for the period of 17 years (1979–1995), prices for consumer goods in cities increased by 3.7 times. The rise in prices especially accelerated after 1984, when the first major attempt to accelerate entry into the market was made. Over ten years (1986–1995), prices for consumer goods increased 2.6 times in urban areas and 2.5 times in rural areas. The fastest growing prices were for food products (grain, vegetable oil, livestock and water products, and vegetables) and, in recent years, for services (utility services, water and electricity, transport, medical care, etc.).

Even though the supreme executive power controlled pricing, price dynamics were not calm and balanced. During the years of reforms, retail trade repeatedly experienced price storms. It was in 1985 when the prices for vegetables, livestock products, and fishery products were released; it was in 1988–1989 and in 1993–1994 when the coupon provision of the urban population with grains and vegetable oil was canceled, and a transition to the market trade in these products at free prices was made.

The rise in inflation above 10% is regarded in China as a threat to macroeconomic stability, requiring decisive measures to localize and overcome it. Believing that, in these cases, it is impossible to bring order to the economy by purely economic methods, the Chinese reformers used harsh administrative measures to suppress inflationary waves. As they gained experience, the authorities started to transition from rapid methods of suppressing inflation to a more complex set of anti-inflationary measures.

In this regard, the experience of the anti-inflationary campaign in 1993–1996 is instructive. The fact that after a huge increase in investment in fixed assets in 1992–1993 (by 42.6 and 50.0%), another overheating threatening the economy was realized by the CPC Central Committee and the State Council back in mid-1993. They authorized the adoption of "16 measures" to prevent an inflationary burst. In December 1994, another "10 measures" were adopted. However, the inflation wave continued rising. Since early 1995, the CPC Central Committee and the State Council have engaged all lower party and executive bodies related to national economy management to suppress inflation. A system of measures to suppress inflation and restore order in the economy was developed. As a result of the resolute implementation of anti-inflationary measures, the aggregate inflation index was reduced from 14.8% in 1995 to 6.1% in 1996.

Carrying out consistent monetization of the economy, the Chinese reformers were able to ensure a crisis-free transition from an administrative system of management to a market one, creating a huge money economy. Although, as a result of this activity, the yuan fell, it started performing all the main functions of money: a measure of value, a means of circulation, a means of payment, and a means of storing and accumulating value. All the listed qualities of money are indispensable conditions for the development of commercial and market relations and, with a normal discount rate, create a favorable investment environment for both domestic producers and foreign investors.

1.3.9 Periodization of China's economic growth compared to the world economy

John Ross provides the following periodization of China's economic growth in comparison with the world economy during the late 20th–early 21st century.

The three fundamental stages of the PRC's development in their connection with international trends can be clearly identified by analyzing the relationship of trends in China with the different periods in the world economy. To illustrate this, Figure 3 shows these periods and provides data for advanced economies prior to the PRC's creation. The exact dating is analyzed below, and there are, naturally, some very slight differences in exact timing between the phases at the international level and the phases in China, but the fundamental periods in the international economic development and their relation to China are clear. Regarding primarily global economic trends, these periods are as follows:

(1) 1913–1950—a period of slow average annual growth in advanced economies (2.0%)

(2) 1950–1978—a period of rapid average annual growth in advanced economies (4.4%)

(3) 1978–2007—a period of slower but still relatively fast average annual growth in advanced economies (2.6%)

(4) Post-2007 period—very slow average annual growth in advanced economies (1.1% in 2007–2016, and the IMF expected 1.3% in 2007–2021)

Thus, the data in Figure 3 clearly demonstrate why the situation since 2008 should be seen as a new and complex period in China's development, interconnected with a new period in the world economy.

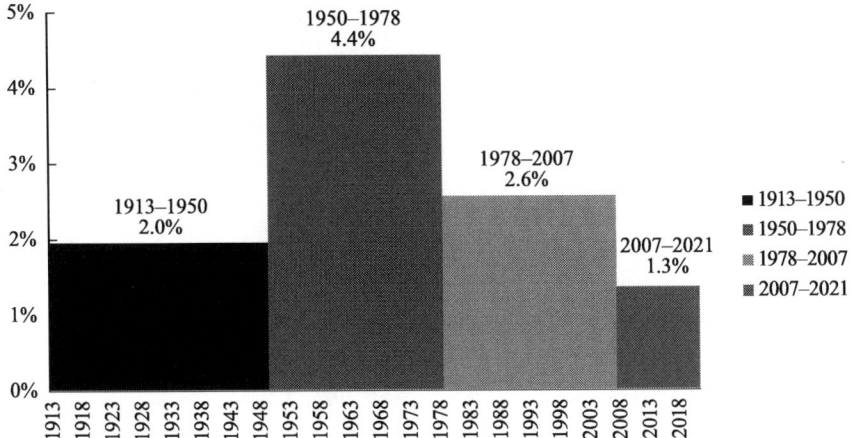

Figure 3   Average Annual GDP Growth in Advanced Economies

Source: Calculated from Angus Maddison Historical Statistics of the World Economy AD 1–2008 and IMF World Economic Outlook, April 2017.

An analysis of these very sharp differences between fundamental periods in the world economy also clearly demonstrates the interconnection between international events and events in China.

To show this interconnection, the fundamental periods in the development of the world economy and their connection with China will be briefly considered; then, the impact of these trends on the current situation will be analyzed.

Four periods in the development of the international economy

Each of the four distinct economic periods in the world economy over the past century, which are given below in chronological order, also had clear consequences for the trends in China and was interconnected with them.

The **first** period, which started after 1913, is the crisis of the international economic system, marked by World War I, the crash of 1929, and World War II. This period of fundamental instability finished with the onset of a stable post-war boom in advanced economies. This period was characterized by a radical fragmentation of the world economy, both because of the war and widespread protectionism after 1929. The starting point of this period is World War I, while its international end and the beginning of a stable boom after World War II can be referred to about 1950. The events in China, which culminated in the creation of the PRC, were clearly not independent of these processes in the international economy but related to international events and their geopolitical consequences.

The creation of the PRC in 1949 was directly related to this period, its culmination in a fundamental historical sense. During this historic period, average annual growth in advanced economies was low (2.0% per annum). However, this was not a low stable average rate but a statistical result of extreme fluctuations between booms and recessions. Thus, this general international period can be attributed to 1913–1950.

The **second** global period is the stable boom of the "golden age" in the developed Western economies after World War II. The pure "boom" phase, characterized by relatively uninterrupted rapid economic growth in all major advanced economies, took place between 1950 and 1973. "Keynesian" economic methods dominated during this period in Western economies. After 1973, there was a start of economic instability, after which in 1979/80, Reagan/Thatcher started pursuing a radical new economic policy with the re-introduction of "neoliberal" methods in Western economies and a clear displacement of Keynesianism. Almost simultaneously in 1978, China embarked on a radically new economic policy that was very different from neo-liberalism, with a "socialist market economy" created by "reform and opening-up." Thus, this economic period could be limited to either 1950–1978, in line with internal events in China, or 1950–1980, in accordance with international events—the last date was the election of Reagan. Since the focus here is on the relationship between international and domestic trends in China, 1950–1978 would be used for statistical purposes, although if they were defined as 1950–1980, it would be of little significance. During this period of 1950–1978, the average annual growth in advanced capitalist economies was high and amounted to 4.4%, and there were no major recessions until 1973. In China, this was a period of planned economy, which provided average economic growth only slightly higher than the growth rate of the world economy: in the period of 1950–1978, global economic growth was 4.6%, advanced economies growth was 4.4%, and China's growth was 4.9%.

The **third** economic period lasted from 1978 until the outbreak of the international financial crisis in 2008. In the advanced economies, this period was characterized by neoliberal policies initiated by Reagan/Thatcher and, in contrast to this, by the "socialist market economy" policies initiated by Deng Xiaoping in China. During this period, growth in the advanced economies slowed significantly compared to the post-war boom, averaging 2.6% per annum, but remained higher than in the period of the deep crisis that began with World War I. During this period, China's socialist market economy model far outperformed neoliberal policies in advanced economies: China's average annual growth in 1978–2007 amounted to 9.9%. To compare with the analysis more commonly used in China, it can be noted that this internationally recognized period of 1978–2007 covers most three of the five domestically defined leadership periods.

In 2008, the international financial crisis began. As already analyzed, growth in advanced economies since that period was extremely low, averaging 1.1% per annum in 2007–2016 and, according to IMF forecasts, 1.3% in 2007–2021. This average growth rate was much lower than during the great crisis in the advanced economies, which started with World War I. However, the low average rate in the current period was created after the recession of 2007–2009 by very slow but relatively stable growth, rather than the low average rate created by the extreme swings of boom and recession seen in the crisis that began with World War I. Given this extremely slow recovery from the international financial crisis, the term "Great Stagnation" is most relevant to the current period since 2008. This stage in the global economy certainly creates an international context for the "new normal" in China.

The relationship between international and domestic factors for China during all these periods is obvious—our goal was simply to establish the international features of the third period of this development, starting with the international financial crisis of 2008. To do this, the following clarifications are necessary.

No serious scholar suggests that the founding of the PRC in 1949 was connected with the great period of international crisis that started with World War I, continued through the Great Recession after 1929, and ended with World War II.

All analysis in China marks the great turning point of 1978 and Deng Xiaoping's "reform and opening-up." While some authors pay insufficient attention to the fact that this almost exactly coincides with the great reversal in Western economies in 1979/80 initiated by Reagan/Thatcher, our experience is to consider the fact that Chinese scholars note that such a fundamental turnaround both in China and Western economies, occurring almost at the same time, cannot be a coincidence. Despite the explanation given, it is obvious that 1950–1978/80 is a period in the history of both China and Western economies, and a new period began in 1978/80.

As noted, both in China and other countries, the international financial crisis of 2008 was the largest peacetime financial crisis since 1929. But in some research, this was explicitly or implicitly inaccurately interpreted as just a temporary episode, a rather large "uprise" in countries with developed economy, followed by a "return to normal life." Compared to the well-known discussion in China, it is implicitly or implicitly assumed that after 2007, advanced economies entered a V-shaped period, a sharp decline followed by a return to relatively fast growth rates. Instead, we previously found that, in comparison to the discussion in China, in terms of growth rates, advanced economies entered a more L-shaped pattern after 2007—a recession that was not followed by a return to a fast average growth rate. These facts suggest that the years since the 2008 international financial crisis represent a single historical period characterized by new low average growth rates in advanced economies. This represents a new period in the international economy and therefore in its relationship with China.

It is obvious that in advanced Western economies, this situation has serious implications for the situation that China faces. As was analyzed above, it is for this reason that the development of the PRC in terms of international trends can be analyzed in relation to three periods:

(1)   1949–1978
(2)   1979–2007
(3)   2008–

In this context, China's current policy is a response to this new period after the international financial crisis.

The key trends of the new international period that China's economy is facing
The fact that China, as well as advanced economies, was experiencing a long period of slow growth, establishes a clear link between the general nature of this period and immediate events. It also demonstrates that China's international initiatives are not individual or uncoordinated but form a coherent structure. However, to complete this picture, these international trends must be integrated with China's cumulative domestic economic achievements, since it is obvious that each of these fundamental international periods also corresponds to a particular stage of China's domestic development:

1949–1978 was a period of "social miracle" in China, which has no precedent in world history. Life expectancy is well known in economics as the most sensitive general indicator of social conditions since it sums up in one figure all positive (economic prosperity, good education, good health care, environmental protection, etc.) and negative trends (poverty, poor education, lack of health care, environmental pollution, etc.) grew in China for the period of 29 years from 1949 until Mao Zedong's death in 1976 from 35 to 64 years. Life expectancy in China increased by more than one year every past chronological year, rising from 73% of the world average in 1950 to 105% in 1976. However, the tremendous social gains of this period were not accompanied by exceptionally rapid economic growth. As already noted, in 1950–1978, China's overall GDP growth was only marginally above the global average—China's GDP grew at an average annual rate of 4.9% compared to the global average of 4.6%, and average annual growth of China's GDP per capita was 2.8% compared to a global average of 2.7%.

In 1979–2007, China's socialist market economy was well ahead of the economic growth of Western economies, with an average annual GDP growth rate of 9.9% compared to 2.6% in advanced Western economies. With the very rapid economic growth, China successfully made the transition from a "low-income" economy to an upper middle-income economy according to the international classification and almost reached "high-income status."

Since 2008, China moved toward achieving "moderate prosperity" by 2020 and shortly thereafter received the status of "high-income" according to the World Bank criteria. In brief, a period of the "Great Stagnation" in Western economies will simultaneously lead to China's rise to the ranks of high-income economies. This transition to "moderate prosperity" and then to "high-income" status, according to international criteria, represents a key Chinese feature of the current period.

Thus, the new period starting from 2008 is characterized by the following:

(1)   From the point of view of the domestic economy, China's transition from the status of a "middle-income" country to the status of a country with a "middle level of well-being" and then to the status of a "high-income" country according to international criteria

(2)   In terms of international economic development, a very slow growth in developed Western economies

This combination is economically very different from any of the earlier periods of 1950–1978 or 1978–2007.

Consequences of the new period. There are numerous consequences of the interaction of these domestic Chinese factors and the current extremely slow growth in Western economies, which are too numerous to analyze here, but key examples are provided below. Purely economic trends are to be analyzed in the first instance, followed by their geopolitical results, and finally, their effects and attractiveness to countries other than China:

The current period in the advanced economies is characterized by slow average growth, but not by the boom and bust of growth and decline, as in the last period of very slow growth in the advanced economies since World War I. Although a significant acceleration in advanced economies should not be expected, there is no reason to expect a large-scale economic crisis like in 1929: the crisis that began with World War I was caused by the collapse of the world economy both during the war and after 1929 due to for widespread protectionism. There are currently no such conditions. Therefore, the main prospect is long-term slow growth in advanced economies, but not a sudden deep *recession*.

Since China is going through an important period during which the growth in advanced Western economies is expected to be low, while a sudden recession is not expected, the prospects for growth in Chinese exports to these countries will be relatively limited.

The continued slow growth of the US economy is creating protectionist tendencies in it, although other advanced economies, which are most important in terms of the size of the European Union (EU), are still strongly opposed to this.

These international trends create a common global context for the "new normal" of China's economic development.

So far, the relationship between the international economy and the Chinese economy has been analyzed mainly in terms of its implications for China. However, there is, obviously, an increasingly strong cause-and-effect relationship in the opposite direction—China's influence on the world economy and China's neighboring countries. This, in turn, naturally affects China. This cause-and-effect relationship has been greatly amplified by two complementary processes that have taken place since 2007:

(1)   The growing importance of China in the global economy
(2)   Slow growth in Western economies

The result of these processes is the fact that in terms of PPP in 2007–2016, 31% of global GDP growth was driven by China, compared to 10% for the US: at current dollar exchange rates, 44% of global GDP growth in 2007–2016 was driven by China. The IMF predicts that 27% of global GDP growth at PPP in 2016–2021 will be in China compared to 14% for the US.

Thus, a new feature of the current period is a very strong direct influence of China on the world economy and the objective interest of other countries in cooperation with it. This fact ensures a clear relationship between key international initiatives.

The emphasis on the "community with a shared future" is correct from a fundamental theoretical and long-term perspective, as it stems from the fact that the benefits of a division of labor mean that international economic cooperation becomes mutually beneficial. This cooperation corresponds to reality due to the advantages of the international division of labor, since in the economy, "one plus one equals more than two," and in reality, there are "win-win results," and not the concept of "zero-sum game" of American neoconservatives. More directly, however, the concept of the "community of common destiny" also opposed the protectionist strategies of the key members of Donald Trump's administration. It is for this reason that Xi Jinping's speech at the 2017 World Economic Forum in Davos, in which he strongly defended globalization, received wide international support.

Slow growth in advanced economies creates a special form of other countries' attitudes toward both China and the US. China's economy is growing at a much faster pace than the US, but the US maintains global military dominance. Thus, China's attractiveness to other countries is largely economic, while the US has military power. To put it aphoristically, China offers other countries to join the Belt and Road Initiative (BRI) or the Asian Infrastructure Investment Bank (AIIB), while the US offers a "stick" in the form of a military attack or a "carrot" in the form of a military alliance.

The slow growth analyzed above is specific to advanced economies. Growth in developing countries is much faster. Thus, the specific characteristic of the current economic period is slow growth in advanced economies and much faster growth in a number of developing countries. This clearly demonstrates the strategic importance of key initiatives for China, such as BRI, AIIB, and the BRICS New Development Bank (NDB). The growth potential of the B&R region, both in percentage terms and in absolute terms, is far greater than that of North America and Europe, giving other countries a strong incentive to take advantage of it.

Very slow growth in advanced economies creates the context of the "Washington Consensus" that is promoted by the US, but which, as evidence shows, has been much less successful in generating economic growth than China's socialist market policy, resulting in a growing number of countries under her influence. Therefore, it is important that China actively promotes its economic policy at the international level.

Conclusion. The data cited by John Ross demonstrates that after analyzing the de-facto situation in the world economy, the various trends of the current period are not separate but integrated and interconnected with the domestic trends in China. China's response to them is also not just a series of isolated initiatives. On the contrary, it logically stems from the fundamental nature of the new period of the world economy and its relationship with China.

It should be noted that an accurate understanding of the trends operating both internationally and within China meets the requirement of both Chinese and advanced Western ideas that any situation must be understood from the point of view of the totality of forces acting in it, including both internal, as well as international forces. This contradicts the fallacious analysis that attempts to analyze a situation by considering only one or a few (usually internal) forces acting in it.

Applying this method to a comprehensive analysis of trends in the world economy and in China clearly demonstrates the trends and sheds a clear light on the global economic outlook facing China. However, it is obvious that only the Chinese should decide whether such an international analysis of the three fundamental periods of China's development in relation to the international economy is useful for China. Nevertheless, at the international level, it clarifies the connection between trends in China and the fundamental periods of world economic development.

NOTES

1. *China Statistical Yearbook* (Beijing, 1991), 34.
2. Identified based on "Factors Explaining Rapid Economic Growth of China in Recent Decades," March 22, 2021, https://www.tutor2u.net/geography/reference/factors-explaining-the-rapid-economic-growth-of-china-in-recent-decades
3. Ibid.
4. *China Statistical Yearbook* (2001), 61.
5. Ibid.
6. National Taxation (Beijing, 1995), 170.
7. Ibid., 173.
8. Ibid.
9. *China Statistical Yearbook* (1991), 235.
10. Ibid.
11. *Twenty Years of Economic Reform in China* (Beijing: Foreign Languages Press, 2000), 41.
12. *China Statistical Yearbook* (1991), 416.
13. Ibid., 27.
14. Ibid., 34.
15. Ibid., 346.
16. *Economic Daily*, April 22, 1990.
17. *China Statistical Yearbook* (1998), 389.
18. *Twenty Years of Economic Reform in China* (Beijing: Foreign Languages Press, 2000), 26–29.
19. *China Statistical Yearbook* (1993), 664.
20. Ibid., 302.
21. *National Taxation* (Beijing, 1995), 179.

22. I. B. Shevel, *China Tax System Reform* (Moscow: Institute of Far East of the RAS Publ., 1993), 91–110.
23. *China Statistical Yearbook* (1998), 302, 317.
24. *China Statistical Yearbook* (1991), 130.
25. Ibid., 135.
26. P. Sorokin, *The Basic Trends of Our Time* (M.: Nauka, 1997), 350.
27. *Twenty Years of Economic Reform in China* (Beijing: Foreign Languages Press, 2000), 41–42.
28. *Accelerate the Change in the Mode of Economic Growth* (Beijing: China Planning Press, 1996), 4.
29. *Studying the Strategy of the 10th "Five-Year" Plan*, vol. 1 (Beijing: China Population Press, 2000), 87.
30. Where to Go (Beijing: China Today Press, 1997), 53.
31. *Accelerate the Change in the Mode of Economic Growth* (Beijing: China Planning Press, 1996), 3–4.
32. *China in 2020* (Beijing: People's Publishing House,1999), 539.
33. Accelerate the Change in the Mode of Economic Growth (Beijing: China Planning Press, 1996), 41–64.
34. *People's Daily*, March 20, 1996.
35. *China Statistical Yearbook* (2001), 281.
36. *Economic Daily*, February 29, 2000; March1, 2001.
37. *China Statistical Yearbook* (2001), 597.
38. Ibid., 588.
39. *China Statistical Abstract* (2001), 156.
40. Ibid.
41. *China Statistical Yearbook* (2000), 718.
42. *A Report on the Development of China* (Beijing, 2000), 88.
43. *People's Daily*, March 18, 2001.
44. Ibid.
45. Ibid.

CHAPTER 2

Characteristics of the Chinese Model of Transition from Directive to Market Economy

2.1 Background Information

Compared with market transformations in other countries with economies in transition, the transformation of the PRC's economic system is distinguished by several characteristics. The following should be mentioned among the most important of them.

(1) An important prerequisite for China's reform is the adoption at the national level of pragmatic decision-making, adherence to common sense, and the rejection of dogmatism were important prerequisites for reforms in China. Conditions for the development of various schools and directions of economic thought were created in the country, and none of them were declared forbidden, scientifically untenable, or bringing discredit on itself as an instrument of scientific knowledge, etc. Various aspects of the theory and practice of economic reform were widely and purposefully discussed in China in an atmosphere of free exchange of opinions.

As a result, the fear of a discrepancy between real economic practice and outdated but still influential theoretical views, inevitable under conditions of rapid changes, was overcome. The country's leaders, in a short notice, managed to perpetuate in the public mind the rejection of a number of dogmatic attitudes hindering progress, unlike most other reformed countries, where some dogmas were replaced by others, often even more absurd. Thus, in Russia, the myth about the maximum effectiveness of directive planned management of the country's economy was replaced by the myth about its a priori inefficiency. In fact, this is a question of the degree of effectiveness of various methods of managing economic development, depending on the objective conditions and existing competitive advantages.

It is also important to emphasize that the leaders and most scientists of the PRC managed to avoid a very common thesis in other countries about the self-sufficiency of the transition to market methods of managing the economy, which in the PRC, unlike many post-socialist countries, were considered only as a means of solving specific socio-economic tasks facing the country, but never taken as an end in itself.

(2) The initial goal of the reforms was not the growth of social welfare, but the rise in production and the development of productive forces. At the same time, it is the growth of production, and not the compliance of economic regulation and its structure with various a priori formed models, that is the highest criterion for the correctness of the ongoing transformations.

(3) The most important feature of the market transformation of the PRC's economy is its manageable nature and the controllability of the ongoing transformations to the control actions of the state power. This circumstance allows, when necessary, to correct the logic of ongoing reforms and achieve the goals set. A network of state bodies, including the National Development and Reform Commission, similar committees or local offices, and research centers under the central and local governments, was created in the country to develop and implement economic reform. The reform was actively popularized, which significantly contributed to raising the level of economic thinking of practitioners and management personnel at all levels.

(4) Both the reform as a whole and its individual areas are experimental in nature. When embarking on market transformations, the country's leaders did not have a clear idea about the structure of the economic model to which the transition was being made. Therefore, most decisions regarding current changes in the economic regime, made at the level of macroregulation, were tested in certain regions of the country or on a limited number of economic entities. Depending on the testing results, ongoing initiatives could either be ceased or extended to a wider range of territorial subjects. During the reform, there was a careful consideration of regional and local economic conditions,

achieved due to the multivariance and diversity of local implementation of uniform principles dictated by national legal norms and economic decisions.

(5) The PRC's leaders invariably prove their adherence to socialist values (collectivism, humanism, social responsibility, etc.). This circumstance served as a guarantee that during market transformations, the interests and needs of various social groups were fully considered. Sociological surveys of the population's reaction to the reform were constantly conducted in the country, and their results were actually taken into account by the country's leaders. Such an approach provides a broad social basis for reforms and their support by the overwhelming majority of the population.

This significantly distinguishes the Chinese reform from the market transformations in post-socialist countries, in which the population, who suffered as a result of the reforms, was persistently inspired by an idea of the need to sacrifice to join the achievements of civilization, build a modern market economy, etc. Unlike Western experts and the governments of reformed countries, which were implementing their recommendations, the Chinese leaders considered this way of implementing reforms unacceptable and dangerous.

At the same time, many experts note[1] the contradictory nature of China's social policy, caused by the desire to combine socialist ideas about social justice with the market principles of functioning of the economy, under which the paternalistic functions of the state cannot be a predominant tool for social security.

The distinctive features of the economic reform in the PRC, which determine its dissimilarity with the reforms in European countries, are the balanced nature of the measures taken and the gradual nature of the transformations, which were vividly and strongly manifested in the economic liberalization. The pricing reform at the preliminary stage (1978–1984) was carried out without changing the pricing *mechanism*: pricing departments raised prices for scarce goods and lowered prices for the goods produced in excess in a directive way, thereby ensuring that the planned prices for these goods approached equilibrium prices. In 1985, the pricing reform entered its second stage. The main content of the pricing reform at this stage was the gradual release of prices for end products and material resources, the formation of a "dual track" pricing system, in which prices for the planned part of a particular product are determined by the government, and for unplanned one by the market. By 1996, goods whose prices were completely determined by the market accounted for 93% of total retail sales, 79% of total purchases of agricultural products, and 81% of total sales of capital goods.

Chinese economists argue that the pricing reform was carried out according to the principle of "trying to leap a *chasm* in two jumps."[2] The main problem was the fact that the pricing system reflected the sectoral structure of production. Therefore, immediate price liberalization carries a lot of risks. In particular, it jeopardizes the interests of economic agents interested in maintaining stable and low prices for the factors of production, which causes hidden or open opposition to reforms and leads to an economic recession. In other words, if the *chasm* between planned (deformed, subject to correction) and market prices is too big, it will be impossible to leap it in one jump, and there will be a serious danger of falling into it.

That is the reason for choosing the path of reforming prices associated with the transition to a "dual track" system. Prices for goods produced in excess of the established plan were free, and the endowment of enterprises with a number of economic freedoms gave them an opportunity for development. Therefore, most enterprises were not at all against an unplanned system of resource allocation and market prices. Market price legalization required the regulation of target prices and provided an appropriate system of guidelines (market signals), and therefore, it became possible to reform target prices on the scale and in the ways (for example, granting subsidies) that enterprises can withstand.

Since the rapid growth of the economy was mainly attributed to non-state sectors outside the sphere of direct planning, the scope and range of market prices were continuously expanded. Therefore, even if the total volume of regulation through the system of planned prices remained unchanged, following the continuous contraction of the relative share of planned regulation, its influence on economic performance was constantly decreasing. In addition to this, by gradually adjusting planned prices, the state constantly reduced the difference between planned and market prices, which made the divergence of economic interests associated with the existence of a dual-track price system insignificant. Meanwhile, the "chasm" was already almost filled up, and it was possible to cross it safely in two jumps. Although this method led to a delay in the macroeconomic environment reform in the process of transformations in China, it generally provided low risk and, therefore, low cost for achieving the main objectives of the reforms: to maintain stable growth in the physical volume of production and prevent mass enterprise failure.

Liberal reforms in other areas were carried out similarly. Liberalization of the banking system was preceded by the interest rate regulation. The tax system creation started with reforming the volume of direct non-tax deductions.

A good example of a combination of consistency and gradualism is China's currency reform. Initially, to stimulate the activity of economic organizations in earning foreign currency, the independence of enterprises in the field of its use was expanded, and a system for preserving a part of the earned currency was introduced. In 1988, the currency redistribution market was officially allowed, which led to a steady expansion of the internal circulation of currency in the country, until the exchange rate unification in 1994. Thus, even before a unified exchange rate regulated in accordance with the market level was formed, 80% of the foreign currency circulating in the country had already gone through the foreign exchange market with its market rate. At the same time, after repeated adjustments to the official exchange rate, the gap between the official and market exchange rates significantly shortened. This is the main reason why the transition to a unified exchange rate, rather painful for most reformed countries, went quite smoothly in China.

At the same time, it would be wrong to believe that the economic reform in China proceeded "in a linear fashion." Sporadically, there was a need to go back and carry out transformations that seemed already completed. The revival of economic life was followed by a frequent spread of chaos, which created the danger of an overheated economy and therefore was suppressed by the government, focusing on GDP growth as the most important criterion for the success of ongoing reforms. After reforming the economic mechanism at the micro level, enterprises had their own interests and the desire to increase production volume and gross profit. In a situation where the price of money is still artificially low, as soon as the government loosens its control over lending and investment, enterprises actively seek loans to expand production, while underdeveloped infrastructure (energy, transportation) and, to a certain extent, even the raw materials industries are not able to satisfy their demand, so that bottlenecks are formed in the economy, and inflationary tendencies (demand-pull inflation) arise, requiring government intervention, which regulates and compulsory restrains the investment process.

Government measures to streamline the economy include the following milestones:

(1) Price control, allowing to stabilize consumer prices, prices for the means of production, interest rate, and exchange rate

(2) Return of economic rights delegated to enterprises (In some cases, the government limits the rights delegated to individual departments for resource allocation.)

(3) Strengthening control over the scale of lending (Due to the fixed interest rate, demand and supply in the money market require direct state control,

which is achieved only by increasing state intervention in economic agents' activities.)

(4)   Slowdown in the development of non-state sectors of the economy (This measure is an inevitable consequence of the state's desire to prioritize the *planned* needs for resources, which causes discrimination against non-state enterprises in providing resources.)

Perhaps the most profound retreat of this kind took place in the mid-1980s, during a period of the so-called administrative decentralization. The aforementioned set of measures, which embodies, as they say in China, "the suppression that follows chaos," causes an outflow of resources from relatively efficient non-state sectors. Enterprises face a lack of energy; they incur losses, prices are again unable to regulate supply and demand for the factors of production, growth rates slow down, difficulties in filling the state budget arise, etc. Therefore, the "suppression" is followed by what Chinese economists call "stagnation" (fading out of business activity), in which there are increasingly loud calls and more vigorous actions at the micro level demanding the transfer of rights to enterprises, and non-state sectors intensify their struggle for resources. Liberal reforms of the economic mechanism and the system of resource allocation connected with the transfer of rights to enterprises and allowing them to dispose of profits were encouraged again. Thus, "stagnation" is again followed by recovery, and conditions for the repetition of the same spiral "recovery—chaos—streamlining—stimulation—recovery" arise.

The following important lessons of Chinese economic reform, which are undoubtedly of international significance (although they cannot be idealistically transferred to the economic practice of other countries), should also be highlighted:[3]

(1)   The controlled nature of the reforms, the active regulatory role of the state, which directs economic transformations and determines the rules for the economic entities' activities

(2)   Comprehensive consideration of the objective economic interests of various social strata and groups and social orientation of the reforms

(3)   Formation of a favorable investment climate, a system of legal and financial guarantees for domestic and foreign investors, as well as institutional forms of domestic market protection

(4)   Development of a mixed economy, forms of establishing cooperation between the state and business, between large and small businesses, and between economic entities of various forms of ownership

(5) Creation of free economic zones, intensive development zones, technopolises, science incubators, and other regional growth poles

(6) Various forms of attracting the population savings for internal lending to ensure economic development and the safety of these deposits are guaranteed by the state

(7) Experience in the conversion of defense enterprises and application of dual-use technologies

(8) Forms of cooperation between the state and the overseas Chinese diaspora

(9) The experience of multilateral political consultations, the creation of structures of a broad patriotic front of all population segments in the interests of ensuring internal political stability and strengthening international relations and the authority of the country

The economic reform in China was carried out not in accordance with some ideal model or predetermined timeline. New, effective ways of allocating resources and the incentive mechanism cannot instantly manifest their effect in all economic sectors at once. First of all, they start acting in the form of an increase in national income created in the sectors that began transformations earlier than others or arose as a result of the reforms. Chinese economists invariably emphasize the "incremental" nature of the reforms, the meaning of which is not to redistribute the existing volume of resources, but to increase the role of the market mechanism in the creation and distribution of an increasing part of resources. This approach makes it possible to ensure the "Pareto-optimal" nature of economic transformations: minimal damage to economic agents that gradually start focusing on market feedback signals and, consequently, minimal resistance to the ongoing reforms.

The role of the "visible hand" and "invisible hand" in managing the economy was the subject of long and intense discussions in the Chinese scientific community. Especially during the "landing" of the economy after its rapid growth and acceleration in 1992–1995, discussions about the interaction between the plan and the market in the national economy management revived in the scientific circles of China once again. A voluminous (826 pages) collection of reports and articles by 74 famous Chinese economists entitled "On the Socialist Market Economy," published in June 1995 by the "People's Publishing House" of Henan Province, stands out among numerous studies on this topic.[4] One of the concepts that received wide circulation in the PRC was presented by Professor Liu Guoguang, then Vice President of the Chinese Academy of Social Sciences. The essence of his concept lies in the fact that "heading for the market, it is by no means possible to create a cult out of it; while firmly following the planned economy, it is also by no means possible to idealize it."[5]

Arguing with those who believe that the market and the law of value will naturally put everything in perspective, Liu Guoguang provides examples of when the market is powerless to correct the situation. Among such problems, he, in particular, named the general balancing of the national economy, the settlement of large proportions and its structure, the establishment of relations between justice and efficiency in distribution, the creation of conditions for fair competition, and the maintenance of ecological balance and environmental protection. According to Liu Guoguang, the market in its pure form is fundamentally inapplicable to the Chinese economy. He wrote that while carrying out market transformations, the role of "guiding" plans and government management cannot be neglected.[6] Considering the negative experience of several attempts to accelerate "jumping" into the market, Liu Guoguang believed that the most acceptable economic system for China would be the creation of a socialist planned commodity economy. Figuratively paraphrasing the idea of Deng Xiaoping about the plan and the market as two methods of management, Liu Guoguang substantiated the concept of managing the economy with two hands—"visible" (plan) and "invisible" (market).[7] Later, the idea of "two hands" in managing the economy was supported by other economists.[8]

Considering the rich and extraordinary experience of applying planned and market methods in managing the economy, the PRC leaders and scientists are currently intensively studying the issues of their interaction, using the positive aspects of both. Planning tasks and a strategic line are being actively developed, and the role of the government in managing the economy is being specified.

In accordance with science-based recommendations, the responsibilities of the National Development and Reform Commission of the PRC (the modern Chinese State Planning Committee) should include the following areas. The **first** area is the development of a strategy for the economic and social development of the country; transformation of the structure of production; development of the regional economy and providing technological modernization; conservation of natural resources and environmental protection; establishment of international economic and scientific and technical relations, as well as competition.

The **second** area is the consistent replacement of the system of directive indicators with indicative and guiding indicators, including the determination of such macro indicators as the rate of economic growth and inflation, the total volume of investment in fixed assets, the total value of exports and imports, revenues, expenditures and the state budget deficit, natural population growth, and urban growth.

The **third** area includes the development of a policy of macroeconomic stabilization, income distribution, and international economic relations. The modern Chinese state plan was entrusted with the implementation of targeted policies in the fields of finance, money, investment, prices, and international trade. Reports prepared by the State Planning Committee and materials regulating the economy should contain specific political and economic proposals for the implementation of the developed strategy for macroregulation.

The **fourth** area is investment policy, capital investments in fixed assets, including their filling with material and monetary resources and their rational and efficient use. The duties of the State Planning Committee included determining the total volume of investments in fixed assets on a scale of the whole society and the scale of the public sector of the economy and regulating and controlling the entire investment process from its sources to the finished product output. Particular attention is drawn to the need to streamline the structure of investment, construction of state key facilities, and recovery and improvement of the information system in the field of investment. According to the nature of investment in the planned market conditions, it is proposed to divide the constructed facilities into competitive, basic, and generally useful, and the investment itself into political (i.e., state) lending and commercial lending. Regarding foreign investments, it is proposed to use them rationally and avoid risk. State foreign credits are fully subject to planned distribution.

The **fifth** area covers the formation of a system of macroregulation and control. The functions of the State Planning Committee include the development of systems of indicators for control, forecasting, and analysis of the sources and structure of incomes of the population, the state of market prices, the balance of supply and demand, as well as economic development for a month, quarter, half a year, or a year. Tracking economic development, the State Planning Committee is obliged to warn in a timely manner of impending problems and propose measures to prevent them and to ensure the stable functioning of the national economy.

In the last, **sixth** area, the demand for raising the scientific level of planning and its democratization is expressed.[9]

At the same time, according to the developers of the reforms, building a socialist market economy involves using the role of the market, the laws of value, supply and demand, and market competition in the rational allocation of resources in recovering the economic activity of enterprises and the entire economic system at the micro level. The plan, according to them, should be "oriented" to the market and consider its requirements. It must lead, regulate, and control the market, limiting the uncontrollable behavior of market forces and their destructive actions.

Under the new conditions, the role and functions of the government in the economic system are specified. Non-interference of the government in the direct economic activity of enterprises does not mean, according to scientists, the withdrawal of the government from the economy. On the contrary, the government should delve deeper into the essence of the economic system. The market system created in China, in their opinion, "is a market system regulated by the government."[10]

As can be seen from the economic history of the PRC, in the most critical periods of market reforms, when the economy was spontaneously out of control, threatening collapse, the government, using all permissible measures—economic, administrative, political, and in the most severe and uncompromising manner, introduced relative order in it.

From the considered Chinese experience of the market economic reform, it follows that the idea of a rapid comprehensive liberalization of economic activity and non-intervention of the state in the economic process as decisive factors for the success of reforms is a delusion. Indeed, liberalization acted as an important element and even a condition for systemic transformations; it liberated the personal initiative of people and gave impetus to the formation of an entrepreneurial class in post-socialist countries. But at the same time, liberalization posed the risks of destabilizing the economy and the development of many well-known negative phenomena. Therefore, the socio-economic situation today is much better in those countries where liberalization was carried out in a balanced way, combined with state control over the unfolding processes and actions of business entities, where the destruction of the old management mechanisms did not cause chaos in the economy and social sphere but was accompanied by the creation of a system of public administration which was adequate to market conditions and the effective performance of the new duties to regulate socio-economic development by the legislative and executive state bodies.

E. V. Pivovarova notes that the main features of the Chinese reform, which contributed to significant socio-economic progress in the country, were the following.

Firstly, the PRC did not waste its energy on destroying and criticizing the past but concentrated on creating the future.

Secondly, the Chinese reform immediately focused on the needs of the population. The tasks of providing it with food and consumer goods became the key ones in the activity of the newly created economic structures. This guaranteed nationwide support for the reform even at its initial stages.

Thirdly, the country's leaders did not initiate implementing the reform based on someone else's recipes but, having studied both their own and international experience, concluded that it was necessary to proceed from the characteristics of their country and resolutely embarked on the path of "building socialism with Chinese characteristics." The latter required serious consideration of such a fundamental factor as the massive population with the extremely limited resources of the country.

Fourthly, there was no dramatic liberalization in the PRC, and the main method was a step-by-step, experimentally tested advance to the market, the transition from small to big, from specific to general, a gradual but decisive expansion of the scope of the reform and its deepening. Here, this method was figuratively called "crossing the river by touching the stones."

Fifthly, the creation of market entities in the PRC was carried out not by destroying existing state structures but mainly by filling existing gaps, i.e., from the first steps, the reform was aimed at reducing the deficit of the country's economy. Not only were internal reserves mobilized for these purposes, but foreign capital was actively attracted as well.

Sixthly, by stimulating economic initiative at the micro level, the Chinese leadership did not lose sight of macrocontrol and, in periods of dangerous growth in economic imbalance, took additional measures to strengthen it.

Seventhly, the practice of the first years of the reform demonstrated that the most natural path to the market is the development of various types of entities (collective, individual, private, joint Chinese-foreign) in terms of forms of ownership. It not only ensured the rapid growth of the market participants but also, by changing the structure of the national economy according to the forms of ownership, corrected the structure of investment and production to bring it closer to the real needs of the population.

The world-recognized successes of the economic reform in the PRC are the best evidence of the fruitfulness of the Chinese choice, which lies in determining the strategy of socio-economic development to proceed "not from subjective wishes," not various foreign model, not from dogmatic interpretations of certain provisions of Marxist writings" but be guided by the principle "practice is the criterion of truth."[11]

2.2 Specific Macroeconomic Mechanisms

China's economic miracle is a clear example of the embodiment of the theory of convergence of the capitalist and socialist systems—the antipodes of the previous world economic order. The dialectical synthesis of opposing relations of production based on the selection of creative mechanisms for economic development gave a strikingly effective result in the formation of a new world economic order. Its definition as an "integral system" emphasizes its typical target function of the system of state management of economic development—the unification of people, as well as the ruling and productive elite, to achieve the goal of increasing the general welfare, as well as the desire of the state to integrate the interests of various social groups into a harmonious system of relations of production.

The radical transformations in the relations of production that took place, notwithstanding the prevailing theoretical ideas, and the emergence of a new progressive form of socio-economic structure that surpassed in efficiency the global systems of socialism and capitalism that competed in the last century, need theoretical understanding. First of all, it is necessary to clarify the basic concepts of socialism and capitalism.

If we proceed from the Marxist view of the key role of property relations, then it is necessary to admit that neither capitalism nor socialism exists in the world anymore. In the capitalist world, family private enterprises of the 19th century were substituted by transnational corporations, where ownership rights were divided between numerous shareholders and concentrated in impersonal funds. In socialist countries, the State Planning Committee and the State Committee for Material Technical Supply were abolished, giving enterprises market freedom. In all countries, mixed forms of ownership prevailed both in relation to structural enterprises and to the economy as a whole. At the same time, state-owned enterprises operate in a competitive market environment, while private business is strictly regulated by the state. It proves to be much more sensitive to the regulatory influences of the state than state-owned enterprises, whose leaders, in turn, are afraid of being unprofitable, no less than private entrepreneurs. According to the academician V. L. Makarov, a mixed type of economy is more consistent with its complexity as a management object compared to homogeneous systems, whether market or centralized ones.[12] Therefore, as a rule, it is more efficient and sustainable in modern conditions.

Numerous theoretical and empirical studies unequivocally are indicative of the inadmissibility of absolutization of either the market or the state in attempts to improve the modern economic system. In the integrated system that formation we are witnessing, its development management is based on finding a reasonable balance between private and state interests, developing productive forms of public-private partnership, and regulating market relations based on national interests. A well-known modern specialist in the field of management theory, R. Musgrave, admits: "One market mechanism cannot perform all economic functions. Public policy is necessary to manage, correct, and supplement certain aspects of it. This fact is important to understand since it means that the appropriate size of the public sector is largely a matter of technical rather than ideological order."[13] J. Stiglitz had a similar idea: "I wrote it (a textbook—*editor's note*), convinced that understanding the issues raised in it is central to any democratic society. Issues of sound public-private balance and how governments can achieve their goals more effectively are among the most important of them."[14]

A gradual denationalization of the economy took place in the PRC based on the rapid development of private enterprises while maintaining significant public sector and state planning functions. In 1982, according to the *PRC Constitution*, the presence of two public sectors of the economy—the state and the collective ones was recorded in the country. Along with them, a sector of mixed enterprises with the participation of foreign capital and purely foreign capitalist enterprises arose. In 1988, an amendment to the existence of private farms in the Chinese economy, which was declared an addition to the socialist economy, was made to the Constitution of the PRC. Later, in 1999, all types of private entrepreneurship were united under the single term "non-public sector," which is supervised and controlled by the state that also directs its activities. In 1993, the state sector of the economy was renamed into a sector of the economy based on state ownership. Such a renaming meant the expansion of the rights of enterprises, granting them operational independence, releasing them from the dictates of the state plan, but not from state control. The provisions on the subordination of the activities of public sector enterprises to the strict implementation of the state plan were also excluded from the PRC Constitution. Currently, according to the Constitution of the PRC, the functions of the state include the formation of a market economy, the development of economic legislation, and the improvement of macroregulation.[15]

An important feature of the Chinese model of transition to the market economy was the preservation of state control over the banking system, which became the main channel for financing investments in economic development. As the structure of the latter became more and more complex, the selective ability of the banking system increased, and the flexibility of monetary policy increased.

Their role was gradually becoming more complex and increasing as economic activity intensified, enterprises were reconstructed, and new construction was launched, trade, economic, scientific, technical, and financial relations with international financial structures, foreign companies, and monopoly associations were expanded. Along with the system of modern enterprises, the banking system became a financial framework that ensured the expanded reproduction and stable functioning of the socialist market economy system created in the PRC, the formation of a single national market, and its connection with the world market.

The experience of reforms demonstrated the fact that the financial and banking system in the hands of the PRC leaders became a powerful means of macroregulation of the most complex economic processes and an instrument of economic reform. The tasks of ensuring normal, stable, and free of inflationary bursts commodity-money circulation, centralization of financial resources dispersed in society and improving the quality of capital, and stable supply of investment projects with money were set and successfully solved by the financial and banking system of the PRC.

Currently, the banking system in China is a complex structure in terms of its organization. It includes five groups of financial institutions. The first group includes one single financial institution—the PBC, the central bank, the bank of banks, founded on December 1, 1948. The second group is represented by a very heterogeneous group of banks: three political banks, four state commercial banks, 12 joint-stock banks, and 18 urban cooperative banks. The third and largest group of financial institutions are urban and rural savings cooperatives. There are 4,647 of the former and 50,800 of the latter. The fourth group includes nonbank financial institutions, including 96 securities trading companies, 244 trust companies, 64 financial companies, 16 financial leasing companies, and 13 insurance companies. The rapidly increasing group of Sino-foreign and foreign monetary financial institutions, brought into existence by the implementation of the policy of openness, forms the fifth group. In 1997, 527 various foreign financial organizations set up operations in the PRC, including 156 organizations with a capital of $30 billion (including eight insurance companies) with the right to conduct operations. In turn, Chinese commercial banks and insurance companies opened more than 500 offices and branches in other countries. It would be wrong to ignore another, the sixth in a row, expanding and growing group of financial institutions—money (stock) markets (exchanges). With the formation of the system of modern enterprises and their accelerated corporatization, the markets for the shares of enterprises and government bonds, as well as currency, real estate, futures markets, etc., were becoming more and more active.

One of the most important among the numerous complex tasks facing the banking system and banks was to prevent the suspension of industrial and agricultural production during the transition to market relations and to provide enterprises operating in the key sectors of the national economy with the necessary working capital.

During the banking system reform, on the one hand, there was a progressive increase in the number and size of monetary institutions, clarification of their functions, rights, and obligations, and on the other hand, streamlining the entire monetary system and endowing it with a central organizing orientation. Along with the creation of a system of modern enterprises, the reformed banking system became an important mechanism for the formation and functioning of the socialist market economy system under creation and an effective tool in the hands of the central government for managing the national economy, accumulating money, improving the quality of capital, and its targeted application for the scientific and technical rise of the economy.

The main institution entrusted with the management of the country's rapidly growing monetary economy at a new stage in the PRC development was the PBC, which performed the functions of a central bank. In the 1990s, two laws on the PBC were adopted; the last one was adopted on March 18, 1995. The law once again confirmed the fact that the PBC was a state-owned bank. Article 8 of the law states that "the capital of the PBC is fully funded by the state and is the state property." At the same time, in the spirit of separation of powers between the enterprise (PBC) and the state, Article 7 states that *under the leadership of the State Council and in accordance with the law, the PBC independently conducts monetary policy, performs the functions entrusted to it and expands its activities without interference from local governments, government agencies of various levels, public organizations and individuals* (emphasis added). It should be noted that to protect the PBC from the pressure of the provincial leaders regarding funds allocation, the branches of the PBC in the provinces were liquidated in 1999. Instead of 30 such branches, nine were created, and the provinces were grouped accordingly. This is one of the measures taken recently by the central government to fight undaunted parochialism.

The law specifies the relationship between the government and the PBC. The PBC should not provide on-call (short-term) financial loans to the government and should not directly purchase and sell state bond loans and other government bonds. Article 29 states that the PBC should not grant loans to local governments, non-governmental departments at various levels, nonbank financial institutions, other organizations, and individuals, except in cases determined by the decision of the State Council.

The PBC operates with an independent budget reviewed and approved by the financial authorities of the State Council and included in the central budget. The budget of the PBC is controlled by the financial departments of the State Council. Net income after revenues less expenses is transferred in full to the central budget. The losses of the PBC are compensated by the central budget.

The rules of emission and its use are prescribed by the laws. Its volume is approved at the annual sessions of the NPC. The emission is used as the share premium of the state. The application of the funds emitted should be carried out based on orders from higher authorities. No organizations or individuals are allowed to violate the established order.

According to the law, the PBC was granted greater rights to manage and control all financial institutions. It regulates and supervises financial institutions and their operations, providing stable and healthy functioning of the monetary sphere. As necessary, the PBC has the right to audit, inspect, and control financial institutions on the status of deposits, loans, settlements, non-cash debts, etc.

Being directly subordinate to the government, the PBC was granted the right to apply all means (economic, legal, and administrative), including emergency ones, to perform its functions.

An extraordinary innovation during the third stage of the reform was the establishment of three political banks in 1994: the *China* Development Bank (CDB), the *Export-Import Bank of China* (Chexim—China Exim Bank), and the Agricultural Development Bank of China (ADBC). There were banks in the PRC whose functions included the activity areas of the new banks. In the 1980s, the *China Construction Bank*, the Bank of China (engaged in foreign economic activity), and the Agricultural Bank of China were recreated. However, after it became clear in the early 1990s that a significant part of the assets of these banks was so-called "political" loans (67% of all assets of the Bank of China, 51.2% of Agricultural Bank, 58% of China Construction Bank and 25% of Industrial and Commercial Bank of China in 1991) issued by order of the State Planning Commission of the PRC, the country's leaders decided to entrust the financing and lending of strategically important facilities to specialized financial institutions, and political banks were fulfilling this functions.

According to the authorities, these banks were started not for profit. Their tasks include the implementation of the state structural and regional policy and the implementation of large projects that require significant funds with long construction periods, low economic efficiency, and slow returns, which are not of interest to commercial banks due to unprofitability or lack of necessary funds. Such management areas include the development of new agricultural areas, construction of extensive infrastructure, key facilities, etc. The capital of political banks is formed from the state budget and the sale of government bonds.

The authorized capital of the CDB is 50 billion yuan, which was raised from state construction funds. In 1996, the value of the bank's property reached 280.3 billion yuan. The main task of the CDB is to create a long-term sustainable source of capital, meet the financial needs of key construction projects, credit the construction of key strategic facilities (political facilities, as they say in China), provide discount loan services, regulate the total volume of investments in fixed assets and their structure, gradual creation of a mechanism of self-restraint and responsibility for the regulation and risks in investment, and increase the efficiency of investments in bottlenecks that limit economic development in accordance with the principles of the market economy (including large objects of basic industries that directly affect the increase in state power, large high-tech facilities in the urban economy and other major interregional strategic facilities). After selecting suitable facilities for investment, the CDB evaluates the funds, developing the logic of their distribution and lending conditions.

The head office of the political bank China Exim Bank is in Beijing, with branches in several major cities. Its authorized capital at registration was 3.38 billion yuan. In 1996, the bank's property was estimated at 20 billion yuan. The immediate task of China Exim Bank is to facilitate the export of high-tech products, products of key industries (engineering, electronics, petrochemistry, building materials), and complete equipment.

The authorized capital of the political bank of the ADBC in 1994 amounted to 20 billion yuan. In 1996, the entire property of the bank was already estimated at 705.7 billion yuan. The bank's capital was formed on the refinanced funds of the PBC. The tasks of the bank include lending for the purchase and creation of a state system for special storage of grain, cotton, oilseeds, meat, sugar, and other important agricultural products, lending for the development of poverty areas, as well as lending for irrigation construction and technical reconstruction of the rural area, determined by the state.

Along with the allocation of special functions and special status, the task of all political banks includes the concentration of capital dispersed in the national economy. The CDB should carry out this work in the field of investment of fixed assets. It is also entrusted with such a large-scale task as determining the total volume of investment and rational distribution.

The former specialized banks (Industrial and Commercial Bank of China, Agricultural Bank of China, the Bank of China, and China Construction Bank) were transformed into state-owned commercial banks. New commercial banks, as well as joint-stock and urban cooperative banks, were established. The most important event in the organization of the banking system was the "Law of the People's Republic of China on Commercial Banks," adopted on May 10, 1995. The law determined the statutory provisions, the scope of their activities, subordination, and the establishment procedure. According to the law, commercial banks are enterprises that are legal entities and are engaged in loan and deposit activities, as well as the implementation of settlement and similar operations. Among the goals of the law, the need for *achieving the normative nature of the commercial banks' activities, improving the quality of credit assets, strengthening regulation and supervision, ensuring the healthy and stable functioning of commercial banks, supporting order in the monetary sphere, and promoting the development of the socialist market economy* (emphasis added)[16] are indicated. A commercial bank, by law, is an independent enterprise that carries out independent management and bears independent responsibility for risk, profits, losses, and self-regulation. Any organizations and individuals are prohibited from interfering in the conduct of the operations of commercial banks permitted by law. At the same time, the law says that in the process of carrying out their activities, commercial banks are required to comply with all approved legal provisions and must not harm the interests of the state and society by their actions. Meanwhile, by law, commercial banks are subject to supervision and control by the PBC. The latter is responsible for their activities to the government and the NPC Standing Committee.

Throughout the history of the PRC, and especially after 1978, the banking system in the hands of the Chinese leaders has been the most important lever for managing the economic and social processes in the country. Under conditions of intensive development of commodity-money relations, deepening monetization and commercialization of economic relations, the banking system and the PBC objectively bear a great responsibility for the stability of monetary circulation, the stability of the national currency, the provision of funds to the largest industrial enterprises that form the supporting framework of the entire national economy and society. The new reform of the banking system, which was carried out in 1994, is aimed, on the one hand, at streamlining and stabilizing the financial situation in the country and, on the other hand, at solving strategic forecast tasks in the 21st century. One of the general tasks of the reformed banking system is to establish the closest financial and monetary connection with production, to provide production with money resources and to manage it, considering the combination of centralized and local management and providing a certain freedom for the economic initiative of direct producers—enterprises. Nevertheless, the main task of the banking system was and remains the financial and monetary support of strategic national programs. The solution to these issues can be exemplified by the use of credit resources by Chinese banks.

With the development of production, the increase in monetary aggregates, and the deepening of monetization, monetary resources in the PRC were rapidly increasing. In 1998, compared with 1994, the volume of bank deposits increased by more than 2.2 times and reached 11,042.05 billion yuan, exceeding the value of GDP volume in 1998 by almost 1.4 times. Over the years, the loan volume increased from 3997.6 billion yuan to 8652.4 billion yuan. In 1998, 6,061.3 billion yuan, or 70% of the total credit resources, were used for short-term loans, and 2,071.8 billion yuan, or 23.9%, for medium and long-term loans. In 2000, banks' credit resources reached 9937.1 billion yuan, including medium and long-term loans that amounted to 2793.1 billion yuan (about 28%). In contrast, it is necessary to note that in Russia, medium and long-term loans account for only about 3% of the total loan volume.

One of the major recipients of loans was industrial enterprises, which borrowed 1,782.2 billion yuan, or 29.4%, which accounted for more than 75% of the value of current capital in industry. Trade (32.6%) received a significant share of short-term loans, followed by construction (2.7%), agriculture (7.3%), township and village enterprises (9.2%), and individuals and private traders (0.78%). Chinese huaqiao (person or people of *Chinese* ethnicity living in a non-*Chinese* country) enterprises and foreign capital accounted for 4.1% of loans. At the same time, the main funds are concentrated in state banks. In 1995, 72% of all deposits in the country were concentrated in state banks.

Despite the great progress in reforming the banking system in the PRC and its huge role in the development of the economy and society, it cannot be considered complete and well-established, since it is in the process of constant development. It has a lot of purely internal and external financial problems. The first and most pressing problem is the delay or non-payment of loans, the growing debt of industry to banks, which is now approaching 3 trillion yuan. In this situation, state-owned and state-joint-stock banks feel more secure. They will always be provided with state support, and the State Council will protect them from *failure*. New urban commercial banks and rural credit cooperatives are in much worse conditions. Many of them are in critical condition. According to the survey, more than 50% of loans issued in rural areas are "bad," i.e., there are difficulties with their repayment. Approximately 30% of rural cooperatives have losses exceeding 50% of the funds required to pay interest to shareholders. Newly created urban commercial banks face numerous difficulties. The main problems include the low quality of authorized capital and even its shortage, low profitability of banks, shareholder fraud, and the facts of capital embezzlement. The bank's staff are low-qualified people, and the material and technical base and management methods, as a rule, do not meet modern requirements.

It was the state of the banking system of China by the late 20th century. However, these seemingly unsolvable Western economists' problems turned out to be nothing more than growing pains in the Chinese economy. With the implementation of investment projects and the increase in output, as well as the growth of incomes and savings of the population, these problems were solved in a natural way: loans were returned, bad debts were restructured, losses were compensated for by an increase in lending, personnel improved their professional skills, and the banking system was becoming more and more efficient.

NOTES

1. V. Y. a Portyakov, *Economic Reform in China* (1979–1999) (M.: Institute of the Far East of the Russian Academy of Sciences, 2002), 130.
2. Lin Yifu, Cai Fang, and Li Zhou, *The China Miracle: Development Strategy and Economic Reform* (Shanghai: Gezhi Publishing House. 1999), 336.
3. M. L. Titarenko, *China: Civilization and Reforms* (M.: Respublika, 1999), 113–114.
4. *On the Socialist Market Economy* (People's Publishing House), 1995.
5. Ibid., 38.
6. Ibid.
7. Ibid.
8. *Accelerate the Change in the Mode of Economic Growth* (Beijing: China Planning Press, 1996), 38; Twenty Years of Economic Reform in China (Beijing: Foreign Languages Press, 2000), 32.
9. *Twenty Years of Economic Reform in China* (Beijing: Foreign Languages Press, 2000), 35.
10. Ibid., 36–37.
11. *People's Daily*, September 22, 1997.
12. V. L. Makarov, *Social Clasterism, Russian Challenge* (M.: Business Atlas, 2010).
13. R. A. Musgrave and P. B. Musgrave, *Public Finance in Theory and Practice* (M.: Business Atlas, 2009).
14. J. E. Stiglitz, *Economics of the Public Sector* (M.: MSU, 2011).
15. B. N. Kuzyk and M. L. Titarenko, *China-Russia 2050: Co-Development Strategy* (M.: IFE RAN, IES RAN, 2006), 18–19.
16. *Economic Daily*, May 12, 1995.

China's Economic Rise in the Modern World

Comparative Analysis of the Socialist Countries' Transition to the Market Economy

THE EVOLUTION OF DIFFERENT STATES OF THE DISINTEGRATED WORLD system of socialism has demonstrated in practice a wide variety of trajectories of transition from a directive to a market economy. Economic theory rarely succeeds in experimentally testing any given hypothesis, which results in the scholasticism and speculation of its numerous directions. The period of the late 20th–early 21st century provided the richest empirical material, whose significance is still underestimated by economic science. In fact, a global experiment to test the validity of the main economic theories was set up.

The most popular in the Western academic community, the neoclassical theory of market equilibrium, the so-called mainstream in its most consistent version of market fundamentalism, was taken as a "guide to action" in Russia, Ukraine, the Baltic States, and the Eastern European CMEA member states. At the same time, the experiment was staged under different conditions: Russia and Ukraine carried out the transition independently, while other Eastern European states were absorbed by the EU. In turn, within each of these experiments, there were additional differences. In Russia, the transition was carried out under conditions of an authoritarian political system, and in Ukraine, it was under conditions of parliamentary democracy. Among the Eastern European states, a special case is the GDR, which was absorbed by its Western neighbor.

The transition to a market economy in China, Vietnam, Belarus, and Uzbekistan is an experimental test of another economic theory known as economic theory or physical economics. This theory is distinguished by a pragmatic approach to the study of economic phenomena free of speculative abstractions like market equilibrium models.

Finally, there were two socialist countries where market reforms were superficial or not conducted: Cuba and North Korea. When assessing the experiment results, they can be used as a "control group." It is interesting that, despite the serious blow that hit these relatively small economic systems with the collapse of the USSR and the world socialist system, they not only survived, but retained a considerable potential for development. Cuba is showing solid economic growth, while North Korea manages to survive despite economic sanctions and enormous political pressure. Furthermore, Cuba has a powerful political influence on the countries of Latin America, many of which are successfully developing socialist institutions of state ownership and planning.

Figure 4 demonstrates GDP growth rates in some countries with economies in transition against the backdrop of the US, which until recently was considered the most stable market economy. It clearly shows the failures in the economic dynamics of the post-Soviet states that chose an ultra-liberal model of transition to the market and the successes of states that retained the central planning system, combining it with the evolutionary development of market relations. Table 18 complements these comparisons of inflation rates, which is considered the most important indicator of macroeconomic policy success.

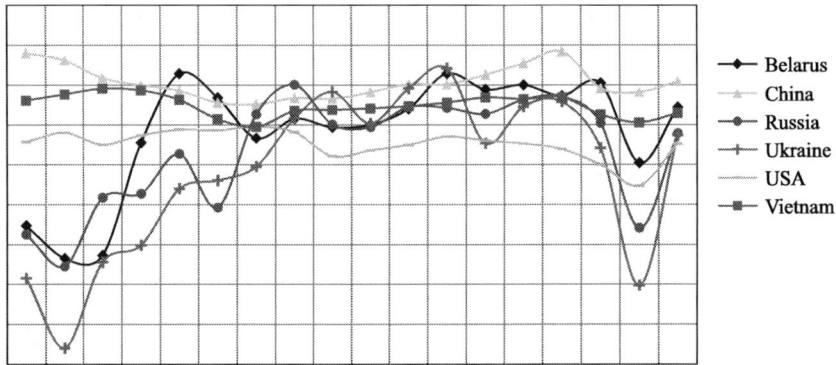

Figure 4   GDP Growth Rates in 1993–2010 (as % of the Previous Year)

Source: International Monetary Fund, World Economic Outlook Database, October 2010.

COMPARATIVE ANALYSIS OF THE SOCIALIST COUNTRIES' TRANSITION ... 91

Table 18   Average Annual Growth Rates of Consumer Prices (as %)

Countries	1990	1991	1992	1993	1995	1997	1999	2000
Bulgaria	24	339	79	72.8	62.1	1082.3	0.3	9.9
Hungary	29	32	22	22.5	28.2	18.3	10.0	9.8
Macedonia*	608	...	1927	349.8	15.9	4.4	–1.1	10.5
Poland	586	60	44	35.3	27.8	14.9	7.3	10.1
Romania	5	...	199	256.1	32.3	154.8	45.8	45.7
Slovakia	10	58	....	23.2	9.9	6.1	10.6	12.0
Slovenia	552	247	93	32.9	13.5	8.4	6.1	8.9
Croatia*	610	...	...	1,517.5	2.0	3.6	4.2	6.2
The Czech Republic	10	52	...	20.8	9.1	8.5	2.1	4.0
Yugoslavia*	580	...	...	1,165×1012	78.6	21.6	44.9	85.7

Source: S. Glazyev, ed., *Marketing Research* (M.: Ekonomika, 2004).
Note: * Consumer prices.

Followers of the neoclassical paradigm were unable to provide a convincing explanation for the striking differences in the results of the transition to a market economy in different countries. The explanations for China's successes and Russia's failures come down to frivolous discussions about the inconsistency of the "shock therapy" policy in Russia and absurd hypotheses about the consistent implementation of the doctrine of market fundamentalism in China. There are similar attempts to explain the relatively successful development of Belarus by energy subsidies from Russia, although despite receiving energy at lower prices, the neighboring Smolensk and Pskov regions demonstrate dismal results.[1]

In contrast to the neoclassical paradigm, the evolutionary paradigm makes it possible to logically explain the striking differences in the results of the transition from a directive to a market economy in different countries, depending on the chosen ideology of the reforms. As already noted, from the point of view of evolutionary economics, each point on the trajectory of economic development is determined by the entire prehistory of evolution and "natural selection" of the population of economic entities operating in the conditions of the corresponding economic environment. At the same time, the performance of economic entities is formed in the processes of search and "natural selection" combined with the economic environment.

To explain the differences in the results of the transition to a market economy in various post-socialist countries, it is necessary to compare the above classification of states according to different methods of transition to a market economy with the classification based on the objective results of this transition. If the latter is formed based on the parameters of GDP per capita and final consumption, which reflect the level of economic development and standard of living, respectively, then comparing their levels at the beginning and end of the transition period (which can be conditionally defined from 1990 to 2001), six groups of states can be distinguished (Table 19).

Table 19   Classification (Reform Results in Countries with Economies in Transition)

Class	Countries
1	China
2	Hungary, Poland, Slovenia, Estonia
3	Slovakia, Croatia, Belarus, Latvia
4	Albania, Bulgaria, Romania, the Czech Republic, Yugoslavia, Bosnia and Herzegovina, Macedonia, Uzbekistan, Lithuania
5	Russia, Armenia, Kazakhstan, Kyrgyzstan
6	Ukraine, Moldova, Azerbaijan, Georgia, Turkmenistan, Tajikistan

Source: S. Glazyev, ed., Marketing Research (M.: Ekonomika, 2004).

To explain the various results of the transition to a market economy in 2001, they were analyzed based on the economic policy pursued. In this regard, correlation matrices of the most important macroeconomic parameters were calculated for individual countries and for classes that unite different countries in accordance with the classification. Based on the calculations, conclusions regarding the statistical relationship of various macroeconomic indicators for individual countries and groups of countries, published in the collective monograph Marketing Research, were drawn. The results of these studies are provided below.

As a result of this analysis, which covered data for the specified period for all countries with economies in transition, the following conclusions were drawn.

(1) The analysis findings suggest that a decline in the physical volumes of production is one of the key factors of inflation, but the decline in inflation,

although generally beneficial for economic dynamics, is unable to ensure economic growth. Moreover, in some cases, to achieve the goals of economic growth, there is no need to suppress inflationary processes. Sometimes, the inflationary heating of the economy itself, carried out within narrow, carefully detected limits, acts as a stimulus for economic growth, which to a certain extent confirms the theoretical correctness of the Keynesian interpretation of the processes under consideration. An example of this situation is the Chinese economy, with a stable *positive* correlation between GDP growth rates and inflation rates of 87%.

In general, no significant correlation can be found between GDP growth rates and consumer price growth rates for any group of countries divided into classes in accordance with the classification. As for individual countries, a negative correlation between these indicators is observed in Bosnia and Macedonia, as well as in the republics of the former USSR, apart from Russia, Belarus, Moldova, and Georgia, and a positive correlation is found in China and Vietnam. Thus, it is obvious that the relationship between high inflation and economic recession is not a general pattern but a consequence of a certain logic of economic reforms.

(2) An analysis of the ratio of the money supply to GDP dispels any illusions about the need to limit the money supply for successful macroeconomic stabilization. The leader in this indicator is China, where the volume of M2 in the last three years is 1.5 times higher than the GDP level. It is followed (based on 2001 data) by the Czech Republic (73.7%) and Slovakia (67.6%), followed by a dense group (43%–50%) of successfully reformed Eastern European countries (Slovenia, Croatia, Poland) and Vietnam that did not face economic recessions.

A comparison of the Central and Eastern European countries (CEECs) based on this indicator only confirms the general conclusion. In 2000, Romania had the smallest ratio of M2 to GDP among the countries of this region (23.2%), while in terms of inflation rates in the same year, it firmly dominated, being 4.5 times ahead of Bulgaria and Hungary, which followed it. Among the Baltic countries, the ratio of M2 to GDP was higher in Estonia, where reforms were more successful compared to its immediate neighbors, which is confirmed by both classifications.

Among all countries with economies in transition, only Ukraine and Latvia demonstrated a positive correlation between inflation rates and the ratio of M2 to GDP, and in Poland, Slovenia, and China (in these three countries, it was more than 80%), as well as in Romania and Croatia, the correlation was negative. A positive correlation between inflation rates and the total money supply M2 could be found in Ukraine and Romania, and a negative correlation—in Hungary, Slovenia, the Czech Republic, Slovakia, Moldova, Azerbaijan, Kazakhstan, Estonia, Lithuania, China, Vietnam, as well as in Latvia and Russia.

Studies conducted by World Bank experts also demonstrated a well-defined *inverse* correlation between the amount of money in circulation (money supply as a percentage of GDP) and the inflation rate: the less money in circulation, the higher the inflation rate.[2] This fact, which contradicts the usual monetarist ideas, naturally needed an explanation. The World Bank experts had to use Keynesian rather than monetarist concepts to explain this anomalous (from the point of view of neoclassical theory) situation. They presented the case in such a way that the countries with the highest inflation rate experienced the largest decline in production, which was accompanied by a significant decrease in the demand for money. Under these conditions, although the central banks of these countries reduced the amount of real money in circulation, they did not do it to the extent that the demand for money decreased. Thus, although the money supply was shrinking, it was still in surplus.

As demonstrated in *Marketing Research*, this explanation could be considered plausible if two conditions are met, neither of which is true. Firstly, it implicitly relies on the fact that there is a positive correlation between the inflation rate and the decline in production, which is inconsistent with the measurement results. *Secondly*, for its confirmation, this explanation requires the detection of the phenomenon of "flight from money" in transition economies with high inflation. However, such a hypothesis also contradicts the realities of transformational processes. For instance, in Russia, with the greatest decrease in the volume of the money supply and a liquidity crisis in the corresponding years, the lack of working capital of enterprises led to a crisis of non-payments and the naturalization of economic relations (barter).

In fact, it is quite simple to explain the feedback between M2 volume and inflation. A restrictive financial policy aimed at shrinking the M2 aggregate does not entail a reduction in the volume of the money supply, but only causes a deterioration in its quality. Instead of liquid monetary aggregates, the channels of monetary circulation are filled with financial illiquid assets, money surrogates, and various debt obligations, which accumulation leads to a non-payment crisis. In Russia ,in the mid-1990s, for instance, the total volume of "quasi-money" in circulation reached, according to some estimates, half of the total money supply, and in some sectors, it accounted for 80%–90% of the total volume of operations of Russian enterprises.[3] The non-payments crisis causes a deepening of the economic recession, and it, in turn, acts as a key factor in inflationary processes, since it increases the disproportions between the amount of money in circulation, which remains practically unchanged (despite M2 shrinking), and the volume of their commodity coverage.

Those economists who follow the monetarist paradigm normally explain the long-term failure of the attempts at financial stabilization in Russia by the fact that all the components of the standard package of stabilization measures recommended by the IMF were not fully implemented. But the same is true for any country that succeeded in fighting inflation: none of them was an orthodox follower of the IMF's recommendations.

Moreover, it can be noted that the CEE countries that carried out the most drastic restriction of the amount of money in circulation (Bulgaria and Romania) experienced the greatest problems with inflation, as well as with overcoming the decline in production. Almost no CEE country (with the exception of Poland and Hungary) managed to reduce the money supply for more than a year. In many of these countries, inflationary *stimulation* of economic growth, contrary to the monetary logic of financial stabilization, turned out to be a reality.

(3) The budget deficit was considered one of the key factors of inflation in many countries with transition economies. However, in fact, only countries that experienced a severe deflationary shock demonstrate a negative correlation between inflation rates and the ratio of the state budget surplus to GDP: Poland, Azerbaijan, Armenia, Kazakhstan, Kyrgyzstan, Tajikistan, Estonia, and Lithuania, while Slovakia and Slovenia show a positive correlation. In addition, of all groups of countries, only the last two (the fifth and sixth) demonstrated a significant, naturally negative correlation between these parameters. This indicates that in countries with weak state regulation of transformation processes, the growth of the budget deficit provokes inflation, and in more successfully reformed countries, where the influence of the national government on the logic of the ongoing transformations is quite strong, the budget deficit is not so significant, or, in any case, a fast-acting inflation factor.

This position is also supported by the results of other studies, which object to the developed countries of the world: in the countries where the government keeps the macroeconomic situation under control, there is no direct correlation between the level of budget deficit and inflation rates. According to a sampling of 48 countries that collectively account for 9/10 of the world's total GDP, no statistically significant correlation could be found between the levels of budget deficits and inflation.[4]

(4) In the same way, the logic of economic reforms predetermines the relationship between final consumption and inflation, which, in practice, is not as obvious as it should result from general theoretical considerations. A positive correlation between the growth rate of consumer prices and the volume of per capita final consumption was demonstrated by Ukraine, Moldova, Tajikistan, and Turkmenistan, and a negative correlation was shown by other countries, except for Russia, Belarus, Lithuania, Macedonia, Azerbaijan, Georgia, and Kazakhstan. It is easy to see that in the most successfully reformed countries, the correlation between inflation and the level of final consumption is negative; countries with average results (and somewhat worse than average) do not demonstrate any correlation, and in outsider countries, it is positive. This is natural since feedback mechanisms work better in leading countries, and bursts of inflation immediately reduce final consumption. In other countries, the lag between these changes is significant; the macroeconomic system reacts to price increases with a delay, and, in addition, non-monetary incomes play a significant role in total final consumption in most of them.

(5) Spasmodic liberalization of the economy, facing competition from highly developed economies and a natural deterioration in the investment climate, causing a chronic lack of investment (especially for large long-term projects), hit the most modern industries producing technically complex products very hard. It was here, in the sphere of high technologies and in modern industrial sectors, where the lagging behind the Western countries was the most pronounced. The lack of investment resources, which was accompanied by a sharp decrease in the accumulation rate in the economy for modernization, caused their collapse and degradation (Table 20).

On the other hand, the energy and raw materials industries and the life-supporting sectors of the local and national economic infrastructure were in a more favorable position. The former turned out to be quite competitive in the world market, given the light dumping they used; the latter was simply necessary to finance in order to avoid complete economic and social collapse.

Table 20   Gross Domestic Investment in CEE and CIS Countries in 1990 and 1995 (as % of the GDP of Respective Years)

Countries	1990	1995
CIS countries		
Armenia	47.1	9.0
Azerbaijan	27.8	16.0
Belarus	27.4	25.0
Georgia	no data	3.0
Kazakhstan	42.6	22.0
Kyrgyzstan	23.8	16.0
Moldova	no data	7.0
Russia	30.1	25.0
Tajikistan	23.4	17.0
Turkmenistan	40.0	no data
Ukraine	27.5	no data
Uzbekistan	32.2	23.0
Some CEE countries		
Bulgaria	25.6	21.0
The Czech Republic	28.6	25.0
Hungary	25.4	23.0
Poland	25.6	17.0
Romania	30.2	26.0

Source: *Human Development Report for Europe and the CIS* (UNDP, 1999), 16.

As stated in the extensive study *Marketing Research*, which summarizes the experience of various countries with transition economies, most European countries had to pay a high price for the economic mechanism liberalization. The reaction of the economy to the accelerated destruction of the usual mechanisms of control in the absence or weakness of new market institutions and inadequacy of the indirect levers of macroeconomic regulation turned out to be extremely painful. As a result, most of the countries in the first years of transformation were in a deep economic crisis. Its main manifestations were the rapid increase in inflation, which in some countries threatened the collapse of public finance, and the fall in production volumes. There were also serious problems in the social sphere.

These consequences of liberalization were natural, taking into account the peculiarities of the economic environment that existed at the time of its implementation. Thus, obtaining the expected effect from the price liberalization without accompanying losses would be possible only under conditions for free competition when the market is equally open to all buyers and sellers, and there are no obstacles to the redistribution of resources and capital movement. In this case, a mechanism of price competition would automatically arise in the struggle for consumers, and producers would have a desire to reduce costs and prices (or to increase output and product quality at a constant price). However, a perfectly competitive environment does not exist in real life, and in countries with transition economies, it was completely absent at the start of reforms. Therefore, price liberalization everywhere, albeit to a different degree, led to stagflation, i.e., rising prices while reducing production volumes.

In addition, price liberalization was carried out in economies highly prone to inflation. This was caused, firstly, by the inherited imbalance of the sectoral structure, which caused a disequilibrium between supply and demand for various groups of goods, and, secondly, by the "monetary overhang" that was formed in many countries at the end of the administrative-command system existence—a significant excess of money supply in enterprises' accounts and population savings over the mass of commodities in the domestic markets. Goods shortage at a stable level of administratively set prices gave rise to latent, suppressed inflation, which, after the liberalization of pricing, took an open form. Additional and very significant price growth factors at the initial stage of the reforms were: 1) a drop in state revenues due to a reduction in production and weakening of financial discipline in the national economy, and 2) covering the state budget deficits arising as its result, mainly due to currency issue. The role of the systemic inflation factor, associated with the preservation of state support for enterprises during the transition period and the rare use of bankruptcy procedures in real economic practice, gave rise to a non-market reaction of enterprises to demand restrictions (primarily in the form of non-payments) was also significant.

The sharp inflation surge in the late 1980s and early 1990s occurred in all CEE and CIS countries. However, the scale of inflation that followed price liberalization varied across countries. They depended on the inflationary potential accumulated in the economies and the nature of the current monetary, foreign exchange, and budgetary policies. The differences were in the rate and duration of inflation and ultimately in the ability of the government to manage this process.

Only in Hungary, annual inflation rates in the most difficult years practically did not exceed 30%, while in the Czech Republic and Slovakia, a higher inflation rate of 60% was only in 1991, after which its rates decreased noticeably. In other CEE countries, inflation was more significant. In Poland, Bulgaria, and Romania, it was of a galloping nature and was expressed in three-digit figures. In 11 countries, including the Baltic states, inflation was above 200% for at least one year, and in Estonia, Bosnia, Croatia, Serbia, and Bulgaria, inflation peaked above 1,000%. At the same time, most of these countries managed to curb inflation relatively quickly. Thus, starting from 1996, it no longer increased by 10% in Slovakia, Serbia, Croatia, Bosnia, Slovenia, and Macedonia, and in the Baltic countries after 1997, it fell below 8%.

A completely different picture was observed in the CIS countries. In 1992–1994, annual inflation rates in all CIS countries, except for Belarus, exceeded 300%, and peak values exceeded 1,000% per annum. At the same time, in Kazakhstan, Georgia, Azerbaijan, and Ukraine during the same period, inflation rates did not fall below 900% per annum. In Turkmenistan, annual inflation rates were about 3,000% in 1993–1994, and the peak value of inflation in Georgia surpassed the 15,000% mark in 1994.

The most important result of the liberalization measures carried out in the foreign economic sphere was the stratification of the sectoral structure of production in most countries with transition economies into two groups of industries—export-oriented (mainly resource industries) and oriented to the domestic market. Both developed countries, which consume most resources exported from less developed countries, and the governments of transitional states are interested in the development of export-oriented industries, since it is these industries that bring the lion's share of export foreign exchange earnings, a part of which is an important item of the country's budget income. Only national governments and the population of the respective countries are interested in the development of industries oriented to the domestic market. At the same time, lobbying the interests of their producers in foreign markets, more developed countries most often seek to undermine the domestic markets of countries with transition economies and capture them by imposing their own rules of the game.

As a result of the above circumstances, the aggregate GDP of the CEE countries decreased in 1989–1993 by 20% (Table 21), and the decline in industrial production was twice as large. Heavy industry, which in most countries was the backbone of the economy, was particularly affected. Domestic demand for its products fell, mutual supplies between post-socialist countries, which large enterprises were traditionally oriented sharply decreased after the collapse of the CMEA and the Soviet Union, and in Western markets, goods from Eastern European countries, with a few exceptions, could not compete due to low quality and high prices.

Table 21   Changes in Real GDP Level, 1990–1999

Countries	1990	1992	1993	1994	1995	1996	1997	1999
Armenia	100.0	54.7	49.9	52.6	56.2	59.5	63.0	64.0
Azerbaijan	100.0	72.6	55.8	44.8	39.5	40.0	42.2	53.0
Belarus	100.0	84.7	78.3	68.4	61.4	62.9	66.0	83.0
Georgia	100.0	51.7	36.5	39.8	41.0	45.7	50.2	37.0
Kazakhstan	100.0	88.8	80.7	65.6	60.3	60.6	61.8	62.6
Kyrgyzstan	100.0	80.8	68.2	54.5	51.6	54.5	56.2	63.1
Moldova	100.0	66.6	65.8	45.3	44.5	40.9	40.1	32.8
Russia	100.0	80.2	73.3	63.9	61.3	57.9	58.2	59.4
Tajikistan	100.0	64.7	53.5	46.7	40.9	34.0	32.7	53.4
Turkmenistan	100.0	127.3	129.1	107.0	96.3	96.4	92.5	no data
Ukraine	100.0	84.5	72.5	56.0	49.2	44.3	42.0	40.8
Uzbekistan	100.0	83.5	81.2	77.1	76.2	77.4	79.9	94.7
The Czech Republic *	100.0	80.0	80.4	82.6	86.6	90.1	91.4	...
Poland	100.0	95.5	99.1	104.4	111.6	118.3	125.2	...
Yugoslavia	100.0	64.4	44.6	45.8	47.5	49.6	50.1	...

Source: Human Development Report for Europe and the CIZ (UNDP, 1999), 14; Russia in Figures (M., 2000), 281–382.
*Note: * In 1992—Czechoslovakia.*

The rate of decline in GDP in most CIS countries in the 1990s turned out to be much higher than in the countries with transition economies in Central and Eastern Europe and is comparable only with the rate of decline in GDP in Yugoslavia, which in the last decade experienced the state collapse and several bloody wars.

In Russia, the minimum GDP over the past ten years amounted to 58% of the 1990 level (this happened in 1998), 41% in Ukraine, 36% in Moldova, 48% in Kyrgyzstan and Armenia, 28% in Georgia, 61% in Kazakhstan, and 65% of the 1990 level in Belarus. The gradual economic recovery that began in 1994 could partially compensate for the transformational decline and bring production in some CEE countries to the pre-reform level only by the late 1990s. By 2000, none of the former republics of the Soviet Union was able to surpass the level of 1990, and in 2001, Uzbekistan (103% of the 1990 level) and Estonia (102%) succeeded.

Thus, the systemic crisis was less profound in the CEE countries than in Russia and the CIS. Differences between countries within the Eastern European region were also very significant both in terms of the scale of the transformational recession and the pace of overcoming it. This is partly explained by objective reasons related to the initial conditions of systemic transformations, the general level of economic development, the specific features of the sectoral structure (including the share of the military-industrial complex), the depth of the existing macroeconomic imbalances, the degree of reformation of economic systems and the psychological readiness of the population for a change in the social system.[5] In Central and Eastern Europe, as well as in the Baltic States, these conditions were generally more favorable than in Russia. In the Czech Republic, Hungary, and Poland, they contributed to a more successful "market entry" than, for instance, in Romania or Bulgaria. An external factor also played an important role, including the scale of support for reforms by international financial institutions.

However, most researchers agree that these factors were not decisive for the course of systemic transformations and economic dynamics. The decisive role was played by the degree of understanding, the quality of setting and the will to implement transformational tasks by the authorities, as well as the economic policy pursued by the state.[6]

Due to the timely and consistent work to create a regulatory and legal framework for the economy, Hungary, Poland, and the Czech Republic, which were leaders in the systemic transformation, were able within a minimum time period to fill the "institutional vacuum" formed after the dismantling of the administrative-command system, create favorable conditions for economic activity and relatively reliable security system. Examples include tax law, the insurance system, the corporatization of property, and a number of other institutions that adequately work in the countries that were the leaders in the transition process, unlike most CIS countries. The timeliness of institutional transformations helped governments to prevent or minimize some of the negative features manifested in the economy of Russia and some other countries that delayed institutional reforms: conducting economic activities according to informal and often harmful rules for society, deep criminalization of the economic sphere, and large-scale corruption.

Simultaneously or immediately after liberalization, *macroeconomic regulation* became the main function of the state. The task of financial stabilization, which was solved primarily through monetary and budgetary policy instruments, was the priority of state economic policy in all CEE and Baltic states, as well as in most CIS countries. The obligations of the central authorities in relation to their compliance with other parameters of budget balance (limits or prohibitions on lending to governments by central banks, restrictions on building up domestic public debt, external borrowing, and budget deficit) were formalized, and tax reforms were carried out. However, monetary methods alone were not enough for macroeconomic stabilization, since at the beginning of the transition period, non-monetary factors of inflation (structural, systemic, external debt, etc.), which could not be quickly eliminated, played a key role. Therefore, along with limiting budget deficits and currency issues, many countries used such "non-market" methods as administrative regulation of prices and wages, as well as freezing ("anchor") or softer forms of fixing ("corridors," "crawling peg," etc.) exchange rates.[7] Experience has shown that these were the countries that had implemented a comprehensive approach in their anti-inflationary policy and achieved sustainable results in stabilizing the economy earlier than others.

An important task of the post-socialist states that faced the problem of a decline in production was to *stimulate economic growth*. At the first stage of market transformation, governments tried to solve it mainly by means of monetary and tax regulation (in particular, after relative financial stabilization, they followed the path of a cautious increase in the money supply). The investment, industrial and scientific, as well as technical policies necessary for the structural adaptation of production to the requirements of the domestic and world markets, were almost not carried out, both due to the lack of funds and ideological prejudices. During this period, the erroneous opinion that the best industrial policy is its absence prevailed in the ruling circles of most transition economies.

However, as mentioned above, the peculiarity of the transformational decline lay in the fact that along with inefficient and obsolete industries, modern industries, especially in high-tech engineering, fell into decline. Therefore, the state authorities of many post-socialist countries had to be engaged not only in an active industrial policy but also in support of production beyond the usual functions performed by the state in a developed market economy. Similarly, the monetary authorities of a number of post-socialist states, free of liberal mythology, introduced currency restrictions in response to capital flight. According to the development practice of many post-socialist countries, the set of possible tools used by the state in these areas is quite diverse.

In the conditions of an undeveloped and unstable financial market, the state in all the reformed countries *took on the function* of supporting the development of the private sector, which was arising on its own basis. In all countries, they tried to simplify the rules for registering and doing business. Small businesses received financial assistance in the form of guarantees for commercial loans, subsidizing a part of the interest rate on loans and direct soft loans; simplified taxation schemes were introduced for them, and tax benefits were established; measures were taken to facilitate their access to leasing funds and capital markets, to tenders and competitions for public procurement contracts; to assist their activities, information and advisory systems were created, entrepreneurs were trained in business management, and assistance was provided in connecting to international programs for the development of small businesses. Particular attention was paid to targeted support for socially significant activities of small businesses, entrepreneurial projects in economically depressed areas, projects aimed at creating new jobs, introducing innovations into production, and export activities of small businesses.

According to the aforementioned research, contrary to liberal theory, the practice has refuted the assertion of a direct relationship between a reduction of state participation in the redistribution of national income and an increase in economic growth rates. The share of public spending in GDP in post-socialist countries with positive economic dynamics (Poland, Hungary, and Slovenia) was 45%–50% during the transition period and 25%–35% with negative or stagnant ones (Bulgaria and Romania). During the years of transformational recession, the share of budget expenditures in the GDP of most countries even increased. For example, in Hungary in the period of 1990–1994, it increased by almost 9% and reached a maximum level of 62%. There was, although not so significant, an increase in Poland, Slovenia, Croatia, and Macedonia. Of the countries under consideration, this share at the first stage of the reforms significantly decreased only in the Czech Republic and Slovakia—from 64.5% in 1989 to 43.3% and 48% in 1994, respectively.

Unlike the European post-socialist states, the transition to a market economy in China and Vietnam was carried out only on a pragmatic basis. According to the researchers, the transition to a market economy in China was not carried out in accordance with some ideal model or a predetermined time schedule. Chinese economists invariably emphasize the "incremental" nature of the reforms, the meaning of which is not to redistribute the existing volume of resources but to increase the role of the market mechanism in the creation and distribution of an increasing part of resources. This approach makes it possible to ensure the "Pareto-optimal" nature of economic transformations: minimal damage to economic agents, gradually beginning to focus on market feedback signals, and, consequently, minimal resistance to ongoing reforms.

Liberal reforms were similarly carried out in other directions. The liberalization of the banking system was preceded by the interest rate regulation. The creation of the tax system began with reforming the volume of direct non-tax payments. The best example of consistency and gradualism is China's monetary reform. Initially, to stimulate the activity of economic organizations in earning foreign currency, the independence of enterprises in the field of its use was expanded, and a system for retaining a part of the earned currency was introduced. In 1988, the currency redistribution market was officially allowed, which caused a steady expansion of the internal circulation of currency in the country until the exchange rate unification in 1994. Thus, even prior to a single exchange rate formation that was regulated in accordance with the market level, 80% of the foreign currency circulating in the country had already passed through the foreign exchange market with its market rate. At the same time, after repeated adjustments to the official exchange rate, the gap between the official and market exchange rates significantly reduced. This is the main reason why a rather painful transition to a unified exchange rate went quite smoothly in China.

The Chinese experience has confirmed the above conclusions regarding the negative effectiveness of the privatization campaign carried out in Russia. Unlike Russian reformers, who focused on the privatization of established state-owned enterprises, the focus in China was on creating a favorable environment for the creation of new enterprises. According to the experience of various countries with transition economies, the result of economic reform largely depends on the ratio of newly created private enterprises and privatized state enterprises. The larger the share of the former (the example of China, Vietnam, Poland, Slovenia, and Hungary), the higher the rate of economic growth. In other words, the countries where reforms create conditions for the development of new types of activity and do not concentrate entrepreneurial energy on the redistribution of previously created ones are successful.

An analysis of empirical data confirms the above hypothesis that there is no direct relationship between privatization and economic growth rates. For instance,

Slovenia and Poland—the states where the privatization process was slower than in other countries of Central and Eastern Europe—demonstrated higher rates of economic development.

The actual data confirmed the reality of the threats of the participation of foreign capital in privatization. Foreign investors often acquired enterprises with the aim of moving environmentally harmful and ergonomically hazardous industries to post-socialist countries. The transfer of control over the basic sectors of the economy to foreign capital intensified structural deformations, caused first-class specialists' drain to foreign firms, and led to the appropriation of a significant part of the resource rent exported from the country in the form of transfer of profit, dividends, and royalties by foreign investors. In all post-socialist countries, there were cases when foreign investors acquired enterprises that were their potential or existing competitors to bring them under control or liquidate them.

The data provided in Table 22 illustrate mass privatization campaigns in various post-socialist countries. By the middle of 1998, the economy of almost all countries of the former CMEA, Albania, and Mongolia became predominantly private. At the same time, the share of the private sector in GDP varied significantly—from 20% in Belarus to 80% in Hungary. No connection between the share of the private sector and economic efficiency was found. At the same time, a number of post-Soviet states with low rates of privatization (Azerbaijan, Belarus, Uzbekistan, and Turkmenistan) demonstrated relatively better macroeconomic indicators.

The analysis carried out in the monograph *Marketing Research* shows that privatization has a positive economic effect only if it is accompanied by the timely creation of institutions for competition and capital accumulation and the development of market infrastructure.

A comparison of the methods of conducting monetary policy for macroeconomic stabilization is of particular interest in explaining different results of the transition to a market economy. In the same study, based on a generalization of the experience of all countries with transition economies, three variants of this policy are distinguished: orthodox monetary policy, heterodox monetary policy, and structural and production monetary policy.

The **orthodox** approach emphasizes reducing the government budget deficit both by reducing government spending and by increasing the revenue base. At the same time, a tight fiscal policy is accompanied by a restrictive monetary policy, including administrative planning of the money supply, binding money emission to the growth of foreign exchange reserves, and the use of money supply sterilization technologies through the sale of government securities on the stock market.

Table 22   Results of Privatization in Transition Countries

Countries	Privatization methods		The assets of state enterprises privatized in 1997, %	Number of large and medium-sized enterprises privatized in 1994–1997 (their share by late 1997, %)	Number of small enterprises privatized in 1994–1997 (their share by late 1997, %)	Cumulative share of the private sector in GDP in the middle of 1998, %
	Main	Auxiliary				
Albania	SO, MEBO	MP1 (interrupted in 1997)	less than 25	71	5,600	75
Bulgaria	SO (DS)	MP1	20.0	n.d.	(21.1)	50
The Czech Republic	MP1	SO (DS)	More than 50	1,680 (74.2)	no data	75
Slovakia	MEBO (DS)	MP1, SF	62.0	1,281 (79.4)	no data	75
Bosnia and Herzegovina	undefined (MP, MEBO, SO, restitution)		no data	no data	no data	35
Croatia	MEBO	SF	Up to 50	1,600 (67.5)	no data	55
Macedonia	MEBO	DS, SF	Up to 50	70.8	no data	55
Slovenia	MEBO	SF, MP, SO, BP	More than 50	(72.0)	no data	55
Hungary	SO (DS)	SB, MEBO	More than 50	1,566	(87.7)	80
Poland	MEBO	MP1, SO (DS)	More than 50	(35.7)	no data	65
Romania	MEBO	SO (DS)	Up to 50	(28.4)	(95.5)	60

(Continued)

Country						
Armenia	MP1	MP2, MEBO	Up to 50	1,010 (72.3)	(77.8)	60
Azerbaijan	MP1	DS, MEBO	70% of assets, 3,200 enterprises by the middle of 2,000		(71.0)	45
Georgia	MP2	MEBO (DS)	More than 50	876 (73.1)	(93.8)	60
Kazakhstan	MP1	SO (DS)	0	no data	(100.0)	55
Kyrgyzstan	MP1	MEBO	Up to 50	(63.8)		60
Estonia	SO (DS)	MEBO, MP	More than 50	(99.0)	(99.6)	70
Latvia	MP1	SO (DS)	8.2	1,351	no data	60
Lithuania	MP1	MEBO, DS	Up to 50	1,034	no data	70
Belarus	MEBO	MP	n.d.	(25.5)		20
Moldova	MP2	SO (DS)	Up to 50	1,100	no data	45
Russia	MP2	SO, MEBO	More than 50	35,000	115,000	70
Ukraine	MP1	MEBO	Up to 25	7,800 (72.4)	no data	55
Tajikistan	MEBO	MP	Up to 25	(11.3)	(50.0)	30
Turkmenistan	MEBO	DS	n.d.	15	1,779	25
Uzbekistan	MEBO	MP, DS, BP	Up to 50	18,264	no data	45
Mongolia	MP	MEBO	no data	470 (70.0)	n.d.	no data

Source: Transformation of Ownership Relationship and Comparative Analysis of the Russian Regions (M., 2001), 21.

Note: MP1—mass (voucher) privatization with equal access for all citizens, MP2—mass (voucher) privatization with significant benefits for insiders, MEBO—management and employee buyout, SO—sale to outside, DS—direct sale, SB—secured borrowing, BP—bankruptcy procedure, SF—transfer of stocks to social funds.

The **heterodox** approach focuses on the policy of price and income stabilization, which, along with orthodox methods, uses their temporary "freezing" by administrative methods. This approach can give a quick anti-inflationary effect, but it also generates negative results: the system of price impulses and estimates is deformed. Confidence in the state may be undermined in case of a "freeze" of obligations on government securities.

By the time of the weakness of the world system of socialism, the world practice had accumulated considerable experience in the use of various policies of macroeconomic stabilization. In particular, in the 1970s–1990s, Latin American countries carried out stabilization programs of both orthodox and heterodox types, often with their rotation or interweaving. This experience demonstrates that both orthodox and heterodox financial stabilization measures can be successful and unsuccessful. At the same time, they do not provide a long-term economic effect, which allows us to conclude that to ensure sustainable economic growth, a set of measures that is not limited only to financial stabilization is needed.

It is believed that most Central and Eastern European states chose a heterodox type of financial stabilization.[8] In a number of cases (in particular, Poland, the Czech Republic, etc.), a tight fiscal and monetary policy was pursued in combination with income restrictions (for example, in Poland, by taxing the growth of wage funds in the public sector, as well as underestimating the indexation of income compared to inflation rates). To be more precise, such a policy is a combination of orthodox and heterodox approaches. As a result, it resulted in a number of positive shifts in curbing inflation, but its application invariably caused a dramatic decline in production. In Poland, for instance, with a decrease in inflation from 600% in 1990 to 30% in 1994, the volume of industrial production in 1990–1991 decreased by about 35%. In the Czech Republic in 1991–1992, it fell by almost 30%, and in Romania, it fell by more than 40%.

The catastrophic consequences of the policy of macroeconomic stabilization in Russia by orthodox methods were discussed in the first section of this book.

In contrast to the monetary variant, the **structural and production** variant of macrostabilization is not so widespread in countries with transition economies. Modern China, which is carrying out a powerful modernization of its production and economic potential under conditions of strengthening the market principles of the economy within the framework of the established social system, is an example of its application. Prior to this, similar approaches to macrostabilization were applied in Japan and South Korea, which pursued an active, purposeful policy of restructuring the economy and developing productive forces during the post-war decades.

There are the following characteristics of the structural and production variant of macrostabilization:

(1) The active role of the state in the implementation of the structural transformation of the national economy by pursuing a structural and investment policy and stimulating promising areas for manufacturing modernization

(2) Comprehensive stimulation of industrial investments, including through the direct participation of the state in capital investments, providing guarantees to investors, subsidizing R&D, and creating "growth points"

(3) Support for domestic producers, stimulating the supply of goods and services, protecting the domestic market, and stimulating competitive national advantages in the global economic division of labor

(4) Stimulation of final demand, both from firms and households

(5) Pursuing a comprehensive policy to overcome inflation, including limiting cost growth

These characteristics of the structural-production variant of macrostabilization, as a rule, are linked with the course toward an evolutionary, gradual transformation of the economic system, which does not allow its abrupt collapse, which is fraught with control loss. This option acts in the transformational aspect as an antipode of "shock therapy," and in the aspect of macrostabilization—as an antipode of the monetary variant of stabilization. Its theoretical basis is such areas of economic theory as Keynesianism, institutionalism, and evolutionary economics, as well as a number of trends in socioeconomics (from technocratic to social democratic ones). Based on methodological grounds, this variant is opposed to purely liberal and monetarist approaches to macroeconomic stabilization based on the neoclassical theory of market fundamentalism. According to this approach, the privatization of state property, price liberalization, and foreign trade are considered from a purely pragmatic and not ideological position, as in the orthodox variant of stabilization. Within the framework of this option, financial stabilization becomes not a self-sufficient but an accompanying constituent component, and the implementation of anti-inflationary policy is based on achieving the goals of economic growth and raising living standards.

The structural and production variant of macrostabilization involves the development and implementation of the economic strategy of the state aimed at using the country's competitive advantages in the world economic division of labor. This strategy directs the action of market mechanisms at achieving the strategic goals of economic development and is accompanied by purposeful efforts of the state in structural and investment activities. It is worth noting the important role of programming the key areas of development, the participation of the state in the intersectoral flow of resources, stimulating private investment, regulating the volume and timeframes of capital renewal, etc.

The active structural, production, and investment policy of the state ensures the modernization of productive forces, the reduction of production costs, the increase in the domestic products competitiveness and, ultimately, the growth of product supply, which achieves an anti-inflationary effect. At the same time, measures to stimulate the effective demand of the population, solve social problems, and increase state demand and the demand of enterprises (primarily through working capital restoration) are taken.

This policy necessitates easing credit restrictions and a manageable money supply and may be accompanied by a short-term rise in inflation. The experience of applying this variant of macro stabilization demonstrates the possibility of keeping inflation within reasonable limits through constant monitoring of macroeconomic dynamics, control over prices for the products of natural monopolies, development of non-cash forms of payment, etc. Financial stabilization is achieved when production revives and rises. An example of the successful application of this approach is the Chinese economy, where it is possible to keep inflationary processes under control despite the growth in money supply, which significantly outpaces the growth in physical volumes of production throughout the entire period of reforms.

Thus, the anti-inflationary effect is achieved as a result of general macrostabilization carried out in the structural and production variant on the basis of expanding the capacity of the domestic market, increasing production volumes, and building up national competitive advantages in the world economic division of labor. The criterion for the success of macroeconomic stabilization is not the achievement of certain quantitative values of monetary indicators (inflation rates, the state budget deficit, the stability of the national currency), but economic growth and an increase in the standard of living of the population.

According to the results of an extensive comparative study of the experience of transition of different states from a directive to a market economy, generalizing excerpts from which are provided above, there is nothing surprising in the fact that, contrary to the expectations of the reformers and society, as a result of radical reforms, Russia rolled back the decades. The relations of production that developed as a result of the reforms turned out to be unable to use the country's intellectual, scientific, and production potential. Hundreds of thousands of first-class specialists who went abroad, millions of involuntary unemployed, half-loaded production facilities, abandoned fields, hundreds of billions of dollars of capital exported from the country—all this testifies to the inadequacy of the economic management system resulting from the reforms to the level of the existing economic potential. Even worse results of the reforms can be observed in the Ukrainian economy. Similar processes of the degradation of the economy and the productive forces of the society took place in the Baltic and Eastern European states, despite their entry into the EU and colonization by European capital.

Thus, the results of the radical reforms in Russia and other post-socialist countries, which implemented the doctrine of market fundamentalism based on the neoclassical paradigm under the leadership of the IMF, turned into an economic disaster and were contrary to the stated goals and expectations. Instead of improving economic efficiency, they got its sharp decline, instead of an increase in economic activity—a two-fold decrease, and instead of new horizons of development—a monstrous degradation. At the same time, the new system of economic regulation turned out to be unable to master the inherited industrial potential of the country. The most complex and scientifically advanced industries underwent the deepest destruction, and the economy rapidly degraded to the primitive forms of production—the extraction and export of minerals and raw materials of low-level processing.

The previous section provided the details of the goals and motives of economic behavior, which were formed in the specific conditions of the collapse of the Soviet state and the mass privatization of its wealth. Incredible opportunities for quick enrichment opened up for the most active and immoral ones. The winners were those who, by abusing their official position in the relevant state authorities or using connections and bribing officials, were able to privatize the most profitable state-owned enterprises. Those who tried to create their own business with their own honest work failed and, to a large extent, simply went bankrupt in macroeconomic conditions that were unfavorable for increasing their own production. Most of the richest and most influential people in the post-Soviet states made their fortunes through the privatization of state property, natural rent from the export of raw materials, overpricing, or other forms of embezzlement of other people's property or income.

It is obvious that such a "natural selection" of entrepreneurial behavior could not lead to highly efficient forms of management. On the contrary, the stereotype of appropriation of the unearned, which was formed on the basis of the criminal privatization of state property, inevitably led to an endless struggle for the redistribution of property, in which the long-term interests of the development of production faded into insignificance. Following the privatization of state property applying the same methods and with the participation of corrupt institutions of state power, raider seizures of other people's private property became widespread. This fact discouraged conscious entrepreneurship and made investments in the development of production senseless. After all, as soon as the latter started bringing noticeable profits, there were immediate attempts to capture it through professionally developed technologies of raider attacks with the participation of tax and law enforcement agencies.

Given the prevailing stereotypes of the behavior of the most successful part of the business class, it is difficult to expect economic growth. It should be repeated that the owner's attitude to the property is largely determined by the source of its acquisition. If it is acquired by "blood, sweat, and tears," then the attitude toward it is quite thrifty—the owner takes care of increasing this wealth. And if it is stolen, then there is no thrifty motivation. The illegal owner is mainly concerned with how to quickly liquidize this property and hide it somewhere abroad, away from law enforcement agencies and competitors who can claim it.

Accordingly, the macroeconomic results of such entrepreneurial behavior will be fundamentally different: in the first case, there is economic growth; in the second one, there is the export of capital and the degradation of production. The first variant of the transition to a market economy was implemented in China, where the private sector of the economy was created not through the redistribution of state property but based on personal entrepreneurial energy under favorable conditions created by the state. The second one was implemented in most former Soviet republics, where the private sector grew out of the ruins of the state sector. The results turned out to be the opposite: in the first case, a rapid economic recovery, and in the second, a catastrophic decline. At the same time, China attracted up to a trillion dollars of foreign investment into its economy, while Russia lost the same amount of exported domestic capital.

To understand why most post-socialist countries implemented an obviously damaging and contradicting national development goals variant of transition to a market economy, it is necessary to consider the patterns of economic behavior of the population.

Over the decades of Soviet power, most citizens had formed certain stereo-types of behavior, determined by the stability of socio-economic relations and confidence in a prosperous life if they followed once and for all set rules. Not only ordinary citizens but also managers acted in the conditions of infrequently changing industrial relations in accordance with the established decision-making procedures. Although the USSR economy grew at a relatively high rate, new activities were created every year, thousands of new factories were built, and dozens of new professions were mastered, the socio-economic environment itself remained stable. It encouraged loyalty to the authorities, a conscientious attitude to one's duties, and the desire to move up the party and economic career ladder.

Both the piratical attitude toward property privatized by a doubtful method and the monstrous impoverishment of the majority of the population were unexpected for the radical reformers. Indeed, what prevented the fully literate and qualified population from taking a massive part in the privatization and subsequent management of the former public property? Why, in just a few years, the main part of the national wealth was under the control of only a few dozen people, while most citizens lost their rights not only to their part of the once common property but also their savings? And for what reasons, instead of increasing the efficiency of production and multiplying the property received from the state, its new owners chose the path of plundering it and exporting capital abroad in most cases?

Widespread neoclassical ideas about the economy as a community of profit-maximizing economic entities operating in formal conditions of free competition do not provide intelligible answers to these questions. Meanwhile, an analysis carried out from the standpoint of evolutionary economics proves that the results obtained were predetermined by the pursued policy of "shock therapy" and became its natural result. If carefully cultivated fields are abandoned, one should not be surprised at the rapid growth of weeds. Dominating predatory forms of entrepreneurial activity turned out to be the most effective in terms of gaining wealth in the conditions of the chaos that arose and during the "natural selection." The consequence of this was a whole range of phenomena analyzed in the previous section, which were anomalous from the point of view of the generally accepted theoretical ideas of economic science and that deteriorated the meaning of the radical reforms carried out.

Gradually, the society adapts to the new system of socio-economic relations. But this process of studying takes time. In cases where economic reforms are ahead of the ability of society to master new forms of constructive activity in a rapidly changing environment, social tensions and dysfunctions arise due to inadequate motivation of economic entities. Conversely, if the processes of teaching society new forms of economic activity correspond to the pace of socio-economic and political transformations, then positive results can be expected. By understanding a new meaning of their activity and being guided by the principles of fair competition and the rule of law, people can achieve outstanding and highly beneficial results for society.

A comparative analysis of the market transformation of the Russian and Chinese economies, which was carried out in fundamentally different ways at the same time, simultaneously with the developing global economic crisis, is of specific interest to economic science.

Under these conditions, the result of any economic transformation was determined by a combination of its results with technological shifts that laid the foundation for the future path of economic development. In Russia, the transition to a market economy was accompanied by the destruction of institutions that ensured the reproduction of scientific, industrial, and intellectual potential. In China, these institutions were not destroyed but modernized and adapted to function in the conditions of market competition, along with the growth of new institutions of a market economy. At the same time, the state policy was aimed at preserving and developing the scientific and production potential and focused not on formal transformations but on practical results.

Creating conditions for enhancing the creative potential of the individual and entrepreneurial abilities through the targeted activities of the state allowed China to considerably increase production since the start of reforms. In Russia and most other post-socialist countries, the transition to a market economy based on the appropriation of state property by a small group of people close to authorities could not ensure economic success.

As rightly pointed out by a friend and associate of mine, John Ross, the overwhelming economic superiority of countries that implement or are influenced by the Chinese socialist development model demonstrates that the PRC economy has outperformed all available alternatives in terms of efficiency.

A detailed theoretical analysis of the reasons why the Chinese development model outperforms existing alternatives is given in John Ross' book *The Great Chess Game—A New Perspective on China's Destiny* (2016).

The Chinese "strategy of socialist development," which began in 1978 with economic reforms, is radically different in its structure and critically opposed on key policy issues to the policy of "shock therapy" imposed on Russia and other post-socialist countries, based on the principles of the Washington Consensus." According to Xi Jinping's statement on economic policy, China used both hands—the "visible hand" and the "invisible hand"—not only market mechanisms but also a comprehensive system of state regulation and control. Throughout the years of reforms, the instructions of the 3rd Plenum of the 18th CPC Central Committee have been working: "We must firmly consolidate and develop the state economy, maintain the dominant position of state property, and fully give the state-owned economy a leading role."[9]

The Chinese economic management system is characterized by the following principles aimed at stimulating economic growth:

(1) China does not rely solely on the market and deliberately uses public infrastructure spending to boost the economic level of its less developed inland provinces.

(2) Legally, China guarantees private property, but a key economic role has been given to the public sector.

(3) Politically, China is a socialist state.

Since 1978, China's growth rate has exceeded the global indicators by an average of 6 times, and since 1989, China has outpaced other countries' average growth rate by 3 times.

Not only the average GDP growth per capita was impressive, but the eradication of poverty as well. Since 1981, China has lifted around 750 million citizens out of poverty. Following the Chinese model of governance, Vietnam has lifted 30 million people out of poverty. Other countries that followed the dominant model of the Washington Consensus promoted by the IMF lifted only 120 million people out of poverty. As a result, the number of Chinese living below the poverty line has decreased by 85% and only by 15% in capitalist countries.

These data refute the claim that "capitalism" promotes rapid economic growth and reduces poverty. The real engine of rapid economic growth and poverty reduction is the socialist system of management with a market economy, created in the PRC and successfully reproduced in a number of other countries.

In the competition between the two systems, the Chinese "model of socialist development" was a huge success, while the primitive capitalist "Washington Consensus" was defeated. This can be clearly seen in a comparative analysis of GDP per capita growth rates in developing and post-socialist countries (Table 23). Economic development remains the most fundamental issue for most of the world's population: according to the World Bank data, 84% of the world's population lives in developing countries. Therefore, any objective analysis based on the desire to maximize the development potential of countries must be compared with the Chinese "model of socialist development." The facts of world economic development show that China's development policy is based on the key role of the public sector, a large-scale elaborate program to eradicate poverty, and the socialist political orientation that has become the most successful in the field of economic growth and poverty reduction.

Table 23   Countries with the Highest GDP Growth per Capita

	Average annual GDP growth per capita with consideration of inflation					
	Rating 1			% of growth		
Countries	1978– 2015	1989– 2015	1993– 2015	1978– 2015	1989– 2015	1993– 2015
China	1	1	1	8.6	8.8	8.8
Cambodia	no data	no data	2	no data	no data	5.5
Vietnam	no data	2	3	no data	5.4	5.4
Lao PDR	no data	3	4	no data	4.8	5.2
India	5	4	5	no data	4.7	5.2
Mozambique	no data	7	6	no data	4.3	5.2
Ethiopia	no data	16	7	no data	3.3	4.7
Sri Lanka	6	5	8	4.0	4.5	4.6
Belarus	no data	no data	9	no data	no data	4.3
Poland	no data	no data	10	no data	no data	4.3
Mali	11	13	11	2.8	3.5	4.2
South Korea	2	6	12	5.2	4.4	4.0
The Slovak Republic	no data	no data	13	no data	no data	4.0
Kazakhstan	no data	no data	14	no data	no data	3.9
Uzbekistan	no data	28	15	no data	2.4	3.9
Bangladesh	13	10	16	2.8	3.6	3.8
The Dominican Republic	17	15	17	2.8	3.3	3.7
Peru	41	20	18	1.4	2.8	3.6
Romania	no data	no data	19	no data	no data	3.6
Bulgaria	no data	37	20	no data	2.0	3.5

(Continued)

Total countries according to the data[1]	70	85	94			
Country average[2]				1.6	1.8	2.3
Average by country[2]				1.5	1.6	2.0

Source: Calculated from World Bank World Development Indicators.
Note: 1. Ranking is based on unrounded growth figures; 2. Countries without oil production with a population of less than 5 million people in 2015, with the data for the period indicated.

China has a three-tier economic development support system. In addition to the fiscal and monetary duopoly typical for the capitalist countries of the West, the PRC has an additional investment mechanism regulated by the National Development and Reform Commission. This is possible due to the public sector, which dominates the development management system. It is this ability to pull the "lever" of investment due to a large public sector, in contrast to the investment decline of the US, Japan, and Russia, that determines the fact that the latter countries are characterized by a sharp decline in economic growth rates, while China, on the contrary, demonstrates stable outstripping development.

It is the large public sector that distinguishes China from any capitalist economy. In November 2013, at the 3rd Plenary Session of the 18th CPC Central Committee, it was unequivocally emphasized that "we must firmly consolidate and develop the state economy, maintain the dominant position of state property, and fully give the state-owned economy a leading role." Western analysts, in their comments, tried to belittle the merits of the state in stimulating economic development in the PRC. But life itself revealed their craftiness: most countries dominated by private companies—Africa, Latin America, and much of Asia— remained in poverty. No major country with an economy based on private property has ever achieved such rates of economic growth as China during a long period of time.

In China, the state monopoly on large banks is fundamental to lowering the cost of capital for manufacturing companies. The lower cost of capital for manufacturing companies in the PRC is ensured by controlling interest rates and limiting high profits. By providing relatively cheap capital inflows as well as superior infrastructure, i.e., material conditions for markets, Chinese state-dominated economic structures create favorable conditions for the development of private business. Regarding the public and private sectors of the economy as complementary rather than opposing ones, China has achieved economic growth that has never been achieved by Western countries. This, in turn, explains the high level of optimism in China about its development compared to the pessimism that currently pervades all Western research.

The Chinese approach to managing economic development sets an example for other countries. The ability of China to neutralize the consequences of crises confirms the PRC development model's efficiency. The results of overcoming the consequences of the pandemic in 2020 are demonstrated above. China also overcame with dignity the global financial and economic crisis that erupted in 2007. Between the 2nd quarter of 2007 and the 2nd quarter of 2014, China's economy grew by 78% compared to 8% in the US. At the same time, the US had the best indicators among the G20 countries.

This chapter analyzes China's economic miracle based on generally accepted macroeconomic indicators. For clarity, the economic development of the PRC is compared with that of Russia, which legally became the successor of the USSR. These countries represented the two poles of the old world economic order, forming its bipolar core. After the collapse of the USSR, Russia in fact dropped to the periphery of the American-centric system of regulation of the world economy. Comparisons with it are interesting as an indicator of the likely dynamics of the PRC economy's evolution if the leadership of the PRC followed the recommendations of American advisers and the IMF instead of maintaining the socialist system.

As a result of a comparative experiment on the practical application of two different theoretical doctrines, diametrically opposite results were obtained: if Russia experienced more than a twofold drop in the main indicators of scientific and technical potential, then there was multiple growth in China. This proves the inadequacy of the theoretical ideas of the neoclassical paradigm, based on which the doctrine of the Washington Consensus and the policy of "shock therapy" in Russia were implemented, to the principles of modern economic development. The doctrine of rational management, which corresponded to the evolutionary paradigm and underlying the Chinese policy of transition to a market economy, on the contrary, made it possible to consider and use these principles. Their comprehension is a prerequisite for assessing the correctness of the economic policy pursued.

Market reforms began in the post-Soviet space later than in the PRC and immediately became of a radical nature. In contrast to the pragmatic evolutionary approach of "leaping a chasm in two jumps" typical of the Chinese leaders, Russia took the path of the revolutionary dissolution of the Soviet system, jumping in "shock therapy" headfirst. For the PRC economy, the transition to a market economy was not a chasm but a rise. For most of the national economy of the USSR, the shock of the libertarian reforms turned out to be fatal, and the therapy turned into euthanasia.

The fact that the market reforms, which freed up the entrepreneurial energy of Chinese society and created the conditions for improving its well-being, had disastrous consequences for Russia and other post-Soviet republics for the majority of the population and economy sectors may surprise a Chinese reader. It seems that the same instruments of economic regulation—free pricing, the stock exchange, the liberalization of foreign trade and foreign exchange regulation, the dual banking system, private property, share capital, and the stock market—gave completely different results on Chinese and Russian soil.

For three decades, the volume of GDP in China increased 10 times, investment 28 times, industrial production 40–50 times, agricultural production 7 times, exports 38 times, and high-tech exports 115 times. During the same period, the Russian economy significantly degraded: GDP increased 1.2 times, industrial production was 90% of the 1991 level, agricultural production increased 1.1 times, and exports 6 times, including high-tech 3 times (compared with 1996).

The position of China and Russia in the international division of labor has also changed, respectively. The share of China in the world economy increased from 1.6 to 16% (of Russia, it fell from 2.2 to 1.8%) in high-tech products export, the share of China reached 25% of the global volume, and the share of Russia decreased to 0.3%.

The use of the same instrument in the hands of an experienced doctor can cure the patient of the disease, and in the hands of an amateur or an executioner, it can lead to fatal injuries and mutilations. The IMF and Western advisers guided market reforms in Russia. It was at their insistence that the simplest way to implement reforms was chosen through the simultaneous liquidation of all institutions of centralized management of the national economy, the liberalization of prices, domestic and foreign trade, and the privatization of state enterprises. The state ceased its funding, transferring credit to spontaneously created commercial banks and limiting itself to the regulation of money issues.

Russian reformers promised to transfer to a developed market economy based on the model of the US and the EU in 500 days. In reality, the Russian economy plunged into chaos. In the very first year of its independent existence, production volumes halved, investments fell fivefold, and household incomes decreased by more than a third. The waves of galloping inflation devalued wages—a significant part of the working population plunged into poverty. 20% of the population was in poverty. The student youth that faced the lack of demand for many previously prestigious specialties was in the most difficult situation. The mass privatization of state property, which was carried out by free vouchers distributed to the population, led to the criminalization of relations of production and the seizure of enterprises by unscrupulous and incompetent adventurers. Instead of organizing production, they began plundering the property of enterprises that were in their ownership, transferring their income to offshore companies, and converting them into real estate objects. Until recently, a society of universal equality and prosperity underwent a sharp income differentiation, succumbing to the Latin American level of property differentiation and to the African level of social security.

To understand the peculiarities of the rise of China and the post-reform economic decline in Russia, the dogmas of the neoclassical mainstream of economic thought that seized the minds of Russian reformers must be contrasted with the principles of long-term economic development. The theory of evolutionary economics demonstrates that a dogmatic approach to economic transformation inevitably leads to its destruction. The complexity of the modern productive forces is incompatible with the primitive recipes of monetarists and libertarians, who ignore the significance of scientific and technological progress and the peculiarities of organizing high-tech production, denying the role of state policy for economic development.

Based on the discovery of the regularity of the periodic change of technological orders made by the author of this monograph, the essence of the ongoing structural crisis of the world economy is revealed, and the optimal strategy for the national economy development is substantiated. During this period, the advanced countries were faced with capital depreciation in obsolete industries and the depression of the economy, which lost its development direction. For the backward countries, the opportunity for a breakthrough opens based on the outstripping growth of the production of a new technological order and the subsequent rapid rise on a new long wave of economic growth. This is how all the economic miracles were performed after the Industrial Revolution of the 18th century, including the rise of Russia, Germany, and the US in the late 19th and early 20th centuries, Japan and the Asian Tigers in the second half of the 20th century, modern China and the countries that followed its path of socialism with a market economy.

China has managed to build a complex economic development management system that combines strategic planning and market self-organization, public credit system and private enterprise, public infrastructure development, and private property in competitive activity areas. Soviet and American economists half a century ago dreamed of the convergence of socialism and capitalism—the creation of an integral system that combines the best qualities of two alternative formations and does not have their shortcomings. The Communist Party of the Soviet Union (CPSU) leaders rejected this idea as a revisionist one and pushed the Soviet economy to the limit of expanding the ossified structure of the national economic complex. Its technological diversity entailed a drop in efficiency with expanded reproduction, which eventually led to the collapse of the USSR.

A quarter of a century after the collapse of the USSR, China's economic miracle is an experimental confirmation of missed opportunities and the correctness of the theory of convergence. Those superficial observers who compare China's successes with the Soviet NEP (New Economic Policy), referring to the transitional state of the Chinese economy, are wrong.

Against the backdrop of China's indisputable economic successes, the slyness of the concept of a "transitional economy" introduced by Western puppeteers is clearly visible. From the very beginning of market reforms, "socialism with Chinese characteristics" was built in the PRC: a socialist market economy, the development guidelines for which were determined based on the prospect of the middle of the 21st century. In Russia, the reformers were going to move from a directive to a market economy in 500 days, seriously counting on achieving the parameters of the socio-economic development of the US and Western Europe. They initially considered market reforms as mechanisms for transferring the economy from the state of an advanced socialist power to an aggregate of developed capitalist countries. They did not realize that the latter already lost their development prospects and were clearly losing to the PRC, which was creating a new progressive world economic order. All countries following the PRC's path of forming this integral world economic order have been demonstrating rapid development for the past three decades.

In other words, by choosing the path of "shock therapy," the then-Russian leaders led the country into a historical impasse. The consequence of this fatal mistake was the degradation of the Russian economy and social degeneration, which total damage is comparable to the losses of the USSR due to the Nazi invasion. The revival of the political independence of Russia and its military and technological power, taking place in recent years under the leadership of President V. V. Putin, suggests a way out of this historical impasse. After a quarter of a century of being in the dead water of Washington financial institutions, the Russian economy has sunk to the periphery of the US-centric system of liberal globalization. It is used by the US and the EU as a cash cow, and they have deprived it of more than a trillion dollars of capital, millions of brains, and billions of tons of non-renewable natural resources.

NOTES

1. E. Fedosov, "Innovative Path of Development as a Global Trend," *Herald of the Russian Academy of Sciences*, no. 9 (2006).
2. A. V. Buzgalin and A. I. Kolganov, "Introduction to Comparative Studies," in *Research and Comparative Analysis of Socio-Economic Systems: Methodology, Theory, Application to Transitional Economies* (M., 1997), 203.
3. A. Yakovlev and F. Glisin, "Alternative Forms of Settlements in the National Economy and the Possibility of Their Analysis by Methods of Subjective Statistics," *Statistics Issues*, no. 9 (1996), 21–31.
4. Ibid., 254.
5. In a number of CEE countries, the task of market reforms was facilitated by the fact that during the socialist period of development they retained elements of the market system in the form of a private sector in agriculture (Poland, Yugoslavia) and small private entrepreneurship in cities. In Yugoslavia, Hungary, and Poland, the reform of the planned economy began long before the revolutionary transformations of the late 1980s. By the beginning of the systemic transformation, some market instruments had already been introduced into the economic mechanisms of these countries, and economic entities had the skills to operate in a "semi-free" economic environment. Yugoslavia, where enterprises were managed by labor collectives and enjoyed relatively broad independence, came closest to a market economy.
6. O. T. Bogomolov, *Reforms in the Mirror of International Comparisons* (M.: Economics, 1998); *Ten Years of Systemic Transformation in the CEE Countries and in Russia: Results and Lessons* (M.: IMEMO RAS, 1999).
7. The Czech Republic, Hungary, Poland, Slovenia, and Slovakia used various centralized exchange rate regimes, which helped them to ensure greater stability and sustainability of the economy than Bulgaria and Romania, where, after the introduction of internal currency convertibility, exchange rates were freely formed in the interbank foreign exchange markets.
8. K. Zukrowska, "Transformations of the Transition Period: Theory and Practice," *Mirovaya ekonomika i mezhdunarodnye otnosheniya*, no. 6 (1995): 115.
9. Published by the Embassy of the People's Republic of China in the Russian Federation (URL: http://ru.china-embassy.gov.cn/rus/ztbd/sbjszqh/ (Accessed: June 1, 2022 г.).

CHAPTER 4

Comprehensive Development as a Means of Enhancing People's Well-Being

E MBODYING THE IDEA OF PROSPERITY IS SOMETHING CHINA HAS BEEN striving for for many years. In 2021, Xi Jinping stressed that through the joint efforts and hard work of the CPC and the Chinese people, China was able to achieve the first "centenary goal" of building a complete "moderately prosperous society in all respects" ("Xiaokang").[1] It was stated that absolute poverty had finally been eradicated, and China then turned its energies to realizing its second "centenary goal," namely the establishment of a modern, strong socialist state.[2]

The concept of "Xiaokang," or the construction of a "middle-income" ("middle prosperity," "middle wealth") society, has deep historical roots and a special meaning for the Chinese nation based on its distinctive features and traditional culture.[3]

In different periods of time, the goals and objectives underlying the implementation of this concept varied depending on the conditions and level of development of the country, but what remained constant were the common and understandable ideas of justice, common prosperity, China's own unique path, etc. The following variants of interpretation of the achievement and assessment of the "Xiaokang" period of China's modern development are distinguished:[4]

(1) The early years of "reform and opening-up." Deng Xiaoping first used the term "Xiaokang" to define his vision of Chinese modernization: "By Xiaokang, we will mean GNP per capita of $800." This goal and the construction of a "Xiaokang" society were to be achieved by the end of the twentieth century.

(2) In 1982, "Xiaokang" became the overall goal of Chinese economic development.

(3) In 1987, a three-phase strategic plan for China's modernization and further improvement of people's living standards was created, including the following steps:

- By the end of the 1980s, doubling the 1980 level of GNP and providing the Chinese people with adequate food and clothing
- By the end of the twentieth century, doubling the 1990 level of GNP and ensuring "average prosperity"
- Raising per capita GNP to the level of average developed countries, creating a relatively prosperous life for people, and implementing basic modernization by the mid-21st century
- By 1992, fully meeting the basic needs of the Chinese people

(4) In 1997, a new three-phase strategic plan for China's economic development was created with the following:

- By the end of 2010, double the level of the GNP of 2000, ensure the growth of people's welfare, and establish a functioning socialist market economic system
- Further development of the economy and all previously established systems continued by the centenary of the CPC
- By the middle of the twenty-first century, to carry out basic modernization and transform China into a modern, strong, prosperous, democratic and culturally advanced socialist state
- By the end of the twentieth century, reach a basic level of "average prosperity" as planned

(5) In 2002–2007, the basic level of "average well-being" remained rather low, fragmented, and unbalanced. The goal was set to build a "moderately prosperous society in all respects." For this purpose, a plan was put forward specifying the details and requirements for the level of economic, political, cultural, social, and environmental development.

(6) China's "New Era" and Xi Jinping's presidency: building an all-round developed and fulfilled "middle-wealth" society by 2021. It is the main and First Goal of the Century, so the Five-Sphere Integrated Plan, or China's overall plan to build a "Chinese-style" socialism and promote the country's development in the economic, political, cultural, social, and environmental fields and the Four-Pronged Comprehensive Strategy, or China's strategic plan to build a "Chinese-style" socialism were created to achieve it, aimed

at completing the construction of "middle-class" society, furthering reform, consolidating the supremacy of the "middle-class" society and promoting social welfare. It identifies areas that serve as indicators of achieving full "Xiaokang," namely sustainable economic development, democratic development, enhancing culture as China's "soft power," further increasing living standards and prosperity, and making progress in building a resource-saving and environmentally friendly economy.

In 2017, the results of a comprehensive analysis of the progress made toward full Xiaokang were presented. On this basis, the strategy for consolidating the progress made and the subsequent transition to the construction of a modern socialist state was defined. This work certainly highlighted the important role of Xi Jinping as the ideological inspirer and wise leader.

Achieving full "moderate prosperity" or "medium prosperity" symbolizes the following:[5]

(1) From a historical perspective: the end of a long period in the chain of "living wage-partial (fragmented) welfare—full-fledged average welfare on the way to shared prosperity." Given China's densely populated population, realizing the goal of "average well-being" within the country can be seen as making the impossible a reality.

(2) In ideological terms: an important step toward the realization of the "Chinese Dream" of a "great rebirth of the Chinese nation"[6] and a reflection of China's historical transformation (from a deep "periphery" of the world economy to a strong, prosperous, and rapidly growing state).

(3) In the national dimension: the joint achievement of all the Chinese people, which has strengthened and inspired them to continue to struggle for national rebirth and the construction of socialism "with Chinese characteristics" as well as material and spiritual progress, embodying the hard work, responsibility, resourcefulness, determination and heroism of the Chinese people, their devotion to the ideals of socialism and their trust in the course of the Party.

(4) On the development side: deepening reforms and effective coordinated action in five key areas simultaneously (i.e., economic, political, cultural, social, and environmental progress), a substantial rise in living standards, and China's ability to keep up with its progress.

(5) In terms of governance: the landmark achievement of the CPC (the largest and most influential party in the world), which demonstrated its responsibility, ability to solve problems, **keep promises made,** and win the trust and support

of the people (party and people unity). The happiness and common welfare of the Chinese people is defined as the Party's mission.

(6) In the aspect of the transformation of the world order: an important contribution to the development of the world economy and international relations from the private (national economic development) to the common (impetus for building a "community of common destiny" as the common future of the world's countries and joint development). China shares its unique experience of reform and achievement with the world.

It is stressed that the idea of full "average well-being" would not be possible without awareness of the following facts and the implementation of the relevant tasks:

(1) **"Xiaokang" as an outcome of comprehensive development.** This is reflected primarily through the creation and implementation of the Five-Sphere Integrated Plan and the Four-Pronged Comprehensive Strategy. In order to raise the standard of living, **a strong, efficient economy** with a strong emphasis on substantial scientific and technological progress (with the construction of innovation centers, the development of basic and applied research and their adequate and sufficient funding), industrial and infrastructure development; a developed democracy with **a high ideal of social justice and a guarantee of respect** for citizens' rights are essential; **a high level of cultural development** with a strong ideological foundation, knowledge of and reverence for cultural traditions, large-scale involvement of the population in cultural events and tourism (which implies their accessibility) and international impact (culture as China's "soft power"); **improving living standards and taking care of people** as the first and foremost task of the CPC and the State, which implies increasing incomes and a comfortable full life for every citizen, a steadily developing labor market and increasing the quality of the labor force, a decent level of education and its accessibility and social protection, and the availability and high quality of medical services; **environmental objectives and principles** (improving and protecting the environment, controlling pollution, caring for the ecosystem, choosing and implementing a green development path).[7]

(2) **"Xiaokang" as a distinctive common good** with the characteristics of non-excludability and indivisibility, expressed in the objectives of welfare for everyone (including poverty alleviation and harmonious all-round personal development), integrated urban and rural development (including the

improvement of rural well-being, urbanization processes, closer urban-rural interaction), coordinated and balanced regional development (through the appropriate.[8]

(3) **"Xiaokang" as a reward for the hard work** of the Chinese people and the CPC working on the principle of "putting the people first" and aiming to serve the people. To this end, Sound Policies and Strategies shall be formulated and implemented, considering the accumulated experience and internal and external conditions, formulating adequate and phased objectives, analyzing and evaluating intermediate and overall results, solving problems, and eliminating risks. Furthermore, it should be understood that the implementation of "reform and opening-up" and "Xiaokang" are complementary processes running in China in parallel with its interaction with the outside world. Of particular importance to the "Xiaokang" is the succession of generations sharing and understanding the significance of China's independent path, ready to make sacrifices and work hard together to achieve the common goal under the leadership of the CPC.[9]

(4) **"Xiaokang" as an impetus for international development**[10] (China as an economic giant, providing more stable and prosperous development, having proposed and successfully implemented its "recipe" for fighting poverty, supporting mutually beneficial cooperation, sharing its experience of modernization with partners, ready to build a global "community of one destiny").

However, it should be clearly recognized that the realization of the idea of "middle-class welfare" is only an intermediate goal in the "chain" of China's modernization and national renaissance. Despite significant achievements and a new level of achievement, China continues to face the following serious problems and challenges:[11]

(1) Internal
- Unbalanced development (income inequality, imbalance in urban and rural development, the problem of regional inequalities within the country, etc.)
- Unfulfilled reform targets in a number of key areas
- The problems of insufficient innovation capacity for high-tech development
- Agricultural development issues
- The need for additional efforts in the area of green economy and environmental protection

- • Weaknesses in social management and maintenance and welfare policies
(2) External
  - • The impact of the coronavirus pandemic
  - • Entrenched and growing conflict in the world, expressed in the development of collective international sanctions regimes, trade wars, open military confrontations, etc., and increasing instability and uncertainty in the world
  - • Changes in technological and world economic patterns
  - • Struggle between the trends of globalization and regionalization

All the challenges and threats listed above make the path to further development difficult. However, China is optimistic about the future, and it has all the possibilities and resources to realize its goals. In the new stage of development, by improving its philosophy and stimulating economic growth, China plans to make impressive progress once again. It is on course to reach a basic level of socialist modernization by 2035:[12]

(1) Substantial growth in economic and scientific-technological potential and per capita income, a technological leap forward in key areas of the national economy that will give China global leadership in innovation, new industrialization, greater use of IT, accelerated urbanization and agricultural modernization, and the construction of a modern economic system is expected.[13]

(2) The national public administration system will be modernized, and more opportunities will be created for equitable citizen participation; the rule of law and respect for people's rights will be adequately protected.

(3) The country will take the lead in culture, education, human development, sports, and health care. It is committed to the all-round individual development of each individual as a worthy member of modern society, and to raising the level of culture as an effective component of China's "soft power."

(4) It is intended to introduce the principle of "eco-friendly" everywhere, both in the work of organizations and institutions and in the way of life of citizens. In this way, it will be possible to achieve the goal of a "Beautiful China" and ecological civilization, to stop the growth and further substantially reduce environmental pollution (especially various emissions) and significantly improve its condition.

(5) A new, more progressive phase of "reform and opening-up" is looming, which will unlock the country's potential to participate more effectively in

international economic cooperation and strengthen its competitive edge and international influence.

(6) There will be a significant increase in the share of the middle-income (middle-class) population and an increase in per capita GDP to the level of developed countries. In addition, there is a commitment to ensure equal access to basic public services and to reduce the "development gap" between urban and rural areas and different regions of the country.

(7) It is stressed that the "peaceful China"[14] initiative will continue at a higher level but with a modernization of the national defense and armed forces.

(8) The Chinese people are expected to live better lives, with great opportunities for both all-round personal healthy development and shared prosperity and common well-being.

(9) It is predicted that by the middle of the twenty-first century. China will emerge as a modern, prosperous, "beautiful," harmonious, strong, democratic, highly cultural socialist state.

The concept of China's economic rise is inconceivable without a comprehensive spatial development management system, which has a number of specific features[15] that make the Chinese experience interesting and useful for Russia.

Firstly, it cannot be separated from the overall course of China's economic development, with the following stages representing a transition in economic history:

(1) Toward a "planned market" economy strategy and major reforms (1976–1989)

(2) Toward an export-oriented strategy (1992–2005)

(3) Toward stimulating domestic demand (2006–2013)

(4) Toward a "New Normalcy" with a new quality of economic growth (from 2014);

(5) Toward a "double-circular" growth model relying on domestic consumption, including domestic (stimulating domestic demand and establishing production "chains" to meet it) and external (expanding the network of regional and bilateral trade and economic agreements, reducing investment barriers, increasing competitiveness, etc.) contours[16]

Secondly, the development of China's regions is carried out in stages, as noted by Deng Xiaoping. Initially, the provinces on the east and southeast coasts of the country, which are more closely linked to foreign markets, were chosen as the experimental sites. Special economic regions (Shenzhen, Xiamen, Zhuhai, Shantou) were first designated, and later open economic zones were established. This approach (including the use of economic zoning since the 1980s) made it possible to accelerate economic development and enhance the investment attractiveness of the allocated regions, as well as to intensify foreign economic activity.

Thirdly, the donor-recipient algorithm is applied to regional development when resources accumulated in the regions with advanced development are reallocated to the catching-up regions, which, among other things, allows shifting the focus from some regions to other regions or, in other words, creating "waves of economic returns." At the same time, it is crucial to accumulate experience in dealing with debt burdens arising in the advanced regions of outstripping growth. Western regions are currently expected to grow with a focus on extensive factors and coastal regions at the expense of productivity based on the STP factor.

Fourthly, urban agglomerations and their development play an important role. Between 1980 and 2018, China's urban population grew from just over 19% to almost 60% and is expected to reach 66% by 2030. This urbanization trend has pulled up other important indicators such as labor productivity, income levels, consumption, and investment (including R&D). The four largest urban agglomerations are currently being actively shaped and developed,[17]

Fifthly, there is a link between the achievement of "Xiaokang" and China's spatial development strategy. Not only does the implementation of the strategy lead to poverty alleviation, but also the goal of fully building a "middle-income" society gives impetus to balanced regional development.

Finally, the organization of regional authorities is of particular importance. It is characterized, for example, by greater autonomy in administering budgets and a mechanism for selecting staff for executive positions (including examinations for applicants and civil servants).

To summarise this part, it must be stressed that by the early 2020s, China had completed only **the first important step** in the movement toward "Xiaokang"— the **elimination of absolute poverty** in the country, which is linked to the biological survival of people.[18]

Currently, China continues to actively **develop a concept and strategy to combat relative poverty** (in other words, poverty compared to others) and thus seeks to address social inequalities.[19]

The anti-poverty strategy implies a clear understanding of the causes and specificities of poverty in the country. In the mid-2010s, force majeure (e.g., natural disasters) and social problems (education, employment, and morbidity) were the main drivers of poverty in China. Given the high population size and wide spatial distribution, the depth of poverty, the problems of regional poverty (including the presence of "continuous" poverty areas) and old-age and child poverty, and the exacerbation of structural poverty types (due to the long-standing "two-branch structure" of cities and villages and separate governance) and "illness," the elimination of absolute poverty can be assessed as the next "Chinese miracle."[20]

As shown above, China has continuously improved its strategy of poverty alleviation and achieving full-fledged "Xiaokang" as part of the goal of eliminating absolute poverty. One of the next stages of this process since 2013 reveals the following distinctive features of the new model and direction of poverty alleviation:[21]

(1) Strengthening the principle of targeting measures
(2) Strengthening the system of accountability for the achievement of the objective
(3) Securing the resource base and increasing investment
(4) Increasing the effectiveness of anti-poverty work
(5) Developing internal capacities to overcome poverty from within (unlocking the potential of the poor)

NOTES

1. "China's Epic Journey from Poverty to Prosperity," The State Council Information Office of the People's Republic of China, September 2021. Available at: https://www.mfa.gov.cn/ce/cehu/hu/xwdt/P020211011852905009033.pdf (accessed 05.05.2022).
2. "China's Epic Journey from Poverty to Prosperity," 1–4. Available at: https://tass.ru/mezhdunarodnaya-panorama/11793915?
3. A. Voskresensky, "Realisation of the 'Chinese Dream' during the 'Xi Jinping Era': What Should Russia Expect?," *World Economy and International Relations* 63, no. 10 (2019), 5–16.
4. Highlighted based on "China's Epic Journey from Poverty to Prosperity," 4–10.
5. Based on "China's Epic Journey from Poverty to Prosperity," 1–4.
6. A. Voskresensky, "Realisation of the 'Chinese Dream' during the 'Xi Jinping Era': What Should Russia Expect?," *World Economy and International Relations* 63, no. 10 (2019), 5–16.
7. Details, "China's Epic Journey from Poverty to Prosperity." The State Council Information Office of the People's Republic of China, September 2021, 10–42.
8. Ibid., 42–56.
9. Ibid., 56–67.
10. Ibid., 67–71.
11. Based on "China's Epic Journey from Poverty to Prosperity," 71–75.

12. Ibid.
13. https://rg.ru/2020/11/10/kitaj-zavershit-socialisticheskuiu-modernizaciiu-ekonomiki-k-2035-godu.html?ysclid=l39tzmtgel.
14. See also the discussion of the concept of the "peaceful rise of China" in https://globalaffairs.ru/articles/chzhungo-hepin-czzyueczi-mirnoe-vozvyshenie-kitaya/?.
15. Based on V. A. Yasinsky and M. Y. Kozhevnikov, "Spatial Development: China's Experience," *Economic Strategies*, no. 2 (2021): 6–15. https://ecfor.ru/publication/prostranstvennoe-razvitie-kitaya-yasinskij-kozhevnikov/.
16. Formulated also taking into account: S. A. and E. O. Zaklyazminskaya, "Transformation of China's Socio-Economic Model under Pandemic Conditions," *Contours of Global Transformations: Politics, Economy, Law* 13, no. 6 (2020): 198–216, DOI: 10.23932/2542-0240-2020-13-6-11.
17. V. A. Yasinsky and M. Y. Kozhevnikov, 9.
18. L. Boni, "Eradicating Poverty in China, Part 1" *ASIA AND AFRICA TODAY*, no. 8 (2020): 5, https://www.ifes-ras.ru/files/abook_file/boni-asia-1.pdf.
19. L. Boni, "Eradicating Poverty in China, Part 2," *ASIA AND AFRICA TODAY*, no. 9 (2020): 7, https://www.ifes-ras.ru/files/abook_file/boni-asia-2.pdf.
20. L. Boni, "Eradicating Poverty in China, Part 1&2."
21. L. Boni, "Eradicating Poverty in China, Part 2."

CHAPTER 5

Factors of Economic Growth in the PRC

THE MOST IMPORTANT GROWTH FACTORS OF THE CHINESE ECONOMY ARE the development of labor specialization and production cooperation, manifested in a relative increase in the production of intermediate products; capital investment; labor input and scientific and technological progress, manifested in the growth of factor productivity.

The outstripping growth in the production of intermediate goods in the PRC, based on the advantages of the division of labor, is based on an increase in the size of the domestic market. In turn, it is based on outstripping growth in capital investment. First of all, in the development of transport infrastructure, increasing the capacity of roads and railways. Priority development of infrastructure was provided by the system of strategic planning, of which spatial planning is an integral part.

While in the early days of reform and opening-up, the FDI factor was of great importance for the growth of the Chinese economy, the impact of the global financial crisis sharply reduced the share of trade in the Chinese economy. The share of exports of goods and services in Chinese GDP fell from 35% in 2007 to 23% in 2014, and the share of imports fell from 27% to 19%. As a result of giving greater importance to domestic market development, China has become less dependent on the international division of labor than before.

Investment in fixed capital is the most important productive factor in economic growth. As shown above, at the beginning of China's economic upturn, they were financed by targeted credit issuance. As people's incomes have risen, savings have played an increasing role in financing investments. The Chinese government has made a concerted effort to fine-tune the mechanism for transforming savings into investment, including by raising corporate yields, thereby minimizing the cost of money to the economy as a whole and channeling significant savings to finance investment in large projects.

The factor of labor is multiplied by the growth of its quality, which plays an increasing role in increasing its factor productivity. The primacy of labor quality over labor quantity is an important priority in managing the development of the Chinese economy. It is becoming more knowledge-intensive and technology-intensive, which puts a high demand on vocational training and engineering training. Scientific research and advanced development are stimulated (the share of public expenditures in the PRC for this purpose is constantly increasing), which is the most important factor of growth through the increase in innovative activity.

An analysis of the contribution of factors of production to China's economic development belies neoliberals' blind faith in the market and entrepreneurship and their ability to ensure expanded reproduction with little or no state intervention. The patterns observed in China's macroeconomic dynamics have often been and continue to be the subject of fierce debate, the main bone of contention being the degree of state involvement in organizing capital investment in development. In the early days of China's economic ascent, many experts argued for the Chinese government to rely primarily on private investment. The global economic crisis has shown the fallacy of this approach. In times of crisis, it is the state, not business, that assumes the main responsibility for organizing the money supply to enterprises investing in the development and expansion of production, as well as the adjustment of cooperative chains—the same investments in the internal division of labor that have timely and very successfully supported economic growth in the PRC.

The evaluation of FDI in the development of the Chinese economy is a subject of ongoing debate. In "The Relationship between Interest Rate, Exchange Rate, GDP, and FDI in Relation to the Chinese Economy,"[1] it is argued that the Chinese economy develops not so much through FDI but through its sovereign public funds. Therefore, changes in the flow and speed of foreign investment into the PRC economy do not have a critical impact on it. The opposite is true: the Chinese economy is strengthening more than before, thanks to its own reserves and low level of public debt. Moreover, the Chinese economy is the largest driver of the US economy; any macroeconomic fluctuations are instantly relayed to the US as well. This is because China is the largest global investor in the US debt market. The analysis shows that China's economy is objectively insensitive to global shocks for the foreseeable future, as it was in 2008, which was possible precisely because it has formed its own sources of funding for capital operations. In other words, China has taken advantage of the opportunities of globalization to strengthen its own position in the global economy.

Before "reform and opening-up," China was a poor backward country, virtually isolated from the outside world, not least because of ineffective economic policies.

Until 1979, China under Mao Zedong followed a command economy and centralized planning. The state-controlled the bulk of production, setting goals and targets, allocating resources, and regulating prices. In the late 1950s, the so-called "three banners" were raised as benchmarks: The "General Line," the "Great Leap Forward," and the People's Communes.[2] By 1978, almost three-quarters of industrial production was being created centrally by state-owned enterprises in line with the targets. China's aim was to make the national economy relatively self-sufficient, and foreign trade was largely limited to imports of scarce goods.

Such policies led to serious "distortions" in China's economy, which faced excessive "tutelage" from the state, a lack of effective redistributive mechanisms, low-quality production, and low worker motivation. Maddison estimated that the average annual real GDP growth between 1953 and 1978 was about 4.4%. China's economy also suffered a real "shock" due to the "Great Leap Forward" (1958–1962), which caused famine and the deaths of some 45 million people, and the "Cultural Revolution" (1966–1976), which wreaked political and economic havoc. Between 1958 and 1962, the standard of living in China fell by 20.3%, and between 1966 and 1968, it fell by 9.6%.

In 1978, it was decided to change economic policy considerably by "trying on" the state and market to achieve high economic growth and prosperity. Deng Xiaoping acted as the "architect of economic reform" in China and uttered the historic phrase: "It doesn't matter what color the cat is, as long as it catches mice." The phrase can also be interpreted in this way: it does not matter how you classify the resulting type of economy as long as it works to achieve its goals.[3]

Since 1979, the situation has changed dramatically; suffice it to mention that China has become one of the fastest-growing and developing economies in the world. The results of this transformation have been called the "Chinese miracle." This economic growth has enabled China to double its GDP on average every eight years and to lift some 800 million people out of poverty. China has become the largest economy in the world (as measured by purchasing power parity), with a high level of production and trade and a huge stock of foreign exchange reserves, as well as one of the most important partners of the US.

The economic reforms initiated since 1979 have involved, among other things, the following areas:

(1) Implementation of price and property incentives for farmers
(2) Creation of special economic zones to attract foreign investment, increase exports and imports of high-tech products
(3) Ensuring trade openness
(4) Transfer of part of the control and regulatory functions to the local level
(5) Encouragement of private initiative and entrepreneurship
(6) Conducting local market experiments
(7) Implementation of tax and other incentives
(8) Price liberalization

China's reform strategy is based on the principle of gradualism, i.e., gradualism in economic policy implementation, or what Deng Xiaoping figuratively described as "crossing the river by groping for rocks." Among the drivers of China's economic growth, large-scale capital investment and productivity growth stand out in particular.

The results of "reform and opening-up" are indeed impressive. Suffice it to mention that China's economy, thanks to timely and effective government measures, was able to confidently withstand the processes and consequences of such a powerful and large-scale external challenge as the global financial and economic crisis, the acute phase of which occurred in 2008–2009.

Furthermore, for China, the term "openness" further implies not only transforming the national economy from within but also implementing a "go global" strategy, i.e., deepening cooperation and bringing mutually beneficial changes to the global economic order. This idea is also consistent with the implementation of the BRI and the construction of a "community with a shared future."

However, as China has evolved, its economic growth has gradually begun to slow down. For example, while it was just over 14% in 2007 (as measured by real GDP growth), it dropped significantly to 6.6% in 2018, and according to IMF estimates, it will fall to 5.5% by 2024. China was prepared for this turn of events and called it a "new normal" in which to exist. However, the need was recognized to move toward a new economic growth model with a focus on private consumption, service sector development, and innovation rather than on fixed-asset investment and exports. Such reforms were supposed to help China avoid falling into the "middle-income trap," which occurs when a country reaches a certain level of economic development and gets "stuck" in it, experiencing a steady decline in economic growth and being unable to tap new sources of growth.

China has thus identified innovation as a priority source of economic growth. As part of this innovation, the "Made in China 2025" initiative, or an ambitious plan to modernize China's manufacturing through enhanced state support, was introduced in 2015, covering ten key sectors of the economy:

(1) New-generation information and communication technologies
(2) High-performance automated control systems and robotics
(3) Aerospace and aviation equipment
(4) Marine engineering equipment and high-tech manufacturing of marine vessels
(5) Modern railway equipment
(6) Energy-efficient vehicles
(7) Electrical equipment
(8) Agricultural machinery and equipment
(9) New materials
(10) Biopharmaceuticals and high-performance medical devices

However, many (especially in the US) see the goal of this strategy as not to develop a national economy and international cooperation but rather to reduce China's dependence on foreign technology and dominate global markets. In 2017, the Trump administration launched an investigation into the PRC under Section 301 of the US Trade Act[4] and noted that China's policies on innovation, rights protection, and the use of intellectual property were considered harmful to US interests. The US and PRC subsequently "exchanged" duties on each other's goods, leading to a sharp decline in their bilateral trade in 2019, and after Trump signed the memorandum "On Combating Chinese Economic Aggression," a full-scale trade war was launched.[5]

According to experts, a prolonged and progressive trade conflict between the US and China will have negative consequences for both parties involved due to their interconnectedness in the global economic system.[6]

Furthermore, China faces additional challenges, such as an incomplete market economy, manifested primarily in industrial policy and state-owned enterprises, elements of excessive state control, and bottlenecks in the monetary and financial system, corruption, and environmental and demographic challenges.[7]

However, strict currency controls and capital export restrictions are an integral part of China's economic development management system. Without it, the Chinese financial and banking system would not have been able to increase its lending to investment and production growth at such a high rate. A ban on foreign exchange transactions on the capital account is necessary to prevent capital flight, speculative attacks against the renminbi, and the inflation of financial bubbles and to ensure the stability of the national currency. It is necessary to keep interest rates low and to prevent long-term lending to enterprises because it prevents the creation of vortices of currency speculation that pull money out of the productive sector. Finally, currency controls and restrictions on capital exports act as a barrier to the embezzlement of credit and working capital of companies, preventing them from hiding misappropriated funds abroad.

In this case, what seems anachronistic to Western economists are, in fact, elements of the management system in the new world economic order, which is an order of magnitude more effective in ensuring economic development than the previous one, which persists in the US, the EU and peripheral countries in relation to them.

As John Ross points out, China's economic development has a unique character—its "Chinese characteristics." This character lies in a particular combination of economic forces that are global in nature. Those who created China's economic policy, especially Deng Xiaoping, were right to assert both the uniqueness of Chinese policy and to act according to the "universal laws" of economics. From this follows the possibility of replicating China's economic success, not by blindly copying it but by creatively reinterpreting and recycling it.

China's policy of "opening up" is rooted in the fact that the domestic and international division of labor, reflected in the growth parameters of intermediate products, is the most powerful force for economic development. The policy of "opening up," which marks participation in the international division of labor, more so than import substitution, can serve as the basis for rapid economic growth.

The above substantive analysis of the growth factors of the Chinese economy is appropriately complemented by econometric analysis.

Of particular importance for planning and regulation in China is an analysis of the processes and drivers of economic growth. This is important not only for properly setting national development goals but also for tracking the dynamics of major global economic indicators and regional trends, as the "Chinese miracle," achieved through special economic policies and "reform and opening-up," has propelled the country into the ranks of global economic leaders. Although China is often still referred to as the world's largest developing country, it has already made the transition from the "rapid economic growth" stage to that of creating high-quality products. China has now entered another level of transformation, the path and logic of which are again unique.

Despite the difficult period of 2020–2021 due to the negative external factors of the "double whammy" (the coronavirus pandemic and the surge of protectionism), which was a real test of strength even for highly developed countries, and the internal challenges (issues of maintaining economic growth shifting toward the L-shaped trajectory, stability and positive effects of the results achieved), the Chinese economy remains "thriving" and resilient to "shocks."[8]

The following key drivers of China's economic growth currently stand out:[9]

(1) The level of consumer demand (CD). For example, according to expert estimates, because of COVID-19 in 2020, more than 60% of China's total GDP decline is attributable to falling SP, while during 2013–2019, the opposite was true: on average, about 60% of GDP growth was generated by SP.

(2) The development of the tertiary industry or service sector. While its share reached almost 46% in 2012, surpassing for the first time the tertiary sector, which has long been the backbone and driver of China's economic development, in 2019, it increased to 54%.

(3) Investment in the real estate market. In the initial stages of urbanization, they significantly stimulated economic growth, but with the saturation of the property market, their role in stimulating China's economy has diminished. However, the overall positive effect this factor can have should not be underestimated either. It is recommended that China partially shift its focus from urbanization and real estate market development to other factors of economic growth.

(4) R&D expenditure. Their impact on economic growth in the short and medium term is insignificant, but in the long run, they contribute to STI, having a positive effect on economic development. One possible way of reducing the time lag between these expenditures and the expected results is to accelerate the application of STI achievements in practice, which requires an increased level of cooperation between universities and research organizations with industry and business.

(5) Deepening financial reform. The case of China's western regions shows that the current level of financial development hinders economic growth, so continued reform of the financial sector of the economy is necessary.

(6) Development of a green economy and environmental improvement. At one time, the rapid development of industry led to increased pollution, increased emissions of various harmful substances, environmental degradation, and, as

a consequence, a considerable increase in the costs of eco-management and projects. China has made environmental commitments and is now aiming not only for a sustainable economy but also for future economic growth to be "green."

NOTES

1. K. Vidhya and S. B. Inayat Ahamed, "The Relationship between Interest Rate, Exchange Rate, GDP, and FDI with Respect to the Chinese Economy," *International Journal of Innovation Technology and Engineering Research* 8, no. 11S2 (September 2019).
2. Y. V. Yaremenko, *The "Great Leap Forward" and the People's Commune in China* (Moscow: Politizdat, 1968).
3. "China's Economic Rise: History, Trends, Challenges, and Implications for United States," Congressional Research Service, June 25, 2019, RL33534.
4. https://news.rambler.ru/asia/40171613-voruet-li-knr-u-ssha-intellektualnuyu-sobstvennost/?ysclid=l3lhnqcyfj.
5. https://interaffairs.ru/news/show/19596?
6. "China's Economic Rise: History, Trends, Challenges, and Implications for United States."
7. Made based on "China's Economic Rise: History, Trends, Challenges, and Implications for United States."
8. Li M., Sun H., F. O. Agyeman, M. Heydari, A. Jameel, and H. Salah ud din Khan, "Analysis of Potential Factors Influencing China's Regional Sustainable Economic Growth," *Applied Sciences* 11, no. 22 (2021): 10832, https://doi.org/10.3390/app112210832
9. Ibid.

The PRC as the Nucleus of a New Technological and World Economic Order

Changing Technological and World Economic Patterns as an Objective Basis for China's Rise

G LOBAL COMPETITION IS NOT SO MUCH BETWEEN COUNTRIES AS BETWEEN transnational reproduction systems, each of which brings together, on the one hand, the national education systems of the population, capital formation, and scientific organizations of the countries concerned, and on the other hand, the production, business and financial structures operating at the scale of the world market. Several such systems, which are closely linked together, determine global economic development. They form the core of the world economic system, concentrating intellectual, scientific-technical, and financial potential. The countries that are not part of it form the periphery, deprived of internal integrity and opportunities for independent development.

The concentration of transnational capital and production has reached a qualitatively new level, which allows us to talk about the formation of a new world order in which international capital, transnational corporations, and international organizations associated with the core of the world economic system play a decisive role. The countries outside of it form the periphery, deprived of internal integrity and opportunities for independent development. The relationship between the core and the periphery of the world economic system is characterized by non-equivalent economic exchange, in which the countries in the periphery have to pay for the intellectual rent contained in imported goods and services at the expense of the natural rent and labor costs contained in the raw materials and low-tech goods they export.

By dominating the periphery, the core "pulls" from it the most qualitative resources—the best minds, scientific and technological achievements, property rights, to the most valuable elements of national wealth. Having technological advantages, the countries of the core impose convenient standards on the periphery, securing their monopoly position in the sphere of technological exchange. By concentrating on financial power, the core imposes capital flows and the use of its currencies, including for forming foreign exchange reserves, on the periphery, thus gaining control over the financial systems of peripheral countries and appropriating the proceeds of the global economic system. Deprived of their main internal sources of development, peripheral countries lose the possibility of conducting sovereign economic policies and managing their own growth, becoming an economic space to be exploited by international capital.

US global competitiveness is now based on a combination of technological, economic, financial, military, and political superiority. Technological leadership allows US corporations to be the most competitive in the global marketplace and to capture intellectual rents by funding R&D in order to stay ahead of competitors on the broadest possible front of STI. By holding a monopoly on the use of advanced technology, US companies have a competitive advantage in world markets, both in production efficiency and in the supply of new products. Economic superiority provides the basis for the dominant position of the US currency, which is defended by politico-military methods. In turn, through the appropriation of global seniority from the emission of the world currency, the US finances inflated military expenditures, including expenditures on advanced research and development. In this way, a positive feedback loop is maintained between all components of national economic competitiveness.

The global crisis that is currently underway, replacing the long economic recovery of developed countries, is a natural manifestation of the long waves of economic activity known as the "Kondratiev waves."[1] Each of them is based on the lifecycle of the corresponding technological mode—a reproducible integral system of technologically linked productions. The politico-military crisis, in turn, is a manifestation of a change of centuries-old cycles of accumulation, each of which is based on a different institutional world economic order—a system of interrelated institutions ensuring expanded reproduction of capital and determining the mechanism of global economic relations. The superposition of these two cyclical processes in the crisis phase creates a dangerous resonance that threatens to destroy the entire system of global economic and political relations.

6.1 Patterns of Technological Change

In the history of world development, starting with the Industrial Revolution in England, life cycles of five successive technological modes can be distinguished (Figure 5), including the information and communication technological mode dominating the structure of the modern economy.[2] Its life cycle is coming to an end, as manifested in a structural crisis of the global economy, stagnation of the advanced economies, financial turbulence, and a technological revolution. In the throes of the latter, a new technological stage is being born.

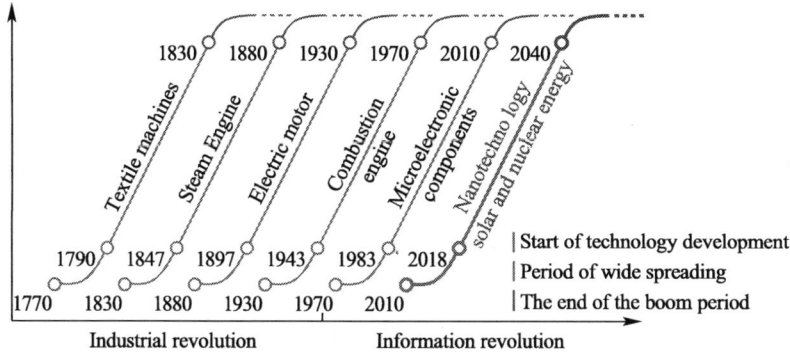

Figure 5   Shift in Technological Modes in the Course of Modern Economic Development

Source: S. Glazyev and V. Kharitonov, eds., *Nanotechnology as a Key Factor of a New Technological Stage in the Economy* (Moscow: Trovant Press, 2009).

We can already see the key areas of the new, sixth technological paradigm, whose growth will ensure the rise of advanced economies in a new long wave of economic growth: biotechnology, based on advances in molecular biology and genetic engineering, nanotechnology, artificial intelligence systems, global information networks and integrated high-speed transport systems (Figure 6).

Their implementation ensures a multiple increase in the efficiency of production, reducing its energy and capital intensity.[3]

At present, the new technological order is moving from an embryonic stage of development to a growth phase. Its expansion is constrained both by the small-scale and untested nature of the technologies concerned and by the unpreparedness of the socio-economic environment for their widespread application. However, despite the crisis, the costs of absorbing the latest technologies and the scale of their application are increasing at a rate of around 20%–35% per annum.[4]

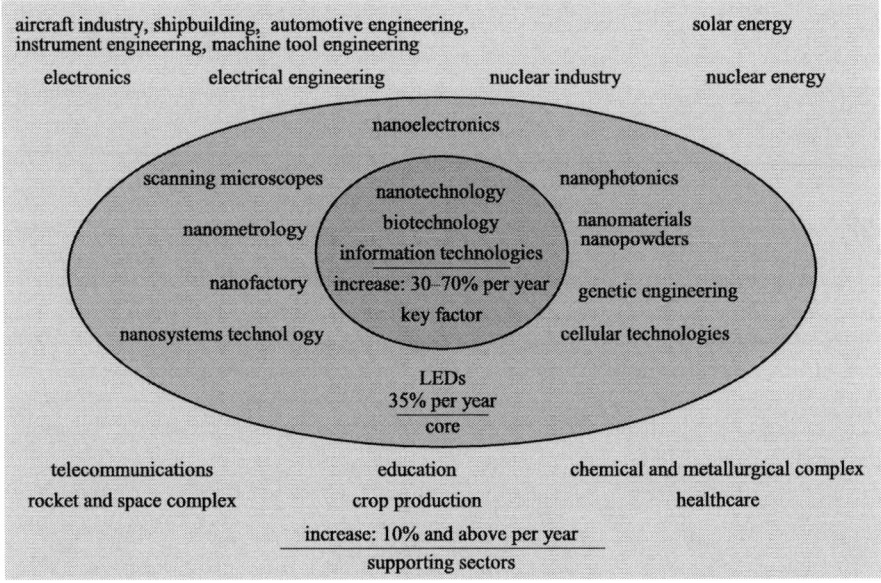

Figure 6   Structure of the New Technological Order

The further unfolding of the crisis will be determined by a combination of two processes: the destruction (modernization) of the structures of the former technological mode and the formation of the structures of the new mode. The cumulative work along the product lifecycle chain (from basic research to the market) requires a certain amount of time. The market is conquered by those who are able to pass this way faster and produce a product in a larger volume, at a lower cost, and of better quality. The sooner financial, economic, and political institutions adapt to the growth of new technologies, the sooner a new long wave of economic growth will rise. Not only the technological structure of the economy will change, but also its institutional system and the composition of leading firms, countries, and regions. Those who will be able to enter the growth trajectory of the new technological paradigm and invest in its components in the early stages of development will succeed. Conversely, entry for "outsiders" will become more expensive each year and will close with the maturity phase.[5]

Research shows that in periods of global technological change, it becomes increasingly difficult for the former leaders to maintain their favorable and familiar dominant position as the new wave of growth is taken ahead by other countries that have succeeded in preparing the prerequisites for its emergence. Unlike the champion countries, which are facing a crisis of capital over-accumulation in obsolete industries, the challenger countries have an opportunity to avoid massive capital depreciation and concentrate as much as possible on breakthrough growth-promising areas of the new technological paradigm.

In order to maintain their leadership, the "champions" have to intensify the power component of their foreign policy and economy. First of all, a sharp increase in spending on R&D and investment in shaping the growth trajectories of the new technological paradigm is needed. Given the high risk of exploratory developments, the government should take the bulk of its funding, helping private capital to master new technologies. Under the liberal-democratic political-economic system prevailing today in the advanced countries, they have no other way to do so except for defense and security purposes. It is no coincidence that military-political tensions and risks of major international conflicts rise sharply in times of changing technological paradigms. The tragic experience of two previous structural crises of the world economy can serve as an instructive example.

Thus, the Great Depression of the 1930s, caused by reaching the growth limits of the "coal and steel" technological mode that dominated in the early twentieth century, was overcome by the militarization of the economy, which resulted in its technological restructuring based on extensive use of internal combustion engine and organic chemistry, transition to oil as the main energy carrier and to the car as the leading means of transport. The transition of the economies of the world's leading countries to a new technological mode passed through the disaster of World War II, which entailed a cardinal change of the entire world order: the destruction of the system of European colonial empires and the formation of two opposing global political-economic systems. The leadership of American capitalism in the emergence of a new long wave of economic growth was ensured by the extraordinary growth of defense orders for the development of new technologies and the inflow of global capital into the US, with the destruction of productive capacity and the depreciation of the capital of its main competitors.

The depression of the mid-1970s and early 1980s, caused by the exhaustion of the potential of this technological stage, entailed an arms race with extensive use of information and communication technologies, which formed the core of the new fifth technological stage. The subsequent collapse of the world system of socialism, which failed to switch over the economy to a new technological mode in time, made it possible for the leading capitalist countries to use the resources of former socialist countries for "soft transplantation" into a long new wave of economic growth. The export of capital and the brain drain from the former socialist countries and the colonization of their economies facilitated the structural reorganization of the economies of the core countries of the world capitalist system. In the same wave of growth of the new technological mode, the newly industrialized countries rose up, managing in advance to create their key productions and laying the foundations for their rapid growth on a global scale. The political outcome of this structural transformation was liberal globalization with the dominance of the US as the issuer of the main reserve currency.

The exhaustion of the growth potential of the dominant technological mode has caused a global crisis and depression in the leading countries of the world in recent years.[6] The current phase of the birth of a new technological pattern appears on the surface of economic phenomena as a combination of financial turbulence accompanied by the formation and bursting of financial bubbles, economic depression characterized by declining profitability and volumes of customary industries, falling incomes, and prices, including those for basic energy and construction materials, and the rapid spread of fundamentally new technologies in the initial stages of their scientific and productive development.

Figure 7 shows a diagram of the technological stage life cycle. The upper part reflects fluctuations in the economic situation, known as the long Kondratiev waves, and the lower part shows the change in technological modes generating these fluctuations. The shaded area reflects the period of technological change, which is now coming to an end.

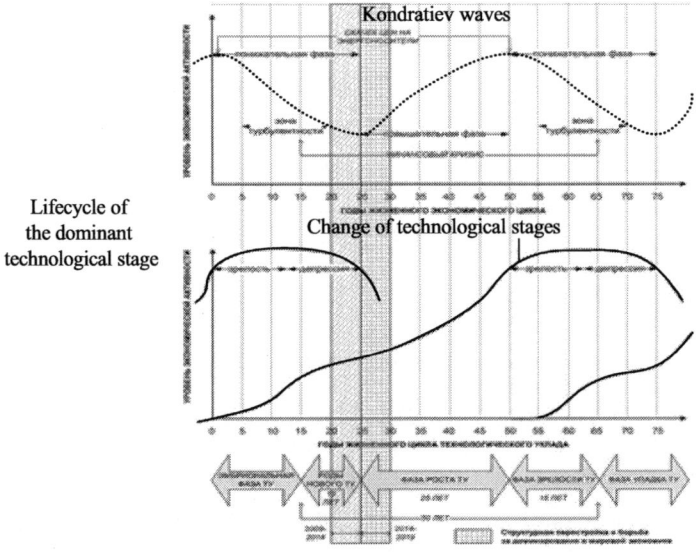

Figure 7   Lifecycle of the Technological Stage

Recovery from the current depression will be accompanied by large-scale geo-political and economic changes. As in previous cases, the "champion" countries demonstrate an inability to cooperate in major institutional innovations that could channel the released capital into the structural restructuring of the economy based on a new technological pattern, continuing to reproduce the existing institutional system and serving the economic interests embodied in it.

The US and its G7 allies have by now exhausted the possibilities of siphoning resources from the post-socialist countries, where their corporate structures have developed and privatized the remnants of their productive potential. The financial war that Washington is waging on insecure national financial systems, tying them to the dollar by imposing monetarist macroeconomic policies through its dependent IMF, rating agencies, leverage agents, etc., is also exhausted. The capital inflows thus artificially stimulated into the US economy are no longer sufficient to service the avalanche-increasing obligations of the federal government, the costs of which are approaching a third of the US GDP (Figure 8).

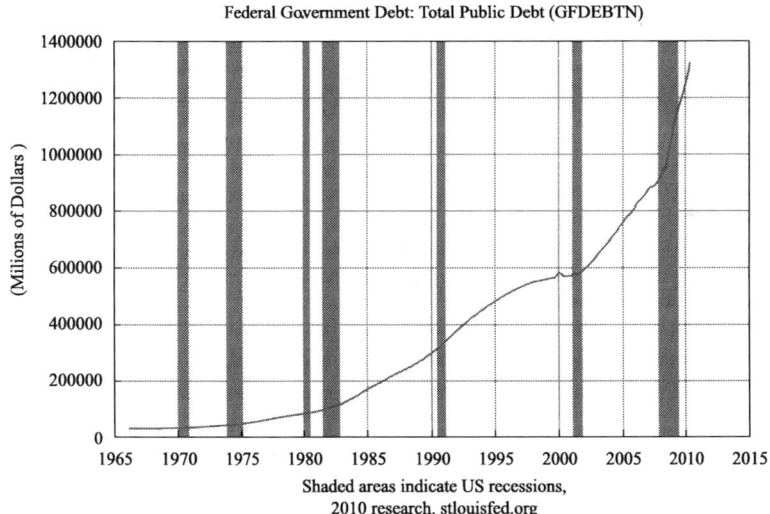

Figure 8   US Public Debt Dynamics

Source: US Department of the Treasury, Financial Management Service.

At the same time, the countries that have retained their economic sovereignty (China, India) have not opened their financial systems, showing strong growth in the crisis. The major economies of Latin America and Southeast Asia are following suit, resisting the takeover of their assets by speculative capital. China is rapidly developing its international payments system through bilateral currency swaps.

The room for maneuvering of the US Federal Reserve is inexorably shrinking: The US economy has to bear the brunt of the depreciation of capital concentrated in obsolete and redundant industries, financial pyramids, and the liabilities of distressed countries.

Based on the above, we can conclude that the crisis will unfold further according to the internal logic of the current global economic system. Three theoretical scenarios are theoretically possible.

(1) The optimistic scenario of a rapid emergence of a long new wave of economic growth. It would allow the leading countries to channel the recession into obsolete sectors and peripheral regions of the global economy, channeling these resources to boost innovation activity and accelerate the growth of a new technological pattern. This will drastically change the architecture of the global financial system, which will become multi-currency, as well as the composition and relative weight of the leading countries. State institutions of strategic planning and regulation of financial flows, including on a global scale, will be considerably strengthened. Globalization will become more manageable and balanced. A sustainable development strategy will replace the doctrine of liberal globalization. Terrorism, global warming, mass hunger, disease, and other threats to humanity will be among the goals that unite the world's leading nations.

(2) The catastrophic scenario, accompanied by the collapse of the US-centric financial system established after World War II, with the formation of relatively self-sufficient regional monetary and financial systems, destruction of most of the international capital, the sharp decline in living standards in "golden billion" countries, deepening recession and erection of protectionist barriers between the regions.

(3) An inertial scenario, accompanied by growing chaos and destruction of many institutions, both in the core and on the periphery of the global economy. If some institutions of the existing global financial system are preserved, new centers of economic growth will emerge in China, India, and other countries that have managed to be ahead of others in forming a new technological pattern and "ride" a new long wave of economic growth.

The inertial scenario, combining elements of optimistic and catastrophic scenarios, may prove catastrophic for some countries and regions and optimistic for others. It should be understood that the core institutions of the global financial system will try to survive by siphoning off resources from peripheral countries by gaining control over their assets. This will be achieved by exchanging the issuance of global reserve currencies for the property of host countries. If necessary, to maintain this exchange, forceful political techniques will be used, as has already happened with the assets of Iraq, Afghanistan, and Libya, transferred by the occupation authorities to the control of US corporations. Today, the same process can be observed in Ukraine, where the puppet government set up by the US secret services has announced mass privatization of remaining state property in favor of American capital.

So far, events are developing according to an inertial scenario, which is accompanied by a stratification of the leading countries of the world according to the depth of the crisis. The biggest damage is borne by the countries with open economies, where the fall in industrial production and investment reached 15-30% during the acute phase of the crisis. China and other countries with autonomous financial systems and large domestic markets, protected from attacks by financial speculators, continue to grow and increase their economic weight.

To reach the optimistic scenario, the formation of global regulatory institutions capable of curbing turbulence in global financial markets and mandated to adopt universal rules for financial institutions is needed as soon as possible, including managerial responsibility, transparency of stock options, elimination of internal conflicts of interest in institutions assessing risks, limitation of credit leverage, standardization of financial products, cross-border bankruptcies, etc.

In any of the scenarios, the economic upturn emerges on a new technological basis with new production capabilities and qualitatively new consumer preferences. The crisis will end with the outflow of the remaining capital from the collapse of the dollar financial pyramid and other "financial bubbles" into the production of a new technological paradigm.[7]

As noted above, the new (sixth) technological stage is based on a set of nano-, information and communication, additive, digital and bio-engineering technologies. Although the main sphere of application of these technologies lies in health care, education, and science, not directly related to the production of military equipment, the arms race and increased military expenditures are habitually becoming the leading means of state stimulation of the formation of the new technological paradigm.

The liberal ideology dominating the ruling circles of the US and its NATO (North Atlantic Treaty Organization) allies leaves no other reason for the state to expand its intervention in the economy except for the needs of defense. Therefore, faced with the need to use state demand to stimulate the growth of a new technological paradigm, the leading business circles have resorted to the escalation of politico-military tensions as the main way to increase state purchases of advanced technology. It is from this perspective that the reasons for Washington's spinning the flywheel of the war in Ukraine, which is not a goal but a tool for the global task of maintaining US dominant influence in the world, should be considered.

6.2 Regularities of the Change of World Economic Paradigms

The spread of a new technological pattern fundamentally changes the entire system for managing socio-economic processes. On the one hand, there are opportunities for total control over the behavior of citizens on a global scale. American special services are actively working in this direction, spying on millions of people all over the planet through wiretapping of phone calls, monitoring of social networks, and built-in computer equipment of the American production of pads.

On the other hand, the emergence of private cross-border systems to manage economic, social, and political processes affecting the national interests of states and their associations is becoming possible. The basis for such systems is provided by global social information networks, internet commerce, cryptocurrencies, and blockchain, taking international trade and financial flows beyond national jurisdictions. Citizens can dispense with state systems of control by relying on networked structures, using blockchain and smart contracts.

Government regulation is clearly lagging behind the challenges of new technological capabilities, not only in cybersecurity, e-commerce, and Internet regulation but also in the use of bioengineering technologies, unmanned vehicles, 3D printers, etc. Public consciousness is agitated by films about out-of-control robots, cyborgs, human-computer monsters, etc. Advertisers seduce with smart homes, talking irons, and fridges. Advanced architects suggest governments build smart cities.

As the current crisis of the world economic system unfolds, it is becoming increasingly clear that the development of productive forces requires new production relations and institutions to organize the global economy in a way that will ensure the sustainable development of humanity and repel planetary threats. However, within the framework of both the formational theory, in which the representatives of scientific communism believed, and the modern doctrine of market fundamentalism, which is professed by the apologists of the American-centric picture of the world, there is no answer to this challenge. The collapse of the USSR and the world system of socialism disproved the postulates of the political economy of socialism, and the deepening world financial crisis proves the inadequacy of the basic dogmas of "economics" about the automatic efficiency of market relations of the capitalist economy. The epochal changes taking place require theoretical understanding, which presupposes the formation of a new scientific paradigm. It can be based on the theory of great cycles in the development of the economy, the sequence of which forms an ascending trajectory of human evolution to increasingly complex structures of social structure with more and more efficient forms of organization of economic activity and perfect technologies.

The patterns of techno-economic development manifested in the long Kondratiev waves generated by technology life cycles have been outlined above.[8] Less studied are the century cycles of capital accumulation generated by the life cycles of world economic modes (WEM).[9]

The concept of the **world economy** is defined as a system of interrelated international and national institutions that ensure the expanded reproduction of the economy and determine the mechanism of global economic relations. The leading country's institutions have a dominant influence on international institutions that regulate the global market and international trade, economic, and financial relations. They also serve as a model for peripheral countries, which tend to imitate the leader and import proven institutions. The institutional system of the world economy permeates the reproduction of the entire world economy in the unity of its national, regional, and international components. It is not homogeneous and may even consist of ideologically antagonistic parts (as was the case in the era of confrontation between the USSR and the US), but at its core, it has common basic elements that determine the development of the economy (in this example—the use of FD[10] to finance the growth of large vertically integrated production systems).

Each world economic order has limits to its growth, determined by the accumulation of internal contradictions within the framework of the reproduction of its constituent institutions. The unfolding of these contradictions entails increasing tensions in the system of international economic and political relations, resolved so far by world wars. At such times, there is a sharp destabilization of the system of international relations, the destruction of the old world order, and the formation of a new one. The possibilities of socio-economic development on the basis of the established system of institutions and industrial relations are exhausted. The formerly leading countries face insurmountable difficulties in maintaining the previous rate of economic growth. As we shall see, this is also the time when the lifecycle of the technological stage comes to an end. The overcapitalization of aging production and technological complexes depresses the economies of the former leaders, and the established system of institutions makes the formation of new technological chains difficult. These, together with new institutions of production organization, are making their way to other countries, breaking through to the forefront of economic development.

The regularity of the periodic change of world economic patterns is manifested in the sequence of century-long SCCA discovered by Arrighi. Each of them was associated by Arrighi with the epoch of dominance of the corresponding country in the world economic system (Spain, Holland, Great Britain, US). Based on the type of underlying international trade and economic relations, we define the corresponding WEM as trade, trade-manufacturing, colonial, and imperial.

World economies differ not only by the type of organization of international trade but also by the system of industrial relations and institutions that allow the leading countries to achieve global superiority and form the regime of international trade and economic relations. The classification of world economic patterns is determined by the institutional systems of the leading countries that dominate international economic relations and form the core of the world economic system. At the same time, other, less efficient, and even archaic institutional systems of organization of national and regional economies can be reproduced at its periphery. The relations between the core and periphery of the world economic system are characterized by the non-equivalent foreign economic exchange in favor of the core, whose countries receive super profits at the expense of technological, economic, and organizational superiority in the form of, respectively, intellectual and monopoly rent, entrepreneurial and emission income. Therefore, the countries of the core form the center of the world economy, which dominates international economic relations and determines global socio-economic development.

The centuries-long cycles of capital accumulation discovered by J. Arrighi reflect the rhythm of capitalism that emerged about half a millennium ago at the periphery of traditional society. The entrepreneurial spirit, focused on the constant search for new opportunities for personal enrichment, undermined traditional society and the imperial institutions of state power that held it back. Beginning with the religious wars and the Inquisition in Europe and the Great Troubles in Moscow, all the world empires were destroyed in five hundred years of private capital accumulation and replaced by the institutions of civil society. But capitalism has not remained an unchanging society of homo economicus, preoccupied with profit maximization. The systems of institutions that determine the reproduction of capital and economic development were periodically changed revolutionary as a result of world wars, which radically changed the world economic-political system and the leading countries forming successive world economies.

The historical scheme of centuries-long cycles of capital accumulation and corresponding world economic patterns, conventionally named after the type of the then dominant system of international trade and economic relations, is shown in Figure 9. It shows the matrix of the industrial civilization wave developed by A. E. Aivazov, which he also called a periodic system of capitalism. It combines life cycles of World Economic Order (WEO) and Technical Principles (TP), their corresponding Arriga and Kondratiev cycles with the indication of dominant countries and world centers of capital reproduction.

Why does the process of change in the world economy occur once in a century and is accompanied by social revolutions and world wars that mediate the change of the institutions governing the reproduction of the economy? There is still no definite answer to this question. During the life cycle of WEO, four generations of people change according to the definition of the generation length adopted in demography. A change in WEO is always accompanied by a dramatic renewal of the ruling elite. Assuming that the elite position in society is largely inherited and accompanied by ideological continuity, in the fourth generation, the ruling elite perceives its dominant position in society as something self-evident and eternal, not subject to fundamental changes. By the end of the WEO life cycle, the dominant country's power is held by people born after its formation and raised in an environment of stability and prosperity. And they are naturally resistant to political changes that threaten their dominant position at home and in the world.

Unwilling to change anything, the ruling elite of the world's leading country, in a bid to maintain its hegemony, would commit any crime against humanity, up to and including wars aimed at destroying competitors. These wars were considered world wars because they were fought between the core countries of the mature WEO. But their domination could not last forever, due to the gradual exhaustion of opportunities for expanded reproduction of the economy on the basis of the institutions of the existing world economic order and the emergence of new leading countries through the formation of more effective institutions of economic organization, forming a new center of world economic relations. As a result of these world wars, the leadership in the new WEO was transferred to the third country, which was on the periphery of the previous WEO, that entered the world war at the final stage and won due to its more effective system of management, formed on the basis of the institutions of new WEO.

The most recent historical examples of this kind are World Wars I and II, which were instigated by the British intelligence services to mutually destroy Russia and Germany, regarded by the British ruling elite as major competitors for their geopolitical dominance. However, with the Socialist Revolution and the formation of the USSR, as well as the flight of capital and minds from Europe to the United States, two varieties of a new, more efficient system for managing economic development on a global scale emerged. Although World War I ended with the triumph of Britain, the main beneficiary was the US, which entered the war in its final phase to participate in the redivision of the world's spheres of influence.

World War II completed the transition from colonial to imperial WEO, accompanied by the disintegration of the British Empire, even though it was again among the victors. Similarly, the transition from imperial to integral WEO is now underway, with the center of the world economy shifting to China and Southeast Asia. Attempts by the US ruling elite to maintain global hegemony by provoking international conflicts between rivals can no longer stop this process.

In light of the aforementioned theory, the current crisis of the world economic system is explained by the current change in technological and world economic patterns. During such periods, the system of international relations is sharply destabilized, the old-world order is destroyed, and a new world order is formed. Opportunities for socio-economic development based on the established system of institutions and technologies are exhausted. Previously leading countries faced insurmountable difficulties in maintaining previous rates of economic growth. Overcapitalization of aging industrial and technological complexes is depressing their economies, and the established system of institutions is making it difficult to form new technological chains. These, together with new institutions of production organization, are forcing their way into other countries that are breaking through to the forefront of economic development. The arms race, typical of the change of technological patterns, with an increase in military and political tensions, turns into a world war, which is a logical phase of the change of world economic patterns.

In terms of historical analogies, the decade after the global financial crisis of 2008 is similar to the Great Depression preceding World War II. Although the issuers of the world's currencies were able to mitigate the structural crisis and avoid a steep decline in production thanks to a huge pump of money, the economies of the world's leading countries are in a state of prolonged stagnation. The accumulated loss of potential GDP over the decade is quite comparable to the damage of the output decline of the 1930s, which was overcome relatively quickly.

Figure 9   Industrial Civilisation Wave Matrix

Source: S. Glazyev, A. E. Aivazov, and V. A. Belikov, "Cyclical-Wave Theories of Economic Development and Prospects of the World Economy." *Scientific Proceedings of the Free Economic Society*.219, no. 5 (2019): 177–211.

Since 2014, the global crisis has turned into an open US financial aggression against Russia, accompanied by a de facto occupation of Ukraine under the guise of a neo-Nazi coup d'état. In essence, the US ruling elite is waging a global hybrid war in order to maintain its global hegemony by weakening and destroying countries that do not obey it. US intelligence agencies are instigating sectarian and ethnic conflicts in chaotic territories outside their control. The US trade aggression against the PRC that began in 2018, accompanied by escalating anti-Russian sanctions, has given this hybrid war a global dimension. The coronavirus pandemic that has been artificially promoted should be interpreted as a translation of this war into a phase of mobilization of the available financial, industrial, scientific, and technical resources of the countries involved.

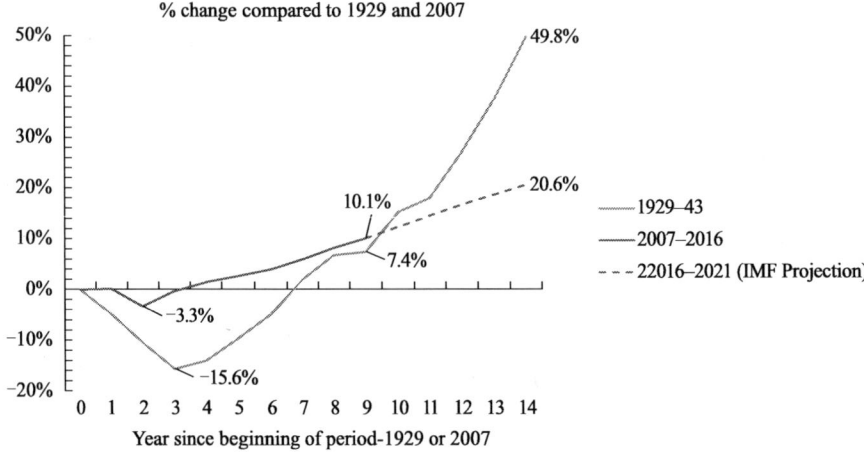

Figure 10   GDP of Developed Economies, % Increase over 1929 and 2007 Levels

Source: Based on Angus Madisson Historical Statistics of the World Economy AD 1–2008; IMF World Economic Outlook, October 2016.

Whereas in the 1930s, the exit from the Great Depression happened quickly and abruptly due to the enormous increase in state demand resulting from the militarization of the economy in the run-up to and during the world war, the hybrid war going on today is mainly conducted in the field of humanitarian technology and does not need to produce large quantities of weapons and military equipment. It is not accompanied by enormous losses of population and material wealth, thus avoiding the rising costs of reconstruction. Leading countries are trying to maintain economic activity through quantitative easing, pumping cheap credit into the economy, and increasing social spending by issuing budget deficits.

However, the threats to humanity posed by the profound structural changes in the global economy should not be underestimated. The synthesis and release of a coronavirus, with hundreds of thousands of casualties already attributed to the pandemic, is an ominous harbinger of a possible humanitarian catastrophe through the latent use of biological, cognitive, and cyber weapons.

In the last century, Britain's ruling elite tried to preserve its global hegemony by provoking wars between its main rivals: Japan against Russia, Germany and Austria-Hungary against Russia and the USSR, and Japan against the US. To contain the latter, the British Empire imposed an embargo on American imports in the 1930s. Today, the US leadership is trying to do the same with respect to Chinese goods. Similarly, US intelligence agencies are provoking conflicts between their main competitors by pushing Vietnam and Japan into conflict with China and cultivating Russophobe regimes in the former Soviet Union with the aim of dismembering and destroying Russia.

This historical analogy is quite instructive, as it reflects the objective patterns of structural changes in the world economy, affecting the reflexes of the ruling elite of the Anglo-Saxon world. The previous period of the change of world economies began with World War I, which resulted in the collapse of all mainland Eurasian empires (Russian, German, Austro-Hungarian, Ottoman, and, finally, Chinese) and strengthened the US, Japan, and Great Britain, which reached the peak of the power of their global maritime empire. Then, in the wake of the global triumph of British imperialism, British geopoliticians, too, had a sense of the end of history, reflected in the far-fetched concept of the dominance of the peoples of the sea (Thalassocracy) over the peoples of the land (Tellurocracy),[11]

The current period of change in the world economy begins with perestroika in the USSR, culminating in its collapse and the collapse of the world system of socialism. China, India, and, most of all, the US, which has reached the peak of its global financial and corporate empire, have strengthened.

From this observation, we can conclude that in the first phase of transition, the country dominating during the life cycle of the existing world economic order reaches the peak of its power, fully realizing the socio-economic development potential inherent in it. The global hegemony of this country creates the illusion of "the end of history." But in reality, it is only the life cycle of the existing world economic order that is entering its final phase. At the same time, on the periphery of the world economic system, a fundamentally new, qualitatively more efficient system of institutions for managing reproduction and economic development is emerging.

In the next phase of transition a transition to a new world economic order takes place. Thus, as a result of World War II, the British colonial empire collapsed, and a new bipolar imperial world economic order was formed, with its centers in the USSR and the US. In the present situation, the destruction of its remaining American-centric part, which imposed liberal globalization on the world in the interests of the US power and financial elite, will be accompanied by the formation of a new WEO, which will develop in competition with socialist China and democratic India.

Despite victories in two world wars, the British Empire disintegrated, reaching the peak of its power by the middle of the last century. This was due to the hopeless backwardness of the system of colonial governance it had created, which proved far less efficient in its ability to ensure economic development than the institutions of the new world economic order that had emerged in the USSR and the US. The latter find themselves in a similar position today. Having reached the peak of its power after the collapse of the USSR, the US is hopelessly losing the economic competition to China, which has created a more effective system of economic development management. The imperial world economic order is giving way to an integral one with a substantially more complex mixed system of economic development management.

The structure of the new world economic order and the system of its constituent institutions is now becoming clearer. It corresponds to the interests of sustainable and harmonious development of mankind, providing for the primacy of public interests over private ones. It manifests itself in state control over the main parameters of capital reproduction, a combination of planning and market mechanisms, and systematic stimulation of innovative activity. Public-private partnership is subordinated to the public interests of economic development and improvement of people's welfare and quality of life. Accordingly, the ideology of international cooperation is also changing: the paradigm of liberal globalization in the interests of the private capital of the world's leading countries is being replaced by the paradigm of sustainable development in the interests of all humanity. The new integral world economic order differs from the previous one in the restoration of national sovereignty in the regulation of the economy on the one hand, and in the strict observance of international law, on the other.

Unlike the US institutional system, focused on serving the interests of the financial oligarchy, parasitizing on the dollar issue as the world currency, the institutional systems of China, India, Japan, South Korea, Vietnam, Malaysia, and other countries of the new world economic development center, which is forming before our eyes, are focused on ensuring the public interests of socio-economic development. They are aimed at harmonizing the interests of various social groups and building partnerships between businesses and governments to achieve socially significant goals.

The most important achievement of the closing imperial WEO was the invention of FD, which opened up the possibility of unlimited lending for economic development. The significance of this invention for the economic system can be compared to the hypothetical discovery of the philosopher's stone in alchemy. If properly applied, FD can be used to finance sustainable economic growth for the progressive improvement of social welfare. If privatized, FD becomes an instrument of enrichment and a source of power for a financial oligarchy.

The monetary authorities of the world's leading countries create money against government and business debt in order to finance the expanded reproduction of the economy. In conditions of structural crisis, they resort to an extensive monetary issue to stimulate investments in the development of a new technological mode. Its main channel is the purchase of low-yield government debt by central banks to finance budget deficits. As part of their quantitative easing policy, the US Federal Reserve and the European Central Bank (ECB) are also issuing money to purchase the liabilities of large banks and corporations. China and other successful new WEO countries are issuing money against the investment plans of economic agents according to centrally set priorities.

Unlike countries issuing world currencies, which print a large part of their money for export and advocate free cross-border capital movements, the emerging countries of the new WEO have strict capital export restrictions that protect them from the spasms of the global financial system. They operate on the principle of a nipple—they let in foreign investment without restrictions and let it out according to certain rules, blocking speculative attacks against the national currency and financial market. The financial storm that originated in the US is "immune" to such countries. Amid a stock market crash by a factor and a half in the US and by a factor and a half in Russia, the Chinese market sat at 10% during this global financial market slump.

Whereas in the US, the economy continues to stagnate despite a five-fold increase in dollars over the last decade, the PRC combines the highest levels of monetization of the economy, savings rates, and output growth. Focused on maximizing current profits, the US financial oligarchy is clearly inferior in terms of managing economic development to the Chinese communists, who use market mechanisms to boost people's welfare through increased production and investment. And also the Indian nationalists who have created their own version of an integrated economic development management system with a democratic political system.

As noted above, the lifecycle of the world economy can be represented in the form of the Arrighi open SCCA[12] discovered by Arrighi, which stretches over a century and takes the form of a century-long wave. In its rising phase, which J. Arrighi called "the phase of material expansion," the economy develops primarily in the productive sphere, in the real sector of the economy. During the British JLCC, the British economy reached its greatest heyday in the 1850s–1970s (the "Victorian Era" in the British Empire), when British industry produced half of the world's industrial output. During the American SCNC, the "golden age of capitalism" came in the 1950s and 1960s (the "Welfare Society"), when American corporations were already producing half the world's industrial output.

The material expansion phase of the world economic order coincides with the growth phase of the technological order. The new global leader is surging ahead in the upward phase of the long Kondratiev wave, using progressive institutions and methods of economic development management to accelerate the mastery of the basic innovations of the new technological pattern. This expansion of capital in the sphere of real production ensures rapid growth of the economy until the possibilities of expansion of the corresponding technological mode are exhausted, after which it is dragged into depression. The capital that did not find a profitable application in real production goes into the "financial cloud," concentrating on financial bubbles of speculative operations. The second phase of the SCCA, which J. Arrighi called the era of "financial expansion," begins. Domination of the real economy provides the basis for domination of the global financial market. In this phase, the leading country makes super profits on non-equivalent foreign economic exchange, lending capital to the periphery of its economic system and profiting from its exploitation. However, it creates opportunities for peripheral countries to import advanced technologies and to rise on the wave of growth of the next technological stage. Thus, the foundations for the emergence of new global leaders are being laid. They challenge the existing ones during the next structural crisis, when the old leaders are faced with massive depreciation of capital in obsolete industries and their management system proves incapable of organizing capital overflow into the creation of new technological stage industries. Capital in the financial cloud of the leading country is in no hurry to come down to earth, preferring the risks of technological innovation to the super-profits of financial market manipulation. At this time, the peripheral countries using progressive institutions and more efficient methods of governance challenge the leaders, creating the core of a new WEO. This becomes possible during another change of technological modes, when the economy of the leading country sinks into a deep depression, and the successfully developing peripheral countries, free from the excess burden of obsolete industries, concentrate available and imported resources in the key productions of the new Technical Orders (TO). They outpace the former leader in their absorption and, in a long new Kondratieff wave, surge ahead, creating the core of the new WEO.

The world experienced a period similar to the current expansion of the global financial market at the turn of the nineteenth and twentieth centuries. This phenomenon was explored by R. Hilferding in his Financial Capital.[13] Later, based on Hilferding's research, Lenin made his famous summary of "the end of history" in his work "Imperialism as the highest stage of capitalism."[14] However, as A. Aivazov and V. Belikov point out[15] that Lenin was wrong in his main conclusion, since it turned out that this was not the highest stage of capitalism as a socio-economic formation, but the last stage in the development of the British SCCA. The US economy was already breathing down its neck, gaining momentum on the basis of the deployment of the institutions and production relations of the new ICC, taking the lead in the change of technological modes during the Great Depression and World War II.

At the turn of the twentieth and twenty-first centuries, the world economy is again going through a phase of financial expansion, only within the framework of the American CCNK. The financial expansion since the second half of the 1980s has been astonishing in its unprecedented scale. The market capitalization of global stock markets peaked in December 2019 at $94.4 trillion (Figure 11). The bursting of financial bubbles has been accompanied by a fall in the relative capitalization of industrial companies, which can be clearly seen in the declining share of industrial corporate capitalization in the benchmark US stock market index. On the global market scale, this process can be observed in terms of the share of industry in the capitalization of the global market (Figures 12, 13).

At the same time, the countries of Southeast Asia, which achieved an economic miracle during and after the structural crisis of the 1970s and 1980s by relying on imports of advanced technologies from the US, are now forming the core of a new Global Economic Structure (GES). Using its advantages, they organize advanced economic growth based on investment in the expansion of new technological modes of production.

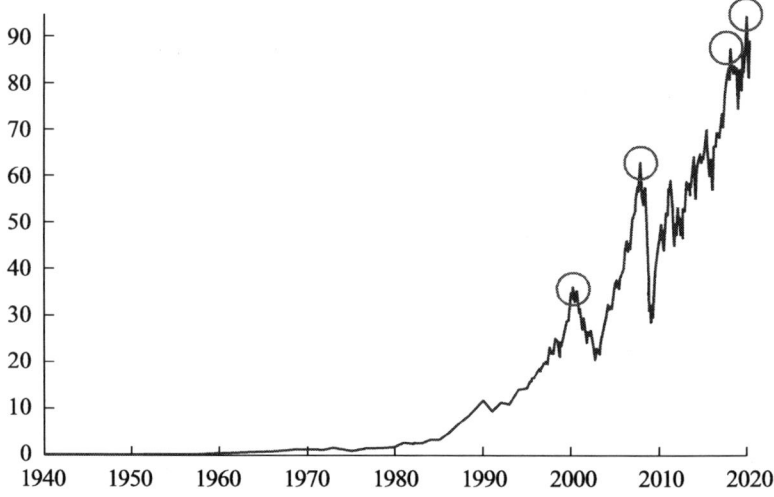

Figure 11   Global Stock Market Capitalization

Source: BofA Global Investment Strategy, Global Financial Data.

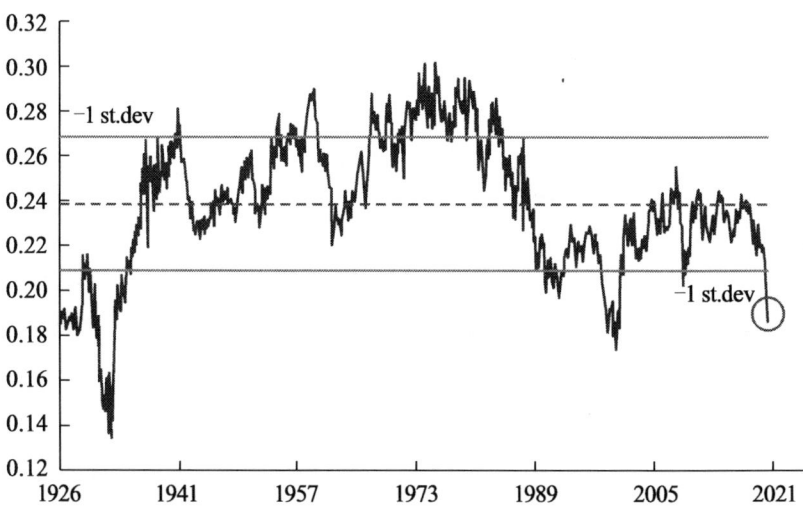

Figure 12   Share of Industrial Corporations in the Index of Largest US Companies (S&P500), in Relative Prices

Source: BofA Global Investment Strategy, Global Financial Data; Bloomberg.

Figure 13   Industry Share, as % of Global Market Capitalization

Source: BofA Global Investment Strategy, Global Financial Data; MSCI, Data Stream.

As A. Aivazov and V. Belikov point out, in the phase of "financial expansion," the mainstream is set by libertarian ideology, and in the phase of "material expansion" by dirigist ideology. They explain this by saying that financial capital needs complete freedom to move, while it is important for productive capital to enjoy the protection and support of the state. Libertarian ideology, by demanding freedom from state regulation, stimulates the rapid growth of stock indices, the erection of financial pyramids, and the inflation of "financial bubbles," through which financial capital reaps maximum profit. When a critical mass of these "bubbles" is reached, a crisis of financial capital over-accumulation takes place, leading to the collapse of financial markets as it happened in 1929.

The theory of change of technological modes reflects the regularities of reproduction of industrial society, the formation of which began with the Industrial Revolution in the late 18th century.[16] Nor is it certain that this pattern will continue in a post-industrial society—it is possible that the sixth technological mode currently emerging will prove to be a transition from the industrial to the information and digital society, in which scientific and technological progress may take a smoother course, and the inertia of large technological systems will be overcome by flexible production automation systems, additive technologies, and full lifecycle planning.

6.3 Systemic Changes in the Rhythm of Global Economic Development

Likewise, centuries of capital accumulation cycles may become a thing of the past along with capitalism, and the hypothesis of a changing world economy may become irrelevant. Any system has a finite life span, and capitalism is no exception. In his time, analyzing the production relations of the Colonial World Economy and the British SCCA, K. Marx concluded that the end of capitalism was inevitable. And the end did come, but not to capitalism, but to the British SCCA, which was replaced by the American SCCA. Now, we hear again that capitalism is coming to an end. This message is being heralded by such an elite organization as the Club of Rome, according to a recent report.[17] The report is the first of its kind to contain many sound judgments about the inability of the capitalist system to cope with the increasing economic, social, and technological threats to the existence of humanity. The report refers to the degeneration of capitalism, in which financial speculation has become the main source of profit. The Club of Rome report argues that 98% of financial transactions are now speculative in nature, between $21 trillion and $32 trillion are hidden offshore, and there is an oversupply of capital in fictitious but profitable areas, while the areas on which the future of the planet depends are cash-strapped. The report believes that global rules binding on all countries are inevitable: individual states are not free to do as they please, especially when it comes to the consequences affecting the whole planet. At the same time, the Club calls on governments to forget about borders and join forces for shared prosperity.

In fact, the good wishes contained in the report are being realized in the successful practice of forming an integral MHI in the PRC and other Southeast Asian countries. It can accurately be argued that the end has come, not of capitalism, but of the American SCCA.

On the basis of the long-term downward trend in the rate of return discovered by K. Marx, the currently observed decline in interest rates to zero or lower can be regarded as a "marker" of the end of capitalism. Today, global interest rates are at their lowest historical level, and judging by the yield curve, central banks will keep them there for the foreseeable future[18] (Figure 14).

With all the doubts about the validity of the data before the 17th century, even more so a millennium ago, the long-term downward trend in interest rates and yields of financial instruments is beyond doubt. By now, this trend seems to have reached its limit. In the past decade, the real yield of US treasury bonds, reflecting the minimum price of money on the world market, averaged 1.3%.

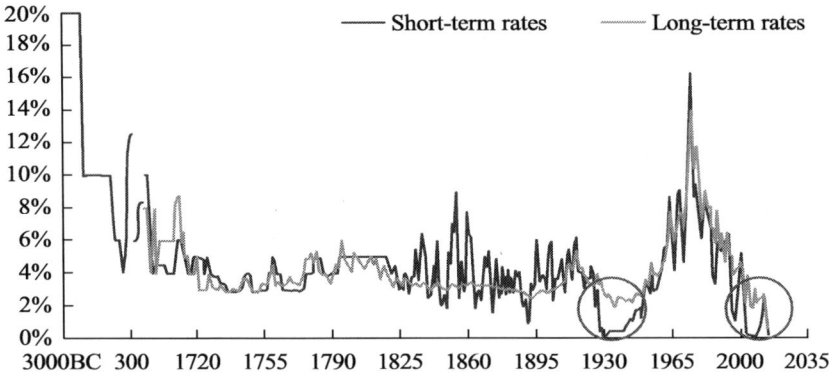

Figure 14   Interest Rates since 3000 BC

Source: Bank of England, Global Financial Data; Sidney Homer and Richard Sylla, *A History of Interest Rates* (New York: John Wiley & Sons, 2011).

Sovereign bond yields are tending toward zero in all major capitalist countries, which limits the demand on the part of market players. National central banks have become the main buyers of government bonds, which means a shift to purely inflationary financing of budget deficits. The authors of the study conclude from this that the resource of stimulating economic growth (or at least the financial segments of national economies) by artificial pumping of money is close to being exhausted everywhere (Figures 15–19).

Figure 15   US 10-Year Treasury Bond Yields since 1790

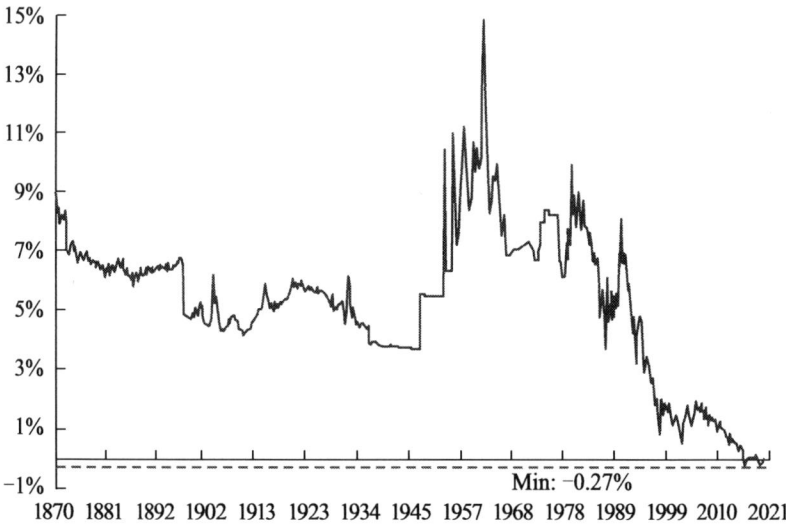

Figure 16   Japanese 10-Year Government Bond Yields

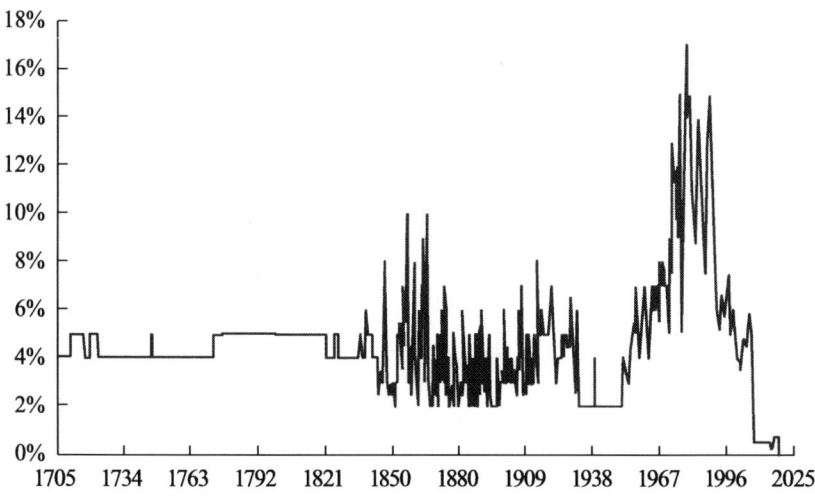

Figure 17   Bank of England Base Lending Rate

They also point to a fundamental shift in socio-political priorities: "The trend induced by populist electoral politics and the greater presence of the state in the economy is probably the best indicator of an impending change in the governance model."

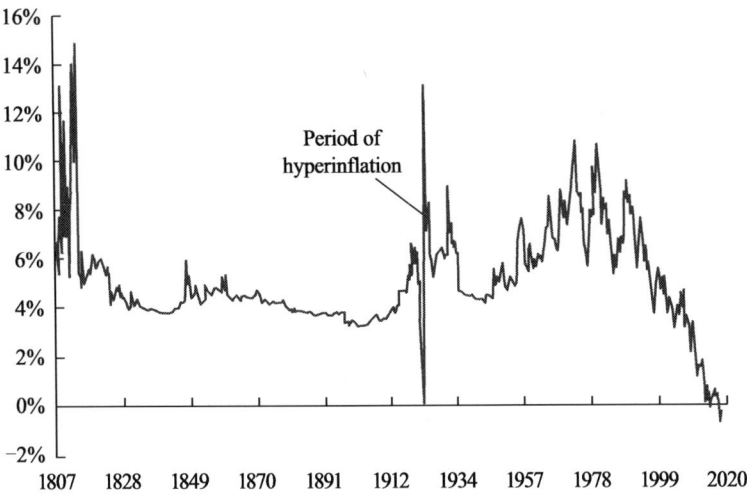

Figure 18   German 10-Year Bond Yields

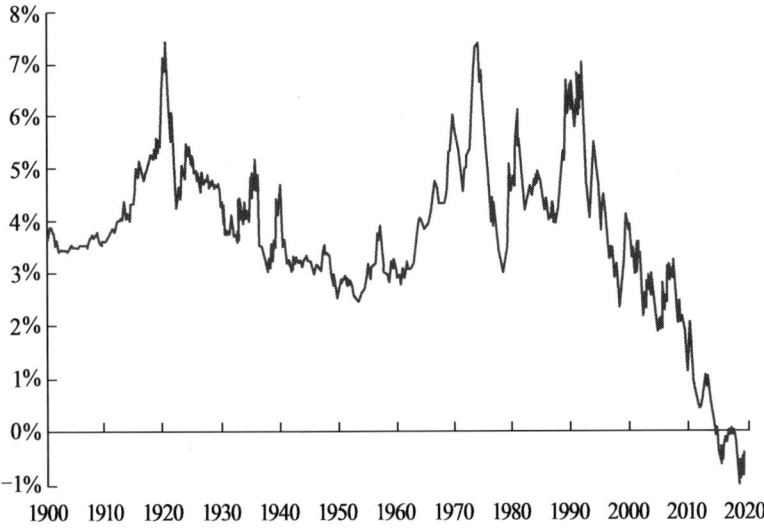

Figure 19   Swiss 10-Year Government Bond Yields

Source: BofA Global Investment Strategy, Global Financial Data, and Bloomberg.

The predictions of the authors of the study thus confirm our conclusions about a shift in world economic patterns. But the change may be even more far-reaching: Moving the interest rate into negative territory makes it impossible for capital to grow itself, which really does mean the end of capitalism.

K. Marx justified the downward tendency of the rate of return, which he discovered by the growth of the organic structure of capital with technological progress.[19] In fact, Marx observed this trend against the background of the downward phase of the Kondratieff wave, reflecting the end of the life cycle of the second technological order. Following the technological revolution brought about by the electrification of the economy, new opportunities for economic growth opened up. The profitability of investments in the expansion of the third technological mode of production rose again to an acceptable level. And so each time, as the technological stage becomes obsolete, the average rate of return falls and then, with the change of technological stages, rises again.

However, the current decline in returns on all financial market instruments to negative values is unprecedented. One way or another, the long-term retention of interest rates and returns on invested capital in the negative zone finally turns money into a technical instrument for financing economic activity, depriving it of its function of capital accumulation.[20] (Fig. 20–22)

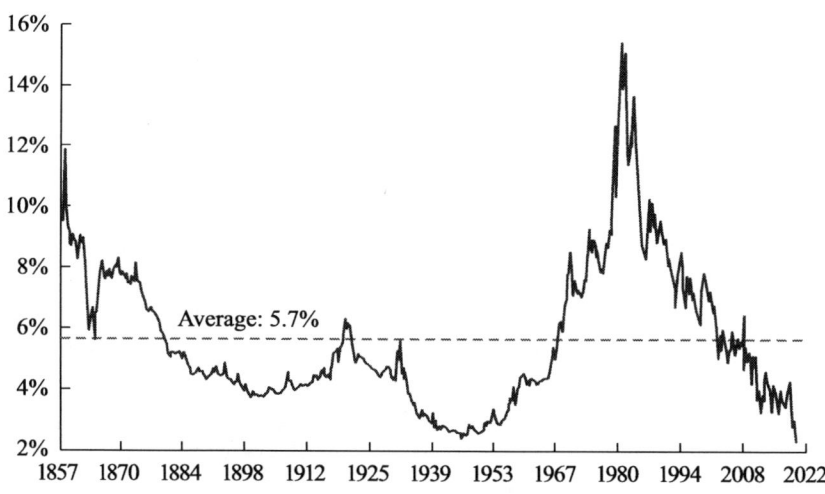

Figure 20   AAA Corporate Bond Yield

Source: BofA Global Investment Strategy, Global Financial Data.

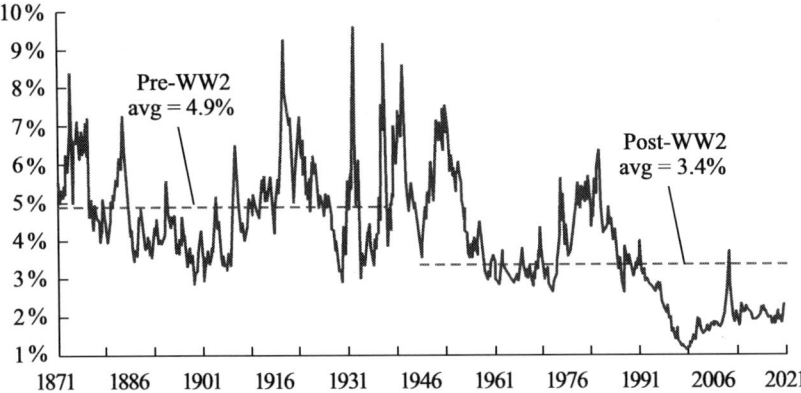

Figure 21   Dividend Yield

Source: BofA US Equity & Quant Strategy, Global Financial Data, Bloomberg.

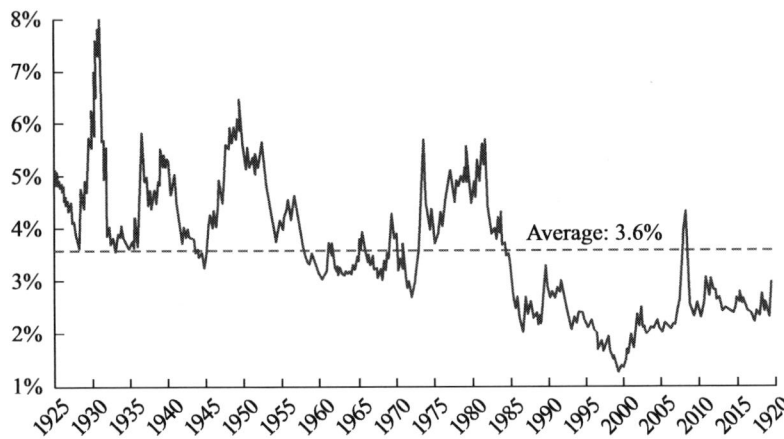

Figure 22   Global Equity Dividend Yield

Source: BofA US Equity & Quant Strategy, Global Financial Data, Datastream.

The hypothesis of a pattern of change in the world economy, on which this paper is based, seems similar to the Marxist formational theory. However, the latter is refuted by the collapse of the world system of socialism a quarter of a century ago and is not supported by historical data. For example, the trafficking of people was at its peak not in the phantom Ancient Rome, but in the epoch of capital accumulation described by Marx in the 19th century. The primitive communal formation also differs greatly from the communist idyll described by the classical Marxists, not to mention the naïve notions of a rapid transition to a communist society with a leap from the realm of necessity into the realm of freedom because of socialist construction. The characterization of feudalism in the formational theory reflects only a fragment of the age of decay of traditional society in Western Europe with a communal way of life, religious consciousness, and an imperial socio-state structure. Marx's treatment of this order as an Asian mode of production is nothing more than a manifestation of a European superiority complex, since the same exact order had defined the life of the population of Europe two centuries before "Capital."

In connection with the increasingly frequent assumptions about the end of capitalism, it is pertinent to mention studies of civilization cycles, which are still poorly understood. The theoretical concepts of Gumilev L. and Yakovets Y.[21] reflect important aspects of these processes in terms of cultural and ethnic attributes. Y. Yakovets argues for the end of the Western half-century era of domination and transition to a new civilizational cycle with the leadership of the East. A. Toffler[22] and D. Bell[23] write about the stages of agrarian, industrial, and post-industrial human development. Many researchers see the current world crisis as the end of human civilization altogether and a transition to a post-humanoid state of the world with new types of cloned and transgenic humans, cyborgs, and artificial intelligence.

With these reservations in mind, the analysis of current events will be guided by the above hypothesis of the change in world economic patterns. According to this hypothesis, the currently unfolding global crisis is explained by the desire of the US power and financial elite to maintain its dominance in the global market by strengthening control over its geo-economic periphery, including the methods of military and political coercion. This entails major military conflicts in which the aging leader squanders resources without achieving the desired effect. The potential new leader, who is by this time on the rise, tries to take a wait-and-see attitude in order to preserve his productive forces and attract the fleeing minds, capital, and treasures of the warring countries. By building up their capabilities, the new leader enters the world arena when the warring adversaries have weakened enough to appropriate the fruits of victory for themselves. This is what we are witnessing as a result of the global hybrid war unleashed by the US ruling elite, the winner of which, according to this theory, will be China, while the beneficiaries will be the countries of Southeast Asia and other successfully emerging institutions of the new world economic order.

By combining the institutions of central planning and market competition, the new world economic order demonstrates a qualitative leap in the efficiency of management of socio-economic development compared to its predecessor systems of the world order: the Soviet one with directive planning and total statehood and the American one dominated by the financial oligarchy and transnational corporations. This is evidenced not only by China's record economic growth rate over the past three decades but also by its rise to the forefront of scientific and technological progress. There are also leaps in the development of other countries that use the institutions of an integrated world economy: Japan before the artificial suspension of its rise by the Americans through a sharp revaluation of the yen; South Korea before the American financial oligarchy provoked the Asian economic crisis in 1998; modern Vietnam, which in many ways is adopting China's experience; India, implementing a democratic model of the new world economic order; Ethiopia, showing record growth rates with the active participation of Chinese investors.

A fundamental feature of the new world economic order is the orientation of the system of economic regulation toward the improvement of public welfare. The primacy of public interests over private ones is expressed in the institutional structure of economic regulation characteristic of the new world economic order. First of all, state control over the main parameters of the reproduction of capital through mechanisms of planning, crediting, subsidizing, pricing, and regulation of the basic conditions of entrepreneurial activity. The state does not so much order, but rather acts as a moderator, forming mechanisms of social partnership and interaction between the main social groups. Officials do not try to direct entrepreneurs, but organize joint work of the business, scientific, and engineering communities to form common development goals and work out methods for achieving them. In their turn, entrepreneurs fit the profit maximization and enrichment motive into ethical norms that protect the interests of society. The use of business institutions focused not on profit maximization, but on socially important results: non-profit organizations, development institutions, and specialized banks targeting investment projects are increasing. Ethical norms are taken into account in the management of money flows, and restrictions are introduced against financing criminal, speculative, and immoral activities. The mechanisms of state regulation of the economy are also adjusted to this.

The state provides long-term and cheap credit, while businessmen guarantee its targeted use in specific investment projects for the development of production. The state provides access to the infrastructure and services of natural monopolies at low prices, while businesses are responsible for producing competitive products. In order to improve its quality, the state organizes and finances the necessary R&D, education, and training while the entrepreneurs implement innovations and invest in new technologies. Public-private partnerships are subordinated to the public interest in developing the economy, increasing people's welfare, and improving the quality of life.

Throughout the world, including in capitalist countries, the fundamentals of the welfare state, which were formed during the transition to an imperial world order, are changing significantly. As Fishman points out,[24] "... in the prototypes of the modern welfare state, those who were most useful to it were primarily cared for, as evidenced not only by the very modest scope of services but also by the fact that social insurance originally existed for the privileged—officials and the military ..." At the same time, care for other categories of the needy was reduced almost exclusively to charity social policies like "laws on the poor," and that did not concern all the poor, but only the honest and industrious. The author goes on to quote Western experts: "Over time, the original narrowly focused concern for the 'poor,' the 'worthy,' and the 'useful' has been transformed into a social policy designed to ensure a decent life for all members of society without exception. Policies implemented in the light of this concept were designed to form a community in which class differences were legitimate in terms of social justice. The point of all this is that inequalities based on inherited (class) advantages are reduced, but instead, a new—and already legitimate—type of inequality emerges."[25] Democratization, on the other hand, has helped to ensure that many previously clearly discriminated against social groups are allowed to make decisions about how to assess their own usefulness. The assistance, which had previously only applied to "real citizens" who were useful to the state, then also began to be extended to those for whom it was not originally intended.

Nevertheless, as the author of another contribution shows, "the utilitarianism described did not and could not disappear under the conditions of the capitalist economy. Its presence can also be found in today's justifications for social policy. For example, universal access to education, health care, care for pensioners, the unemployed, mothers, children and so on are justified economically—as a concern for labor reproduction and as a policy to prevent social conflicts."[26] Another expert echoes this: "If families are relieved of the burden of caring for young, old, and sick relatives, there is increased labor market activity, labor mobility, and economic productivity."[27]

The popular thesis that the main wealth of a country is, first of all, people has objective grounds: the main factor of economic growth is NTT, which is driven by the intellectual potential of a nation and investments in the reproduction of human capital in developed countries have long ago exceeded investments in machinery and equipment, buildings and constructions in volume. Therefore, the growth of social policy expenditure is justified by the need to "invest" in human capital to maintain the competitiveness of the national economy. This is what the European social model, in particular the Swedish experience of economic growth, is set up for, which is quite in harmony with social progress. For example, if there is investment in affordable, quality childcare, economic growth rates begin to improve, including by bringing more women into the labor market. However, such a social policy philosophy, as Fishman concludes, works only when its beneficiaries constantly prove their usefulness intellectually, business-wise, morally, and ethically in relation to the public good and the level of social protection they have received. The question arises: what if this connection weakens and the usefulness of released household citizens for the socio-economic system is called into question?

Indeed, we are witnessing a reassessment of the "necessity" and "usefulness" of labor due to the current shift in technological patterns. The technological revolution is entailing a massive displacement of people by robots and artificial intelligence from routine activities, and there is a dramatic devaluation of human capital in a large number of traditional professions. "By and large, the only factor inhibiting the winding down of social states is human existence itself, which justifies receiving social guarantees," states Fishman.

As Sinyavskaya notes, "models of social justice and social institutions adequate to conditions of seventy years ago do not correspond to new risks and needs of modern societies."[28] It is clear that social clustering, the gender revolution in the public sphere, the reassessment of marriage, and the pandemic and the resulting economic crisis have exacerbated the problem of limited "good" jobs and stable employment. The response to these transformations, together with the tectonic shifts generated by the shift in technological modes, has been the translation into practice of Nobel laureate Amartya Sen's idea that social policy should ultimately contribute to empowering people in advanced economies.[29]

A modern welfare state is not just about redistributing resources to the poor but is primarily concerned with reducing the risks of job and income loss.[30] This model has been called the "social investment welfare state." It assumes that public programs that create employment opportunities and increase productivity increase the economic sustainability of the state. Expenditures on universal health care, education, vocational training, and skills development are seen as social investments that save and increase human capital. As O. Sinyavskaya concludes, the seemingly burdensome social state is being transformed into a resource for economic development.

Another significant difference between the integral world order and the imperial world order, which is recreating national sovereignty as the basis of both international law and the social organization of the modern state, is the reincarnation of national sovereignty. "... Democracy alone cannot preserve the state indefinitely if society is divided and the authorities do not pursue the goals which the population considers vital. This requires a deeper source of legitimacy rooted in a shared sense of national identity. In today's world, the greatest and most enduring source of these feelings and of state legitimacy is nationalism," argues A. Lieven.[31]

Speaking of the origins of progressive nationalism during the formation of the imperial world order, he states that the imperialists generally believed in the need for a new managed "national economy," higher progressive taxation to pay for social reform and military preparations. They also believed in the restriction of free trade to protect industry and imperial economic unity ("imperial preferences").[32]

However, as the imperial world order emerged, global systems of economic reproduction were formed, and national institutions were subjugated. The collapse of the world system of socialism exacerbated this trend. As A. Cooley and D. Nexon noted, "Developing countries could no longer pressure Washington by threatening to resort to Moscow or pointing to the risk of a communist coup to protect themselves from the need for domestic reforms. The scope of Western power and influence was so limitless that many politicians believed in the eternal triumph of liberalism."[33] Professor R. Müllerson of Tallinn University has aptly remarked on this: "Economic liberalism with global uncontrolled financial markets and social liberalism that puts the individual and his interests and desires above those of society are destroying the bonds that held society together. As a result, they are also undermining nation states, the cradle of democracy."[34]

Fascinated by the triumph of liberalism, many authors in the early 1990s were quick to diagnose the collapse of nation-states—the main subjects of international law and sources of relative social justice. The image of Pax Americana began to take shape in global public opinion: "Washington is trying to impose through military force and sanctions against the disobedient, not the noble normative system that somehow worked even during the Cold War (largely due to the existing balance of power), but the so-called 'rules-based' liberal world order, that is an order based on Washington rules and unrelated to international law," believes R. Müllerson.

China and other countries of the emerging new world order are fundamentally dissatisfied with these unwritten rules of the self-proclaimed suzerain. They are consistently and, as the trend of liberal globalization wears off, increasingly asserting their national interests. The new world order resuscitates a system of international law based on the mutual recognition of the national sovereignty of cooperating states. And not the rules of Washington or any other national capital purporting to be the world capital, but treaty-based norms of mutually beneficial, voluntary, and mutually respectful cooperation in the interest of the growth of social welfare will shape the new world order.

6.4 PRC as the Nucleus of a New World Economy

For future forecasting, China is of particular interest, which is not only a leader in shaping the new world economic order but also makes creative use of the experience of both Soviet socialism and Western capitalism. The Chinese communists managed to draw the right conclusions from the collapse of the rigidly centralized system of management of the socialist economy, transferring it to market mechanisms and subordinating their work to the achievement of politically established goals of socio-economic development. At the same time, centralized management remained in the financial, infrastructure, and basic industries, which created the general conditions for the growth of the entrepreneurial sector. Private business is supported by the state through loans, R&D subsidies, access to infrastructure, stable prices for energy and commodities, transport and communication services. This gives dynamism to the economy, and managerial resources are freed from routine planning procedures to focus on strategic management and harmonization of the diverse interests of the social groups that ensure economic reproduction. Unlike the Soviet system, the Chinese economic management system has learned to restructure the economy technologically and institutionally, shut down obsolete productions in time, cut off inefficient enterprises from resources, and help the front-runners to master cutting-edge technologies.

China's rapid economic growth, which continued after the onset of the global financial crisis against the backdrop of a stagnating global economy, is attributed to an effective system of economic management. It combines strategic and indicative plans with targeted lending for investment projects on the one hand, and market competition in an open economic environment with selective government regulation on the other.

China has managed to form a model of a new world economic order that is qualitatively superior to the previous one in terms of efficiency. Its basic institutions and mechanisms of economic reproduction are considerably diverse, combining public and private ownership, centralized planning and market self-organization, control over observance of the public interest and private initiative.

Figure 23 compares the PRC's economic growth with that of the US and Russia. It shows a qualitatively higher efficiency of the Chinese system of economic development management, which ensured an order of magnitude higher growth of investment through a faster increase in the volume of lending to the economy. Against the backdrop of the rapid growth of the Chinese economy, the American economy has been in a state of sluggish reproduction for the last decade and a half. On its periphery, the Russian economy was recovering from the disaster of the early 1990s and then stagnating after the global financial crisis of 2008. The savings rate in both Russia and the US is around 20% of GDP compared with 45% in China. This testifies to the decline of the outgoing MHI, the investment processes both in the core and the periphery, which barely ensure the simple reproduction of the economy against the background of the rapid growth of production and investment in the core countries of the new MHI. Also, twice as much monetization and credit provision of the Chinese economy as in the US and 4 times as much as in Russia testify to the much higher efficiency of the financial-investment system of the new integral WEO, as compared to the outgoing imperial one.

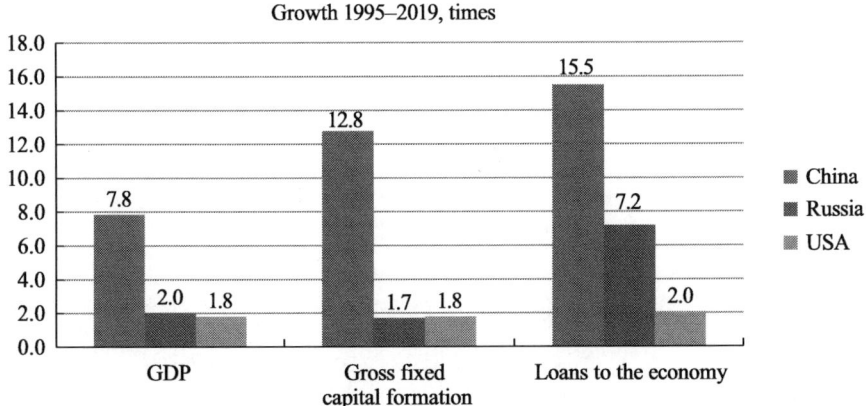

Figure 23   Growth of GDP, Capital Formation, and Credit to Economy at Constant Prices in PRC Compared with US and RF

Source: EEC Macroeconomic Policy Department based on data from World Bank, OECD, IMF, and Bank of Russia annual reports.

. As can be seen in Figure 23, China's explosive GDP growth has been accompanied by even more rapid investment growth and outstripping credit growth in the productive sector. Per unit of GDP growth, there are more than one and a half units of investment growth and two units of money supply and credit growth. This illustrates how the growth mechanism of the Chinese economy works: increased economic activity is driven by investment growth, much of which is financed by increased credit from the state banking system.

China's low inflation against the background of rapid money supply growth was ensured by a steady increase in the efficiency and volume of goods production by keeping money flows in a loop: credit issue–investment growth–volume and efficiency growth–mass growth of goods at lower unit costs of production and prices–income growth–savings growth–investment growth. This was achieved by tying loans from state banks to investment projects for the development of production, observing currency restrictions on capital transactions, the cross-cutting responsibility of state authorities for achieving the indicators of production and investment growth, and systematic combating of corruption.

The Chinese themselves call their formation socialist while developing private enterprise and growing market-competitive corporations. The Chinese Communist leadership continues to build socialism while avoiding ideological clichés. They prefer to formulate objectives in terms of people's welfare, aiming to overcome poverty and create a middle-income society, and subsequently attain a leading position in terms of living standards. They try to avoid excessive social inequalities by maintaining a labor-based distribution of national income and by orienting economic regulatory institutions toward productive activities and long-term investments in the development of productive forces. This is a common feature of the countries forming the "core" of the new world economic order.

At the same time, China, India, Indonesia, and Indochina are showing outstripping growth rates. They are forming the "core" of a new, integral, world economic order. Japan, Singapore, and South Korea took a different historical path to form a similar system of economic reproduction institutions even earlier. The synthesis of market competition mechanisms with state planning on both socialist and capitalist bases gave rise to a convergent system of production relations. While in China, this system is considered socialism with Chinese characteristics, in Japan, no one questions the capitalist character of Japan Incorporated. The Korean chaebol is also considered quite capitalist. All countries, from Vietnam to Ethiopia, following the way of convergent model formation, combining socialist ideology and state planning with market mechanisms and private entrepreneurship, and regulating the latter in order to increase the production of material goods, demonstrate today the advanced sustainable development against the stagnation of the leading capitalist countries. The American century cycle of capital accumulation is being replaced by the Asian cycle, and the center of the world economy is shifting to Southeast Asia.

Unlike the countries of the "core" of the existing world economic order, which imposed a universal system of financial and economic relations as the basis of liberal globalization, the emerging "core" of the new world economic order is characterized by great diversity. This peculiarity is also manifested in the principles of international relations shared by its constituent countries: freedom of choice of development paths, rejection of hegemonism, and sovereignty of historical and cultural traditions. The new world economic order is being shaped on an equal, mutually beneficial, and consensual basis. New regional economic associations are being created according to these principles: the Shanghai Cooperation Organization (SCO), the Eurasian Economic Union (EAEU), Mercosur, ASEAN-China—and international financial institutions: the Development Bank and the BRICS pool of currency reserves, the AIIB, the Eurasian Development Bank (EDB).

The association of countries in major international organizations such as the SCO and BRICS represents a qualitatively new model of cooperation that pays tribute to diversity in contrast to the universal forms of liberal globalization. Its fundamental principles are the firm support of universally recognized principles and norms of international law, and the rejection of policies of coercive pressure and infringement of the sovereignty of other states. The principles of international organization shared by the countries of the emerging "core" of the new world order are fundamentally different from those characteristic of previous world orders formed by Western European civilization, as S. Huntington admitted, "not due to the superiority of their ideas, moral values or religion (to which few other civilizations were converted), but rather due to superiority in the use of organized violence."[35]

The formation of a new world economic order gives rise to a reform of the world economic order and international relations. The revival of socio-economic development planning and state regulation of the main parameters of capital reproduction, active industrial policy, control over cross-border capital flows, and currency restrictions—all this is turning from the "menu" forbidden by the Washington financial organizations into generally accepted instruments of international economic relations. As a counterbalance to the "Washington consensus," a number of academics are talking about the "Beijing consensus," which is much more attractive to the developing countries where the majority of humanity lives.[36] It is based on the principles of non-discrimination, mutual respect for sovereignty, and the national interests of cooperating states, orienting them toward the enhancement of the people's welfare rather than the servicing of international capital. It allows for a variety of national rules on currency regulation of cross-border capital movements, which each country is free to set according to its own sense of expediency. This could lead to a new, more favorable regime for developing countries to protect intellectual property rights and technology transfer. New rules on international trade in energy and natural resources are likely to emerge, stabilizing prices and market access conditions. New agreements could be made to limit emissions, etc.

The restructuring of the global monetary and financial system is key to the transition to a new world economic order. The new architecture of international monetary and financial relations should be built on a legal and contractual basis. Countries issuing world reserve currencies will have to guarantee their sustainability by keeping certain limits on public debt balance of payments and trade deficits. Besides, they will have to comply with demands established on the basis of international law for transparency of mechanisms ensuring the issue of their currencies and their unrestricted exchange possibility for all assets traded in their territory.

It would be wise to classify national currencies, pretending to be world or regional reserve currencies, into categories depending on the compliance of their issuers with the requirements of international law. The new monetary and financial architecture should also cover settlements in digital currency instruments, including the use of a distributed data registry (blockchain) methodology, which implies the introduction of appropriate requirements to ensure their transparency and identification of participants, as well as the harmonization of national regulations. In the future, it is possible to issue a global settlement currency in digital form, linked to a basket of national currencies of the parties to the relevant agreement, gold prices, and basic exchange commodities.

In order to stimulate global dissemination of socially significant achievements of the new technological mode, it is necessary to deploy an international system of strategic planning of global socio-economic development, including long-term forecasts of scientific and technological development, identification of prospects for the development of the world economy, regional economic associations and major national economies, identification of opportunities to overcome existing imbalances, including gaps in the development level between advanced and underdeveloped countries.

The international policy approach characteristic of the countries of the core of the new world economic order (refraining from interfering in internal affairs, military intervention, and trade embargoes) gives the developing countries a real alternative to American-centric liberal globalization on the basis of building equitable and mutually beneficial relations.[37] Many of them are gradually being drawn into the formation of an integrated world economic order, creating an effective system of international cooperation with the countries of its core. All long-term forecasts of the world economy's development point to further outpacing the development of the countries relying on the institutions of the integrated world economic order and forming the Asian systemic cycle of capital accumulation. Despite significant differences in political structure and economic regulation mechanisms, many stable cooperative ties are forming between them, and mutual trade and investment are growing rapidly. The center of global development is shifting to Southeast Asia, which allows a number of researchers to speak of the beginning of a new Asian century cycle of capital accumulation.[38]

As was shown above, regardless of the dominant form of ownership—state, as in China or Vietnam, or private, as in Japan or South Korea—the integrated world economy is characterized by a combination of institutions of state planning and market self-organization, state control over the main parameters of economic reproduction and free enterprise, the ideology of the common good and private initiative. At the same time, the forms of political structure may differ fundamentally—from the world's largest Indian democracy to the world's largest CPC. What remains unchanged is the priority of public interests over private ones, expressed in rigid mechanisms of personal responsibility of citizens for conscientious behavior, clear performance of their duties, compliance with the law, and service to national goals. The management system of socio-economic development is based on the mechanisms of personal responsibility for improving the well-being of society.

Thus, based on the most likely outcome of the global hybrid war unleashed by the ruling elite of the US, not in its favor, the new world economy will be formed in the competition between the communist and democratic varieties, the results of which will be determined by their relative effectiveness in the development of opportunities and neutralizing the threats of the new technological order. The main competition between the communist and democratic variants of the new world economic order is likely to evolve between China and India, the leaders of the current pace of economic development, who, together with their satellites, claim a good half of the global economy. This competition will be peaceful and governed by international law. All aspects of this regulation, from the control of global security to the issuing of world currencies, will be based on international treaties. Countries that refuse commitments and international monitoring will be marginalized in their respective fields of international cooperation. The world economy will become more complex, and the restoration of the importance of national sovereignty and the diversity of national systems of economic regulation will be combined with the fundamental importance of international organizations with supranational powers.

The competition between the communist and democratic variants of an integrated world economy will not be antagonistic. For example, China's BRI, with its "Community with a Shared Future of Mankind" ideology, involves many countries with different political arrangements. The democratic countries of the EU are setting up free trade zones with communist Vietnam. The competitive landscape will be determined by the comparative efficiency of national governance systems.

The change of world economies takes a considerable period of time, which is necessary for a generational change of the ruling elite of the world's leading countries. In the last century, it amounted to more than three decades, from the beginning of World War I to the end of World War II. During this period, the ruling elite of the leading countries of the world changed dramatically. Instead of hereditary aristocrats and capitalists, the technocracy took the leading power and economic position, and the state administration was taken over by a professional bureaucracy. Competition between private companies was replaced by competition between global organizations, whose reproduction was regulated by two global political systems of states.

The collapse of the world system of socialism should be regarded as the beginning of the modern transition to a change of WEM. Today, the imperial world economic order is being finally destroyed, the American systemic cycle of capital accumulation associated with it is coming to an end, and the transition to an integrated world economic order is underway. The contours of the latter have already been formed in China and other countries of Southeast Asia, which are mastering the institutions and creating the management systems of economic reproduction of the integrated world economic order. They are proving their efficiency not only in the dynamics of macroeconomic indicators but also in the successful repulsion of American aggression during the hybrid world war.

Over the last three decades, China has made impressive progress, rising from the deep periphery of the world economy to become a leader. Almost unscathed by the global recession of the last decade, China displaced Japan as the world's second-largest economy in August 2010. In 2012, with imports and exports of $3.87 trillion, China overtook the US to become the world's second-largest economy. The PRC overtook the US with a total foreign trade turnover of $3.82 trillion, displacing it from the position it held for 60 years as the global leader in cross-border trade. By the end of 2014, China's GDP, measured at purchasing power parity, was $17.6 trillion, surpassing that of the US ($17.4 trillion), the world's largest economy since 1872 year.[39]

Over three decades, China's GDP has increased 30-fold (from $300 billion to $9 trillion at the current exchange rate of the yuan to the dollar), industrial production 40–50-fold, and foreign exchange reserves several hundred times (from a few tens of billions of dollars to $4 trillion). In terms of economic development, as measured by GDP per capita, China has risen from the bottom of the list of poorest countries to a place in the top 30 middle-income countries.[40]

According to the theory of long cycles described above, the change of world leaders takes place during crises caused by the change of technology and WEM. As we have already mentioned, a change of technological patterns creates opportunities for countries that are the first to develop the key productions of the new technological pattern. By shaping the trajectory of its growth, they are able to extract intellectual rent on the global market, thereby enhancing its competitive advantages and ensuring global leadership in the new long wave of economic growth.

As early as 1986, China adopted the National High-Tech Research & Development Program, known as the 863 Program, as a response to the global challenges of the new technological revolution and competition. Since 1997, China has been implementing its National High-Tech Basic Research Program to provide a scientific foundation for its future development and rise to the leading edge of technology. The plan to turn China into a scientific superpower by 2050 envisages a decisive step in the next 15 years. During this period, it is planned to reduce dependence on foreign technology and achieve a level of "endogenous" innovative development of strategic high technologies, which will guarantee China's national security and ensure its strong position in global scientific and economic competition. The implementation of these plans is backed by strong financial support from the central government and provincial administrations.

China is catching up with the US in terms of total R&D expenditure. In rapidly increasing its overall R&D spending, China has given priority to funding the development of key new-technology stage technologies.

In terms of government spending on nanotechnology, China has already moved into second place worldwide, behind Japan and Germany. Corporate nano-technology expenditure is also rising rapidly, having increased at an annual rate of one and a half times.[41] It is symptomatic of the Chinese Academy of Sciences initiative to make solar energy the country's main energy source by 2050.

In fact, China is pursuing a mixed strategy in economic development. In the preceding long-wave industries, a catch-up strategy is being pursued, exploiting China's competitive advantage in labor costs. At the same time, with its rise to the forefront of science, the conditions are being laid for a strategy of scientific and technological leadership.[42] Appropriate industrial policy measures have been taken to implement these strategies. With the support of central agencies, 103 enterprises have become experimental innovation centers, "pulling" others behind them. In the next 3–5 years, the number of pilot enterprises will increase to 500.[43]

China is becoming a global engineering and technology hub. The share of the Chinese engineering and scientific workforce in the world's workforce reached 20% in 2007, up from 1420,000 in 2000 and 690,000 in 2000, respectively. The proportion of Chinese engineers and scientists in the world reached 20% in 2007—double that of the 1,420,000 and 690,000 in 2000, respectively. Tellingly, many have returned to the PRC from Silicon Valley in the US, playing a major role in the rise of innovative entrepreneurship in China. It is projected that, by 2030, there will be 15 million engineering and scientific personnel in the world, of which 4.5 million (30%) will be scientists, engineers, and technicians from the PRC.[44] By 2030, China will rank No.1 globally in R&D expenditure and account for 25% of global R&D expenditure. China will become the world's No. 1 research and development nation, accounting for 25% of global R&D expenditure.[45] In May 2015, the Chinese government published its "Made in China 2025" plan to rapidly develop ten high-tech industries, including electric vehicles, next-generation information technology, telecommunications, advanced robotics, and artificial intelligence. The plan aimed to achieve 70% self-sufficiency in high-tech industries and a dominant position in these global markets by 2049. Currently, PRC is leading in new energy technologies such as ultra-high voltage lines, power cells for solar power plants (60% of global production), wind power, promising developments for hydroelectric power plants, and battery production.[46]

China's phenomenal success in science and technology belies the conventional wisdom that it is incapable of generating new knowledge on its own. The US accuses China of industrial espionage and unauthorized copying of advanced US technologies. It is well known that China pays great attention to the training of highly qualified specialists at the best universities in the US and Canada.[47] Over the past decade, however, China has been rapidly shifting to its own scientific and technological basis for developing its economy. Between 2000 and 2016, China's share of global publications in the physical sciences, engineering, and mathematics quadrupled, surpassing that of the US. In 2019, the PRC surpassed the US in patent activity (58,990 versus 57,840). Not only at the macro level but also at the micro level, Chinese companies are outperforming US innovation leaders. For example, for the third year in a row, China's Huawei Technologies Company, with 4,144 patents, is well ahead of US-based Qualcomm (2,127 patents).

In the global race to master the fifth-generation (5G) information and communications technology space, Huawei was the first to release commercial products in February 2019. China's planned 2020 global launch of 5G took place on October 31, 2019. Three local mobile operators began providing access to fifth-generation networks in 50 cities across the country, which not only made China an overnight global leader in the adoption of new technology but also strengthened Huawei's position against which the US announced sanctions. As a result, China has become the world's largest user of the new networks, while in the US, the fifth-generation connection that does not use the solution is only offered in certain areas of some cities. Meanwhile, Shenzhen in China's Guangdong province has become the world's first city with full 5G coverage. According to the China Academy of Information and Communications Technology (CAICT), a total of 93.7 million 5G-enabled smartphones were sold in China between January and August 2020. More than 90% of smartphone shipments in China come from local manufacturers.

The PRC has successfully resisted cyberattacks by US intelligence agencies, attempts by media and bloggers controlled by them to manipulate public consciousness for political destabilization, withstood Trump's trade war, and defended itself against currency and financial threats. Washington's sanctions against Chinese high-tech companies have forced them to push their own R&D into building a national technology base.

NOTES

1. S. Glazyev and G. I. Mikerin, *Long Waves: NTP and Socio-Economic Development* (Moscow: Nauka, 1989).
2. S. Glazyev, *Theory of Long-Term Technical and Economic Development* (Moscow: VlaDar, 1993).
3. S. Glazyev, *A Strategy for Russia's Advanced Development in the Global Crisis* (Moscow: Economics, 2010).
4. S. Glazyev and V. Kharitonov, "Nanotechnology as a Key Factor in a New Technological Order in the Economy."
5. S. Glazyev, *Theory of Long-Term Techno-Economic Development* (Moscow: VlaDar, 1993).
6. S. Glazyev, "On Russia's Economic Development Policy," 2013; S. Glazyev, "Economic Growth Policy in the Global Crisis," 2012.
7. S. Glazyev, "Modernization of the Russian Economy on the Basis of a New Technological Mode as a Key Direction of Anti-Crisis Policy," Analytical Report under the Program of Russian Humanitarian Science Foundation (Project No. 09-02-95650 report), 2009.
8. S. Glazyev, "Methods for Estimating the Dynamic Characteristics of STP," *Izvestia of the USSR Academy of Sciences* (Economic Series), no. 1 (1985).
9. S. Glazyev, "World Economic Patterns in Global Economic Development," *Economics and Mathematical Methods* 52, no. 2 (2016); S. Glazyev, "Applied Results of the Theory of World Economic Patterns," *Economics and Mathematical Methods* 52, no. 3 (2016).
10. Fiduciary money (FD) is a modern form of money whose nominal value is set and guaranteed by the state regardless of the value of the material from which it is made. The main physical property of FDs, which distinguishes them from earlier types of money, is their intangible nature, which allows them to be created in unlimited amounts and to move instantly in space. Although called debt, FDs are not backed by any official collateral. Their issuers are not liable to anyone. The most important economic function of modern FDs is their role as a stimulant of economic activity. The definition is based on the following sources: https://otyrba.livejournal.com/312078.html; D. Golubovsky and A. Otyrba, "The ABC of Financial Sovereignty," *Expert*, no. 39 (2011): 772.
11. H. J. Mackinder, *Democratic Ideals and Reality* (New York: Holt, 1919).
12. S. Glazyev, A. E. Aivazov, and V. A. Belikov, "Cyclical-Wave Theories of Economic Development and Prospects for the World Economy," *Scientific Proceedings of the Free Economic Society*, no. 5 (2019): 177–211.
13. R. Hilferding, *Financial Capital* (Moscow: Gosizdat, 1922), 460.
14. V. I. Lenin, *Complete Works*, vol. 27, 5th ed., 299–426.
15. S. Glazyev, A. E. Aivazov, and V. A. Belikov, "Cyclical-Wave Theories of Economic Development and Prospects of the World Economy," 177–211.
16. M. Hazin, *Memories of the Future: Ideas of Modern Economics* (M.: Ripol Classic, 2019).
17. Ernst Ulrich von Weizsäcker and Anders Wijkman, "Come On!: Capitalism, Short-Termism, Population and the Destruction of the Planet," *The Club of Roman's*, January 2018.
18. BofA Global Investment Strategy, "The Longest Pictures," May 30, 2020.
19. K. Marx, *Capital*, bk 3 (Moscow: State Publishing House of Political Literature, 1951).
20. The accumulation of capital in private hands is no longer possible. Capitalists, in order to preserve their savings, must invest them in the expansion of socially useful productions. The negative value of money means that it must be spent as quickly as possible and dramatically accelerates reproduction processes. This also automatically increases the role of government

regulation of the circulation of money in order to develop the economy, and creates conditions for a more efficient system of government, including the replacement of taxes by the issue of money.

21. Y. Yakovets, *The Political Economy of Civilisations* (Moscow: Economics, 2016).

22. A. Toffler, *The Third Wave*, 1980 (M.: ACT, 2010).

23. D. Bell, *The Coming of Post-Industrial Society: A Venture of Social Forecasting* (N.Y.: Basic Books, 1973).

24. L. Fishman, "The New Heresy of Civic Religion," *Russia in Global Politics*, no. 5 (2020): 90–101.

25. P. Kivisto, "Marshall Revisited: Neoliberalism and the Future of Class Abatement in Contemporary Political Discourse about the Welfare State," *International Review of Modern Sociology* 33, no. 1 (2007): 2–4.

26. J. Blau, "Theories of the Welfare State," *Social Service* Review 63, no. 1 (1989): 35.

27. S. Kuhnle and S. Hort, "The Developmental Welfare State in Scandinavia: Lessons for the Developing World," Social Policy and Development Programme, Paper Number 17, *United Nations Research Institute for Social Development* (2004), 22.

28. O. Sinyavskaya, "Born of the Pandemic," *Russia in Global Politics*, no. 5 (2020): 10–24.

29. A. Sen, "Development as Freedom," edited and afterword by R. M. Nureyev (Moscow: Novoye Izdatelstvo, 2004).

30. A. Hemerijck, "Correlates of Capacitating Solidarity," *Housing, Theory and Society* (2020): 1–11.

31. A. Lieven, "Progressive Nationalism," *Russia in Global Politics*, no. 5 (2020): 25–42.

32. Ibid.

33. A. Cooley and D. Nexon, "How Hegemony Ends," *Russia in Global Politics*, no. 5 (2020): 137–153.

34. R. Müllerson, "How Liberalism Came into Conflict with Democracy," *Russia in Global Politics*, no. 5 (2020): 43–59.

35. S. Huntington, *The Clash of Civilisations and the Remaking of World Order* (1996) is one of the most popular geopolitical works of the 1990s. Emerging from an article in Foreign Affairs magazine, it re-defines political reality and forecasts the global development of all Earth's civilization. The publication contains Fukuyama's famous article "The End of History."

36. J. C. Ramo, "The Beijing Consensus," The Foreign Policy Centre, 2004; "The Beijing Consensus: An Alternative Approach to Development," World Foresight Forum, The Hague, The Netherlands, 2011, Issue Brief No. 02.

37. J. Ramo, "The Beijing Consensus."

38. G. Arrighi, *The Long Twentieth Century: Money, Power and the Origins of Our Times*; A. Aivazov, "Periodic System of World Capitalist Development," Almanac Development and Economics, no. 2 (March 2012).

39. Dilip Hiro, "Why China Is Taking over the 'American Century,'" *The Asia Times*, August 19, 2020, URL: https://asiatimes.com/2020/08/why-china-is-taking-over-the-american-century.

40. V. Sadovnichy, Y. Yakovets, and A. Akayev, eds., "Prospects and Strategic Priorities for BRICS Ascent" (Moscow: Moscow State University—Pitirim Sorokin-Nikolai Kondratiev International Institute - INES - National Committee for BRICS Studies—Institute of Latin America of the Russian Academy of Sciences, 2014).

41. "China Second to US in Nano," March 12, 2007, www.nanochina.cn.

42. A. Rey, "Competitive Strategies of Countries and Firms under Export Oriented Growth," *Voprosy Ekonomiki*, no. 8 (2004): 46–65.

43. http://www.china.org.cn.
44. Tsinghua University Center for Country Studies, *China 2030: Toward Universal Prosperity*, ed. Hu Angan, Yan Yilong, and Wei Xing (Beijing: People's University of China Press, 2011), 30.
45. V. Sadovnichy, Y. Yakovets, and A. Akayev, eds., "Prospects and Strategic Priorities for BRICS Ascent" (Moscow: Moscow State University—Pitirim Sorokin-Nikolai Kondratiev International Institute - INES - National Committee for BRICS Studies—Institute of Latin America of the Russian Academy of Sciences, 2014).
46. "The BRI in the Global Trade, Investment and Finance Landscape," in *OECD Business and Finance Outlook 2018 (Paris: OECD Publishing, 2018)*.
47. D. Boothby, "Who Goes to North America for a Degree and Why," *Foresight*, no. 4 (2007).

CHAPTER 7

World Economy Center Transferring from America to Asia

B ASED ON THE PATTERNS DESCRIBED ABOVE, IT IS POSSIBLE TO DEVELOP A forecast of the further unfolding of the structural changes currently taking place in the global economy. This forecast cannot but be scenario-based because these changes are made by different power-economic, scientific, technological, and socio-political actors guided by their own interests and objectives, which are far from being always and everywhere able to be combined into a common national and all the more so, into a global strategy. Only the Chinese state, which has mastered the institutions of regulation and methods of management of integral MHI, possesses such an ability at present. It effectively unites social groups with different interests around the national goals of the socio-economic development of the country. While the US's two leading political parties were rocking the boat of American statehood, bringing the country to the brink of a civil war, the CPC Central Committee approved the 14th Five-Year Plan with the ambitious goals of strengthening China's leading position by increasing its own scientific and technological potential, advanced development based on the accelerated growth of new technological mode industries.

In the core countries of the declining imperial world order, especially in the US and the EU, social conflicts between people of different views, colors, religions, ages, and places of residence are on the rise. Social differentiation is growing, not only in terms of income but also in terms of opportunities, undermining the foundations of the welfare state and hindering the development of its institutions in accordance with the principles of integral MHI. The oligarchy of power and finance, based on the deep state in the US and the Euro-bureaucracy in the EU, diverges further and further from the masses in its interests. Its striving for world domination amid the emergence of the new WEO and the relocation of the center of world economic development to Southeast Asia results in stagnating incomes, declining living standards for the population, and a worsening state of security. An antagonistic contradiction arises between the cosmopolitan power and financial elite, which concentrates scientific and technological achievements in its interests, including prolongation of life and manipulation of public consciousness, and the people, who rely on a democratic nation-state. This entails a rise in social tensions, which the ruling elite try to suppress in an authoritarian manner, using the coronavirus pandemic to roll back the institutions of civil society.

In the situation of the unfolding global hybrid war, one can only speak with certainty about the forecasts of China's economic development based on the rapid growth of the new technological mode while maintaining socio-political stability. In the US and the EU, on the contrary, growing socio-political destabilization is to be expected. In this case, the concentration of capital and scientific and technological potential among the power and financial elite will encounter resistance from democratic state institutions. The outcome of this confrontation is currently impossible to predict. It may culminate in a social revolution with the establishment of public control over financial, scientific, and technological institutions, or it may end in the creation of an electronic concentration camp for an intimidated, vaccinated, and chipped population.

The US-based power and financial oligarchy is waging a hybrid war in two planes: for world domination and against its own people. It has technologies and agents of influence in all countries and social strata. It is opposed by the Chinese state that consolidated society, relying on more efficient institutions and methods of management of the new world economic order, much more attractive for the majority of countries and humanity as a whole, as compared to the world order of liberal globalization imposed by the power-and-financial oligarchy. The outcome of this confrontation is far from clear and largely depends on the position of both other sovereign countries, including Russia, and the productive elite of the United States and its ability to curb the power-financial elite of this country. And also on the work of the scientists and engineers who created the technological framework of the new world order.

The development of information and communication, bio-engineering, and digital technologies, which are at the core of the new technological stage, has given rise to many opportunities for improving systems of economic and social management, as well as posing serious threats to the future evolution of humanity. Let us try to grasp the intricacy of real and imaginary challenges of the new technological pattern's spread and understand its significance in the productive and social relations of the new world economic order.

Rising unemployment in connection with the robotization of jobs, the automation of management processes, and the growing use of 3D printers is considered a serious threat to public security. While this problem is not new, and since the first industrial revolution, the Luddite movement, which destroyed spinning machines in England over two centuries ago, has been well known, it is of particular concern today. Indeed, in the early days of mass robotization, we can expect to see an appreciable increase in unemployment among workers and employees in certain professions and occupations. Already today, there has been a sharp decline in the demand for fitters, turners, assemblers, packers, and a host of other trades that have been replaced by automated machining centers and robotic complexes.

Well, as the nearly three hundred years of experience of modern industrial development shows, this threat is partly neutralized by other factors.

Firstly, alongside stagnant unemployment in old industries, there is always a labor shortage in new industries. The imbalance in the labor market is sharply exacerbated in times of technological change. At this time, the economy plunged into depression due to the cessation of expansion of business activity in the established directions, reduction of production, and investments in the sectors that provided the main growth of employment for two generations of the working-age population. Then there is the "shock" of a sharp fall in incomes for many previously prosperous working-age groups, many of whom will never be able to recover. At the same time, the growth of the new technological structure ensures demand for labor of other specialties, and workers released from the obsolete technological structure who wish to retrain can learn new, in-demand professions. The state can significantly mitigate the "dissipation" of labor market imbalances by subsidizing retraining programs for people who have lost their jobs and by the timely restructuring of the education system to meet the demand for new professions.

Secondly, robotization, like the digital revolution, is already well underway, destroying millions of jobs in various industries. Since the 1980s, with the rise of the then-new information and communications technology paradigm, automation of production has embraced many manufacturing industries. Flexible automated systems made the work of millions of assemblers, packers, and machinists redundant. The rigid automation of assembly lines has freed millions more people from the monotonous labor of simple, repetitive operations. The progress in computer techniques eliminated millions of jobs of typists, punches, rate-setters, designers, accountants, and other specialties connected with routine calculations according to set algorithms. Tens of millions of people were replaced by automation, but a social disaster like the Great Depression, when the change of technological and economic systems also took place, did not occur. Young people enthusiastically adopted new professions as programmers, operators, and adjusters. Older people retired early. Many have found themselves in the service sector, the rapid expansion of which has been the most visible side of the growth of the new technological stage, giving rise to the view of a transition to a post-industrial stage of economic development. In fact, industry is still the backbone of the modern economy; only its share of the labor market has fallen to 25% in advanced economies due to the automation of production.

The public administration system is facing a major challenge from the technological revolution. The army of millions of civil servants tasked with enforcing regulations ranging from road safety to tax controls may be unnecessary—an incorruptible, all-seeing, all-knowing artificial intelligence will do it much more effectively. Digital technology can make government regulation and control much more effective. It fits perfectly into the system of institutions of the new world economic order, which implies a dramatic increase in the role of the state as a development institution.

For example, the use of blockchain technology will make it impossible to falsify registration and permit documents or to retroactively rework inspection acts. The technology will also eliminate much of the unnecessary costly notarization of transactions. The use of smart contracts will eliminate bureaucratic arbitrariness in public procurement. The use of electronic digital signatures and methods of precise identification of paper and electronic media will rule out document forgery. The entire public administration system will become more transparent and open to public scrutiny. The corruption "field" will be reduced, and the need for officials of supervising bodies will be reduced. Maybe that is why the informatization of public administration systems is going so hard—huge sums of money are being wasted on ineffective and imitative measures.

An example of smart state regulation is the experience of China, where the state has traditionally paid great attention to information security and control, having created, for example, a unique political filter of the Internet (Great Firewall).

Currently, a so-called social credit system is being created for information control and assessment of citizens according to a variety of parameters. In 2014, the government published a plan and objectives for its implementation by 2020, and pilot projects are currently being tested. The main objective of this system is to "build a harmonious socialist society." Integrity is declared to be the core value of such a society and must be manifested in everything from behavior on the internet to honoring one's parents. To develop this quality in the people, the system will assign a rating to each citizen of China. Points will be awarded for not breaking the law, useful social activities, and timely fulfillment of obligations, including repayment of loans. Misdemeanors of varying severity will be deducted. If the total score turns out to be "non-passable," life will become a torment. In 2016, the Chinese government published a refined list of sanctions to which low scorers will be subjected: a ban on working in state institutions, denial of social security, special scrutiny at customs, a ban on holding executive positions in the food and pharmaceutical industry, denial of airfare and sleeping space on overnight trains, denial of places in luxury hotels and restaurants, and a ban on sending children to expensive public schools.

Alongside radical social innovations, the technological revolution now unfolding brings with it the dangers of technological change in the nature of man himself, which has become a favorite subject of fantasy films and dystopias. Let's break them down in order of likelihood of realization.

(1) The threat of genetically engineered technology being used to create microorganisms that are dangerous to humans. It has long existed and is clearly underestimated by national security agencies. Even two decades ago, scientists recognized the possibility of synthesizing viruses that are selective against groups of people with certain biological traits. By combining the DNA of viruses living in symbiosis with human pathogens, it is possible to synthesize viruses that cause disease in people of a particular sex, age group, or even race. By bringing these viruses through food exports into enemy territory, it is possible to induce epidemics among people of a particular ethnic group and thus circumvent the double-edged nature of biological weapons. It appears that, despite the latter ban, such research is being carried out with increasing intensity in US laboratories. In any case, some African leaders sincerely hold Washington responsible for the creation and spread of Ebola. The view that the coronavirus is of artificial origin is shared by many experts, some of whom even see technological continuity in the virus in relation to previously synthesized viruses of SARS, swine flu, and AIDS.

(2) The cloning of humans, including those with certain properties. Scientists first spoke of this threat more than a decade ago, when the cloning of mammals was experimentally demonstrated to be feasible. Today, the cloning of dogs has become a commercially viable enterprise, and human cloning factories are theoretically possible.

(3) The implantation of various cybernetic devices into human bodies. This is already a well-established technology in medicine, with widespread use of pacemakers, hearing aids, prosthetic devices, and sensors. Theoretically, cyborgs—people with devices implanted in their bodies to give them additional computing power, improve their sense organs, identify their identity, transmit information to them, manipulate their behavior, etc.—could theoretically emerge.

(4) Incorporating human organs and their models into robotic devices. This is still as fantastic as Professor Doel's head in A. Belyaev's novel, but models of the human nervous system are being developed intensively, and it is possible that androids with human body elements, as well as humanoid living beings, will appear.

(5) Out-of-control autonomous robotic machine systems capable of self-organization. Robot rebellion could theoretically transform from an art form into a real nightmare in the not-too-distant future. Already today, failures of automated power supply systems plunge large cities into chaos. If artificial intelligence systems are able to self-organize and make autonomous decisions, the consequences are impossible to predict.

All of the above threats to human existence are well-known and have been discussed many times. However, no real proposals on their neutralization have been worked out yet. As Subbeto states, mankind, for the first time in its conscious history, faces the imperatives of the Great Logic of Socio-Natural Evolution, which are "focused" on the imperative of human survival in the 21st century.[1] Obviously, it is unrealistic to stop NTP, even though its consequences for mankind are dangerous, but society can limit it with the framework of the law. In order to be effective, these limitations must be international in nature and apply to all countries with significant scientific and technological potential. Their adoption will be one of the leading directions in shaping a new world economic order.

The current experience of international treaties to curb the proliferation of missile and nuclear technologies, ban bacteriological and chemical weapons, and test atomic weapons is encouraging. Although these treaties do not have effective enforcement mechanisms, the world's leading countries tend not to violate them. With the transition to an integrated world economic order based on mutually beneficial and voluntary partnerships of states and strict observance of international law,[2] the range of such agreements will increase. It could also include international treaties necessary to limit the above-described dangers of digital technology, including those providing for the following:

(1) A ban on the cloning of human beings
(2) A ban on the development of pathogenic viruses as a biological weapon
(3) Introducing international standards for implanting devices into the human body
(4) Monitoring the development of artificial intelligence systems to diagnose and neutralize threats to humanity
(5) The worldwide certification of specialists trained in computer and bioengineering technologies
(6) The development and adoption of international technical regulations and certification procedures for Android robots

The countries of the new WEO, through the SCO, could initiate the drafting and adoption of an international convention on scientific ethics prohibiting research on altering human nature, biological weapons, programming of homing robotic systems aimed at destroying humans, etc.

The digital revolution is a long process that has been unfolding for several decades and is striking the imagination of the impressionable. Digital technologies have embraced virtually all information and finances and are a significant part of the industrial and social spheres. It is increasingly penetrating the domestic sphere. While enhancing opportunities and improving the quality of life of people, they have not yet done much harm to society. Numerous examples of the use of digital technology for inhumane and criminal purposes relate to human action rather than to technology as such. At the same time, their monopolistic use in the private interests of others significantly empowers those individuals and may pose a threat to the national security of states. The neutralization of these human-caused challenges should be done through legal regulation.

The use of digital technologies in the formation of institutions of an integrated world economic order makes it possible to achieve a qualitative "leap" in the evolution of mankind. The digital revolution complements and significantly expands the possibilities of generating, processing, transmitting, accumulating, and assimilating information. The computer does not forget anything, information dissemination costs nothing, and any algorithm of routine human activity can be programmed and transferred to robots for execution. The digital revolution definitively frees humans from the need for monotonous and hard work, not only physical but also office work. It frees up the time previously spent by humans in monotonous labor and opens up the possibility for humanity to shift to purely creative activities. This was the dream of the classics of Marxism-Leninism, speaking of the "leap" from necessity to freedom that they associated with communism.

Ironically, the digital revolution developed after the weakness of the world system of socialism, which could have provided a qualitative "leap" in the efficiency of the system of national economic planning and brought enormous competitive advantages in the competition with capitalist countries. In the USSR, scientific and technological progress was associated with opportunities for increasing people's welfare and increasing the share of free time in the human life cycle. In the post-war period, this share grew consistently with the expansion of the recreational sphere. Although many people drank alcohol in their free time, the ideology of building communism had a solution for filling their leisure time with personal self-improvement, creative and constructive work, education, and participation in public work, including the running of the state. It was not by chance that the USSR became the most reading country in the world, with the best system of mass education, healthcare, and recreation for the working people.

For a capitalist system oriented toward maximizing profits at all costs, the digital revolution creates unsolvable problems. On the one hand, rising productivity increases surplus value. On the other hand, the release of people engaged in productive activities means a corresponding decrease in demand, which puts a limit on the expansion of production and the expanded reproduction of capital. Social inequalities are widened, and society is "divided" between the all-powerful holders of the keys to the application of digital technology and the uninvolved consumers of productive activity. The latter form numerous ranks of the precariat. As consumer demand stagnates, capital flows into the financial sector, where the information revolution has created technological opportunities for the rapid inflation of financial bubbles.

The digital revolution is disrupting economic stereotypes. Whereas in traditional industries, the more resources spent, the more expensive the product, the opposite is true in the digital economy. The more data that is accumulated, the cheaper the product is produced. Neither the law of value nor the law of marginal utility applies. The accumulation of data makes it possible to generate new data with the decreasing value of the additional information generated. The market valuation of Internet companies has no comparable material basis. As the scope and reach of the market expands, the marginal efficiency of investment in information systems increases, not decreases, as in material production. The Internet economy and the information revolution in the financial sector have placed the real sector in the position of a donor through which national income is redistributed into the financial bubbles of virtual companies through financial market mechanisms.

In the US-centric model of the outgoing world economic order, the digital revolution is creating more problems than opportunities for socio-economic development. Even as Western economies pump the economy with fiat (fiduciary) money, the lion's share of its issuance is "sucked in" by the financial sector while productive investment stagnates. The institutional system in the US, Great Britain, and other capitalist countries follows the interests of financial market speculators without trying to mitigate the imbalances associated with its expansion and neutralize the threats listed above. They hinder the productive application of new technologies, which is evidence of the mismatch between the existing world economic order and the possibilities and needs of the development of productive forces. This mismatch is being overcome by the transition to a new world economic order.

As indicated above, in addition to the remarkable technological transformation of China's economy, China's leadership brilliantly managed to mobilize the population to neutralize the coronavirus epidemic by establishing an advanced biosecurity system in a very short period of time. Having repelled the coronavirus epidemic, the PRC launched a counter-offensive by offering to help affected countries supply medical equipment, protective equipment, and disinfectants. They are thus taking the initiative from Washington on the ideological and political front, promoting their concept of harmonious international cooperation as a "community with a shared future for mankind."[3] US attempts to discredit the PRC as the source of the pandemic have collapsed in the face of evidence that the virus originated artificially in US bio-laboratories.[4]

The virus, developed by US special services, caused the greatest number of casualties in the country, which is the author of this biological weapon. Against the background of the rapid growth of the core of the new world economic order, it catalyzed a descent into chaos in the American-centric world order. The mass racial protests that engulfed the US testified to the antagonistic contradictions between different social groups in American society. Blacks against whites, Christians against the LGBT community, the poor against the rich, Democrats against Trump—all combine to undermine a state that clearly falters in the face of growing chaos. This is how analyst D. Lifschultz describes the current situation in the US: "The United States is committing harakiri: 4,000 cities are burning without popular resistance for fear that the army will shoot their lower caste comrades ... they believe it will mean the end of the United States ... most of the industry is destroyed and what is left faces the threat of total ruin." The author points to a four trillion dollar budget deficit with an approved US budget of $7 trillion. The amount of net monetary issue in the three preceding years covering this deficit exceeded the amount of credit issued by the US Federal Reserve in the century of its existence. This economic situation, according to Lifschultz, "is worse than the economic catastrophe of Weimar Germany, which had as an excuse the crippling reparations in favor of World War I victors. The modern US has no such justification,"[5]

The manifesto proposed by activists of the BLM (Black Lives Matter) movement is full not only of socialist slogans, clearly incompatible with the basic values of American capitalism and imperialism, but also of outright ideas of so-called African-American supremacism, which consists of justifying the redistribution of material resources in favor of the newly emerging protesters.[6]

It should be noted that, just as in the case of pre-pandemic preparation of public opinion with apocalyptic stories and films made long before the coronavirus, we can also talk about the purposeful creation of triggers for thematic (BLM) protests in the information space. Thus, in early 2020, the feature film "The Banker" was released in the US and in worldwide distribution—the story of African-American business partners Joe Morris and Bernard Garrett, who, in the 1950s, despite all the oppression from the white majority, managed to succeed in building and managing real estate. Two years earlier, the film The Green Book tells the true story of jazz pianist Don Shirley's journey through the southern United States, where he was confronted with racism at every concert. While the themes of tolerance and the eradication of ugly manifestations of racism from everyday reality are topical for American society, the concentration of American film and media attention on the problems of the African-American population raises many questions.

In essence, it is about undermining the foundations of the prevailing ideology in the United States. A. Lukin, responding to the reflection of the collective West on the (un)normality of "transatlantic slave trade," "settler colonialism" and other manifestations of Anglo-American imperialism—genocide, slave trade, wars of aggression—says, "Racism will be interpreted very broadly—not in the usual sense as a theory of superiority of one biological race over another, but as any attempt to justify domination or simply "progressiveness" of the West. From this perspective, racism is not just the ideology of the Ku Klux Klan or the colonial theory of "white man's burden," but also the theory of democracy as the highest form of political system, market economy, human rights, and generally everything invented in the West."[7]

Thus, the interracial clashes taking place in the US provoke the collapse of the ideology of US supremacy, which even its white intellectual elite is hurriedly abandoning. This thesis is articulated precisely by A. Cooley and D. Nexon in the aforementioned joint piece "How Hegemony Ends": "With the rise of powers such as China and Russia, autocratic and illiberal projects are posing an increasingly tangible challenge to the United States-led liberal international system. Developing countries—and even many developed countries—have an opportunity to seek alternative patrons rather than remain dependent on the generosity and support of the West. And illiberal, often right-wing supranational networks oppose norms and have no piety for the liberal international order that once seemed immutable. To cut it short, US global leadership is not just in retreat; it is falling apart. And the process is no longer cyclical; it is constant."[8]

Things are no better in other segments of the core imperial world order. The invasion of migrants from NATO-defeated Middle Eastern countries is destabilizing its European part. The virtual collapse of the concept of multiculturalism that inspired the Euro-integrators is undermining the core values of the EU, where disintegration trends are gaining momentum.[9] Demonstrations of "yellow waistcoats" shake France, neo-Nazis demand the expulsion of migrants in Germany, nationalist governments in Austria and Hungary try to at least partially restore sovereignty, populist political parties in Italy and other Western European countries try to unite people based on traditional moral values and socialist ideals, separatists in Catalonia demand independence from Spain, and all together—from Brussels bureaucracy.

An already tense situation has been further exacerbated by the pandemic. The coronavirus that entered China boomerangs back to NATO countries, causing panic in the population and halting the mechanisms of economic reproduction. Judging by the disastrous consequences of the epidemic in Italy, the sovereignty-deprived governments of these countries are proving far less effective than the Chinese in mobilizing people and resources to fight against biological weapons.

It should be noted that the manifesto of the "yellow waistcoats" is similar in its demands to those of the protesters in the US in the sense that it is incompatible with the principles of capitalism and Euro-bureaucratic imperialism. The demonstrators cover with their demands the whole range of topics that are important in France: fair taxation and distribution of the national income, cancellation of household debts, a ban on the retail sale of GMO (genetically modified organism) foods, etc. Together with the victories of the so-called "populist" parties in Italy, the Czech Republic, and Hungary, which combine socialist principles and conservative values in their ideology, this all points to a serious shift in the public consciousness of the core countries of the imperial WEO.

The popular masses feel the need for revolutionary changes in the socio-economic system far better than the ruling elites. There is an objective reason for this: the sharp decline in the share of wages in the distribution of GDP against the background of the rapid growth of financial market capitalization and stagnation in the productive sphere. The political shift toward populism, accelerated by the pandemic of 2020, marks a shift in the rhetoric of public figures in favor of workers versus capitalists, isolationism versus globalization, and the priority of health over wealth.[10]

However, the second defeat of the socialist B. Sanders in the primaries of the US Democratic Party shows the inability of even the opposition part of the American political elite to meet the urgent changes in the political and economic structure of society and begin to implement the institutions of the new WEO. In this connection, Lenin's definition of a revolutionary situation comes to mind: the grassroots does not want to, and the top cannot.

The growing socio-political tension in the countries of the core of the imperial world economic order is caused by the long-term stagnation of the population's income, stagnant youth unemployment, growing social inequality, degradation of the cultural and moral environment, which is a consequence of the exhaustion of opportunities for further economic development within the existing system of institutions and production relations. The pandemic has further exacerbated these trends. Despite a sharp increase in public expenditure (Figure 24), approaching the historic high of World War II, in order to mitigate its negative social consequences, social and political tensions in the US are increasing.

In response to the economic contraction and increased public expenditure caused by the pandemic, the monetary authorities of the US and other issuers of world currencies have increased the money supply even further. In just 14 years since the start of the global financial crisis in 2008, the amount of dollars in circulation has risen almost fivefold, the Japanese yen more than fivefold, and the euro and the yuan more than doubled. Against this background, the policy of the Bank of Russia to withdraw money from the economy looks marginal and ridiculous (Figure 25).

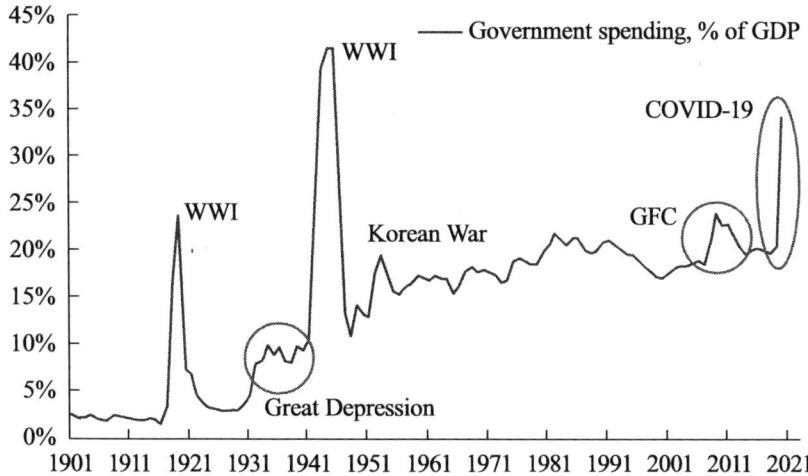

Figure 24   US Government Spending since 1901

Source: BofA Research Investment Committee, Global Financial Data.

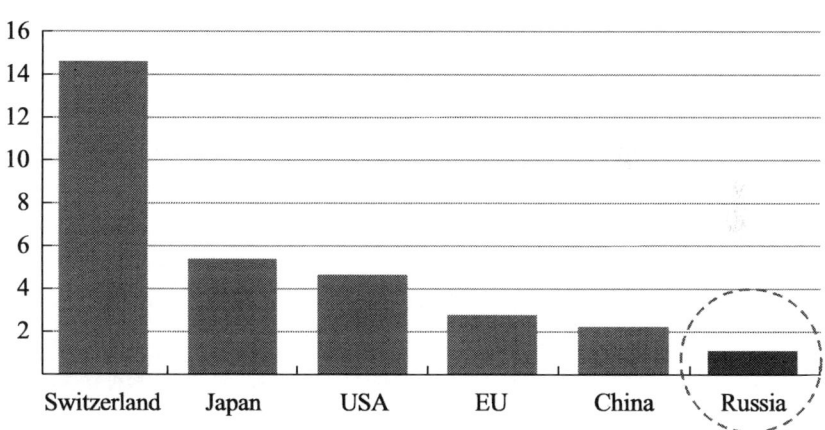

Figure 25   Increase in the Monetary Base of Some Currencies (2007–March 2020), Times

Source: M. Ershov, based on data from respective central banks.
Note: * calculated in US dollars at the corresponding exchange rate, ** calculated with M0.

As a Bank of America study notes,[11] "The Fed's balance sheet as a percentage of GDP ranged from 0% to 3% in World War I, from 2% to 11% in World War II, from 6% to 15% after the Lehman Brothers bankruptcy, from 19% to 36% in

2020. Whereas previously the US Central Bank's balance sheets were only $4 trillion, now they are $20 trillion; the main result has been asset price inflation." (Figure 26).

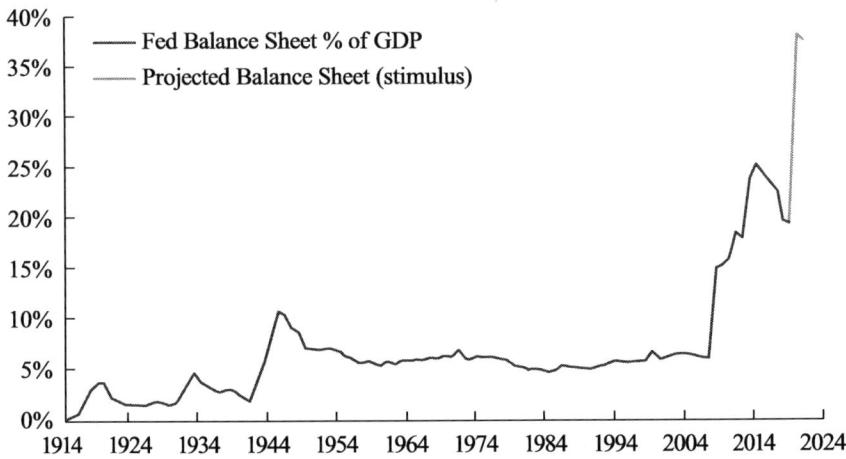

Figure 26   Balance of the Federal Reserve System (FRS) since 1914

Source: BofA Global Investment Strategy, Haver, Federal Reserve Board.

The authors of the study note the loss of autonomy of central banks: under increasing political pressure, they are forced to increase lending to governments, increasing public debt (global debt has reached $255 trillion, i.e., 322% of global GDP). The rapidly growing "financial bubble" of US government debt has gone beyond all conceivable limits of sustainability (Figure 27). Its exponential growth shows that the monetary authorities have lost control of the monetary system. It has clearly entered a turbulent operating mode with spontaneous crisis collapses.

The coronavirus pandemic has focused public attention on issues of public survival and safety, giving the key players manipulating the US financial market an opportunity to quietly begin to burst their bloated financial bubbles. But they do not have full control of the situation. Thanks to the "coordinated" work of financial robots according to set algorithms for decision-making on the sale of securities, the market decline quickly became avalanche-like and uncontrollable, reinforced by a chain reaction of "margin calls" on the networks of bank loans.

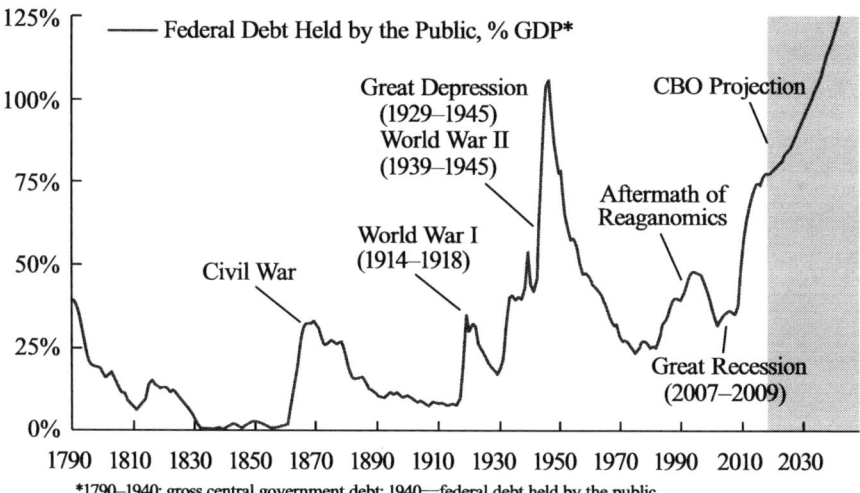

Figure 27   Dynamics of US Government Debt over the Last 230 Years

Source: BofA Global Investment Strategy.

The covenants of most of their corporate borrowers would be "breached," and a growing chain of defaults could trigger an end-to-end insolvency of the banking system. To prevent this, the US Federal Reserve has decided to inject $2.5–3 trillion into it, along with $2.2 trillion in US government support for households. The bulk of these funds will be concentrated in the financial sector and will be spent not to support production but to pump up financial bubbles. Thus, an increase in the monetary base by a factor and a half, unfunded, will not be associated with the growth of commodity production and, according to traditional monetarist ideas, should inevitably cause macroeconomic destabilization.

Another US financial market slump in 2020 is paralyzing the replication of the core of America's age-old capital accumulation cycle, much of which is devaluing, taking away the savings of millions of citizens. Although many observers see the unfolding financial crisis as being managed by the US Fed-linked financial power elite with the aim of sterilizing the excess money supply and redistributing assets in their favor, its scope may exceed the stabilization capacity of the US monetary authorities.

The calculation seems to be that the sterilization of the previously issued excess money supply by the implosion of another financial bubble will cleanse the financial market for the next pump of money. Simultaneously with the deflation of the US financial market by $15 trillion, the US Federal Reserve has launched another bubble. The US Federal Reserve has initiated another large-scale issue of up to $10 trillion to buy new portions of Treasuries issued to finance D. Trump's anti-crisis programs. Thus, the financial oligarchy controlling the Fed, under the guise of fighting the coronavirus pandemic, carried out its usual maneuver by shifting its liabilities to the US government. By shedding their liabilities and dragging the government into new debt, the Fed-linked banks ensured that the financial market recovered, pushing the uninformed players out of the market in the process. This time, however, the situation could spiral out of control. The acceleration of the already unprecedented money issue of the last decade could cause galloping inflation from the financial market to the consumer market. All the more so, a large part of the money issue as part of the anti-crisis policy to deal with the consequences of the pandemic is being used directly to finance consumer spending by citizens.

As many analysts and even IMF and US Federal Reserve officials have pointed out, the US has never seen such a scale of unsecured money issues and financial system bloat in its history.

As can be seen in Figure 28, the US budget deficit could be well above the level of the 1930s when the dollar was pegged to gold, twice as high as in 2009 and comparable to World War II levels. The observed doubling of the Fed's balance sheet in one year in 2020 has never happened in history. According to many economists, the consequences of such a monetary pumping could be disastrous. And most likely, it will be because the expectation of a catastrophe is in the air, or rather even in the public consciousness of Americans.

In order to reduce the cost of servicing the avalanche of public debt, the US President has demanded that the US Federal Reserve further reduce the refinancing rate to negative levels. In real terms, it has been around zero for a long time now, occasionally turning negative. This is causing a systemic failure of all financial risk assessment methods on which investment decisions are based. A continuation of this condition will inevitably cause a profound disruption of the reproduction mechanisms of the world economy. The negative price of money will make it impossible to further accumulate capital in the US-centric financial system and stimulate its outflow to the countries of the new world economic order.

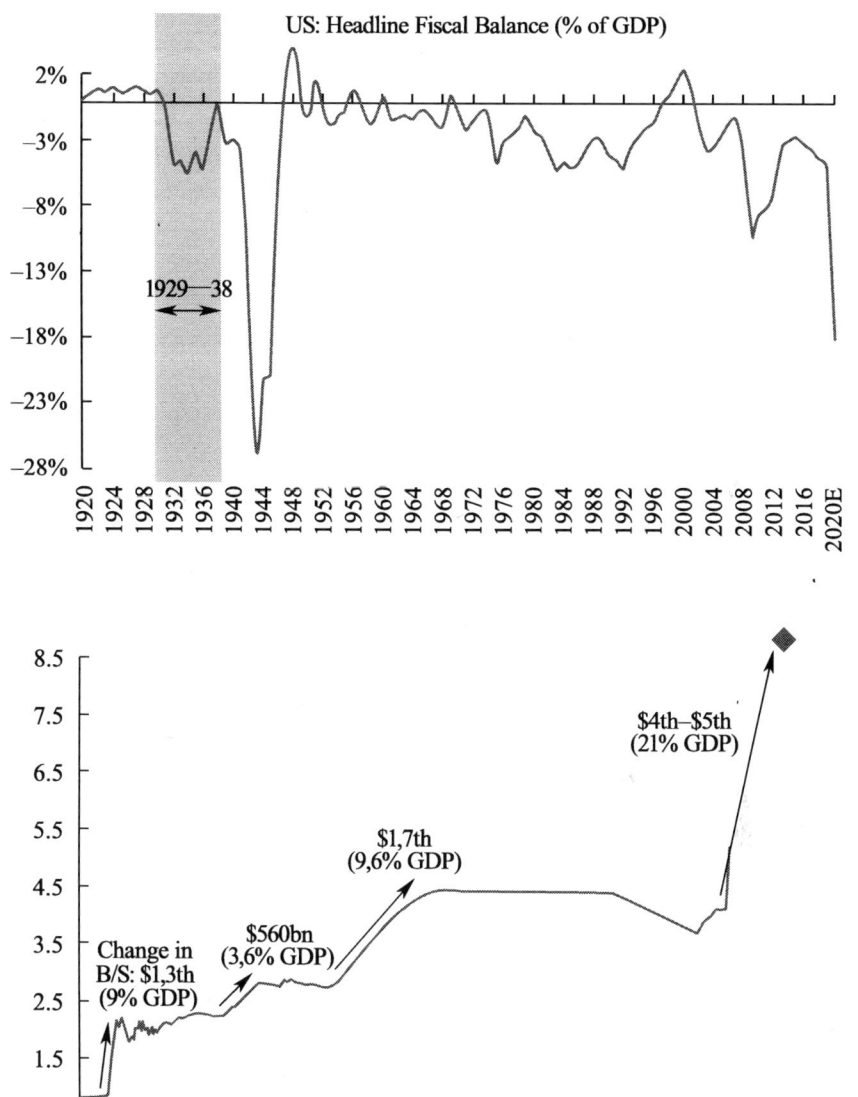

Figure 28   Fed Budget Deficit and Balance Sheet Projections

Source: Chetan Ahya, Morgan Stanley chief economist.

The policy of stimulating economic activity by means of unlimited money supply after the financial crisis in 2008 has so far not caused inflation due to the sterilization of the excess money supply in periodic financial market crashes. The four-step mechanism of monetary policy has been operating: "money issue–increased lending to government and business–implosion and bursting of financial bubbles." The bulk of the dollar issue was tied up in speculative transactions in derivatives "financial pyramids" and "hung on" in the financial market and then destroyed by the bursting of financial bubbles. This process has become rhythmic, indicating that the financial market is moving into a turbulent mode of functioning (Figure 29).

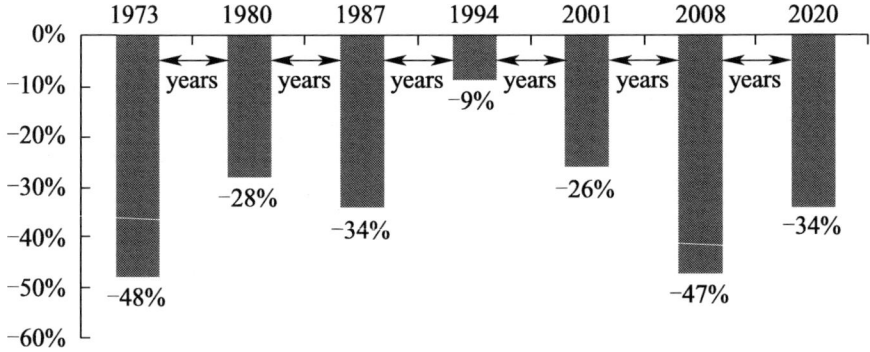

Figure 29   "Cyclicality" of Downturns (S&P 500 Index Performance)

Source: M. Ershov, Bloomberg.

There is no doubt that the ongoing financial crisis will again be accompanied by the collapse of the incredibly inflated financial derivatives bubbles, which have become even larger since the global financial crisis of 2008. As a consequence of the policy of continually postponing the reform of the global financial system and maintaining its reproduction by increasing money supply, system-wide risk, which can be measured in the ratio of off-balance sheet liabilities of the largest, above all US banks to the size of their balance sheets, is steadily increasing. Compared to the beginning of the 2008 crisis, this ratio has increased from 30 to 50 times (Figure 30).

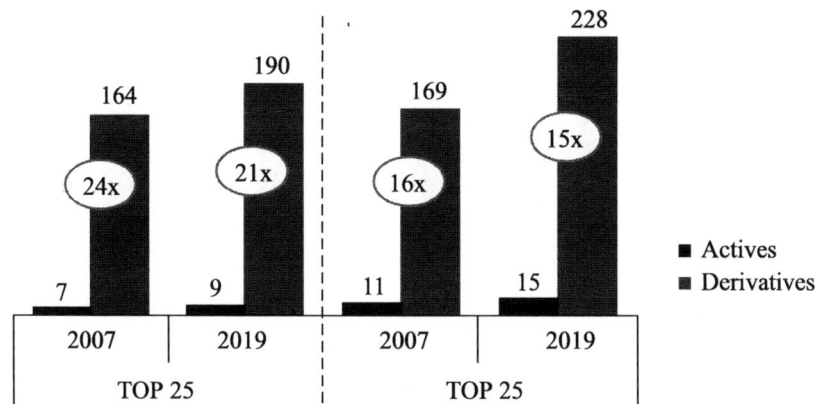

Figure 30   Largest (Top 5 and Top 25) US Financial Holding Companies and
Derivatives Holdings: Derivatives Volume, Assets (Trillion USD) and
Derivatives Mix (Times)

Source: M. Ershov, based on data from the Office of the Comptroller of the Currency.

Today's financial market information technology system is based on automatic algorithms executed by robots whose operations are programmed according to certain rules. The application of these rules is harsh: as soon as the financial bubble stops inflating, the first players leave, followed by an avalanche of speculators and the collapse of the financial market. No anti-crisis measures can stop this mechanism of financial crisis, which becomes spontaneous and leads to the bankruptcy of many funds and banks and a drop in investment activity.

Judging by the low inflation on the commodity market, the bulk of the increase in money is being held in the financial market, which, as shown above, has entered turbulence mode. Although interest rates are at an all-time low, even turning negative not only in real terms but sometimes in nominal terms, the real sector in the core countries of the existing world economic order does not absorb the growing money supply. In order to at least partly tie it up, the IMF imposes tight monetary policies on peripheral countries that force their borrowers, including governments, to apply for loans in world currencies and also create conditions for speculative capital inflows that profit from inflated debt yields (encouraging so-called carry trade).

The unsustainability of the global financial system is still only increasing. The leading public finance systems in the world economy (US, Japan, PIGS countries (Portugal, Ireland, Greece, and Spain) in Europe) operate largely on emission.

For example, in Japan, for every yen generated from tax revenues, almost 2 yen is issued against debt growth; in the US, for every dollar of tax revenues, another dollar is issued against treasury bills; some European countries are almost entirely dependent on inflows from the ECB and external creditors). In essence, the issuers of the world's reserve currencies have embarked on a "pyramidal" principle of increasing public debt, which dooms the entire global financial system, as well as the national systems of public finance, social, medical and pension security of developed countries to self-destruction, which can be triggered by a sharp exacerbation of the global financial crisis during the coronavirus pandemic.

To cushion the negative effects of the previous global financial crisis in 2008, unprecedented measures were taken to bail out systemically important banks. The US Federal Reserve issued, according to congressional committee estimates, $16 trillion, which was injected into 20 US and European banks.[12] To prevent the bankruptcy of European countries, the rest of the G20 countries chipped in with $430 billion, transferred to the IMF to finance an anti-crisis program.

Today, the situation is different. Firstly, the scale of the financial bubbles is much larger than the derivatives pyramid that collapsed in 2008. 30, the monetary base of dollars, euros, and pounds has more than quadrupled, and much of this issuance (with money and credit multipliers) has gone into inflating financial bubbles. Derivative pyramids have become 30%–50% larger. Consequently, the fall of the financial market will also be deeper. In the spring of 2020, its capitalization has fallen by more than a third, and the amount of outstanding liabilities is estimated at $15 trillion, representing 70% of the US money supply.

Secondly, we should not expect the kind of international solidarity against the financial crisis that was evident at the last G20. It is now clear that the G20 is being manipulated by Washington, as all its decisions are prepared by American experts, and officials in other countries are following their lead in convincing their political leadership to follow in the footsteps of the US. The promised reform of the IMF has in fact turned out to be a sham. The Financial Stability Bureau, created at the suggestion of the G7 countries, acts as a supervisor of the financial authorities of other countries and controls the "free" movement of their money. It is unlikely that China, Russia, Argentina, India, and other countries, which last time were persuaded to donate to the EU by the US and its allies, will accept the role of donor again in the hybrid war launched against them by Washington.

Thirdly, the US financial sanctions have discredited the dollar as a global currency. For Russia, Iran, Venezuela, China, and many other countries affected by these sanctions, the dollar has become a toxic currency in which all transactions have become a heightened risk. Measures taken by them to de-dollarize currency reserves and mutual trade provoke a flight from the dollar, which may take an avalanche character and sharply narrow the financial base for servicing the US national debt. The inevitable fall in external demand for their treasuries would then have to be replaced by money emission, which could put the US government debt growth into "aggravation mode" whereby the system loses stability and "goes into a tailspin." The prerequisites for this have been created by the preceding period of US government debt accumulation, which has long been serviced by a "pyramid scheme" of unlimited money emission.

Fourthly, there is a high probability of galloping inflation from the US financial market into the real sector and the consumer market. With the financial market disorganized, the money left over from the bursting of the financial bubbles could flow into the consumption of material goods. Judging by the rapid rise of prices for meat and other foodstuffs (which can only partly be explained by monopolization of the commodity distribution network), this process is already taking place. On the one hand, this will help investment and economic recovery. But, on the other hand, their volume is so much greater than the output potential that it will inevitably cause inflation and disorganize the reproduction of the economy.

The likelihood of a collapse of the dollar financial system is thus greater than ever before. China, Russia, Iran, and other countries against which the US is waging a hybrid war are already taking measures to reduce dependence on the dollar. They are building their own interbank information exchange systems to replace SWIFT (Society for Worldwide Interbank Financial Telecommunication), switching to settlements in national currencies, diversifying currency reserves, and exchanging currency and credit swaps. In this way, they protect themselves from the consequences of the uncontrolled unfolding of the financial crisis, which draws liquidity to the center of the American financial system. In any future scenario, the latter will weaken, and an alternative financial system that is emerging in the Asian capital accumulation cycle will develop. And that means an inevitable contraction of US financial capabilities and a reduction of non-equivalent international economic exchange in their favor. That, in turn, will lead to a sharp decline in the military and political power of the United States, which will have to shed its exorbitant military spending, which generates huge state budget deficits.

So far, the course of events in the US has been characterized by growing chaos. On the one hand, following Trump's decision to withdraw the US from the Transatlantic Trade and Investment and Trans-Pacific Partnership agreements, the trend toward liberal globalization has been reversed. His own decisions to launch a trade war with the PRC have reversed it. In doing so, the US has effectively undermined the foundations of the existing world economic order in which, after the collapse of the USSR, it occupies a central position.

On the other hand, there has been a split in the US ruling elite. The so-called "deep state" has turned the state machine into the former service trajectory of the transnational financial oligarchy with the election of Biden. The unfolding crisis strengthens its position by facilitating a concentration of capital.

However, no amount of tactical maneuvering will ensure that the US wins economic competition with China and other Southeast Asian countries. Despite the enormous issue of global currency, the US financial and banking system is losing out to the Chinese system for financing international cooperation. For example, the AidData study cited by A. Cooley and D. Nexon found that China's total foreign aid from 2000 to 2014 reached $354 billion, approaching the total US aid of $395 billion. Since then, the PRC has managed to overtake the US in the amount of aid given to other states each year. It is important to take into account the quality of that aid and its fundamental orientation: the US mainly subsidizes political projects and feeds the financial market. China, on the other hand, concentrates on creative investments in development—transport, logistics, and geological exploration.

The aggressive policy of the US only enhances the desire of China and other countries to get rid of monetary and technological dependence on the US, encouraging them to force the formation of a new world economy and the development of key industries of the new technological paradigm. They are able to do this much more effectively and faster than the US, whose ruling elite is resistant to institutional change. If Democrats succeed in putting the United States back into the rut of liberal globalization, it will immediately reduce the competitiveness of its economy. Failure to retain leadership in the productive sphere will push the US ruling elite to use non-economic methods against competitors in any case, involving a combination of soft power tools against well-armed and politically independent countries and hard power to retain control over the weak and politically dependent.

Thus, events in the US are leaning toward an unfavorable scenario. The coronavirus psychosis reinforces this trend as it creates conditions for the usurpation of power by the power structures. Once Trump's simple methods of throwing money at the needy show their ineffectiveness, panic and popular discontent may provoke a political crisis, which will increase the aggressiveness of the American power elite.

Up to now, the American leadership has flooded all problems with the issue of money. This policy, as mentioned above, has significantly mitigated the depression that will follow the change of technological modes, keeping the economy in stagnation mode. However, sustainable economic growth cannot be achieved with such policies. And it has limitations, determined by the ability of the economy to absorb the increasing money supply. These limits have long been exceeded, and without a radical restructuring of the socio-economic development management system, continued monetary pumping is fraught with macroeconomic destabilization.

It is interesting to note that the unprecedented growth in cash issuance in the US has not been matched by improvements in payment and settlement technology. China is the world leader in mobile payments, with the US in sixth place. In 2019, the volume of such transactions in China was $80.5 trillion. The projected total volume of mobile payments in the PRC is $111 trillion, and $130 billion in the US. This would seem to indicate that the bulk of US money issuance is tied up in financial market speculative circuits without reaching end consumers.

China's system for regulating economic reproduction has emerged from the pandemic crisis even stronger. Its monetary authorities took advantage of the financial market decapitalization to consolidate national control over foreign-dependent segments of the Chinese economy. It will undoubtedly become even more efficient due to falling energy and commodity prices and more attractive to foreign investment. Although the fall in production due to plant shutdowns during the epidemic is estimated to be $50–70 billion, it is recovering rapidly, while the US and the EU have yet to experience it. The PRC is the only G20 country that has managed to restore economic growth in 2020.

The PRC has managed to avoid the bankruptcies of systemically important banks and state-supported enterprises, which fully control the country's banking system and its transport, energy, and social infrastructure. The leading European, American, and Japanese banks before the current crisis could be closed down by Basel 3 criteria due to insufficient or even negative equity capital. They were kept afloat and could only service their liabilities thanks to a gigantic money supply.

The US administration's attempts to stop China's development through a trade war and economic sanctions have been unsuccessful. Moreover, the US is clearly losing in this war, losing markets in China and worsening the competitiveness of its products due to the loss of Chinese suppliers and the disruption of established technological chains. "What will the US do when Boeing loses the Chinese market?" asks Lifschultz. Of course, he believes, this could be the end of Boeing. "What happens when General Motors is dumped from China?" echoes the analyst with a similar response, as more than half of GM's global sales (7.7 million vehicles) come from China (4 million vehicles). "It will be interesting to see if the US government can effectively block US companies such as Intel, Qualcomm, Xilinx, and Nvidia from continuing to engage with Chinese companies. A total of 40% of their sales come from the Chinese market, and there is some question as to whether they will survive if they lose that market," the analyst reasonably concludes.[13]

In response to US sanctions against Chinese IT leaders (Huawei and ZTE), China has embarked on a technology fast track. In January 2020, Chinese President Xi Jinping announced a new 15-year plan for science and technology innovation to accelerate its national innovation campaign. China continues to develop its knowledge-intensive industry, investing heavily in new factories and technology despite trade tensions and a slowing IT market. China has the most ambitious projects in the world to build high-tech factories and plants (some 30) focused on light-emitting diodes (LED), memory chips, and other technologies that define the element base of modern information and digital technologies.

Against this background, a trade war against China would, as has already been emphasized in this monograph, be devastating for the American industry itself, which is deprived of components, cheap electronic components, jobs, and a market. This reverse effect is already evident in the example of American IT leaders. For example, Apple's shares lost 3% only after hints that Chinese customers will avoid the iPhone if the WeChat app is not supported by the device. As of the second quarter of 2020, China accounts for 30% of iPhone sales and 15% of Apple's total revenue. The latter is heavily reliant on overseas sales, while Tencent (WeChat's parent company) generates 96% of its revenue in mainland China, so the impact of a US ban on it would be negligible.

The further unfolding of the global financial crisis will objectively be accompanied by a strengthening of the PRC and a weakening of the US. As Dr. Wang Wen rightly points out, "The global community sees China growing and the US shrinking on the parameters of international investment, mergers and acquisitions, logistics and currency. Globalization is becoming less Americanized and more Chineseized.[14]

NOTES

1. A. I. Subbeto, "Noospheric Russia: A Breakthrough Strategy," in *Foundations of Noosphere Russian Studies* (SPb.: Asterion, 2018), 164.
2. S. Glazyev, *The Eeconomy of the Future: Does Russia Have a Chance?* (Moscow: Book World, 2017).
3. Concept proposed by General Secretary of the CPC Central Committee Xi Jinping at the 18th National Congress of the CPC in November 2012.
4. "The Nature Medicine," November 9, 2015.
5. David K. Lifschultz, "The US Government's Destruction of Apple Begins,"August 12, 2020, URL: https://operationdisclosure1.blogspot.com/2020/08/the-us-governments-destruction-of-apple.html.
6. "White People, Here Are 10 Requests from a Black Lives Matter Leader," URL: https://www.leoweekly.com/2017/08/white-people/ 16.08.2017.
7. A. Lukin, "The Theory of Universal Racism," *Russia in Global Politics*, no. 5 (2020): 119–136.
8. A. Cooley and D. Nexon, "How Hegemony Ends," *Russia in Global Politics*, no. 5 (2020): 137–153.
9. A. Fursov, World Struggle: *Anglo-Saxons against the Planet* (Moscow: Book World, 2017); K. Malik, *The Quest for a Moral Compass* (Atlantic Books, 2015).
10. BofA Global Investment Strategy, "The Longest Pictures," May 30, 2020.
11. Ibid.
12. F. Smirnov, *The Global Financial and Economic Architecture, Deconstruction* (Moscow: Buki Vedi, 2015).
13. "The US Government's Destruction of Apple Begins," URL: https://operationdisclosure1.blogspot.com/2020/08/the-us-governments-destruction-of-apple.html. August 12, 2020.
14. Wang Wen, "China Won't Watch Globalisation Die," *The B&R News*, June 16, 2020.

CHAPTER 8

The BRI as a Mechanism for Assembling the New WEO

8.1 General Background

China's B&R international cooperation initiative currently involves more than 70 countries. At its core is the implementation of joint investment projects to improve the competitiveness of participating countries and the well-being of their populations. The amount of investment by the PRC in these economies between 2005 and 2018 was about half a trillion dollars[1] compared with 87 billion dollars of investment by the World Bank (Figure 31).

The PRC's investment in the B&R countries is an order of magnitude greater than the much-publicized American Indo-Pacific Vision Initiative (AIPV). The scale of this project pales in comparison to the AIPV, which plans to spend an estimated $4 trillion to $8 trillion. The B&R investment portfolio also dwarfs the Marshall Plan to finance the post-war reconstruction of Western Europe, which at today's dollar value could be valued at $180 billion ($12 billion 70 years ago)[2] (Figure 32).

Not the liberalization of markets in the interests of transnational corporations and foreign investors, but the growth of production based on the realization of joint investments and the creation of joint productions combining the competitive advantages of the cooperating countries is the main motive of international integration in the new world economic order.

■ BRI-participating economies
■ North America
▨ Sub-Saharan Africa (excluding Sub-Saharan African economies identified in the BRI)
■ Latin America
■ Europian Union (excluding EU economies identified in the BRI)
◧ Middle East & North Africa (excluding MENA economies identified in the BRI)
▤ Australia
▨ Other economies

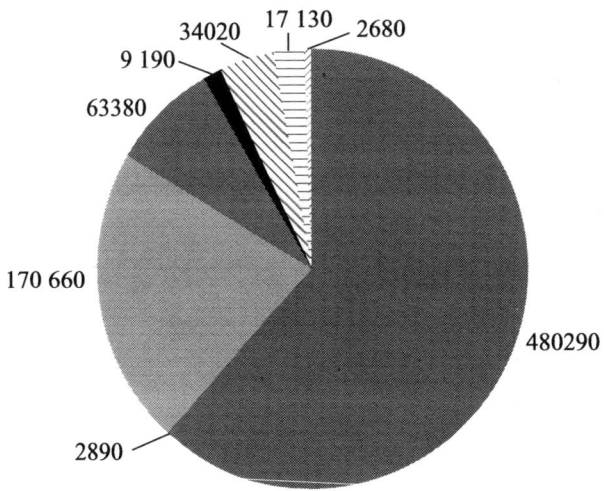

Figure 31   Chinese External Investment in Construction (Cumulative Notional
Amount, Expressed in Millions of USD), 2005–2018

Source: American Enterprise Institute (AEI), China Global Investment Tracker Data Base, 2018.

Mutual respect for national interests, the inviolability of sovereign rights
of states to pursue independent policies, the principle of mutual benefit of
international trade and financial and economic relations, and the norms of
international law are restored. Based on this approach, the SCO, ASEAN, and
EAEU countries form a new world economic order attractive to all developing
countries. The share of the countries participating in the BRI in world GDP and
international trade has reached 1/3, and together with China, it exceeds half.
Already in 2017, in terms of GDP (in terms of purchasing power parity), the
PRC's output exceeded that of the US, and the B&R countries exceeded that of
all NATO countries (Figure 33).

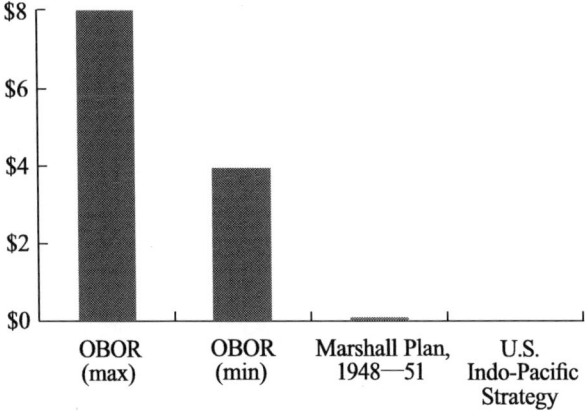

Figure 32   Financing of Investments under the Indo-Pacific Project, the Marshall Plan, and the OBOR

Source: D. Steinbock.

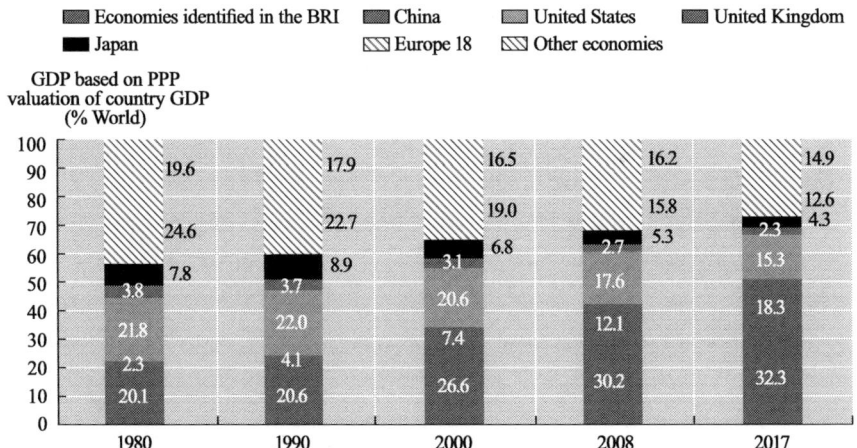

Figure 33   Comparison of GDP Size of Leading One Belt and One Road Countries and Regions of the World, 1980–2017

Source: IMF World Economic Outlook Database, 2017 estimates.

Simultaneously with the rapid growth of the "core" of the integral world economic order, the remaining "core" of the imperial world economic order is relatively shrinking. This process is sustainable and will continue in the future. Table 24 only partially reflects this process: the countries of Indochina, Iran, Pakistan, and in the future, Russia and other EAEU states, Japan, and South Korea can be added to the "core" of the integrated world economic order.

Japan and South Korea have leaped into the ranks of developed states from the periphery of, respectively, the British and American century cycles of capital accumulation and are now participating in the formation of the core of the Asian cycle of capital accumulation. They act as a bridge between the imperial and integral world economies, linking their capital and technology markets. In Table 24, these countries are already included in the core of the new world economic order and the Asian capital accumulation cycle corresponding to it.

Russia, which as part of the USSR was one of the two cores of the imperial world economic cycle, after the collapse of the Soviet Union, found itself on the periphery of the American capital accumulation cycle. Russia's importance in the global economy was leveled accordingly. Having lost its reproducible integrity, the Russian economy is now embedded in the Asian cycle of capital accumulation as a raw material periphery. Theoretically, as a leading country of the EAEU, Russia could still join the core of the integrated world economic order if it manages to master its institutions in time, as well as to create the basic production capacities of the new technological order. Given this potential, the EAEU, including Russia, in Table 25, is also referred to as the core of the Asian capital accumulation cycle.

As Vinokurov states,[3] the BRI, launched by Xi Jinping in 2013, has come a long way in less than seven years. Hundreds of billions of dollars in investment flows have been part of it. The initiative has contributed to strong and sustained growth in trade across the Eurasian continent.

The B&R concept as a single document was developed by the State Development and Reform Committee of China, the Ministry of Foreign Affairs of China, and the Ministry of Commerce of China and presented in March 2015 under the title "Excellent Prospects and Practical Actions to Jointly Build the Silk Road Economic Belt and the 21st Century Maritime Silk Road."[4]

In substantive terms, the OPOP is an idea that can describe China's foreign economic policy for the coming years.[5] It aims to *actively seek a new model of international cooperation and global management and is positioned as a platform for international cooperation to create new drivers for joint development through the increased interconnectedness of infrastructure, trade, finance, and human capital.*

Table 24   Comparison of GDP "Core" American and Asian Capital Accumulation Cycles

Countries	1913	1950	1973	2000	2010	2020	2030
US and EU	54.7	54.4	49.2	43.4	36.5	32.4	18.2
China and India	16.3	8.8	7.7	17.0	28.7	41.1	52.0
Japan	2.6	3.0	7.8	7.2	5.4	4.4	3.2
Russia	8.5	9.6	9.4	2.1	2.4	2.7	3.0

Source: V. Sadovnichy, Y. Yakovets, and A. Akayev, eds., *Prospects and Strategic Priorities for BRICS Ascent* (Moscow: Moscow State University - Pitirim Sorokin-Nikolai Kondratiev International Institute - INES - National Committee for BRICS Studies - Institute of Latin America of the Russian Academy of Sciences, 2014); GDP data are derived from purchasing power parity (PPP) indicators; calculations for 1820–2000 were made by A. Maddison; calculations for 2010–2030 were made by Chinese scholars based on calculations of A. Maddison, *The World Economy: Historical Statistics* (Paris: OECD, 1995).

Table 25   Comparison of a Number of "Core" Indicators of American and Asian Capital Accumulation Cycles (% of World Total)

Indicators	2010	2020	2030
The "core" of the American capital formation cycle (US, EU, Canada)			
GDP	36.5	32.4	18.2
Share of exports	24.1	24.0	21.0
Share of imports	47.5	40.5	34.5
Share of high-tech exports	26.5	20.0	16.0
The "core" of the Asian capital accumulation cycle (China, Japan, India, South Korea, Singapore, Malaysia, the Middle East, the EAEC)			
GDP	33.1	45.5	55.2
Share of exports	16.9	25.4	33.0
Share of imports	15.7	27.5	37.3
Share of high-tech exports	28.0	33.0	38.0

Source: Hu Angan, Yan Yilong, and Wei Xing, eds., *China 2030: Toward Universal Prosperity Center for Country Studies of Tsinghua University* (People's University of China Press, 2011).

The B&R envisages the formation of "seven belts"—**transport, energy, trade, information, science and technology, agriculture, tourism,** and six economic corridors—"**China-Pakistan**" (China-Persian Gulf interconnection), "China-Mongolia-Russia"(connecting the economic zone around China's Bohai Gulf with Eastern Europe), "**China-Central Asia-South-West Asia**" (the corridor covers Kazakhstan, Kyrgyzstan, Tajikistan, Uzbekistan, Turkmenistan, Turkey, Iran, and the Arabian Peninsula countries), "**Bangladesh-China-India-Myanmar**" (China's relationship with South Asia), and "**A 'New Eurasian Land Bridge**" (a transport corridor passing through Russia, Kazakhstan, Belarus, Poland, and Germany, connecting China with Western Europe).

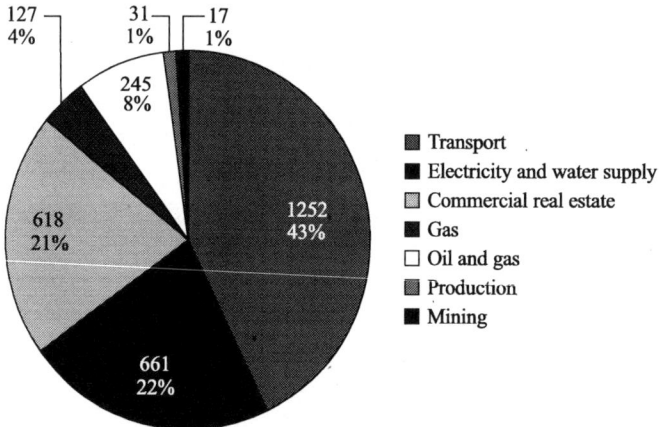

Figure 34   Sectoral Structure of Projects Involving China under the BRI

The BRI has two main objectives, one reflecting China's domestic economic interests and aiming to increase the country's economic growth rate and eliminate regional income disparities, and the other is to form comprehensive economic, political, and humanitarian links between the countries participating in the B&R projects.

8.2 The B&R Docking with the EAEU

8.2.1 The meaning of docking

The EAEU-the B&R interface is one example of multi-regional connectivity: the OPPO project is global in nature but economically promoted and supported by one country, China; the EAEU is an example of regional economic integration with historical, economic, and socio-cultural backgrounds.

For the countries of Eurasia, the BRI identifies **five areas of cooperation**:

(1) Strengthening policy coherence (exchange of views on economic development strategy and tactics, coordination of country economic strategies and elaboration of joint plans, measures to deepen regional integration)

(2) Intensifying road network construction (improving cross-border transport infrastructure to create a transport network linking East, West, and South Asia)

(3) Strengthening trade links (simplifying trade procedures and investment regimes, increasing the speed and quality of external economic transactions in the region)

(4) Reform of currency flows (transition to national currencies in exchange and settlement in current and capital transactions)

(5) Promotion of OSDP ideas among the population (gaining people's support, activating friendly contacts of peoples, strengthening their mutual understanding and friendship)

The initiative "represents one of the most ambitious global infrastructure investment strategies in human history."[6] It covers a wide range of infrastructure and development projects in sectors such as energy, transport, digital technologies, urban development, and water supply, geographically stretching from East Asia to Europe.

One cannot but agree with those experts who believe that China is thus addressing the dual challenge of harnessing its enormous investment potential and gradually increasing its geopolitical influence. China has signed corresponding agreements with 139 countries in all parts of the world. The most important feature of the B&R was the fact that accession to it was not subject to any political conditions or restrictions. Initially, China has demonstrated that it has specific financial resources and mechanisms to implement it (the Silk Road Fund [SRF] was established in 2014 with $40 billion in capital, and the AIIB in 2015 with $100 billion in capital). According to some estimates, China's investment in the B&R in the first five years has averaged $100 billion per year. Naturally, with such a scale of investment, certain difficulties and problems caused by spending inefficiencies could not help but arise. Beijing is aware of the need to make certain adjustments to the B&R, primarily in terms of improving the efficiency of its implementation and information support.

Thus, the April 2021 Boao Asia Forum was essentially an attempt to present the initiative as a "New Silk Road with a Human Face." The focus was on explaining the opportunities for mutual benefits and poverty reduction in the countries participating in the Chinese initiative. The forum showed that Beijing is ready to qualitatively increase transparency and improve procedures at all stages of development, expertise, approval, and implementation of the B&R projects. And recently, in line with the principle, "less is more, but more is better," concrete steps have been taken in this direction. In particular, China has sharply restricted funding limits for the two largest "political" state banks, the CDB and the Export-Import Bank of China, in overseas investment projects. At the same time, there is a trend toward a greater role for Chinese commercial banks with relevant internationally recognized expertise.

As the Chinese initiative has been implemented, a campaign to discredit it has begun to gain momentum in the West. There is an emphasis on the allegedly inevitable negative consequences of Chinese expansion for developing countries (falling into a "debt trap," corrupting local elites, and loss of political and economic independence). However, some Western think tanks take a more sober and realistic view. For example, according to the findings of Investigative Europe, Chinese investments have had a positive impact on the local economy and labor market, while no clear evidence of economic damage or extreme dependence on the countries involved has been found.[7] Furthermore, the German Bertelsmann Foundation estimates that between 2013 and 2017, the ONE PAYE countries received around $290 billion from various Western financial sources, while Beijing received $285 billion. In response to the promotion of the PPI, the West has been somewhat late in formulating alternative programs. Thus, in August 2018. The Vienna Institute for International Economic Studies proposed the creation of a €1 trillion European Silk Road over four years.[8] In June 2021, the Build Back Better World program was announced at the G7 summit, which aims to reduce the infrastructure deficit in the developing world by investing $40 trillion by 2035. There is no doubt that they will ultimately be framed by different political conditions.

Against the backdrop of a deepening confrontation with the US on the external front, China is focusing on developing trade and economic relations with its main economic partners, the EU and Asia-Pacific countries. In this regard, the year 2020 was marked by two critical developments for Beijing. In November 2020, the Comprehensive Regional Economic Partnership (CREP) was signed between ASEAN countries, China, Japan, Australia, New Zealand, and South

Korea. The EU-China Comprehensive Investment Agreement was signed in December 2020. At the end of 2020, trade turnover between the PRC and RCEP countries was $1.473 billion, and between the PRC and the EU was $649 billion.[9] In particular, the agreement with the EU was reached despite opposition from Washington, which sought stricter export controls on joint projects with China and restrictions on Chinese investment in sectors related to dual-use technologies and critical infrastructure (a similar investment agreement has yet to be negotiated between the US and China). The agreement thus already promises Europeans more privileged access to the Chinese market than Americans. It opens the possibility for European companies to invest in a number of sectors previously closed to foreign investors and also removes crucial joint venture requirements with Chinese companies that limit foreign investors' profits. At the same time, China continues to benefit from the openness of the EU market. In the long term, its gain is that EU policy toward the PRC becomes less dependent on the US. However, it should be borne in mind that it will be several years before the agreement enters into force, should the European Parliament ratify it successfully and other legal procedures go through. There is no doubt that the Americans, supported by their satellites in the EU—Poland, Lithuania, and others—will try to hamper the process.

8.2.2 Strategic vision for the docking between the EAEU and China's BRI

The international economic partnership should be based on the principles of harmonization of interests and mutually beneficial cooperation. In addition to the economic basis and institutional framework, the development agendas of the integration association and one of the world's largest economies should have a strategic vision of the directions and mechanisms of cooperation between the EAEU and the PRC. It seems that the practical convergence of the development vectors of the two diverse and multilevel participants should be carried out within the framework of a larger idea defining common key objectives and benchmarks. Such an idea is The Grand European Partnership (GEP), the economic part of which could be the EAEU-the B&R interface. The content of the GEP is largely similar to the B&R objectives in terms of the development of transport infrastructure, the establishment of preferential trade and economic regimes between the countries, and the promotion of industrial cooperation. At the same time, the GEP implements the concept of "integration of integrations," which implies an equal and mutually beneficial dialogue between countries and integration associations with unconditional respect for the national sovereignty of participating countries and non-interference in internal affairs. The GEP is based on a flexible system of legal norms, the operation of common institutions, and the implementation of joint projects for the benefit of all or most of the participants.

In view of the above, it is possible to identify areas for the practical implementation of the EAEU-the B&R interface as an element of the GEP:

(1) Coordinate economic development strategies and policies to implement them

It is important for the EAEU to develop its own interface strategy with the B&R in order to overcome competition from the emerging trade and economic mega-blocs around them. Unlike the B&R, which is not formalized in the PRC as a strategic planning document, the EAEU has a number of general economic and sectoral medium- and long-term development documents: Strategic directions of Eurasian economic integration until 2025, Main directions of industrial cooperation within the EAEU, Protocol on coordinated (coordinated) transport policy, etc. At the same time, some of the B&R projects are taken into account in PRC documents of the current Five-Year Plan, such as the SCO logistics park and PRC-Kazakhstan logistics cooperation. Given the intensification and deepening of the EAEU-the B&R cooperation, joint projects and measures within the B&R framework can be taken into account in the policy and strategic documents of the parties.

(2) The interconnectedness of the infrastructure of the EAEU member states and the PRC

The issue of transport and logistics infrastructure connectivity is a key issue in interconnectivity and determines, in fact, the economic potential of cooperation between the PRC and the EAEU. One of the main development areas of the EAEU is the realization of the transit potential of the member states' territories. To this end, the processes of forming a common market for transport services and implementing a coordinated transport policy within the EAEU have been launched. In addition to agreeing on the main elements of the common market and its regulatory mechanisms, it is necessary to assess the necessary modernization of the existing transport and logistics infrastructure and the construction of new ones.

(3) The mutual reduction of trade barriers and the development of measures to stimulate investment

The EAEU is working purposefully to liberalize foreign economic conditions, achieve preferential trade agreements with third countries, and identify and reduce barriers and restrictions to the free movement of goods, services, capital, and labor within the EAEU. The PRC generally enters into bilateral agreements with individual countries, defining trade and investment regimes. The current agreement between the EAEU and the PRC is non-preferential, but at the same time, it defines approaches to consider reducing mutual exemptions and restrictions. Currently, there are certain restrictions, usually non-tariff ones, in place between the PRC and the EAEU countries, which could be reconsidered from the perspective of EAEU and the B&R alignment.

(4) Deepening monetary and financial cooperation

This element of conjugation is due to the importance of ensuring the financial stability and security of the two regions. At present, trade and economic cooperation between the EAEU and PRC countries is largely serviced by third-country currencies, mainly the US dollar. If relations with the issuing country deteriorate, the risk of various kinds of restrictions increases. In this regard, a gradual transition to the use of national currencies in mutual settlements and investments will facilitate the formation of an independent regional monetary and payment system. A separate aspect of financial cooperation is the creation of joint institutions to provide financial support for the implementation of joint projects.

(5) Digitalization

It is a cross-cutting area that encompasses the above interface elements and is capable of acting as a *process* that ensures interaction between the main actors of the EAEU-the B&R interface, including in the areas of state and supranational regulation, application of customs and tariff, technical, sanitary and phytosanitary requirements, etc., and a separate industry producing digital goods and services both for domestic markets and for export to third countries.

It should be noted that the pairing process is quite heterogeneous and complex:

- Structural interweaving of the development agendas of the integration association and individual country
- Different substantive content of the development program of the EAEU and the PRC
- Differences in goals and expected results of conjugation
- Opposition from internal (monopolies, political pressure groups) and external (Western countries) forces

With this in mind, let us carry out a SWOT analysis of the EAEU-the B&R interface.

Table 26 SWOT Analysis of the EAEU-the B&R Interface

Strengths	Weaknesses
• Strategic geographic location of EAEU countries in terms of overland transit routes to the EU, Iran, Turkey • Proximity of geopolitical and geo-economic goals of EAEU countries and the PRC • Significant reserves of natural resources in the territories of the EAEU member states, including energy resources near the common border of the EAEU and the PRC • EAEU countries are strategically important suppliers of certain types of goods, services, and technologies to China • Existing production chains, as well as trade ties between businesses and companies of the EAEU countries and the PRC • Existence of quality transport infrastructure in EAEU and PRC, with the potential for additional capacity utilization • Trends toward trade liberalization in PRC's tertiary sector • Experience in developing independent financial messaging systems in the Russian Federation and PRC • High level of human development in the EAEU and PRC • Successful experience in implementing joint projects at the corporate and interstate levels	• Effects of EU and US sanctions • Commodity orientation of most exports, limited own unique goods, services, developments, and technologies in the world market • Limited production capacities of the EAEU countries, including in view of their obsolescence and physical deterioration • Weak economic growth rates and low capacity for independent financing of major projects • Relatively low level of investment attractiveness of EAEU economies • The ambiguous practice of implementing Chinese projects in the EAEU countries with the involvement of mainly Chinese labor force, equipment, and technology • China's support of the B&R projects in the areas of its own interests and to promote its products and services; • Prevalence of bilateral agreements between the EAEU countries and the PRC over the dialogue in the P5 format • Lack of coordinated position of the EAEU countries on the directions and mechanisms of cooperation with the PRC • Lack of information about China's market, rules, and procedures for foreign economic activities • Territorial remoteness of some EAEU countries (Armenia, partly Belarus) from the PRC, and, as a consequence, non-obvious benefits from the interface with the B&

(Continued)

Opportunities	Threats
• Accelerated implementation of EAEU objectives through synergies with the B&R, including in terms of the EAEU-2025 Digital Agenda and building the Greater Eurasian Partnership (GEP) • Economic impact of realizing the transit potential of EAEU stations in terms of PRC-EU land routes • Additional inflows of Chinese FDI to EAEU countries, including manufacturing and infrastructure sectors • Increased export potential of EAEU countries, including in terms of supply of high- and medium-tech products, due to easier access to PRC markets; Development of the services sector in the EAEU countries through increased exports to PRC of both transport and tourism services, as well as other services due to the liberalization of PRC regulation; • Creation of new jobs in the EAEU countries by opening new production facilities and implementing joint projects with the PRC • Loading of idle production capacities of EAEU countries; active use of established and formation of additional special economic zones and clusters of EAEU countries • Strengthening regional transport connectivity and expanding interregional cooperation • Opportunities for scientific and technological breakthroughs of the EAEU through increased access of EAEU countries to new technologies, business models, and managerial practices of the PRC • Development of scientific and technological cooperation, including education • Acceleration of commercialization of scientific developments in the EAEU countries	• Admission to the EAEU markets of low-quality and cheaper products from China and, as a consequence, structural and technological degradation of EAEU industries • Uncoordinated positions of the EAEU countries and the PRC in the development of the roadmap for interconnection, which may reduce the number of practically implemented measures • High level of bureaucracy in economic decision-making in the framework of the B&R interface • Deterioration of the environmental situation and increased social tensions as a result of the B&R projects in the EAEU countries • Possible sanctions and opposition to the EAEU-the B&R interface from third countries • Supplies of obsolete technology and equipment to the EAEU market; Relocation of production facilities of the past technological mode (usually labor-intensive) to the territory of EAEU countries • Increase of the Chinese diaspora in the EAEU countries and, as a consequence, possible territorial claims and a sharp rise in Sinophobic sentiments • Lack of compromise in discussing the conditions for the implementation of the B&R projects in the EAEU countries and, as a result, the adoption of conditions that correspond only to the interests of the PRC • Preservation of tariff and non-tariff barriers for EAEU exporters when supplying to the PRC market • Strengthening the economic and financial dependence of EAEU countries on PRC

(Continued)

- Development of financial cooperation and strengthening the financial stability of the PRC-EAEU region by expanding the use of national currencies in mutual settlements, developing financial products and preferential lending in national currencies (primarily RMB), etc.
- Formation of a powerful political-economic alliance promoting the values and standards of Eurasian integration and ONE POLICY - ONE PATH in the international arena
- Reducing the impact of global risks for the EAEU member states and the PRC through coordinated actions
- Forming the contour of energy security and sustainability on the scale of the EAEU-PRC macro-region

- Reducing the political weight of the EAEU (Russia) in the Eurasian region
- Weak development prospects for small and medium-sized businesses as a result of the EAEU-China interface
- Increased competition between the rouble and the yuan as regional currencies in the EAEU

8.2.3 Docking framework of transport and logistics

As Vinokurov points out, China-EAEU-EU transcontinental transit has excellent dynamics and prospects. The dynamics of shipments from China to Europe and back via the EAEU rail network are very strong. The volume of transit traffic could grow by a further 3–4 times. Targeted investments in infrastructure and further regulatory progress are required for this. Next on the agenda is a structural issue for the Russian economy—realizing the potential of landlocked industrial and agricultural centers.

Rail container transit between China and the EU through the Eurasian Union (namely through Kazakhstan, Russia, and Belarus) increased by 43% in 2015, by half in 2016, by 70% in 2017, and by 70% in 2018. The transit of goods between China and the EU (i.e., Kazakhstan, Russia, and Belarus) increased by 30% in 2019. Even in the first quarter of 2020, amid the COVID-19 crisis, it continued to grow! Of course, the growth came from a low base, but today, more than 1.5% of traffic between China and the EU is overland. This share could grow several times more, depending on progress on physical and soft infrastructure. The marginal estimate of the share that overland transit can "take" in total trade between China and the EU is, in our view, 6%. It sounds modest, but it is in fact a major challenge and good business. The low percentage in absolute terms should not be looked down upon: one should keep in mind that we are talking about premium high-margin nomenclature, which already now provides Russian, Kazakhstani, and Belarusian railways with a combined revenue of $2 billion. We are talking about niches of the highest-margin goods—electronics, automotive components, pharmaceuticals, cosmetics, and foodstuffs. So, there is an interesting niche. In addition, entirely new niches may emerge. Reaching transit volumes of 0.65–0.75 million FEU (40-foot containers) is realistic in the next 5–8 years. Moreover, the flows have already gone from Europe to China: BMW takes its car parts to China via the EAEU; Hewlett-Packard is also doing the same with its laptop parts.

Of course, for Russia, topics related to the BRI are not limited to continental transit. The picture of endless freight trains passing through Russia on their way from China to Europe and back is good enough for a newspaper editorial, but does not provide enough justification for serious economic and political investment. What is the overall interest of rail transit in Russia? On this point, E. Vinokurov gives the following reasons why such transit is interesting.

(1) First of all, it is just a small but good business in itself. According to Russian Railways, their revenue from transit in 2018 has already approached $800 million. But it is a fairly low-margin business.

(2) Increasing the level of containerization of the Russian economy as a whole. The Russian railway system is well-developed, but the level of containerization is low, and this prevents it from improving efficiency and fitting into global value chains. Containers account for only 2% of traffic and 6% of revenue in the Russian railway system. This is 2–3 times lower than advanced economies.

(3) As an institutional "framework" to attract Chinese investment in the Russian economy. So far, they are not available in the transport sector in Russia. However, the importance of the B&R for Russia goes beyond transport, and Chinese investments in oil and gas and mining are growing rapidly. We also expect them to grow in real estate and agriculture.

(4) In general, as a tool to enhance Russia's role in the global economy and politics. Russia is interested in the BRI because it makes the world more multipolar.

(5) As part of an emerging "Greater Eurasia," which is also in line with Russian foreign policy priorities. In the current discussions on Greater Eurasia, there is a great deal of rhetoric, whereas cargo transit represents a real item on the current agenda in EU-EAEU-China relations.

(6) The BRI is making serious investments in Central Asia. Russia has a strategic interest in the prosperity of the Central Asian region. Poor and unstable Central Asia poses many risks for Russia. But a prosperous Central Asia gives Russia an attractive 80-million-dollar market at its doorstep.

The book[10] lists the challenges and constraints associated with the further growth of transit traffic under the B&R "umbrella."

First, the explosive growth in container trains and container cargo volumes on China-EAEU-EU routes was largely due to the Chinese authorities subsidization of rail exports introduced in 2013. The actual "zeroing" of the container freight tariff on PRC territory contributed to the prompt switching of Chinese exporters' cargo flows from maritime routes to rail transport. The risk of zeroing or substantially reducing subsidies constantly looms over the growth prospects of freight traffic. Given the small fiscal burden (we estimated the average subsidy at 0.4% of the value of goods transported) and the strategic and economic importance of these processes, maintaining subsidies is desirable. If they are abolished, the tariff will grow from $5.5–6 to $8–85 thousand. For part of the current commodity nomenclature, this would be an incentive to return to sea routes. There is, of course, a hope that during this time, overland transit will become attractive beyond the purely price factor and that there will be positive developments in terms of price related to cost reductions.

It should also be noted that Russia also plans to support transit traffic with its own subsidies. Subsidies at the level of $900 per container per shipment through Russian territory are being discussed.

Second, there is an infrastructural constraint for the prospective growth of trans-Eurasian transit. It is the insufficient capacity of the border crossing points on the Belarusian-Polish border and, in general, the technical weakness of Polish railways. The most intensive traffic of container trains is characteristic of the Brest (Belarus)-Malaszewicze (Poland) border crossing. Almost all routes linking China and the EU pass through it. Investment in Polish railways is completely insufficient.

Third, a rather significant administrative and legal obstacle to the increase in cargo turnover between the EAEU, PRC, and EU countries is the difference in transport regulations and documentation. An important step for the further development of the EAEU interface with the BRI is the decision by the PRC State Railway Administration to start processing all container transcontinental shipments under a single consignment note as of May 1, 2017. (Agreement on international rail freight traffic). The agreement on international rail freight traffic consignment note is used by all container trains from China to Europe and vice versa, with routes passing through Alashankou, Manzhouli, Erlian, Suifenhe, and Khorgos. This progress on soft infrastructure allows trains to achieve a steady 10,000-km route with multiple borders in 15–16 days. But this is only the beginning of the journey: further efforts are needed to unify the regulatory and technical regulations of Eurasian countries (rules for different types of cargo, parameters of the rolling stock used, environmental standards, etc.).

Fourth, there is a structural problem for the development of container exports by the EAEU countries, i.e., a lack of adequate supply of goods that would be in demand in the PRC market and could generate additional cargo flow from the EAEU to China. Commodities account for almost all of the EAEU's exports to the PRC. Fuel (65% of the total), timber (15%), minerals (9%), and mineral fertilizers (4%–5%) account for the bulk of EAEU exports to China (in physical terms). Thus, almost all EAEU exports to the PRC are in bulk and liquid cargo. Only about 1% of rail exports to China are containerized. These are mainly pulp and paper products, lumber, and chemical raw materials. The commodity structure of EAEU imports from China is much more diversified: machinery, equipment, industrial products (25%–30% of supplies), metal products (about 15%), finished chemical products, finished building materials, food, and agricultural raw materials (about 10% each), mineral and chemical raw materials as well as clothing, footwear, and textiles (6%–8% each). This asymmetrical trade structure is a problem. The railways can only partially solve it (for example, by loading empty containers from Russia to China with pulp and lumber). In the long term, the issue of efficiency rests with Russia's change in trade specialization with China—more industrial goods and more agro-industrial products.

So, the first key task facing the EAEU countries and Russia in the first place is to encourage some transit from sea to land through the development of transport and logistics infrastructure, so that goods from China to Europe (and in the opposite direction) go through the EAEU territory. This is a good business niche for logistics companies and railways. There are no insurmountable problems here. Railway networks are quite capable of "digesting" many times the volume of containers, especially if "bottlenecks" are removed, transport and logistics centers are further built, and logistics are optimized (so that containers from China to Povolzhye are not transported via Moscow), etc. There is substantial progress and good prospects here so far.

8.2.4 Docking bottlenecks of EAEU and the BRI

Understanding the patterns of world economic patterns substitution and having empirical evidence of the effectiveness of institutions inherent in the new pattern, we cannot ignore the Chinese experience, as well as the model of broad international non-discriminatory cooperation in accordance with the ideological foundations laid down in the "B&R" concept. Within the framework of the idea of a GEP proposed by the Russian President, the EAEU and the B&R are seen as interlinked and complementary integration projects. Without detracting from the potential benefits of specific mutually beneficial project activities within the framework of the conjugation, I believe it is necessary to go even deeper: to create institutions and management mechanisms for the new world economic order at home, especially since the Chinese model is a derivative of the Soviet model. Having comprehended and adapted the latter, it was possible to form such a system of institutions and management, which harmoniously combines socialist ideology and market mechanisms, giving freedom to private entrepreneurship.

It cannot be denied that cooperation with China, both on bilateral tracks and through the concluded agreement with the EAEU, has strengthened in recent years.[11] For example, cross-border infrastructure cooperation between Russia and China is developing, albeit very slowly: transport channels are expanding, the exchange of specialists and technology is becoming more intensive, and bilateral multidisciplinary cooperation is becoming significantly more active. Six specialized transport "corridors" operate, of which the Silk Road Economic Belt, the Russian-Chinese-Mongolian Economic Corridor, and the New Eurasian Continental Bridge directly pass through Russia, connecting China, Central Asia, and West Asia. The eastern, central, and western sections of the rail link between China and Europe pass through Russia. Cooperation on the construction and development of the "Ice Silk Road" has intensified. Similar projects in the construction of transport arteries, infrastructure, and technology parks affect the economic interests of other EAEU member states.

Economic cooperation between the EAEU and the PRC would benefit from getting rid of unnecessary bureaucratic attributes and burdens that inhibit the implementation of joint large-scale programs. After all, it is these that ultimately determine the project saturation of the idea of Eurasian integration and the B&R, as well as the feasibility of the GEP as a wide area of harmonious cooperation between Eurasian powers that share the principles of an integrated world economic order.

Today, it is clear that the results of projects aimed at the practical implementation of the EAEU and the B&R concept have not yet yielded the expected results: they have a very limited impact, especially in terms of the implementation of Eurasian regional infrastructure construction projects. The share of Russian investment in China and in the BRI is minuscule. There is room for significant expansion in this area, especially in the context of the huge flow of Chinese funding for investments in international projects that China needs to develop its economy. At the end of 2019, China's accumulated investment in the B&R countries exceeded $110 billion, representing about 40% of China's FDI in third countries. In the first six months of 2020 alone, Chinese non-financial investments in 54 countries along the ONE PAYE-ONE PATH reached 57.1 billion yuan (about $8 billion), an increase of 23.8% compared to the same period in 2019. Investments were mainly directed to Singapore, Indonesia, Laos, Cambodia, Vietnam, Malaysia, Thailand, UAE, and Kazakhstan.

Overall, EAEU countries accumulate only 0.7% of accumulated Chinese investment. According to the balance of payments statistics, the stock of FDI accumulated in EAEU economies at the end of 2019 was $749.1 billion, of which only 1.6%, or $12 billion, was accumulated—China's direct investment.[12] Nevertheless, the dynamics of FDI from China to the EAEU countries indicate an increase in their accumulation after the 2015–2016 crisis, which is associated with a 3–3.5-fold increase in accumulated FDI in Kazakhstan. The largest Chinese FDI projects are related to hydrocarbon production and transportation through main pipelines.

Accumulated FDI from China to Russia at the end of 2019 was $3.7 billion, or 0.6% of total incoming FDI. Russia is the second largest recipient of Chinese investment in the EAEU after Kazakhstan, accumulating 31% of total Chinese FDI.

Direct investment from EAEU member states to China is significantly inferior to Chinese investment in EAEU countries. Investments from Kazakhstan into China are 43 times less than Chinese investments; as of January 1, 2020, their cumulative volume was $181.5 million.[13] However, Kazakhstan's investments are more diversified: transport (45% of accumulated investment), ferrous and non-ferrous metallurgy, wholesale and retail trade, fuel complex, and infrastructure.[14]

Russian investment in the Chinese economy is 9 times less than Chinese investment in the Russian economy—$752.1 million in 2019 (including Hong Kong), which is only 0.15% of the total stock of Russian FDI in the world.[15] The main areas for Russian investment in China are manufacturing, construction, and transport.

Thus, we have to state that the investment landscape in the EAEU-China relations is far from fully aligned with the interests of both sides. China is interested in expanding its presence not only in the extractive industries but also in retail, transport, and construction. For Russia's EAEU partner states, the

236 CHINA'S ECONOMIC MIRACLE

additional inflow of Chinese investment is a significant factor in economic growth and increased competitiveness of national economies. In particular, the interest of Chinese investors and the inflow of capital investments in manufacturing, infrastructure, agriculture, and high-tech sectors are strategically important for the EAEU.

The main bottleneck in the pairing of integration initiatives remains the weakness of financial cooperation, which needs to be deepened and expanded many times over, both in the traditional banking sector and in related areas such as insurance, stock markets, and other areas of the financial sector. Transformation of cross-border trade and joint investment activities to settlement in national currencies is needed, which would facilitate closer financial interaction, financial market integration, and interbank cooperation. In order to increase the share of the anchor currency for the EAEU, the Russian ruble in trade and economic relations with the PRC and more broadly with the One Belt One State, a number of technical conditions must be provided, such as integration of national payment systems, hedging currency risks, ensuring deep exchange liquidity in direct currency pairs. As the established mechanisms of international monetary and financial, trade and economic cooperation have collapsed under the influence of anti-Russian and anti-Belarusian sanctions and the trade war against China imposed by the US authorities, the key to the long-term growth of the significance of national currencies is to ensure outstripping growth through economic diversification and reduction of macroeconomic volatility.

The systemic integration of the EAEU and the B&R implies the implementation of a roadmap that is aligned in terms of areas and priority areas of cooperation. What needs to be done?

First, to take into account interfaces within the EAEU strategic development planning system, including an assessment of the economic effects of their implementation for the EAEU member states and scenario projections of the development of national economies. As part of this work, it is necessary to provide a risk assessment for different components of the EAEU-the B&R interface: the implementation of the EAEU transit potential, bilateral or multilateral cooperation with a focus on high-tech sectors, the development of a comprehensive strategic partnership, which includes cooperation in a wide range of areas and sectors.

Second, and most importantly, to form a system for financing the activities of the EAEU-the B&R interface, including through the creation of joint investment funds, development funds, grant support, direct public and private financing, and interstate private partnership mechanisms. Spheres of financing can be determined, including taking into account the current strategic documents on EAEU development. For this purpose, it is necessary to develop and introduce special investment and tax regimes for the implementation of joint projects, to form an effective financing model within the framework of the EAEU-the B&R interface, and to minimize risks of the "Chinese" type of financing (tied loans, non-transparent conditions of transactions, etc.); to create a joint fund for point financing of projects along the interface; to form at the EAEU level a system for promotion of investment interests and projects of the Union countries in Here it is advisable to refer to the experience of using the joint grant system. One example of the formation of joint funding institutions on a grant basis is The EU-China Co-Funding Mechanism (CFM), an initiative launched in 2015 to support joint research and innovation projects between universities, research institutions, and companies in the EU and China in areas of common interest.

In order to make the economic cooperation between the EAEU states and the countries of the core of the new global economic order, the formalization of long-term cooperation should be considered. It seems that the most convenient form is the creation of interstate scientific, technological, and investment consortia (funds). Such consortia could implement major projects of Eurasian importance in the fields of transport, logistics, and infrastructure. These consortia could concession transport corridors to build roads and develop the surrounding area, and finance investments by offering bonds in the financial market of the ONE PAYE and EAEU states, attracting loans from the AIIB, SRF, NDB, and EDB. The role of already existing joint targeted investment funds with the PRC—the China-Belarus Investment Fund, the China-Armenia Regional Development Fund, the Joint Kazakhstan-China Investment Fund, and the Russia-China Investment Fund—should also be defined.

The EEC's prospective agenda for the implementation of the Strategic Framework for the Development of Eurasian Economic Integration until 2025 identifies one of the key activities "Creation of a mechanism for the implementation of joint infrastructure projects, investment and scientific and technological consortia" (clause 6.4.7 of the Strategy). This framework allows to generalize the domestic and foreign experience of forming such structures, to develop standard forms of multilateral contractual agreements, and to prepare specific proposals for the implementation of pilot projects. It is important to assess the feasibility of establishing a Eurasian jurisdiction for joint projects and consortia and to develop transparent and unambiguous mechanisms for the settlement of disputes between participating investors.

NOTES

1. American Enterprise Institute (AEI), "China Global Investment Tracker Data Base," 2018.
2. D. Steinbock, "US-China Trade War and Its Global Impacts," World Century Publishing Corporation and Shanghai Institutes for International Studies China *Quarterly of International Strategic Studies* 14, no. 4 (2018): 515–542.
3. Y. Vinokurov, "Russia and the BRI: Symbiosis of Interests of China and Russia," Analytical Note, May 2020.
4. PRC Foreign Minestry, https://www.fmprc.gov.cn/rus/zxxx/t1254925.shtml.
5. "The EAEU Development Strategy and China's BRI Are Linked," *EEC Macroeconomic Policy Department Report*, February 2021.
6. V. Jasinski and M. Kozhevnikov, "'Dual Circulation'—A Model for Chinese Economic Growth in the Next 15 Years," *Problems of Forecasting*, no. 1 (2022).
7. F. Zieren, "The New Silk Road: The West Should Not Be Afraid of China, But Offer Its Own," *Deutsche Welle*, accessed September 24, 2019, https://p.dw.com/p/3PxpM.
8. Heimberger Philipp, Holzner Mario, and Kochnev Artem, "A 'European Silk Road,'" The Vienna Institute for International Economic Studies, Research Report No. 430, August 2018, https://european-silk-road.eu/key-points/.
9. According to the PRC Customs Administration.
10. Y. Vinokurov, "Russia and the BRI: Symbiosis of Interests of China and Russia," Analytical Note, May 2020.
11. S. Glazyev, M. Ershov, and A. Ageev, "Issues and Status of EAEU and The BRI Pairing Processes as Viewed by China and Russia," MOSCOW: INES, 2019.
12. According to the ECE Statistics Department.
13. Kazakhstan's International Investment Position (IIP) as at January 1, 2020.
14. EAEU and the Eurasian continent: monitoring and analysis of direct investment, 2017.
15. http://www.eurasiancommission.org/ru/act/integr_i_makroec/dep_stat/fin_stat/stat_tables/Documents/Flows_stocks_di/flows_stocks_di1Q2020.xlsx.

SECTION 4

On the Right Track to World Leadership

This section focuses on China's projections for the foreseeable future, based on the 14th Five-Year Plan (2021–2025) and global economic scenarios.

CHAPTER 9

China's Leap into the Future

THE COMMUNIST-LED CONVERGENCE OF SOCIALISM AND CAPITALISM, which has been implemented in China for 40 years now under the names "reform and opening-up," "socialism with Chinese characteristics," and "a new era of socialism with Chinese characteristics," has become one of the largest and most interesting experiments for the whole world, says Tavrovsky, who, probably, knows the preconditions and driving forces of the Chinese economic miracle better than anyone else. It has gone through several stages and, more than once, was on the verge of failure. However, the 70 years of PRC's existence and 40 years of reforms have proved the conformity of socialism with the vital needs of the Celestial Empire. The practice has become the yardstick of truth. The Chinese experiment has clearly succeeded, and while it can still be slowed down, it can no longer be reversed. The Chinese nation is once again making an invaluable contribution to the development of human civilization, paving the way to "da tun"—great unity.

However, despite the above-mentioned successes in economic development, China still has a long way to go to achieve global leadership.

As noted in a remarkable article by Yasinsky V. and Kozhevnikov M., Xi Jinping's 2012 goal of building a "middle-income society" in China by 2021 has been achieved. Per capita income has doubled, exceeding $10,000 a year. The country has eliminated absolute poverty. In November 2020, the PRC President announced a new program—"socialist modernization"—to 2035, which also involves doubling per capita income.[1] The growth model for the Chinese economy for this period is "dual circulation." The emergence of the concept of "dual circulation" is not a spontaneous reaction to the US "trade war" with China. Over the past decade, one of the key features of China's economic development has been the shift toward economic growth generated by domestic consumption, which depends directly on household income. Thus, between 2008 and 2019, the share of merchandise exports in China's GDP fell from 31.6% to 17.4%.[2]

With a population of over 1.4 billion, a third of which is in the middle class, China has an objective opportunity to rely on domestic demand as the main driver of development. It is important to emphasize that China is not a transition economy or state capitalism. The new strategy is being implemented within the socialist development paradigm. "Socialism with Chinese characteristics" is not a decorative sign over the market economy. The state remains the main subject of development with strategic planning, the leading player in scientific and technological progress, science, education, and human capital reproduction. Increasing the welfare of the population and improving the quality of life remain the main development goals. Private business in competitive areas that benefit society is supported but is blocked where it undermines economic stability, increases financial risks, and tries to occupy a monopoly position on the market. At the same time, the conditions for small and medium-sized businesses have been consistently facilitated in recent years. In the course of combating the consequences of the pandemic, new privileges have been granted to this group of millions of entrepreneurs, which are to be maintained in the following period as well. As recent events around China's leading IT companies have shown, the state has the capacity to "convince" even the largest and most successful entrepreneurs to consider the country's long-term development interests and increase their contribution to achieving "common prosperity."

The formation of the national innovation system was accelerated from the early 2000s with the implementation of a large-scale military-technological modernization program ("Program 995"), which was aimed at prioritizing the development of the national defense industry complex (DIC)'s own scientific and technological base.

The breakthrough development of the military-industrial complex could not fail to accelerate the modernization of the associated civilian sectors of industry. Overall, since the start of the reform and opening-up policy, 16 comprehensive and sectoral S&T development programs have been elaborated. This has enabled China to take the lead in the development of a number of key technologies.

Attempts by the US through various kinds of sanctions and restrictions can slow down, but not stop, the further development of the national innovation system. Paradoxically, US sanctions in this area can lead to the opposite result. For example, American obstacles to Huawei's activities in the international 5G market prompted the Chinese company to focus on developing 5G networks in China, and the country has become the undisputed world leader in mastering these technologies.

Nevertheless, the US is stepping up efforts to create the so-called "Anti-China International," or a broad alliance of democracies against authoritarianism. However, it has to be admitted that this process is not going the way it wanted either. The EU's signing of a comprehensive investment agreement with China in particular demonstrates this.

In 2020, Beijing announced a transition to a new economic growth strategy that envisages reliance on domestic demand as the main driver of China's economic development. The new model gives the former drivers—export growth, investment, and foreign economic cooperation—a supporting role. The new strategy is called "dual circulation" (shuāngxúnhuán).

The new development strategy was formulated and legislated in the 14th Five-Year Socio-Economic Development Plan 2021–2025 and the Long-Term Development Goals to 2035 at the March 2021 session of the NPC, i.e., within one year. The speed of making important strategic decisions is nothing short of impressive. To a certain extent, it was dictated by the "trade war" unleashed by the US. At the same time, it is a testament to the effectiveness of the CPC-led political system and the strategic planning experience accumulated in the preceding decades.

We must agree with those experts who argue that the transition to a new economic strategy was not sudden. Its elements have been "maturing" for years and decades.[3] A milestone on this road was the large-scale and ambitious military-technical modernization program initiated by the Politburo of the CPC Central Committee—Program 995 (May 1999). As is known, on May 7, 1999, in the course of NATO's armed conflict with Yugoslavia, an American bomber "by mistake" bombed the Chinese Embassy in Belgrade, killing three people. The program aimed to accelerate the development of a range of breakthrough military technologies. Taking into account the experience of decades of borrowing foreign military and dual-use technologies from Europe, Israel, and the former Soviet Union, Program 995 was focused primarily on the priority development of the national military industrial complex's own scientific and technological base. Tremendous sums of money were spent to implement the program. Thus, between 1999 and 2008, the military budget grew at the fastest rate in China's history, by an average of 16.2% annually.[4] As a result, by the end of the 2000s, China had achieved a high level of self-sufficiency in military equipment and armaments. It is evident that the military-industrial complex's breakthrough development could not but give a strong impetus to the modernization of related civilian sectors.

In addition, after the global financial crisis of 2008, China began to actively discuss the need to rely on domestic demand. In the mid-2010s, the Chinese leadership acknowledged that the economy had entered a state of "new normal," when efforts should be focused not on achieving double-digit GDP growth, but on its quality, finding new resources for development, and placing a bet on improving innovation capacity. An analysis of China's economic growth over the last decade shows that the country has managed to achieve many of its planned qualitative development indicators. In particular, China "relatively reduced exports of finished products of low-tech industries, such as light industry, which for many years was the engine of China's economic miracle, but at the same time successfully implemented import substitution of components used in the production of finished products of all industries. In general, the industries "where China has increased competitiveness over the last decade are medium- and high-tech.[5]

Reliance on domestic demand. Until the early 2010s, exports and increased investment were the main growth drivers. From 2010 to 2020, the share of final consumption in GDP increased from 49.35% to 54.29%, indicating that it is final consumption that is becoming the main source of GDP growth.

At the same time, during the last decade, the ratio of the final consumption shares of households and the government did not change much, amounting respectively to about 70 and 30%. The steady increase in household consumption could not have taken place without a consistent increase in household income in recent decades.

On average, the incomes of all five groups of households rose by 38.4%. At the same time, the incomes of the first and second groups grew faster than those of the first and second groups. As a result of the census, the Chinese authorities have a clear picture of the size of the middle class and the prospects for growth in its share of the country's population. After all, it is the middle class that acts as the main generator of demand for the products in which China seeks to increase its share of the national value added. At the same time, it should be borne in mind that there is no uniform system of criteria for classifying citizens as middle class. Chinese statistics classify households with an average annual income of between 100,000 yuan ($15,200) and 500,000 yuan ($76,000) as middle class. Many countries use different methods of assessment, taking into account such parameters as professional sphere of activity, education, etc. However, in the context of increasing market size, the criterion of disposable income is appropriate.

Using available data on household income and the size of the average household (2.92 people), it has been calculated that the size of the middle class has increased from 270 million to 490 million between 2013 and 2019, according to the above criterion. McKinsey experts predict that the Chinese middle class (household income of 75,000–280,000 yuan per year) could reach 550 million people by 2022.[6]

The increase in the population's income is primarily reflected in the structure of household expenditure. Thus, from 2013 to 2019, households spent more on transport, education, culture, recreation, and healthcare and relatively less on food and clothing. The number of durable goods purchased has also changed (units per 100 households):

(1)   Cars: from 22.3 to 43.2
(2)   Refrigerators: from 89.2 to 102.5
(3)   Washing machines: from 88.4 to 99.2
(4)   Air conditioners: 102.2 to 148.3
(5)   Water heaters: 80.3 to 98.2
(6)   Mobile phones: from 206.1 to 247.4

Furthermore, from the point of view of consumption development, the use of "self-replicating economy" or "circular economy" mechanisms in China seems important. This refers to the establishment of limits on the permissible time of consumption of a number of durable goods and the possession of real estate. For example, the maximum useful life of a residential building is 70 years, after which the building must be demolished. For commercial real estate, the period is limited to 40 years. However, construction waste from demolition must be recycled, as stipulated in the 14th Five-Year Plan. Chinese-made cars must be scrapped after ten years of production. Foreign-made cars after 15 years.[7]

According to Morgan Stanley's research, the biggest potential for growth in domestic demand lies in relatively small (by Chinese standards) cities with a population of between 1 and 3 million (so-called third-tier cities).[8] However, they are where about 34% of the population lives.[9] The reason for this is that the residents of these cities have more opportunities for consumption growth, as they are less burdened by transport and real estate costs compared to the residents of large cities. In addition, it is with these cities that urbanization prospects are linked.

According to China's National Bureau of Statistics, some 244.5 million of the 848 million urban population did not have an urban registration (户口 hùkǒu) in

2017.[10] These are migrant workers with a rural residence permit. They do not have access to social insurance, adequate levels of health services, and education, which causes their increased propensity to save, reducing their consumption potential.

The 14th Five-Year Plan is planned to remove restrictions on urban propiska for rural migrants, specifically in third-tier cities, and some "softening" in obtaining urban propiska for this category of citizens in larger cities. In this way, migrant workers will be able to increase their incomes, which will lead to an increase in their consumption activity.

China is among the countries with the highest savings rate, calculated as gross national income minus total consumption plus net transfers.[11] According to the World Bank, while the global average savings rate in 2018 was 25.1% in China, it was 45%, compared to 19% in the US and 25% in the EU.[12] The Chinese tendency to save is due to a number of cultural and historical factors, including the Chinese mentality. In the recent past, for example, the failure of the "Great Leap Forward" and the economic chaos created by the "Cultural Revolution" convinced the population that the surest means of survival in the current environment were savings.[13] Moreover, the vast majority of today's urban population in Chinese cities is made up of yesterday's peasants who, until recently, were extremely poor.

To overcome the population's historical propensity to save, the Chinese authorities are rightly betting on a steady increase in disposable income and the development of a social insurance system that opens up new horizons for consumption growth.

Development through domestic innovation. Since the founding of the PRC, the modernization of production capacity has been high on the agenda of the authorities of a backward agrarian country with ambitious development goals. In the 1950s, with the help of the Soviet Union, a backbone of enterprises was established, laying the foundation for the development of Chinese industry. After the lost decades of the "Great Leap Forward" and the "Cultural Revolution," the transition in the late 1970s to Deng Xiaoping's "reform and opening-up" meant attracting as much foreign capital and advanced Western technology as possible to all spheres of the national economy.

With the beginning of the reforms, special attention was paid to scientific and technological development. Programs and plans were drawn up to accelerate the modernization of both individual sectors and the national economy as a whole. Their implementation, having become an integral part of the ongoing economic reforms, bore fruit: as a result of sustained high growth rates, China became the "workshop of the world," ranking second after the US in terms of GDP and surpassing them in terms of GDP volume at PPP.

However, it turned out that such a high position in the global economy came with increasing risks of strategic vulnerability, calling into question the prospects for continued growth. For example, the share of national value added in goods produced remained low (especially in high-tech products). In addition, it became increasingly clear that the country was critically dependent on access to advanced Western technology.

One of the first signs that China's leadership was aware of these risks was the adoption of Program 995 in 1999. Its implementation enabled China to create its own technological base and became the foundation for developing its national defense industry, allowing it to reach the leading edge of modern weapons production. A special role in China's comprehensive S&T development is played by the "Made in China" program, which was approved in 2015 and runs until 2025. The program aims to increase the share of key high-tech components produced domestically to 40% by 2020 and 70% by 2025. The program includes priority subsidies, tax incentives, and cheap credit for high-value-added industries.

In the last ten years alone, China has spent enormous amounts of money on overcoming its technological dependency. For example, between 2010 and 2020, R&D expenditure in China rose from 706 billion yuan to 2.44 trillion yuan ($580.9 billion), or from 1.71% to 2.4% of GDP. However, China still lags far behind Japan ($188.9 billion, or 3.5% of GDP), the US ($656 billion, or 3.06% of GDP), and South Korea ($103.6 billion, or 4.64% of GDP) in terms of the share of R&D spending in GDP. In Russia, for example, RUB 1.13 trillion ($44.3 billion), or 1.03% of GDP, was spent on R&D in 2019. In 2019, about 20% of R&D funding in the PRC came from public funds and about 76% from enterprises' own funds.

According to the 14th Five-Year Plan, China plans to increase R&D expenditure by at least 7% per annum, i.e., faster than expected GDP growth. Thus, by 2025, R&D expenditure is set to rise to about RMB3.4 trillion per annum, or $815 billion at PPPs, representing roughly 2.52% of GDP. In addition, the share of basic and exploratory spending in R&D expenditure is rising to an unprecedented 8%, indicating a strong scientific basis for future technological breakthroughs. All of this points to the creation of a powerful innovation cluster in China, a future driver of economic development.

In the new Five-Year Plan, the so-called Key National Laboratories (KNL) are assigned a key role in the development of strategic technologies. Quantum informatics, photonics, micro- and nanoelectronics, network communications, artificial intelligence, biotechnology, pharmaceuticals, and modern energy systems are identified as critical areas for development. Institutes and research groups (both private and public) that achieve KNL status receive direct financial support from the central government. The first KNLs were approved in 1984. The scope of CNLs covers both civilian and military technologies. At the end of 2019, there were 515 KNLs in China.

The developers of the 14th Five-Year Plan are clear about the areas in which China now leads the world, and those in which it still lags far behind advanced Western technologies. For example, artificial intelligence (AI) is a key development priority for China over the next 15 years. The implementation of the AI development program adopted in 2017 involves three phases. In the first stage, by 2020. China should catch up with advanced countries in terms of AI development. Spending on the AI industry should be $22.5 billion, and more than $150 billion on the development of related industries. In the second phase, by 2025, the goal is to achieve a leadership position in some selected areas of AI. Expenditure on the industry will be $60 billion, and $745 billion on related areas. The third phase aims to become a global leader in AI by 2030, with $150 billion invested in the industry and $1.5 trillion in related industries.

AI is not only being used to create new tools for internal and external security. China now has more than 500 smart cities that use AI to analyze traffic and manage infrastructure.[14] During the COVID-19 pandemic, the use of mass surveillance equipment (e.g., thermal scanners in train stations) with AI technologies provided "epidemic maps" that mapped existing and potential hotspots of infection, enabling rapid implementation of point-to-point quarantine measures.

In addition to the development of AI, China is betting on the development of 5G networks for the wireless transmission of large amounts of data. This technology will open up new horizons for industrial automation and enable more complex automated production lines. The introduction of 5G will help China narrow the productivity gap and compensate for its shrinking working-age population. In addition, the development of 5G networks will make more cloud-based technology available, which could reduce the performance requirements of individual devices held by users, thereby offsetting China's technological lag in manufacturing the latest chips with a 5 nanometre or less processor.

By becoming the first country in the world to deploy 5G (86% of the world's 5G users are Chinese to date), China could provide a breakthrough in global satellite internet connectivity. In the first phase, China plans to launch up to

13,000 satellites into orbit by 2022. In the second phase, by 2025, it plans to provide access to satellite Internet worldwide.

China is now the world leader in a number of high-tech fields, with the largest robot market (36% of the global market, China is the world leader in terms of the total capacity of wind and solar power plants).[15] China has the world's longest network of high-speed railways. In 2020, China will produce about 1 million electric cars (410,000 in the US). That year, China overtook Germany to become the country's number one exporter of automotive engineering products (15.8% of the market). China registered 68,720 patents with the World Intellectual Property Organisation last year, compared with 59,230 for the US. Up to 10% of all new patents registered in the US are registered by people with Chinese surnames.

Rising wages, access to quality health care, social security, and quality housing play a key role in attracting the highly educated people needed to develop high-tech industries. For example, China is actively recruiting leading specialists in high-tech electronics manufacturing. By the end of 2020, Chinese companies attracted more than 3,000 engineers from TSMC (Taiwan Semiconductor Manufacturing Company, a world leader in semiconductor chip production), including more than 100 leading engineers and department heads.[16]

In 2000, only 23% of students who went abroad to study returned home. In 2010, 47% returned, and in 2019, 82% returned. In 2019, the number of Chinese students studying abroad was 703,500. Almost half of the Chinese students who have gone abroad are studying at US universities.[17] Their annual graduation rate is 400,000 engineers (2017 year), half of whom have a degree in microelectronics.[18]

The Fourth Session of the 13th NPC, which concluded in Beijing in mid-March 2021, adopted "the Outline of the 14th Five-Year Plan (2021–2025) for National Economic and Social Development and Vision 2035 of the People's Republic of China."

As noted in the Proposals of the CPC Central Committee for Formulating the 14th Five-Year Plan for National Economic and Social Development and Vision 2035 (adopted at the 5th Plenum of the 19th CPC Central Committee, October 29, 2020), "China has entered a stage of quality development with significant institutional advantages, improved management efficiency, long-term economic improvement, a solid material base, abundant human resources, a broad market space, strong sustainable. The document notes the need to "coordinate the overall strategy of the great revival of the Chinese nation and the great changes in the world unprecedented in a century, to have a deep understanding of the new characteristics and requirements caused by the changes in the major contradictions of our society, and to have a deep understanding of the new contradictions and challenges caused by the complex international environment, and to expand risk awareness, to recognize changes precisely, to respond to them scientifically."

"Responding scientifically" to the changes enunciated by the CPC Central Committee in its new five-year action plan means, among other things, comprehensively modernizing the socialist state, moving from catch-up to outpacing development, which, of course, is impossible without a cross-cutting innovation breakthrough in all spheres of life. The Chinese leadership, based on the study of trends in the NTP, correctly identifies the priorities of technical and economic development, combines strategic planning and market competition mechanisms, achieves their implementation, and then adjusts them in a timely manner based on the NTP forecasts.

This science-based approach is the basis for the next Five-Year Plan for the social and economic development of the PRC. A special section of the already cited CPC Central Committee Proposals for the formulation of the 14th Five-Year Plan—Relaxing innovative development and comprehensively shaping new development advantages—formulates the relevant guidelines:

"Adhere to the key position of innovation in China's overall modernization situation, use scientific and technological independence as a strategic support for national development, stand at the forefront of world science and technology … Implement a strategy to rejuvenate the country through science, education, and talent … Strengthen the country's strategy and innovation development strategy, improve the national innovation system, and accelerate the building of scientific and technological strength.

Strengthen national strategic scientific and technological strength. Formulate an action program to strengthen the country through science and technology, improve the new nationwide system in a socialist market economy, fight for key technologies, and improve the overall efficiency of the innovation chain. Strengthen basic research, focus on original innovation, optimize the structure of disciplines and R&D, promote interdisciplinary integration, and improve the delivery system of common core technologies. Target the advanced fields of artificial intelligence, quantum information, integrated circuits, life and health, brain science, biological breeding, aerospace science and technology, deep-sea and deep-sea, etc., and implement a number of promising and strategic major national science and technology projects. Develop and implement strategic science plans and research projects to promote optimal allocation and sharing of research force resources in research institutes, universities, and enterprises. Promote the establishment of national laboratories and the restructuring of the national core laboratory system."

It also defines new priorities of technical and economic development corresponding to the key factors of the new technological mode: "Develop strategically new industries. Accelerate the growth of next-generation information technologies, biotechnology, new energy, new materials, high-tech equipment, new energy vehicles, environmental protection, aerospace, marine equipment, and other sectors. Promote deep integration of various industries such as the Internet, big data, and artificial intelligence; foster advanced manufacturing clusters; create a range of strategic new industry growth engines with unique characteristics, added value, and smart structure, and develop new technologies, new products, and new business formats." And there are even recommendations for organizational forms of industry modernization. It is suggested that "The new model is to promote the healthy development of the platform and sharing economy. Encourage mergers and reorganizations of enterprises to prevent the creation of low-level redundancies."

Thus, one of the fundamentally important points in China's 14th Five-Year Economic and Social Development Plan is the new emphasis on technological "self-strengthening" (technological self-strengthening). The new Five-Year Plan sets very ambitious goals of strengthening the country's scientific and technological strength and making China a leading independent global technological power.[19] The new Five-Year Plan has also emphasized quality, self-reliant economic development, with scientific and technological innovation as one of the main sources of economic growth. Against the backdrop of increasing technological rivalry with the US and other developed countries, the objectives of the new Five-Year Plan reflect the growing urgency to reduce China's technological dependence on external markets and reduce the vulnerability of its supply chains in an increasingly geopolitical tense environment.

In that regard, the plan focuses on achieving breakthroughs in key technologies and outlines systemic changes in China's management, financing, and modernization of its research environment. It emphasizes the importance of S&T self-sufficiency, especially in key technologies of today, which are seen as strategically important to maintaining the country's sustainable development. Increased investment in R&D and prioritization of basic research coupled with the ongoing modernization of the national innovation system define the essence of China's strategic approach to comprehensively strengthen its S&T capacity in the 14th Five-Year Plan. The previous Five-Year Plans focused more on catch-up development. The new Five-Year Plan focuses on making China a global innovation and technology hub and reducing its vulnerability to external shocks by becoming more self-reliant and independent in S&T (self-reliant). In fact, the country's S&T independence is seen as a strategic goal of national development, on the realization of which China's long-term socio-economic and technological security directly depends.

The desire for technological independence means that Chinese companies do not just want to create innovative and competitive products, but want to produce them without having to import core technologies from foreign competitors. Therefore, the priorities of the new Five-Year Plan were to strengthen the country's scientific and technological strength, develop the technological and innovation capabilities of enterprises, stimulate the innovative abilities of scientists and talented professionals, and expand opportunities for basic research and scientific and technological breakthroughs.

When analyzing China's stated goals and objectives in the development of national S&T capacity, it is hardly possible to fully assess the likelihood of their achievement in the foreseeable future. The Biden Administration views competition in the high-tech sector as the main one in the strategic confrontation between the US and China. Washington continues to pursue a policy of restraining China's technological development. In particular, the US is seeking to deny it access to technology and equipment for semiconductor manufacturing because chips are the most important element of most modern information and communication technologies. In fact, the key variable determining the intensity of the rivalry between the two powers is the narrowing of the gap in economic and technological power. Beijing expects Washington to become even more assertive in containing China's rise as the gap narrowed and bridging the scientific and technological gap with the West may be China's major strategic priority at the moment.

There are at least two main scenarios that can be envisaged. In the first scenario, China will gradually catch up and close most of the existing gaps in the development of its own scientific and technological potential, as well as achieve parity in this area with the advanced countries and, possibly, even surpass them in some areas. The second scenario envisages that China would not only catch up with the leading technological powers, primarily the US, but also surpass them to a large extent, becoming the world leader in innovation and advanced technology.

Currently, China has many of the necessary resources to make significant headway in accelerating the development of its own scientific and technological capabilities and steadily increasing its power. Much will depend on Beijing's ability to create a favorable institutional environment that is highly receptive to innovation and to create the right conditions for successful technological "self-reinforcement." However, there is no doubt that the PRC will make every effort and mobilize all necessary resources on the way to realizing the stated goals. China's success is not guaranteed and largely depends not only on extensive government support for R&D but also on the effectiveness of measures to transform the scientific environment, train highly skilled professionals, and provide conditions to motivate Chinese scientists to achieve fundamental breakthroughs. While acknowledging the challenges and obstacles along the way, PRC officials have repeatedly stressed that patience is required to meet the challenges, so there is no expectation of quick success.

The "dual circulation" model of the Chinese economy does not mean abandoning active participation in the international division of labor. An idea of a consistent deepening of this participation is provided by the study,[20] which analyses how the Chinese economy is embedded in global value chains (GVC) in the context of domestic value creation (DVC), based on OECD data. This approach allows us to decompose the DVC process into two effects: direct (contribution of export industries) and indirect (contribution of other ancillary industries). Experts estimate that, first of all, the so-called "smile curve" or U-shaped curve emerges in the emergence of "indirect" effects in the process of DVC creation in all industries, which can be seen as a kind of model reflecting the trajectory of Asian participation in GVC. In this case, the domestic value share to exports declines in the initial phase and gradually recovers in the more mature phase of development, with the "turning point" determined by GDP per capita dynamics. It is noted that the Chinese economy, having successfully overcome the "Central Asian turning point" identified by the authors, has already entered the recovery phase of the DVC effect. In addition, domestic value creation in China has taken place through the development of ancillary industries, among which the service sector, which retains enormous potential for economic growth, plays a special role.

NOTES

1. V. Jasinski and M. Kozhevnikov, "'Dual Circulation'—A Model for Chinese Economic Growth in the Next 15 Years," *Problems of Forecasting*, no. 1 (2022).
2. S. Tsyplakov, "China Chooses Strategy for 15 Years," Nezavisimaya Gazeta, https://www.ng.ru/dipkurer/2020-10-18/9_7992_china.html.

3. A. Lomanov, "Circulation versus Isolation," *Russia in Global Politics* 19, no. 3 (2021): 109.

4. Richard Bitzinger, "Modernising China's Military, 1997–2012," *China Perspectives*, no. 4 (2011): 7–15.

5. A. Bykov, S. Tolkachev, V. Parkhimenko, and T. Shablinskaya, "China's Economic Growth in 2010–2017: Analysis from the Cost-Output Methodology and Modern Monetary Theory," *Finance: Theory and Practice* 2, n0. 25 (2021): 166–184.

6. "How Well-Off Is China's Middle Class?" URL: https://chinapower.csis.org/china-middle-class/.

7. E. Balatsky, "Chinese Model of the Economy of the Future: Development through Permanent Self-Destruction," *Society and Economy*, no. 8–9 (2011): 292–305.

8. "Bullish on China's Lower-Tier Cities," *Morgan Stanley Research*, URL: https://www.morgan stanley.com/ideas/china-lower-tier-cities.

9. "3 Misconceptions About Lower Tier Cities in China," URL: https://agencychina.com/blog/3-myths-lower-tier-cities-china/.

10. "The Number of Migrant Workers in China in 2017 Was 244.5 Million," http://russian.news.cn/2018-12/26/c_137700081.htm.

11. N. Gribova, "Chinese Household Consumption: Major Trends and Pandemic Factors," *Problems of National Strategy*, no. 1 (2021): 33–59.

12. "Gross Savings (% of GDP)," The World Bank, URL: https://data.worldbank.org/ indicator/ NY.GNS.ICTR.ZS.

13. V. Gelbras, "The Economy of the People's Republic of China: The Most Important Stages of Development, 1949–2007," Course of lectures. Ч. 1. Moscow State University, Institute of Asian and African Studies (Moscow: Humanitarian, 2007).

14. P. Strukova, "Artificial Intelligence in China: Current State of the Industry and Development Trend," Bulletin of St. Petersburg University, *Oriental Studies and African Studies* 12, no. 4 (2020): 588–606.

15. V. V. Perskaya and N. S. Revenko, "'Made in China 2025': Chinese Experience of Ensuring National Development Objectives," *Asia and Africa Today* 7 (2020): 19–25.

16. Cheng Ting-Fang, "China Hires over 100 TSMC Engineers in Push for Chip Leadership," URL: https://asia.nikkei.com/Business/China-tech/China-hires-over-100-TSMC-engineers-in-push-for-chip-leadership; Kensaku Ihara, "Taiwan Loses 3,000 Chip Engineers to 'Made in China 2025,'" URL: https://asia.nikkei.com/Business/China-tech/Taiwan-loses-3-000-chip-engineers-to-Made-in-China-2025.

17. S. S. Donetskaya and Li M, "Chinese Students Abroad: Population Dynamics and Purpose of Departure," *Higher Education in Russia* 29, no. 6 (2020): 153–168.

18. M. Makushin, "Microelectronics in China: A New Stage of Development," *Electronics*, no. 7 (2017).

19. N. Gribova, "Prospects for China's S&T Potential in the 14th Five-Year Plan (2021–2025)," *Problems of National Strategy*, no. 6 (2021): 93–114.

20. Taguchi Hiroyuki and Li Jiejun, "Domestic Value Creation in the Involvement in Global Value Chains: The Case of Chinese Economy," *Asian Development Policy Review* 6, no. 3 (2018): 155–168, http://dx.doi.org/10.18488/journal.107.2018.63.155.168, file:///C:/Users/HP/Downloads/ADPR-2018-6(3)-155-168.pdf.

CHAPTER 10

Unsuccessful US Attempts to Torpedo China's Economic Development by Unleashing a Global Hybrid War

10.1 The Legitimacy and Main Directions of American Aggression

As the foregoing suggests, recovery from the current crisis will be accompanied by large-scale geopolitical and economic changes. As it usually happens, the countries dominating the existing world economic order demonstrate their inability to make radical institutional innovations, which could channel the released capital into the structural transformation of the economy on the basis of a new technological order, continuing to reproduce the existing institutional system and to serve the economic interests embodied in it. Meanwhile, the unfolding structural reorganization of the world economy associated with the transition to a new technological mode gives the lagging countries an opportunity for an economic "leap forward" to the level of advanced countries, while the latter are faced with overcapitalization in obsolete production-technological complexes.

By virtue of the laws of global socio-economic development described above, the US is doomed to defeat in the trade war it has launched with China. But the American ruling elite will try to fight for global leadership by all available means, regardless of international law. It has already destroyed international law: by ignoring WTO norms in its trade war with China; by violating the UN Charter with armed aggression in the Balkans and the Middle East; by organizing coups d'état in a number of countries in Europe and South America; by violating the IMF Charter with financial sanctions against Russia; developing biological weapons, cyber-terrorism, and military build-ups in other countries and in space in defiance of international conventions; sponsoring religious extremism and neo-Nazism in order to organize and manipulate terrorist organizations; seizing property and kidnapping unwanted citizens of other countries. As shown above, in full accordance with the theory,[1] this war was initiated by the US ruling elite in order to maintain its global hegemony in the face of the emergence of an order of magnitude more effective economic development management system in the PRC. The question remains: To what limits can the US leaders reach in crimes against humanity in a bid to maintain their domination?

World Wars differ significantly from each other in the technologies used. World War II was a war of motors, which gave a strong impetus to the development of the automotive and organic synthesis industries, which formed the core of a new technological paradigm for that time. By the mid-1970s, it had reached the limits of its growth and began to be replaced by the next technological stage, whose core was the microelectronics industry and information and communication technologies. The "Star Wars" doctrine and the US space and missile arms race gave a strong impetus to its growth, which continued until the beginning of this century. Today, there is a process of replacing this technological paradigm with the next, the core of which consists of digital, information and communication, nano- and bio-engineering technologies. As before, it is being stimulated by the arms race. However, the basic technologies of the new technological order being formed today differ significantly from the previous ones. To stimulate their development, high-precision missiles, targeted biological, cybernetic, and informational cognitive weapons affecting strategic objects, control systems, population, and consciousness of the enemy, are well suited.

It is not difficult to see the current use of these weapons: high-precision weapons in combat operations, biological weapons in the form of a pandemic coronavirus, cybernetic weapons in cyberattacks against financial and energy infrastructure, and cognitive weapons in social media. If it is impossible to use nuclear and chemical weapons, modern world war acquires a hybrid character, including wide use of financial, commercial, and diplomatic methods of crushing the enemy. The US is using its superiority in all the above spheres, seeking to strengthen its advantages in the global economy by weakening the enemy.

A war was waged against Russia on the financial front in the form of financial sanctions, the victim of which was, in particular, the aluminum industry along with Rusal-owned hydroelectric power plants, control over which was taken over by American "partners." Seizures of assets of Russian legal entities and individuals undesirable to Washington, blocking of money transfers, and bans on transactions with them are carried out on a broad front throughout the dollar area. About a trillion dollars of capital taken out of Russia is "captive" in Anglo-Saxon offshore companies.

Trade war tools were used to weaken China, against which Washington imposed additional import duties totaling $300 billion in violation of WTO norms, as well as sanctions on leading computer equipment manufacturers. A trade war technique tested against the USSR in the 1980s was Saudi Arabia's oil price collapse instigated by US agents of influence to undermine Russia's trade balance. Additionally, Saudi Arabia began openly dumping oil on the European market in order to drive Russian companies out of it, on which the US simultaneously imposed sanctions.

An example of the use of cyber weapons was the 2011 accident at an Iranian nuclear power plant, which was caused by a computer virus embedded in an automated process control system imported from the EU. Another example is the disabling of the power control system of Venezuela's capital, Caracas, on March 7, 2019, to provoke riots to stage a coup d'état. Every minute, several cyber attacks are launched by the US NSA against targets in China, Russia, Venezuela, and other countries outside Washington's control. In the global wiretapping network, bugs embedded in computers are no longer a concern.

This year saw the opening of a new front in the global hybrid war involving biological weapons. For example, Zhao Lijian, spokesman for the Chinese Foreign Ministry, made the accusation against the US military. Lijian drew his conclusions after Robert Redfield, the director of the Centers for Disease Control and Prevention (CDC), spoke to the US House Oversight Committee and was arrested immediately after his report.[2]

The development of bioengineering technologies for military purposes was the expected "driver" of the development of the new technological paradigm. Scientists at the Pushchino Scientific Centre of the Russian Academy of Sciences spoke of the possibility of synthesizing viruses with a targeted effect on people of a particular race, age, or sex as early as 1996, justifying the need to develop and adopt a biological security strategy for Russia. The "first swallows" in the form of Ebola, SARS, and, possibly, "bird flu" and HIV flew by long ago.

Back in 2010, the Rockefeller Foundation devised a viral pandemic scenario[3] that is currently being implemented. There is no doubt that a vast network of secret US bio-laboratories scattered around the world is "forging" bio-engineering weapons. These laboratories are mainly scattered in the former Soviet Union and

Southeast Asia. China is in fact surrounded by US military laboratories. To the west of China, the laboratories are in Kazakhstan, Uzbekistan, Afghanistan, and Pakistan. But the closest ones south of China are Thailand, Laos, Vietnam, the Philippines, Cambodia, and Malaysia. Interestingly, the ill-fated bioengineering laboratory in Wuhan is reportedly owned by the well-known British company GlaxoSmithKline (GSK), which co-owns the largest vaccine manufacturer, Pfizer, and is run by the US-based Black Rock and Soros Foundations, which are systemically important in the global financial market. The same funds control the French AXA holding company and own the German company Wintertor, which built the Wuhan laboratory. The circle is closed: the developers of the coronavirus and vaccine manufacturers are affiliated through foundations belonging to the US power-financier oligarchy. They are also the main "customers" of the global hybrid war waged by the US to maintain their global dominance and establish world domination.

The Ministry of Defence of the Russian Federation has published documents of secret US military-biological activities in Ukraine. Thus, laboratories in Kyiv, Odesa, Lviv, and Kharkiv received a total of $32 million from the US. These secret US offshore facilities were chosen by the US Defense Threat Reduction Agency (DTRA) and contractor Black & Veatch as executors of the U-P8 project, aimed at studying pathogens of Congo-Crimean hemorrhagic fever, leptospirosis, and hantaviruses. US military biologists' interest in the project is due, among other things, to the fact that the pathogens have natural foci both in Ukraine and Russia and can be used by masquerading as natural diseases. Ukraine has handed over 5,000 blood serum samples from Ukrainian citizens to the Pentagon-Linked Lugar Center in Tbilisi, and another 773 bio-samples were sent to the UK. In addition, an agreement has been signed with the Leffler Institute in Germany to export unlimited quantities of infectious materials.

The development and use of biological weapons are stimulating the development of advanced bioengineering industries, generating demand for medical research and devices, new vaccines, and drugs. Healthcare, as the leading industry of the new technological order, is getting an additional impetus for growth. It should be noted that against the backdrop of a collapse in production in most industries, there is explosive growth in the production of pharmaceutical products and medical devices in 2020.

The outstripping growth of spending on health care and especially on medical science was noticeable in developed and successfully developing countries even before the pandemic. This is associated with a technological revolution in medicine, with the introduction of cell technologies as one of the key trends in the formation of a new technological paradigm. Their application not only cardinally increases the effectiveness of health care but also creates the possibility of a significant increase in life expectancy. And this, in turn, entails a non-linear increase in healthcare costs for the elderly population. The fight against the pandemic has exposed healthcare bottlenecks—insufficient bed capacity for infectious cases, lack of surge capacity, shortages of personal protective equipment, poor quality, and high costs of tests. Addressing these is associated with even higher healthcare costs. And the need for accelerated vaccine development entails a multiplication of the funding for related bioengineering research.

As illustrated above, healthcare is one of the carriers of the new technological order, which in the future will account for up to 20% of the used GDP.[4] The opening of the biological front of the ongoing global hybrid warfare reinforces the priority of developing public health, medical, and bioengineering science, including for national security purposes.

The widespread introduction of quarantine measures and restrictions on the movement of citizens provides a strong impetus for the development of information technology and computer technology through a dramatic increase in demand for e-commerce services, distance education, home office equipment, and remote workplaces. States are investing enormous sums of money in equipping cities and public places with the means to register and track citizens, recognize their identity, and monitor their movement and state of health. On this basis, artificial intelligence systems are being formed, operating with big data, which require supercomputers and ultra-high-performance software to process. This, in turn, stimulates the development of nanotechnologies and software for the production of computing equipment of appropriate performance, compactness, and energy efficiency.

The arms race, as always in a period of technological revolution, is unfolding in the promising areas of growth of the new technological order. It poses an existential threat to mankind when technology matures into weapons of mass destruction, falling into the hands of immoral politicians. The atomic bombings of Hiroshima and Nagasaki are a prime example of their crime against humanity. The development and use of a coronavirus that affects millions of people demonstrates the relapse of this criminal activity on a modern, advanced technological basis.

The difference from the atomic bombing of Japanese cities is the reverse effect of the biological weapons, which affect not only the enemy's population but also their own. The biological attack on China was intended to destabilize the socio-political situation in the country on the eve of the session of the NPC, which is the highest organ of power, and to sow panic and chaos in order to create conditions for a coup d'état. It can be assumed that the US ruling elite or the so-called "deep state" have their own motives for using it against the Washington-controlled part of the world as well. After the September 11, 2001 attacks in New York with the connivance of the CIA, power structures in the American political system significantly strengthened, having left the control of society and received wide powers. The justification for this partial usurpation of power and restriction of civil liberties was then the "war" on world terrorism, sponsored and directed by the same US intelligence agencies.[5] The victims of this war were tens of millions of people living in countries subject to US aggression—Serbia, Iraq, Libya, Syria, Egypt, and Ukraine. These people lost their homes and jobs and became displaced persons and refugees, pouring into the EU. Frightened European elites closed borders, tightened controls on cross-border migration, and rolled back democratic institutions and freedom of speech to hold on to power.

The pandemic creates even broader grounds for restricting citizens' civil liberties, even to the point of eliminating them altogether. The ruling elite in the core countries of the imperial IHU is also compelled to do so by the objective circumstances of structural changes in the world economy, which threaten its dominant position. The change in technological modes is accompanied by a depreciation of capital and depression. The change in WEM is accompanied by a decline in the efficiency of the institutions that regulate economic reproduction and by a political crisis. The ruling elite needs legal grounds for restricting the rights and freedoms of citizens to maintain control over the situation. This is all the more urgent in the context of the global hybrid war, in which the puppeteers of the US ruling elite aim to deprive their victims of their freedom of action and confiscate their assets. The collapse of the financial bubbles and the financial market has devalued the savings of tens of millions of American citizens, whose potential protest is ideally suited to quarantine. It is possible that the financial oligarchy in power in the US is sacrificing vulnerable sections of the American population in order to paralyze the horror of death by coronavirus against the protest of millions of citizens who have lost their assets and savings.

It is also possible that the American deep state[6] simply did not think about the population of its own country before organizing the coronavirus experiment. Just as the English "deep state," while pandering to Hitler before World War II, did not think about the future victims of the bombing of London and the defeat of the British army in France.

Let us not forget the Anglo-Saxon ruling elite's traditional adherence to the Malthusian ideology that justifies population reduction in order to preserve the habitat of the "golden billion." Mass deaths of the elderly non-working population may be seen as a desirable way of getting rid of "extra mouths" and obligations to fund their entitlements to health care. This is obviously in the interest of health insurance companies, which have saved a lot of money through the mass deaths of chronically ill elderly people whose costs of forced isolation and treatment for the coronavirus have been borne by the state. In the wake of the current pandemic, B. Gates is pushing a project of total population vaccination, according to some experts, using the latest bioprogramming technology.[7] The Rockefeller and Gates Foundations has long been accused of funding global projects to reduce births and sterilize women, including through vaccines recommended by the WHO. In 2014, for example, there was unrest in Kenya among a population suspected of using tetanus vaccines for this purpose.

10.2 COVID-19 Pandemic Linked to US Bioweapon Violations

Investigations into the facts leading up to the coronavirus pandemic suggest that it was systematically prepared. The chronology of Operation COVID-19 dates back to 2010 when the Rockefeller Foundation and Global Business Network report "Scenarios for the Future of Technology and International Development"[8] was released. One of the report's scenarios, entitled Lock Step, essentially presents a simulation of global destabilization through a pandemic virus, "In 2012, we have the biggest pandemic the world has been waiting for years. Unlike H1N1 2009 (the swine flu pandemic virus that emerged in 2009), this new flu strain proved to be extremely dangerous. Even some countries that had prepared themselves for the emergence of such a pandemic were affected, and on a global scale, the virus struck around 20% of the population. Eight million died in the first seven months after the emergence of the new strain ..."[9]

Nature Medicine reported in 2015 that US microbiologists conducted a successful laboratory experiment to create a hybrid form of bat coronavirus capable of infecting humans. "The experiment confirmed the hypothesis that bat coronaviruses can directly infect humans," said the paper, signed by 15 authors, 13 of whom are affiliated with the University of North Carolina at Chapel Hill, and two others are employees of the lead Special Pathogens and Biosafety Laboratory at the Wuhan Institute of Virology. According to the article,[10] US and Chinese scientists were jointly involved in the research. Despite a temporary moratorium by the US government on funding research into enhancements for pathogens, including MERS and SARS influenza viruses, work in this area has received special permission (apparently from US intelligence agencies) and has continued. As ABC News has learned, US military intelligence medical units warned D. Trump in the fall of 2019 about the effects of the coronavirus.

Bill Gates repeatedly heralded the impending pandemic:[11] In a 2018 discussion on epidemics hosted by the Massachusetts Medical Society and the New England Journal of Medicine, Gates presented the results of an Institute for Disease Modelling forecast that showed the new flu could kill 30 million people within six months. On October 18, 2019, in New York City, the Johns Hopkins University Center for Health Security (it is through its information resource that the whole world is now tracking the coronavirus epidemic), in partnership with the World Economic Forum, Gates hosted a strategy game called Event 201"[12] on pandemic response, simulating the spread of the virus through airborne, handshakes and other tactile contact. The features of the virus, according to the strategy game scenario, were the lack of an effective vaccine and the selective mortality of the population, mostly related to immunocompromised individuals.

It is also pertinent to mention the 2011 and then widely promoted blockbuster Infection, which was designed to prepare the public's panicked expectations of a rapidly spreading deadly airborne lung disease.

International financial institutions have also begun to prepare for a simulated pandemic in concert with opinion leaders. Back in June 2017, for example, it was reported that the World Bank had issued specialized bonds aimed at financial support to developing countries as an emergency relief channel in the event of a pandemic.[13]

The question arises: What was the purpose of such a coordinated effort requiring the participation of very influential entities? To answer this, let's look at one of the images of the future in the aforementioned Rockefeller Foundation report. It says,[14] "During the pandemic, national leaders around the world increased their power and imposed the strictest rules and constraints ... Even after the pandemic passed, this more authoritarian control and oversight of citizens and their activities remained and even increased. To protect themselves against the spread of increasingly global problems, from pandemics and transnational terrorism to environmental crises and growing poverty, leaders around the world began to rule more tightly." As written, this is what happens: totalitarian control, accompanied in some places by a formal declaration of a state of emergency;

unprecedented surveillance of all economic and economic activities; subjugation of the social organism to strict rules in the name of security.

But China's leadership emerged from the ordeal with honor, having contained the spread of the pandemic and embarked on the revival of production, trade, and foreign relations with greater vigor. As a result, the bearing structures of the new world order have been strengthened by greater discipline of all social groups, mobilization of resources, shared responsibility, and an increase in the authority of the authorities, whose will has demonstrated the steadfastness of the Chinese political system. Moreover, the Chinese leadership's response to the epidemic has become a model for most countries. China has evolved from a victim to a global leader in anti-pandemic policy, offering its assistance to all countries of the world, including the US.

So, first, a shooting through a predictive report; five years later, the first successful experiment, and another five years later, a pandemic ravaging national economies and households. This is what the already realized scenario of using cognitive bioengineering weapons to demoralize populations for hybrid warfare looks like. And all this without guns, soldiers, and armies, the use of which is currently restricted by international law and cannot be openly used by any state.

The author of this monograph has questioned the "authorship" of COVID-19 attributed to the PRC from the beginning of the pandemic and, despite attempts to marginalize the position, was correct.

The fact that no authoritative international investigation has yet been conducted into the causes of the pandemic, which, due to the highest number of dead citizens, the US is primarily interested in, indicates one thing: to maintain world domination and undermine global supply chains all means are good, even the most misanthropic, neo-Malthusian, for the directors of the "project" of the global virus and the subsequent total vaccination. To keep the world domination, which the US power and financial elite is losing at the current change of world order, their intelligence agencies are frantically trying to create viruses, selectively destroying the unwanted people: the Slavs, Chinese, Africans, etc. As the author reported to the Russian Security Council back in 1996, this is becoming possible with the modern development of bioengineering. Two years ago, in his analytical report, the author of this book substantiated the hypothesis of the artificial origin of the coronavirus developed by American bioengineers. The US is at the forefront of developing new weapons of mass destruction to intimidate other countries and maintain world domination.

Dr. Fauci, who orchestrated the funding of coronavirus synthesis research for the past 20 years as Chief Infectious Disease Officer in the US, still directs US anti-pandemic policy and exerts considerable influence over the WHO. Classified US bio-laboratories continue to operate in all regions of the world in violation of the Biological Weapons Convention. Until we stop these illegal activities that threaten humanity with new man-made epidemics and understand the causes of the coronavirus pandemic and the associated mass psychosis, fighting it will resemble the famous Don Quixote war on windmills, only with other consequences, costs, and casualties.

10.3 Special Features of Modern World Warfare

Faced with the need to suppress China as a successful rival in the struggle for global dominance, the US ruling elite tried all the usual methods of deterrence through "soft power." But as a result of the financial and economic crisis of 2007–2009, the threat of loss of global hegemony has only increased. The rise of China on the wave of the new technological paradigm and the formation of the core of a new century cycle of capital accumulation in Southeast Asia has continued. In order to stop this rise, it was necessary to find a way to paralyze economic activity, which was done through the forced self-isolation of millions of people. This logical sequence of facts and the description of the meaning of the crisis field explains the hypothesis of treating the coronavirus as a biological weapon and the pandemic as a key campaign of global hybrid warfare that becomes a trigger for global change.

This hypothesis fits well with the traditions of the Anglo-Saxon ruling elite. In order to trigger World War I, the British secret services organized the assassination of the crown prince of Austria-Hungary and eliminated the most influential opponents of dragging Russia into the war, including Stolypin and Rasputin, who insisted on ending it. To trigger World War II, the American and British secret services helped Mussolini and Hitler not only to come to power but also to hold it against the generals and to start a war, sacrificing the Czech Republic, Poland, and other European allies. One may also recall the operation with the self-detonation of the US warship Maine in Havana Bay, which the US used as a reason to declare war on Spain in order to seize its American colonies. Or the provocation with the shelling of warships in the Gulf of Tonkin to justify the invasion of Vietnam in 1964.

These criminal provocations, committed at different times, had fatal consequences, setting in motion irreversible processes of global change. They involved those in power in making decisions predetermined by the established routines with catastrophic consequences. The decisions of the heads of the Austro-Hungarian, Russian, and German empires to start World War I following the political assassination in Sarajevo were played out like clockwork. Hitler's actions to usurp power in Germany and then unleash the war in Europe were also calculated and fit the logic of those "ordering" the war. The latter was preparing and triggering a chain reaction of military conflicts in secret, not only from the people involved but also from the parliaments and governments who were forced to make decisions that were predetermined by political logic.

By injecting the coronavirus and spinning panic, the organizers of the hybrid war have put national governments in the position of having to make decisions exactly in line with the Rockefeller Foundation's scenario. Players with "secret knowledge" immediately before the market collapsed shifted their capital from securities to base metals, solidifying their positions and preparing to buy many times cheaper assets. They probably also used their influence to continue developing the coronavirus despite the US government officially terminating the research program.

The leakage of the coronavirus from the super-secure lab linked to the US secret service is somewhat reminiscent of Napoleon's strange escape from the British-blockaded island of Elba, which predetermined further developments in France up to the Rothschild enrichment on the British bond market crash and its subsequent purchase during and after the Battle of Waterloo. The British army had to pay for this with the deaths of many thousands of soldiers and the British treasury with millions of pounds. All in all, Napoleon turned out to be a useful political tool for the British oligarchy, by which France was stripped of its colonies and relegated to a minor land country, while the Romanov dynasty, akin to the British crown, strengthened its unchallenged power in Russia and Central Europe. This historical episode completed the English century cycle of capital accumulation and the establishment of a colonial world order in which Britain took center stage.

However, provocations, fatal in their historical consequences, do not always achieve the results desired by their organizers. World wars are initiated by the countries, the ruling circles of which seek to preserve their dominant position within the existing world economic order and are burdened by the overaccumulation of capital in the production of the existing technological order. However, the winners are the countries that were able to form the institutions of the new world economic order in time and master the basic productions of the new technological order. This period is an opportunity for them to make a leap forward in economic development, riding the new long Kondratiev wave earlier than others and launching a new century-long cycle of capital accumulation.

The last world war was instigated by the British secret services in order to maintain British global dominance. The winners of that war were the USSR and the US, which managed to rapidly develop the basic industries of the new technological paradigm by creating a more efficient management system based on the institutions of the new world economic paradigm. The capacity to mobilize resources by vertically integrated ministries and corporations that organized large-scale production, respectively, in the USSR and the US, was far greater than in the decrepit colonial empires of Western Europe with their family firms and pampered aristocracy. In the first phase of this war, Germany easily defeated and subdued all continental European states thanks to the concentration of resources in the corporate-administrative structures of the Third Reich. However, the Soviet Union's system of national economic planning proved to be more effective: with an order of magnitude less productive capacity than in Europe united by the Nazis, the Soviet Union destroyed the man-hating model of the new world economic order in the form of the Nazi corporate state.

The world wars of the last century were fought over the possession of territory, at least on the part of the main aggressors, Germany and Japan, who proclaimed the goal of expanding the living space of their nations and wanted to enslave the rest of humanity. The current world hybrid war is being waged by the ruling elite of the United States for control of the world economy, and above all, its financial system. By privatizing the function of issuing world currency, the US ruling oligarchy is able to exploit all of humanity through the exchange of the FD it creates for real material goods and assets. The purpose of its aggression is to complete the process of liberal globalization, in which all countries must ensure the free circulation of the dollar as the world currency and the exchange of all national material goods and assets for it. Therefore, combat operations in the current hybrid warfare take place not through the use of tanks, ships, and aircraft, as in the last century, but through the targeted use of financial instruments, trade restrictions, cyber attacks, and cognitive weapons used to manipulate the expert community and the public consciousness. Armed forces are used in the final phase of hostilities for punitive purposes to finally demoralize an already defeated enemy. Biological weapons are used to create panic in the population in order to disrupt governance and stop economic activity, ultimately devaluing the assets of millions of investors and citizens for their subsequent purchase by the global oligarchy.

To date, quarantine and self-isolation regimes have affected almost 50% of the world's population (some 3.9 billion people). Maintaining strict social distancing measures costs 2% of GDP each month. The global economic downturn in 2020 could reach 2%, in a worst-case scenario between 4% and 6%. Production declines in the most vulnerable sectors of the economy reach between 40 and 90% (Figure 35).

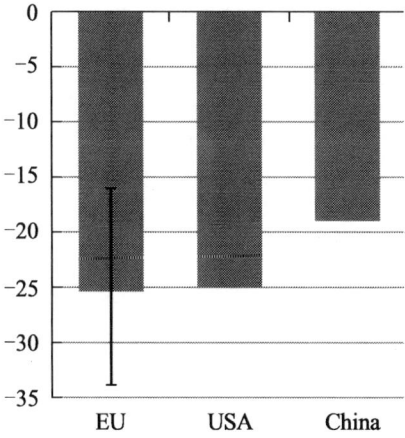

Figure 35   Impact on Economic Activity of a Partial or Complete Stoppage of Production, in % of GDP

Source: OECD.

The global financial market has collapsed by $30 trillion, comparable to the GDP of all Eurasian states. Faced with an acute fiscal crisis, many of these states are lining up for new loans, which the EU and US monetary authorities willingly provide (at the expense of the printing press).

Winning this war for the US would mean the widespread formation of puppet regimes, from which not much is required: strict compliance with IMF recommendations on the openness of the economy and free movement of capital while refusing to create a national monetary management system; privatization of state enterprises in favor of US corporations; transfer of control over media and telecommunications to US agents; acquisition of US military equipment and following Washington's foreign policy in the footsteps. There was no need for the American empire to keep occupying troops in the countries under its control: the indigenous ruling elite, trained in US and British universities, enthusiastically carried out instructions from Washington and received their share of the profits from the exploitation of national wealth by American capital. In return, the

American handlers relieve them of the responsibility of developing the national economy, which is left to foreign investors.

As the historical experience of long-standing US control of Latin American countries shows, it is sufficient for Washington to keep its agents in senior positions in the Central Bank, finance, defense, and foreign affairs ministries to pursue its macroeconomic, defense, and foreign policy, regardless of the heads of state and representative bodies elected by the population. Typical examples of this occupation in modern times are the US-controlled regimes governing Ukraine, Georgia, Iraq, Brazil, and a host of other states, including EU member states.[15]

The economic consequences of such "soft" occupation are comparable to the damage inflicted on defeated countries during the world wars of the last century. For example, Russia's economic losses under the Washington-controlled Yeltsin regime are comparable to the consequences of Hitler's aggression.[16] Only unlike Nazi Germany, which lost manpower and equipment in the occupied territories, the American ruling elite gained control of the trillions of capital taken out of the post-Soviet space and assets retained there without any losses.

Hybrid warfare is far more profitable and comfortable than the armed conflicts of the last century. It fits in well with the business logic of the American power elite, whose power structures and powerful clans are profiting from occupied countries: the CIA on drug trafficking from US-controlled Afghanistan and Colombia; the Pentagon on the oil trade from Iraq and Libya defeated by the US military; the Biden family on privatizing the Ukrainian gas transportation system; the Bush family on the Kuwaiti oil fields.

And these are just isolated examples. US banks and corporations "digest" the assets and resources of US-occupied countries, whose macroeconomic policies ensure that a significant portion of the national income is squeezed in favor of Americans. Their entrepreneurs are forced to use American technology. American collections are enriched with unique pieces from looted museums. Medical clinics receive human organs from countries plunged into chaos for transplantation to wealthy patients. However, it is the American financial oligarchy that makes the most money by manipulating the financial markets of the countries it controls. Even on the bonds of impoverished Ukraine, Soros' wards manage to squeeze out up to 60% of annual income.[17]

Perhaps the most large-scale example of neo-colonial exploitation of the US financial periphery is the squeezing of national income and wealth from Russia. In the 1990s, the super profits of the financial speculation sector were formed and grew on the redistribution of state property through criminal voucher privatization, the state budget through the GKO financial pyramid, and the population's savings through private financial pyramids. The intensity of this redistribution in the interests of the American "partners" and ultimate beneficiaries was extremely high, amounting annually to half of the country's total savings fund and accompanied by the formation of enormous "financial bubbles."[18]

Every rouble invested by speculators close to the privatization agency in the purchase of privatization cheques subsequently brought them tens of roubles of profit on the resale of shares of initially multiply undervalued enterprises, which meant corresponding damage or loss of profits for the state. Having invested these profits in the GKO pyramid scheme of the 1990s, they further boosted their profits and took them out of Russia, driving the state into bankruptcy in August 1998. Having brought down the country's financial system, they then came back to buy up cheaper assets. Another pumping of the Russian stock market, fuelled by rising oil prices, was mistakenly perceived by the Russian authorities and businesses as an economic boom. The rapid growth of stock market capitalization turned out to be a "financial bubble." It burst immediately after the oil price crash and the outflow of foreign speculative capital, once again plunging the Russian financial system into a deep crisis in 2008.

Neocolonial exploitation of peripheral countries through monetary, financial, and price instruments of non-equivalent foreign economic exchange is a characteristic element of the American capital accumulation cycle. But its flip side is the impoverishment of US-controlled countries, which entails the depletion of the global reproduction contours of the established world economic order. In spite of the super profitability of American aggression in the Middle East, CIS countries, and Latin America, the US is doomed to defeat in this hybrid war due to the exhausted capabilities of its management system to provide sustainable economic growth and increase the welfare of the population.

The impoverishment and degradation of the countries that have become victims of Washington's global hybrid war (Iraq, Libya, Ukraine, Georgia) is clear evidence of the decline of the effectiveness of the American-centric imperial world economic order against the background of the successful development of countries integrated by China under the BRI (the Indochina, Pakistan, Mongolia, Sri Lanka, Ethiopia). In order to maintain its global dominance, the US ruling elite is everywhere, destroying the reproductive contours of the countries it does not control through the application of the hybrid warfare tools discussed above. However, it does not set out to create new opportunities for the development of the countries under its control by handing them over to its corporations for exploitation. Having knocked the Chinese out of a number of African countries with Ebola fever, the Americans did not complete the social, transport, and engineering infrastructure started by the PRC, limiting themselves to controlling the sources of their national income. Having cut off Ukraine from Russia, the American puppets did not replace the severed cooperative links and terminated investment projects with new ones, but handed over the most profitable objects of the Ukrainian economy to the American and European capital. For the peoples of peripheral countries, the difference in perspectives of embedding into the integration structures of the new world economy or neo-colonial exploitation by US corporations is becoming more and more evident. The imperial world economy, which has lost its effectiveness, is becoming less and less attractive and is being destroyed as the mechanisms of reproduction of the new, integral world economy are being established and expanded.

10.4 The Inevitability of US Ddefeat in the Global Hybrid War They Have Unleashed

As already noted, the PRC emerged from the pandemic and strengthened its leadership of the global economy. Studies on the impact of COVID-19 on China's economic development stand out. One such study analyses the state of the digital economy (DE) and uses the HP financial index (HP financial index).[19] The authors conclude that despite the spread of coronavirus infection, China's economy has continued to grow, and the area of DE has made tangible progress (especially at the beginning of the pandemic). An analysis of the direct and indirect effects of the COVID-19 and DE pandemic on the Chinese economy showed that digitalization greatly accelerated economic development in China, whereas the coronavirus outbreak and its spread prevented the full benefits of DE from becoming apparent but did not entirely extinguish them. The authors argue that during the pandemic, DE acted as an "intermediary" or "bridge-builder" for the economy, preventing established linkages from being severed and, on the one hand, stimulating China's economic development.

Most interesting are the conclusions drawn by the authors, taking into account the unevenness of China's regional development. For example, the country's high-level eastern region, which had the conditions for DE progress (availability of capital and appropriate technology), developed steadily during COVID-19 thanks to the work of the digital economy. The central region, which received the first blow of the coronavirus, managed to stimulate and improve DE (in particular, online education and the online office) precisely during the pandemic. It was able to assess the situation in the central region and select and implement the most appropriate strategy to respond to the new challenge in a timely manner. As a result, China's economy suffered no significant losses from the coronavirus. Even the economically less developed western region of the country was able to avoid the destructive negative effects of COVID-19 due to its geographical location, but it is still recommended to develop DE more actively in the future.

However, the potential threats that the pandemic continues to pose cannot be ignored, and in order to manage risks more effectively, China needs to take the following measures:[20]

(1) Develop macroeconomic policies and international cooperation
- Establish an effective system to monitor domestic and international trends in the development and spread of coronavirus infection
- Coordinate actions and launch new initiatives in the area of post-conflict development
- Establish effective mechanisms and plans to respond to the next challenges
- Share responsibility between different levels and levels of government effectively for the development and implementation of relevant policies and plans at the national level

(2) Formulate an effective policy and strategy for the development of the digital economy
- Move from implementing an effective short-term ("pilot") policy for the development of DE to the design and implementation of a long-term strategy and policy
- Emphasise "digital industrialization, industrial digitalization, and digital governance" in building a core course for long-term development
- Improve the CE development guidelines for different regions of the country and their respective incentive system
- Move from short-term to long-term state support measures for small and medium-sized enterprises

(3) Manage risks through DE effectively
- Based on big data, artificial intelligence, blockchain, etc., create a system to monitor and respond quickly to potential pandemic risks
- Systematically and timely assessment of the country's capacity to respond (volume of foreign reserves, production, etc.)

- Identify and remedy governance problems similar to those identified as a result of COVID-19 in the health sector
- Build R&D capacity for the development of DE
- Improve the emergency response system to effectively ensure national security

(4) Improve the digital system

- Strengthen "talent support," expand research on advanced technologies, provide effective training, develop the capacity of the DE, etc.
- To accelerate the establishment of a platform for the systematic development of the DE, to facilitate the optimal allocation of resources and coordination of efforts in this direction
- Ensure an effective support system for the development of the DE

What, however, can the US offer to the world instead of the image of the new IHU being formed in the PRC?

The current last phase in the lifecycle of the imperial world economy, in terms of power-economic relations, can be characterized as a period of domination by global finance capital. Since the collapse of the world system of socialism, US-centred liberal globalization has engulfed almost the entire world economy, the reproduction of which is increasingly subject to the interests of transnational corporations, the bulk of which are tied to refinancing by the US Federal Reserve, the ECB, the Bank of England and the Bank of Japan.

In the decade since the global financial crisis began in 2008, quantitative easing policies by the monetary authorities in the US, EU, UK, and Japan have almost quadrupled the money supply of the dollar and tripled it with the euro, the pound, and the yen. Hypothetically, it is conceivable that the increasing flow of money emission could be maintained indefinitely within a relative macroeconomic equilibrium through speculation between these centers of world currency emission with periodic sterilization of excess money supply in collapsing "financial bubbles." Each cycle of money emission generates a corresponding amount of money to the controlling structures, which materialize in the purchase of tangible assets and values, after which the excess money supply is sterilized in periodic financial crises together with the depreciation of savings and the bankruptcy of the entrepreneurs involved in international speculation. This progressive redistribution of property ultimately leads to a concentration of capital on a global scale in the hands of the financial oligarchy that controls the issuance of the dollar and other world currencies.

The 2010s were a decade of minimum economic growth but maximum central bank liquidity and, as a consequence, maximum financial market capitalization. These capitalization rates were boosted by the bursting of financial bubbles in the stocks of so-called high-tech companies, most of which are essentially virtual entities on the internet. The big five US technology companies (Microsoft, Apple, Amazon, Alphabet, and Facebook) are collectively valued at more than US$1 trillion in market capitalization, representing 20% of US stock market capitalization—an unprecedented level of concentration (Figure 36). "Never before in the field of monetary policy has so much been won by so few at the expense of so many," the researchers conclude.

It should be noted that the giant capitalization of these "big five" companies is based on intangible assets, which are usually inflated by classic market manipulation techniques. Using insider information and the general publicity of these companies, some of which are essentially virtual sets of rights and publicity, speculators with unlimited access to credit generated by central banks artificially inflate their stocks. The flow of capital generated by the gigantic money supply is concentrated in the financial market, causing hyperinflation of stocks in its most speculative segments. There is no real growth in economic activity. The large-scale redistribution of wealth in favor of oligarchic clans affiliated with the US Federal Reserve through the appropriation of money from the gigantic money supply is accompanied by a dramatic increase in unemployment and a worsening of the situation of workers. As of April 2020, the US recorded an unemployment rate of 14.7%—the highest level since the Great Depression of the 1930s and 1940s (Figure 37).

The outpacing issue of the dollar and the inflating of financial bubbles in the US market serve as a means of redistributing not only national but also global assets in favor of the same Fed-linked oligarchic clans (Figure 38). About half of the dollars issued go outside the US to buy up the assets of unregulated countries, including Russia. US monetary authorities use hybrid warfare techniques (from sanctions to pandemics) to weaken dependent states in order to absorb their assets. A prime example has been the US Treasury's control of the Russian aluminum industry, along with the major hydroelectric plants that generate energy for it. US financial institutions are using the crisis exacerbated by the pandemic to increase their market clout by shifting their control over assets both within the US and globally. In this way, national wealth is redistributed in favor of the US financial oligarchy to the detriment of other countries.

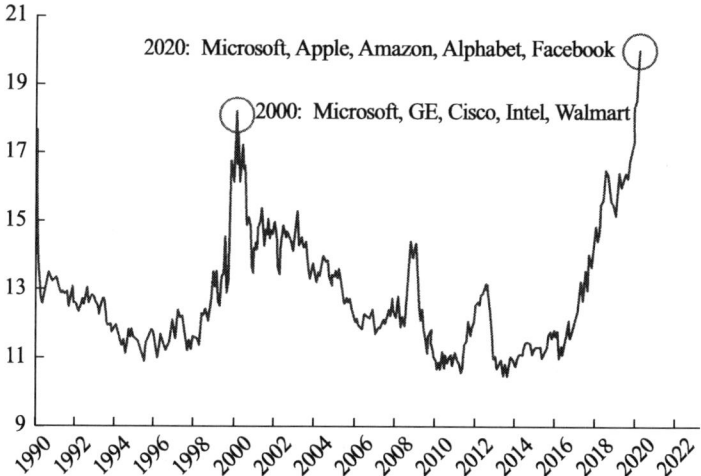

Figure 36   Top Five Companies Ranked by S&P500, as % of Market Capitalization

Source: BofA Global Investment Strategy, Bloomberg.

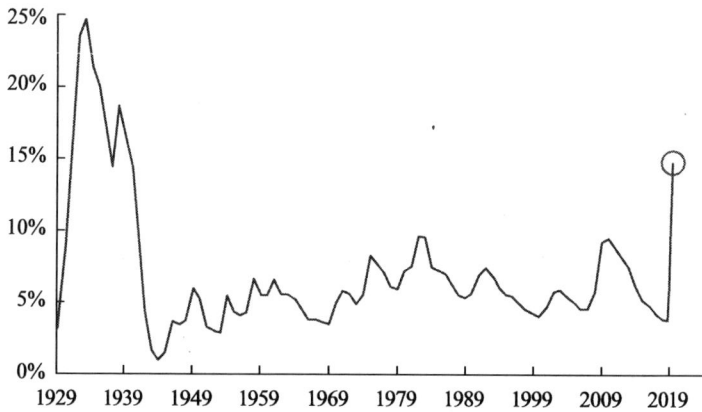

Figure 37   Unemployment Rates in the US since 1929

Source: BofA Global Investment Strategy, Bureau of Labour Statistics, Bloomberg.

The trend toward concentration of capital in the imperial IHU controlled by the US financial and power oligarchy is mirrored in the trend toward impoverishment of the rest of the population, above all wage earners, especially in peripheral countries. Let us analyze the possible consequences of the continuation of these trends in the ongoing structural changes of the world economy.

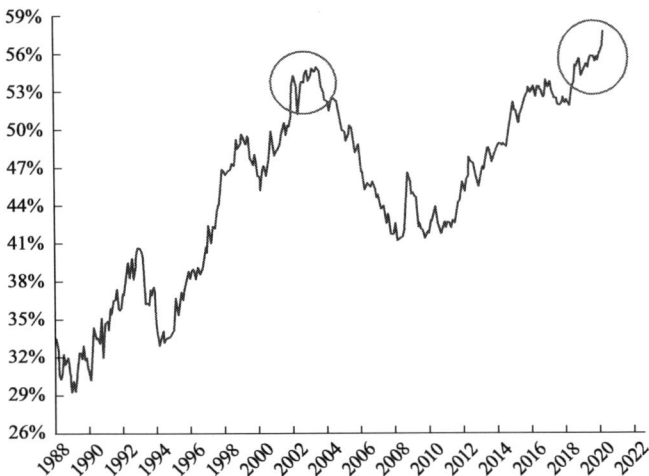

Figure 38   US Share of Global Market Capitalization

Source: BofA Global Investment Strategy, MSCI, DataStream.

10.5 Threats to the Existence of Humanity by the American Power Oligarchy

The literature is replete with anti-utopias and near-scientific concepts of the establishment of world domination by a capitalist oligarchy, from the theory of the "golden billion" to the image of an "electronic concentration camp." Without going into futurological fantasies, we shall state the obvious features of the image of the world order, which the domination of the capitalist oligarchy promises to mankind. They can be constructed by extrapolating the already established trends of forming a unipolar world, taking into account the statements of ideologists and political leaders.

Firstly, this world order will be shaped by the canons of Anglo-Saxon imperialism. The dominance of the Anglo-American system of regulating the reproduction of global capital in today's global financial market is unquestionable.[21] As the financial-pandemic crisis unfolds, the contours of a qualitative increase in the power of the US financial-power elite are emerging. By controlling global currency issuance, it is redistributing global assets in its favor, using the coronavirus pandemic to dump its debt obligations and build up new assets at the expense of sovereign borrowing by states. On the one hand, giant financial bubbles worth up to $30 trillion have been deflated under the veil of the coronavirus fear pandemic. On the other hand, the coronavirus pandemic has paralyzed economic activity in most states and has led to a huge build-up of government deficits, generating demand for large-scale borrowing. To meet this demand, the US Federal Reserve is issuing money. While in the US, it is issued against unsecured government debt, other countries will borrow dollars against sovereign assets. A large part of the loans issued by US banks will be secured by the assets of insolvent borrowers, which will then come under the control of US Fed-linked banks and funds.

Thus, the US financial-power elite is trying to carry out a global redistribution of ownership of valuable assets in their favor. In symbiosis with this elite are the European financial and power elite and also the Japanese, who have powerful international instruments for financial expansion. Peripheral countries that have liberalized, under pressure from the IMF and the Paris and London Clubs of creditors, cross-border capital operations in world reserve currencies will be a field for asset hunting. This includes Russia, where control of much of the private sector has already been taken offshore by the Anglo-Saxons.

Although China, India, and other countries that have mastered the institutions of the new world economy regulate the inflow of foreign capital in accordance with the reproduction purposes of their economies, without allowing foreign capital to absorb systemically important enterprises, the resources of other countries may be sufficient for the American century cycle of capital accumulation to come to a second circle. Most of the post-Soviet states, the Middle Eastern states, and Latin American and African countries that are financially dependent on the US have enough national wealth, which redistribution in favor of American capital could give it a "second wind."

Secondly, the system of global governance built under the control of the capitalist oligarchy will be, in essence, a totalitarian system of power and economic relations. It will have the formal attributes of a democratic and lawful state, but in reality, as the experience of American neocolonialism in the Third World and even in Europe shows, it will be controlled by the oligarchic clans and the special services serving their interests. Through manipulation of public opinion through controlled media, repression of dissidents, bribery of local officials, violent overthrow of unwanted governments, direct aggression, and genocide against resisting peoples and social groups, American ruling elites control the political systems of all their satellites, from NATO members to the Maldives. The escalation of American aggression through the use of all instruments of both "soft" and hard power in the post-Soviet territory, the Middle East, and Latin

America does not cause any doubt about the continuing nature of this totalitarian model of governance. It is also fully manifested in the United States, where after the terrorist attack of September 11, 2001, committed with the connivance of American intelligence agencies, the latter established tight control over the political system and the "deep state."

Thirdly, the domination of the capitalist oligarchy will be anti-social in nature. The capitalist elite has consistently demonstrated its inhuman attitude toward the population under its control throughout the entire period of capitalism. The gruesome pictures of initial capital accumulation described by Marx and the heartbreaking stories of the mass slave trade by Africans, the genocide against Indians, and the spectacular burning of Japanese cities with atomic bombs are by no means a thing of the past. Today, the victims of the American aggression in the Middle East, dictated by the interest of the American ruling elite in the region's oil and gas fields, are millions of dead and tens of millions of citizens maimed and who have lost their homes and property. As it became clear as a result of mutual accusations of Washington and Beijing, the special services of the US conduct systematic working out of selective biological weapons in hundreds (in Ukraine, it is more than tens) of dispersed around the world laboratories. The imposition by the US ruling elite of its order according to the principles of the Washington Consensus always and everywhere leads to the impoverishment and savagery of the population, on the one hand, and to the formation of a comprador local elite under its control, on the other.

Fourthly, the result of the establishment of the Anglo-Saxon model of governance will be a systemic distortion of all the moral and legal foundations of public consciousness. The formation of a false system of coordinates to manipulate public consciousness is the core of this system of governance. Thus, by cynically using stereotypes of religious and national consciousness, Anglo-American political technologists have raised Islamic extremists and Ukrainian Nazis, channeling their energy in the interests of American imperialism. Before that, they succeeded in fomenting World War I by pitting Russia and Germany against each other through a series of political provocations and fomenting false patriotism. The role of the British secret services in the cultivation of Hitler's regime for the purpose of unleashing World War II is well known.[22] The perestroika masterminded by American agents of influence in the leadership of the USSR turned out to be a large-scale deception and resulted, in the words of Vladimir Putin, in the greatest geopolitics. Putin said it was the greatest geopolitical catastrophe of the 20th century.[23] "All current manifestations of American aggression are disguised by false statements about human rights and democratic values while systematically violating international law and ignoring the norms of human morality and morality. Just look at the staging of the consequences of "chemical attacks" in Syria by "White Helmets" and Hollywood clips about the "atrocities" of regimes undesirable to the American oligarchy. Truly, as the scripture says: "He is a liar and the father of lies."[24]

Fifthly, the domination of the capitalist oligarchy will ultimately lead to the destruction of all social groups capable of any kind of solidarity: ethnic, national, class, professional, and religious. As soon as the need to divide and conquer by pitting social groups with different ideologies against each other disappears, the latter will be discredited and their bearers repressed. This is exactly what happened in US-controlled Western Europe, which became a victim of multiculturalism imposed on its people.[25] The social structure of society will be tailored to the needs of the global capitalist oligarchy and will consist of a privileged stratum of politicians, journalists, experts, lawyers, and financiers serving its interests; a technocracy controlling the production processes; a repressive apparatus of the power structures; rentier[26] and precariat.[27] The latter will constitute the majority of the population, and the entertainment industry, the drug business, and the mass media will work to neutralize their social energy. Critically minded scientists will be put under strict control with permanent checks on their loyalty to the control system. As robotics, artificial intelligence systems, and automated process control spread, the number of workers will fall, and specialists will become computer operators. The expansion of the service sector, especially in the health care and information and communications technology sectors, will partly compensate for the loss of jobs. But the sense of class solidarity characteristic of the proletariat and the peasantry will be a thing of the past.

Sixthly, the domination of the capitalist oligarchy and its subordination to the advances of the scientific and technological revolution create the conditions for its gradual transformation into a post-humanoid state. Attempts to extend the life span through cellular technology of tissue regeneration and organ transplantation, desire to clone counterparts, a passion for eugenics, and transgender entertainment of the ruling elite of capitalist countries indicate the qualitative degeneration of their consciousness. The permissiveness for themselves and the tight control of the loyalty of society indicate the emergence of a divine conceit in the capitalist oligarchy. The deification of monarchs and dictators has been commonplace in the history of mankind, especially in traditional societies. However, for the first time, the deification of the ruling elite does not take place on religious or ideological grounds, but on the basis of boundless egocentrism, contrasting their omnipotence with the powerlessness of the rest of society. In the eyes of the capitalist oligarchy, the latter is nothing more than a herd of humanoid beings that can be ruled at will beyond any moral or legal standards. This paves the way for a transhumanist reincarnation of mankind with unpredictable consequences.

It is worth noting that transhumanism is not a product of the current technological revolution, which has, however, given it a powerful push in terms of practical implementation in the sense of a cardinal change in human nature. As V. A. Shchipkov rightly points out, "Transhumanism is part of a humanistic project, in fact, a late humanism. Transhumanism inherits humanism's main principle—anthropocentrism—and uses its main method—the negation of tradition. In this sense, the philosophical foundations of transhumanism are those of humanism."[28] The author continues: "Humanism has declared man to be the source of morality and of all normativity. The ideal and the norm had its source in man himself and ceased to have anything to do with morality understood in the religious sense. The humanists took man as the measure of all things and, indeed, as the measure of himself. On this ground emerged the idea that, during the humanist era, man had reached a high point in his development and had become exceptional "of age." This meant that man (the European, enlightened man) now had the right to decide for himself what was true, beautiful, and moral and to freely create his own religion. Over time, this led the humanist worldview to the concept of "superman" and the birth of fascist ideology.

The negation of tradition becomes the basic method of humanism, the way of thinking for the individual of this culture. Tradition means Christianity itself. The reason for the struggle against the Christian heritage lies in the key position of Christianity that human nature is distorted by original sin and imperfection and that human transformation cannot be accomplished by personal effort alone, without God's help. This undermines the basis of humanism, depriving its rhetoric of its seductive power. Rejecting the Christian idea of man's moral imperfection, humanists proclaimed that every human being is intrinsically good and beautiful and that only his ignorance (ignorance) or adverse social conditions prevent him from showing himself at his best. To "transform" man, therefore, humanists called for a change in the world around him, in the external conditions of his life, and sought to portray the external beauty of his body rather than his soul. Humanistic anthropology was the source of the ideas of transhumanism, which continued to develop the doctrine of human perfection by external means without recourse to the will and moral sense.[29] According to V. A. Shchipkov, "The ideology of transhumanism after militant secularism and postmodernist emancipation considers itself no longer bound by any restrictions in the face of traditional culture, starts with the denial of religious, timeless values and ends with the denial of the individual himself."

Thus, the rebirth of humanism into transhumanism was only a matter of time before secularized rational thought was finally freed from its inner moral constraints. The transition to an industrial society had removed the resource constraints on the rearrangement of the world around it, while the development of capitalism had subordinated the evolution of society to the purposes of expanded reproduction of capital. Freed from moral and religious constraints, the European ruling elite turned most of the world's population into slave laborers and slaves during the British systematic cycle of capital accumulation. The transition to an imperial world order was marked by the emergence of eugenics and mass human experimentation in German and Japanese concentration camps. Fascism became the official ideology of a united Germany in Europe, whose defeat by the Soviet Union only temporarily halted the transition to transhumanism.

After the weakness of the world system of socialism and the formation of a unipolar US-centric model of imperial WEO with the ideology of liberal globalization, transhumanism became mainstream in the evolution of public consciousness. The same study points out that modern liberal democracy allows the social aspect of self-determination to be implemented, changing people's behavioral patterns not only to those not peculiar to traditional society but also to those contradicting people's natural (natural) identity. The author states: "Modern medical technology encourages this process, offering procedures for partial or complete alteration of primary and secondary sexual characteristics, facial features, skin color, hormonal background ... Gender reassignment has no practical significance but is important as an acceptable option in modern society, as a demonstration of human power over nature and social status, and as an advertisement for transhumanist ideas. This breaks anthropological boundaries, opening the way for such biological and social experiments that will allow a person to cease to be human, to go 'beyond the human.'"[30]

The technological basis for practical transhumanism is the transition to a new technological order, the core of which, as shown above, is a complex of bioengineering, information and communication, nano-, digital, and cognitive technologies. By penetrating to the atomic-molecular level, bioengineering technologies make it possible to synthesize new organisms, as well as to change the nature of existing ones, including humans. As V. A. Shchipkov points out, transhumanism refracts the ideas of technologicalism in the field of anthropology. In this sense, transhumanism, like technologicalism, takes itself out of the moral coordinates, claims to be universal, and is inspired by the belief that technology can give man a sense of infinite power over the world and man himself. The author states: "In transhumanism, man becomes a machine not so much as a result of biotechnological modifications to his body and his nature, but after he has abandoned the action of his free will in the process of satisfying his needs. Such a person surrenders his will 'to external control' to technology, which always and instantaneously satisfies the need, providing the necessary result without participation in this process by the will of the person himself. The terms 'man-machine' and 'transhuman' mean mainly the moral state of man, not his external appearance."

In essence, transhumanism denies human nature any normative attributes, ends the anthropological quest, and turns anthropology into the realm of scientific and technological experimentation and free construction. Transhumanism deliberately takes the very notion of the human being out of acceptable discourse and bans it, just as in some Western cultures today, they try to taboo the idea of the biological field and publicly ban the division of people into male and female. In this sense, transhumanism denies anthropology because it denies human beings.[31]

The phenomenon of human life is also subject to a semantic distortion by the philosophy of transhumanism. From transhumanism's understanding of life as something that has an absolute limit, the human right to dispose of his life as any other object of possession without restriction is derived: both the right to ephemeral biological "immortality" and the right of anyone to very real suicide or euthanasia. This refers to a person's right to dispose not only of biological life but also of life as such, ontologically, which is unacceptable in Christian ethics, where life is a divine gift. "Transhumanism creates its own natural-scientific utopia, assuming the achievement of such a level of scientific development that will make it possible to fulfill many conceivable desires of modern man," concludes V. A. Shchipkov. The utopia of transhumanism has been swallowed up by futuristic pictures of man gaining superpowers and unlimited power over his own nature and the world around him. Transhumanism is preoccupied with dreams of being able to translate any human thought into material reality, and its utopia is filled with speculation about technology rather than man. It does not create an overall picture of the ideal human condition but only reflects fragmentary elements of that condition, such as pride ("dignity") and power ("unlimited possibilities").

Thus, the utopia of transhumanism can be characterized as a technological singularity or as a state of "post-culture." This, as it appears to the quoted researcher, is a state of high-tech savagery, i.e., absolute animal freedom, identical to total unfreedom. It means the abolition of taboos and moral restraints that are the basic elements of any culture. Man is not human without culture, so postculture means the end of man himself—his transition to a state, to use the transhumanist vocabulary of the transhuman or posthuman. The technological singularity is the "post-end of history" state in which the existence of man, nature, and culture becomes impossible and meaningless, as man in this state ceases to be human.

Finally, the domination of the capitalist oligarchy inevitably entails the destruction of the Russian state.[32] The combination of chronic Russophobia of Anglo-Saxon political science with the desire for universal domination predetermines the anti-Russian focus of the global hybrid war unleashed by the ruling elite of the US. It is Russia, with its Orthodox humanitarian tradition, according to Anglo-Saxon political technologists, that is the main obstacle to the establishment of world domination of the capitalist oligarchy. It must be said that this opinion corresponds to their own conviction of the Orthodox consciousness about the role of Russia as the final deterrent against the coming of the Antichrist.

As became clear after the collapse of the USSR, it is not anti-communism but Russophobia that is the main component of the ideology of Anglo-American imperialism. Or, as the philosopher A. A. Zinoviev aphoristically put it, "They were aiming for communism but ended up in Russia." After the surrender of the CPSU, Russia was never accepted into the club of developed capitalist "golden billion" countries. It was given a place as a raw material periphery without the right to have any meaningful influence on world politics. The US puppets in power were happy to exploit this place in their own interests, profiting from the exploitation of the natural, productive, and human potential of the post-Soviet space. V. V. Putin succeeded in restoring Russian statehood, which immediately triggered American aggression, the victims of which were Ukraine and Georgia. The US does not hide the fact that the purpose of this aggression is to establish control over these territories in order to turn them into a springboard for the escalation of anti-Russian aggression and further dismemberment of Russia and destruction of the Russian identity.

Thus, the limit of further evolution of the existing world order according to the scenario of world domination of the capitalist oligarchy is incompatible with either the national interests of Russia or the survival of human civilization. Some may be inspired by a transhumanist future, but for the vast majority of humanity, it promises nothing but transformation into a manipulated herd of humanoid beings.

To avoid accusations of conspiracy, we have set aside the most radical versions of this scenario, which are preached by neo-Malthusians obsessed with reducing the world's population.[33] Including the voluntary and compulsory sterilization of women of childbearing age through compulsory vaccination in developing countries, the invention of viruses that selectively affect persons of a certain gender or ethnic group, and the triggering of regional armed conflicts.[34]

The anti-human ideas of the neo-Malthusians, highly influential in the Anglo-Saxon power and financial elite, have no scientific basis: the possibilities of the new technological order radically push the ecological limits to socio-economic development, including the provision of nutritious and clean habitats even when humanity doubles in number.[35] But even without the threat of ecological disaster and the artificial depopulation of humanity, this scenario cannot be considered acceptable beyond the horizon of the "end of history." It would indeed mean the end of the history of human civilization. An alternative scenario is more likely, involving a transition to a new world economic order, which is discussed below as the only acceptable and legitimate one.

NOTES

1. S. Glazyev, *The Last World War: The US Starts and Loses* (Moscow: Knizhniy Mir, 2016).
2. URL: https://www.kp.ru/daily/27083.5/4155093/.
3. "Scenarios for the Future of Technology and International Development," The Rockfeller Foundation, Global Business Network, May 2010.
4. Nanotechnology as a key factor in a new technological order in the economy.
5. D. Chiesa, *What Instead of Disaster* (Moscow: Tribune, 2014).
6. "The deep state" (also parallel state) is an alleged group (or order-type organization) of powerful informal coalitions in the US establishment, political system and elite, consisting of high-level components of the intelligence services (US and foreign), US military, security services, judiciary, financial and political mafia. The concept of "deep state" is similar to that of "state within a state" (Latin imperium in imperio, English state within a state), but is somewhat narrower, as it actually represents an order-type organization that has been operating for several generations.
7. "Bill Gates Talks about 'Vaccines to Reduce Population,'" URL: https://www.warandpeace.ru/en/exclusive/view/44942/ (4 марта 2010 г.).
8. "Scenarios for the Future of Technology and International Development," The Rockfeller Foundation, Global Business Network, May 2010.
9. Ibid.
10. *The Nature Medicine*, November 9, 2015.
11. "Bill Gates Has Been Warning of a Global Health Threat for Years," URL: https://www.businessinsider.com/people-who-seemingly-predicted-the-coronavirus-pandemic-2020-3.

12. The Johns Hopkins Center for Health Security, URL: http://www.centerforhealthsecurity.org/event201/.

13. World Bank (International Bank for Reconstruction and Development) official site, URL: https://www.worldbank.org/en/news/press-release/2017/06/28/world-bank-launches-first-ever-pandemic-bonds-to-support-500-million-pandemic-emergency-financing-facility, Washington, DC, June 28, 2017.

14. "Scenarios for the Future of Technology and International Development," The Rockfeller Foundation, Global Business Network, May 2010.

15. S. Glazyev, *Ukrainian Catastrophe: From American Aggression to World War?* (Moscow: Book World, 2014).

16. S. Glazyev, *Genocide* (Moscow: Terra, 1998).

17. "The Country's Shadow Power: Soros' Cuckoos in Ukraine's Nest," Ukraine.ru, accessed July 13, 2020, URL: https://ukraina.ru/exclusive/20200630/1028126128.html.

18. S. Glazyev, *Lessons of Another Russian Revolution: The Collapse of the Liberal Utopia and the Chance of an Economic Miracle* (Moscow: Ekonomicheskaya Gazeta Publishing House, 2011).

19. Xu Aidi, Qian Fangbin, Pai Chih-Hung, Yu Na, and Zhou Pan. "The Impact of COVID-19 Epidemic on the Development of the Digital Economy of China-Based on the Data of 31 Provinces in China," *Frontiers in Public Health* 9, (January 2022), Article 778671. https://www.frontiersin.org/articles/10.3389/fpubh.2021.778671/full.

20. Based on Xu Aidi, Qian Fangbin, Pai Chih-Hung, Yu Na, Zhou Pan, "The Impact of COVID-19 Epidemic on the Development of the Digital Economy of China-Based on the Data of 31 Provinces in China," *Frontiers in Public Health* 9 (January 2022), Article 778671. https://www.frontiersin.org/articles/10.3389/fpubh.2021.778671/full.

21. A. V. Kuznetsov, *Russia and Anglo-Saxon Globalism: A Monograph* (Moscow: Knorus, 2019).

22. Charles Higham, *Trading With The Enemy: An Expose of The Nazi-American Money Plot 1933–1949* (New York, 1983).

23. "Message from the President of the Russian Federation, V. V. Putin to the Federal Assembly of the Russian Federation," Putin's Address to the Federal Assembly of the Russian Federation, April 25, 2005.

24. "You are of your father the devil, and your will is to do your father's desires. He was a murderer from the beginning, and does not stand in the truth, because there is no truth in him. When he lies, he speaks out of his own character, for he is a liar and the father of lies" (John 8:44).

25. A. Fursov, *World Struggle: Anglo-Saxons against the Planet* (Moscow: Knizhniy Mir, 2017).

26. Rentiers (French rentier from rente) are individuals who live off rents, i.e., income derived from capital, usually placed in the form of bank deposits, securities, profitable real estate, land, businesses, as well as from income derived from copyrights and royalties. John Keynes used the phrase "functionless investor" to describe the term "rentier." He believed that his role was limited to exploiting the value of scarcity.

27. The precariat is a class of socially disadvantaged people without full-time secure employment. Pre-cariat are workers in temporary or part-time employment, which is permanent and sustainable.

28. V. A. Shchipkov, "Secular Foundations and Utopian Features of Transhumanism Ideology," Bulletin of Moscow University Series 12, *Political Sciences*, no. 3 (2018): 7–24.

29. Ibid.

30. Ibid.

31. Ibid.

32. E. Primakov, A World without Russia? What Political Short-Sightedness Leads To (Moscow: Rossiyskaya Gazeta, 2009).

33. I. Blumin, Neo-Malthusianism at the Service of Warmongers: Critique of Bourgeois Political Economy, 3 vols. (Moscow: Publishing House of the Academy of Sciences of the USSR, 1962); A Critique of Modern English and American Political Economy, vol. 2, 267–272.

34. In the speech "Renewing to Zero" at a closed-door conference in Long Beach, California, called the TED2010 Conference, the founder of the global vaccine and immunisation alliance, B. Gates stated literally the following: "First we got population. There are 6.8 billion people in the world today. That number will grow to about 9 billion. Now, if we really do a great job on new vaccines, health care, reproductive health services, we will reduce it by perhaps 10 or 15%. Gates' neo-Malthusian ideas are shared by a whole class of "philanthropists" belonging to big capital

35. N. Klukin and V Gutnikov, "Evaluation of Biological Capacity of Agrosphere in Order to Determine the Population Limit of the Earth," Public Administration, Electronic Bulletin, no. 69 (2018): 482–497.

The China-Russia Strategic Partnership as the Basis for a GEP and the Emergence of a New MHI

CHAPTER 11

Ending Global Hybrid Warfare

11.1 Specifics of Modern World Warfare

The specificity of hybrid warfare is that it can be waged simultaneously against any number of adversaries. The US is currently waging war on all continents. Against Russia in Europe, effectively occupying Ukraine and threatening a new world war. Against China, whose political system is being tested by the "umbrella revolution" in Hong Kong and Japanese provocations over the disputed islands. Against the Arab world, where a full-scale religious war is being waged, exacerbating the chronic confrontation between Shiites and Sunnis and provoking the creation of a full-scale terrorist "Islamic State." Against Venezuela, Brazil, and Bolivia, where political forces undesirable to the US are in power. And this is alongside the occupation of Iraq and Afghanistan and the longstanding conflicts with Iran, North Korea, and Cuba. Signs of attention to the latter should be taken as a sign of large-scale interference in domestic affairs being prepared after the death of F. Castro, as it happened in Libya after the "warming" of relations with Gaddafi.

The US is waging a hybrid world war on multiple fronts, relying on its monopoly on the issue of world currency. This enables them to finance their military, propaganda, organizational, and other expenses of war at the expense of other countries holding American treasury bonds, including the victims of American aggression. And the war itself is based on the principle of self-sufficiency. Mineral deposits, infrastructure, and domestic markets are transferred to US corporations. The Fed organizes the circulation of money, tying the issue of national currency to the growth of foreign exchange reserves in the form of US bonds. The people of enslaved countries have to pay for the activities of the occupation authorities, and pseudo-elections are imposed on them to legitimize the power of American puppets.

The occupation of Iraq is a classic example of American hybrid warfare methodology. Immediately after the capture of that country, carried out with almost no losses thanks to the bribery of the military leadership of the Saddam regime, who betrayed their leader in fear of imminent defeat at the hands of vastly superior NATO forces,[1] the US interim coalition administration, led by US State Department official Lewis Paul Bremer, took control of its economy. On his orders, hundreds of state-owned companies and natural resources were privatized in favor of US corporations. Economic regulation was radically liberalized, and American GMOs were forcibly imposed on farmers.[2]

In Afghanistan, the payback of the occupation is achieved through the production and export of narcotics, the sales of which have increased by more than an order of magnitude since the Taliban period. According to FDCS statistics, 150 billion doses of heroin are produced annually in Afghanistan. According to the UN Office on Drugs, Afghanistan had a record opium poppy crop in 2014, with a total crop area of 224,000 hectares: 6,400 tonnes of opium. There is no doubt that Central Asia, the Caucasus, Russia, and Ukraine will account for most of the sales.

It is worth noting that when foreign forces led by the United States entered Afghanistan in 2001, they listed the elimination of terrorism and the fight against drugs as goals of their intervention. The fact that the number of opium poppy crops and the number of drugs produced in Afghanistan increased more than 40 times after the entry of the military contingent and statements that terrorism in Afghanistan is fueled by drugs are indicative and need no comment. According to the UN Office on Drugs and Crime (UNODC), Afghanistan produces $7 billion worth of drugs every year (from 2001 to 2010, the value of drugs produced was $70 billion).

Fractured Yugoslavia has been left to the EU, which must both bear the costs of maintaining the unsustainable economies of the former SFRY republics and tolerate a criminal regime in Kosovo that has metastasized to the skins of many residents of nearby European countries. The Baltic republics, which have lost most of their economies, have also been taken over by the EU. In addition, whether it will survive Georgia, Moldova, and Ukraine, which were forcibly forced to sign Association Agreements with it, will become clear in the near future.

Thus, when unleashing aggression against a sovereign country, the US appropriates the spoils and profits from the exploitation of its resources, while leaving the financing of the costs to its people and partners. This even allows them to partially privatize the use of criminal methods of warfare to avoid excessive political risks. American invention was the private military companies (PMCs), which are widely used as a strike force for covert operations in which the US is trying to hide its involvement. PMCs not only supply products to the military but also provide services to conduct combat or punitive operations, consult "indigenous" forces, protect facilities, and provide customers with the required military expertise. PMCs operate in areas where overt actions of the US military, for whatever reason, are considered inappropriate.[3] In essence, the US revived the centuries-old political cover of the English Crown's loyal pirates, who seized Spanish, Portuguese, and Dutch ships and shared the spoils with the English throne.

According to the American Center for Public Transparency, since 1994, the US Department of Defense has signed more than 3,600 contracts with 12 American PMCs for a total value of $300 billion. This is obviously only direct contracts through the military department. Other contracts may be awarded by other US government agencies. According to rough estimates, the volume of services and supplies of American private military companies during the Bush presidency was about $100 billion a year. However, no one can provide exact figures.

Due to the specifics of its activities, PMCs, to a large extent, are staffed by former military personnel or descendants of the state military-industrial complex. Since the business of private military companies is based primarily on the exploitation of military conflicts of low intensity, PMCs are interested in continuing such conflicts, provoking and supporting them by lobbying the authorities. Only officially, since 1999, $12.4 million was allocated by PMCs for various election campaigns, including the presidential campaign.

The policy of the US administration regarding private military companies is encouraging. In December 2005, while giving a lecture on the situation in Iraq at the School of Advanced International Studies at Johns Hopkins University, the US government also gave a lecture on the situation in Iraq. J. Hopkins and P. Nitze, US Defense Secretary D. Ramfeld, touched upon the activities of PMCs in Iraq. He said the private military companies act within the laws relating to the conduct of Americans abroad, have the ability to attract human and other resources, both Iraqi and other countries, and not use their services would be unwise.

Most notorious in the light of recent Ukrainian events was the activity of the largest US PMC—Xe Services LLC (Blackwater), which receives 90% of orders from government agencies, while the remaining customers are oil producers, insurance companies, and other private organizations. Xe employees took part in the Afghan war, but an incident of their participation in the Iraq war, related to the killing of civilians and arms smuggling, received wide publicity. Another example of criminal activity of American PMCs is MPRI, whose members participated in Operation Storm, which resulted in the dissolution of the Serbian Krajina and the Republic of West Bosnia. In July 2008, MPRI trained the Georgian army before the conflict in South Ossetia.

Private military companies have a prototype in the political history of the Anglo-Saxons—English pirates. They were widely used by the English Crown to undermine the power of Spain. Although English pirates have plundered the English Channel and adjacent waters for centuries, the main history of English piracy is linked to the era of the colonial wars. It can be divided into three phases. The first is at the end of the eighteenth century, the time of the first Anglo-Spanish skirmishes; the second is the late seventeenth and early eighteenth centuries; and the third lasted until piracy was eradicated in the mid-nineteenth century. During the first two phases, England sought to use corsairs to fight its foreign enemies. The instigator of the first phase, Queen Elizabeth, even knighted the pirate Drake after his successful return from a round-the-world pirate voyage in 1580. It would be wrong to think that Drake's piracy was hushed up; on the contrary, Elizabeth proudly called him my "pirate." Drake's pirate operations were primarily directed against the Spanish. Up until the eighteenth century. "national piracy" was even encouraged, despite the fact that it took on a truly global scale: the shores of Africa and India, the coasts of North America, and the islands of the Pacific.

Within the framework of the current US-dominated world order, the Americans always have the upper hand in a conflict with any rival. The effectiveness of their hybrid warfare with half the world is based on the conformity of its technology with the institutions of the existing world economic order. On the financial front, the US has an overwhelming advantage by controlling the issuance of the world currency and the IMF, which determines the rules of operation of the world and most national currency markets, including Russia. Together with its geopolitical allies, Japan, Great Britain, and the EU, whose currencies also have the status of world currencies, it controls the overwhelming part of the global monetary and financial space and has a majority vote in international financial institutions.

On the information front, the global monopoly of the US media allows it to shape public opinion and thereby influence voter preferences, shaping the political landscape in most democracies. Where this influence is lacking, complementary techniques described above—from financing and promoting their agents of influence to assassinating their political opponents and staging coups—are used to obtain the desired US result.

And on other crucial fronts of hybrid warfare—cultural, ideological, food, energy, communications—the US has tangible advantages. No country with an open economy and a democratic political system can win a conflict with the US in a hybrid war. The convenience of the latter lies in the fact that it does not need to be declared and can be conducted stealthily and even strangle the enemy in the embrace so that he is not aware of the ongoing war against him until the last moment. Hybrid war allows the aggressor to avoid not only losses but also responsibility for the consequences, which are blamed on the "native" politicians. This war can be arbitrarily stretched over time, broken up into phases, stopped, and started again at any time, depending on the circumstances. As the American victorious campaigns against the USSR, the SFRY, and Ukraine have shown, an unprepared enemy, even a very strong one capable of inflicting unacceptable damage, proves unable to defend itself in a hybrid war. It is impossible to use tanks against television or missiles against money.

Thus, within the existing world economic order, no country is immune to American aggression. Only countries with a closed financial, information, and political system can effectively resist it. However, self-isolation leads to technological backwardness and economic degradation, which entails falling living standards and already internal political risks. It is possible to curb the aggressiveness of the United States only through the transition to a new world economic order with a restructuring of the main institutions of the functioning of the global financial and information systems, as well as the creation of mechanisms of responsibility for compliance with the norms of international law.

11.2 Building an Anti-war International Coalition

An anti-war international coalition for the transition to a new world economic order could include the following countries:
(1) EAEU and CSTO countries closely linked by their historical destiny and national interests to Russia
(2) SCO countries, well aware of the danger of another Western aggression
(3) BRICS countries, whose economic recovery could be torpedoed by US-organized destabilization

(4) Indochina countries that have no interest in deteriorating relations with Russia

(5) Some remaining sovereignty-holders in the Near and Middle East, for whom a world war would mean an escalation of their own regional conflicts

(6) The Latin American countries of the Bolivarian Alliance, for whom the unwinding of a new world war means a direct US invasion

(7) The developing countries of the Group of 77, heirs to the Movement of Non-Aligned Countries, traditionally opposed to wars for a just world order

(8) European countries whose political elites are capable of acting in their own national interests, for whom another world war in Europe is totally unacceptable

The motivation for creating such a coalition should be the threats of global hybrid warfare, common to all its participants, that the US is unleashing. An important condition for the successful creation of such a coalition, as mentioned above, is to deprive the US of its monopoly on ideological domination by consistently exposing the anti-human consequences of its interventions, the massacres of civilians committed by its servicemen, and the destructive results of the rule of US proxies in various countries. It is necessary to destroy the image of American infallibility, to expose the cynicism and deceit on the part of American leaders, the disastrous consequences of their policy of double standards, and the incompetence and ignorance of American officials and politicians.

Religious organizations working against the imposition of the cult of permissiveness and debauchery and the undermining of family and other human values could be influential allies in building an anti-war coalition. They would help the participants of the coalition to develop and offer the world a new unifying ideology based on the restoration of inviolable moral limits of human arbitrariness. International humanitarian and anti-fascist organizations could play a constructive role. An ally might be the world's scientific and expert community, which speaks from the position of sustainable development and generates projects of development that unite mankind.

The actions of the anti-war coalition should be aimed not only at exposing and destroying the political dominance of the US but, above all, at undermining the American military and political power based on the issue of the dollar as the world currency. In case of continued US aggressive actions to foment world war, coalition members should abandon the use of the dollar in mutual trade and the use of dollar instruments for the placement of their gold and foreign currency assets.

The anti-war coalition must work out a positive program for the global financial and economic architecture based on the principles of mutual benefit, justice, and respect for national sovereignty. In other words, we need a consensus on the foundations of the formation of a new world economic order. To avoid a global catastrophe in the chaos of hybrid war, a consensus is needed on the critical issues of the global economic order: climate, energy, finance, food, water, population, and recycling.[4]

We have already mentioned above the necessary measures for financial stabilization, more effective regulation of the financial market, banking, financial, and investment institutions, stimulating the growth of a new technological pattern and progressive structural change, and the formation of appropriate new institutions. They must eliminate the fundamental causes of the global crisis, the most important of which are the following,

(1) The uncontrolled emission of global reserve currencies, leading to the abuse of the monopoly position of issuers in their own interests at the cost of growing imbalances and destructive trends in the global financial and economic system

(2) The inability of the existing mechanisms of regulation of the operations of banking and financial institutions to protect national financial systems from speculative attacks aimed at destabilizing them, the excessive risks of cross-border flight of speculative capital, and the formation of financial bubbles

(3) Exhaustion of the growth limits of the dominating technological model and inadequate conditions for the emergence of a new model, including a lack of investment for the widespread implementation of the clusters of basic technologies that make it up

The anti-war coalition must put forward a positive program of measures to overcome the global crisis by eliminating its causes and creating stable conditions for the functioning of the world financial market and international monetary and financial exchange on a mutually beneficial basis, the development of international production cooperation and world trade in goods and technology. These conditions should enable national monetary authorities to arrange credit for the development of industries of a new technological pattern and modernization of the economy on its basis, stimulating innovation and business activity in promising areas of economic growth. For this purpose, the countries issuing world reserve currencies should guarantee their sustainability by keeping certain limits on public debt, balance of payments, and trade deficits. They should also comply with relevant requirements for transparency of their currency issuance mechanisms, allowing for their smooth exchangeability for all assets traded in their territories.

An important requirement for issuers of global reserve currencies should be to comply with rules of fair competition and non-discriminatory access to their financial markets. Meanwhile, other countries that comply with similar restrictions should be allowed to use their national currencies as an instrument of foreign trade and monetary exchange, including their use as a reserve asset by other partner countries. It would be appropriate to classify national currencies that claim to be global or regional reserve currencies into categories depending on the requirements their issuers meet.

At the same time, introducing requirements for issuers of global reserve currencies, it is necessary to tighten control over capital movement in order to prevent speculative attacks that destabilize the global and national monetary and financial systems. For this purpose, coalition countries should impose a ban on transactions of their residents with offshore zones, as well as prevent banks and corporations established with the participation of offshore residents from being admitted to refinancing schemes. Restrictions on the use in international settlements of currencies whose issuers are not compliant would also be advisable.

In order to define requirements for issuers of global reserve currencies and monitor compliance with them, the international financial institutions need to be deeply reformed to ensure fair representation of member countries according to an objective criterion that takes into account the relative weight of each of them in global production, trade, finance, natural capacity, and population. By the same criterion, an IMF basket of currencies could be formed for the issue of new special drawing rights—SDRs (see Chapter 12 for more details), against which all national currencies, including global reserve currencies, could be determined. Initially, this basket could include the currencies of those coalition countries that agree to commit themselves to compliance.

Implementing such ambitious reforms requires appropriate legal and institutional backing. This can be done by making the decisions of the coalition internationally binding on the countries concerned and by relying on the UN institutions and mandated international organizations.

In order to stimulate global dissemination of socially significant achievements of the new technological mode, it is necessary to deploy an international system of global strategic socio-economic planning, including long-term forecasts of scientific and technological progress, identifying the prospects for the world economy, regional associations, and major countries, identifying opportunities to overcome existing disparities, including disparities between the development levels of advanced and underdeveloped countries, and choosing the priorities and areas of cooperation.

It is obvious that the US and G7 countries will oppose the implementation of the above-mentioned proposals to reform the global monetary and financial system, which will undermine their monopoly right to issue world currencies without control. The present regime of exchange of results and factors of economic activity between developing and developed countries suits the latter very well. While the leading Western countries benefit greatly from the emission of world currencies, they are holding back access to their own markets for assets, technology, and labor by imposing further restrictions.

As the US policy shows, it prefers the reform of the world financial system on the principles of justice, mutual benefit, and respect for sovereignty to foment a global chaotic war in order to protect its dominant position. To be effective and efficient, an anti-war coalition must, therefore, have sufficient defense capability to repel US aggression and attempts at politico-military destabilization anywhere in the world. For this purpose, it is desirable to expand the format of the Collective Security Treaty Organization (CSTO), engage China, Vietnam, Syria, Cuba, Uzbekistan, Turkmenistan, and Azerbaijan, and create mechanisms of partnership for peace with India, Iran, Venezuela, Brazil, and other countries threatened by American aggression. For all the heterogeneity of these countries, the formation of their anti-war coalition could take on an avalanche character—small and unable to defend themselves, countries would be interested in taking part in it if they were convinced of the seriousness of the superpowers' intentions to create it.

The balance of power between the US and the anti-war coalition depends critically on the position of European countries. Bound by NATO, they are rigidly following in the footsteps of US foreign and military policy. At the same time, the hybrid war unleashed by the US against Russia is contrary to their interests. US aggression in Ukraine poses serious threats to the security of European countries. US-initiated sanctions against Russia primarily hit their economic interests. That is why the efforts made by Russian President Vladimir V. Putin to explain to the leaders of Russia are so important. Putin to explain to European leaders the perniciousness of the US policy toward Ukraine.

But even without European countries, with military-political and economic power comparable to NATO, the anti-war coalition could win the confrontation imposed by the US and, regardless of their wishes, start reforming the global financial currency system in the interests of sustainable economic development of both the world and all national economies. If the G7 countries refuse to "move" in the governing bodies of international financial organizations, the anti-war coalition should have sufficient synergy to create alternative global regulators.

Such a coalition could be initiated on the basis of BRICS, starting by addressing the following economic security issues:

(1) Establishing a universal payment system for the BRICS countries and issuing a common BRICS payment card uniting China's UnionPay, Brazil's ELO, India's RuPay, as well as Russian payment systems

(2) Establishment of an interbank information exchange system independent of the US and EU, similar to SWIFT

(3) Switching to the use of their own rating agencies

11.3 The Logic of US Defeat in a World War

The pandemic is undermining the reproduction mechanisms of the American cycle of capital accumulation. Its antipode in the outgoing world economic order—the USSR—was destroyed by a mental epidemic of Gorbachev's "virus" of perestroika, which ruptured the reproductive contours of the world socialist system. The erosion of the ideological contours entailed the rupture of the political and, in its wake, the destruction of the legal and economic contours of the reproduction of the Soviet empire.

The coronavirus pandemic is eroding the ideological contour of the American empire, demonstrating its weakness in the face of a magnificently mobilized China. Financial market collapse could become systemic as countries fence off from one another, affecting the financial system as well. Having moved beyond fiscal sustainability through budget deficits, sovereign states would rely on building domestic sources of credit to protect their markets from the onslaught of financial speculators and capital flight. The restoration of restrictions on cross-border capital transactions will break the economic reproduction loop of the US capital accumulation cycle. A legal circuit already severed by hybrid warfare will not protect it from an avalanche of nationalizations of US assets in countries affected by US aggression. Their refusal to use the dollar will provoke the collapse of the financial pyramid of US government debt, which will entail the compression of their military expenditures and the destruction of the political reproduction circuit of their global dominance. The processes of destruction of the reproduction system of the American capital accumulation cycle will accelerate as the countries exploited by the US ruling elite get out of their control.

If we again resort to historical analogies of the previous period of world economic change, its final phase (analogous to World War II) could take up to seven years. So far, these analogies are surprisingly confirmed. The first phase of the transition period, which coincides with the last phase of the life cycle of the current world economy, begins with perestroika in the USSR in 1985 and ends with its collapse in 1991. In the previous cycle, it began with World War I in 1914 and ended in 1918 with the collapse of four European monarchies, preventing the global expansion of British capital.

This is followed by a second phase of transition, during which the world's dominant country reaches the peak of its power. After the end of World War I, British hegemony was established for two decades, continuing until the Munich Treaty, which launched World War II. In this phase of transition, the outgoing world economy reaches the limits of its evolution, while at its periphery, the nucleus of a new world economy emerges. In the previous cycle, it emerged in three political formats: socialist in the USSR, capitalist in the US, and national-corporate in Japan, Italy, and Germany. It is now also emerging in three political formats: socialism with Chinese specificity, Indian democratic nationalism, and the global dictatorship of the mondialists, who have pulled the trigger to escalate the global hybrid war by throwing in a coronavirus. Like the last time, this phase took two decades, beginning with the collapse of the USSR and the temporary establishment of Pax Americana in 1991.

Finally, the third and final phase of transition is associated with the destruction of the core of the dominant WEO and the formation of a new one, the core of which forms the new center of world economic development. In this phase, the leading country of the outgoing WEO unleashes a world war in order to maintain its hegemony, as a result of which the countries of the new WEO win, and global leadership passes to them. In the last cycle, this phase begins with the Munich Treaty in 1938 and ends with the collapse of the British Empire in 1948. If the Nazi coup in Kyiv, their de facto occupation of Ukraine, and the imposition of financial sanctions against Russia are considered the beginning of the global hybrid war unleashed by the United States, then the final phase of the current transition period begins in 2014 and is expected to end in 2024. As predicted by Pantin, who predicted in advance of the global financial crisis of 2008, the peak of American aggression against Russia should be expected in 2024. It should be noted that this year is also a change in the Russian political cycle in connection with the presidential elections.

Let us look more closely at the historical analogy of the previous change in world economies, which began with the dragging of the leading countries into World War I. After the socialist revolution in Russia, a prototype of a new world economy with communist ideology and total state planning emerged. A decade and a half later, in order to overcome the Great Depression, the US implemented the New Deal, forming another type of new world economic order with the ideology of the welfare state and state-monopolistic regulation of the economy. Parallel to this, Japan, Italy, and then Germany are forming its third type, with Nazi ideology and a state-private corporate economy.

All these changes took place during the final period of the British cycle of capital accumulation and its underlying colonial world economy. The British ruling elite, occupying a central position in the world economic system, seeks to resist the changes that are undermining its global dominance. An economic blockade was imposed against the USSR, and only cereals were allowed to be imported from it in order to provoke mass starvation. A trade embargo is imposed against the US. An anti-communist Nazi coup is fostered in Germany, and in order to counteract the influence of the USSR, the British secret service protects and promotes Hitler to power. With the same intentions and in anticipation of large dividends, American corporations invest heavily in the modernization of German industry.[5]

The British are engaging in traditional divide-and-conquer geopolitics, provoking a war between Germany and the USSR. They hope to repeat their success in unleashing World War I, preceded by London's provocation of Japan's attack on Russia. World War I resulted in the self-destruction of all of Britain's main rivals in Eurasia: the Russian, German, Austro-Hungarian, Ottoman, and, finally, the Chinese empires. But immediately after the outbreak of World War II, the qualitative superiority of the Third Reich over all European countries, including Great Britain, in managing the economy and mobilizing all available resources for military purposes became clear. The British forces suffered humiliating defeats not only from Germany but also, together with the Americans, from Japan, which was soundly superior to the Anglo-American alliance in its organizational and technological capability for large-scale warfare in the vast territory of Southeast Asia. Although Britain, thanks to its alliance with the US and the USSR, was among the victors, it lost its entire colonial empire after World War II—more than 90% of its territory and population.

The Soviet system of managing the national economy proved to be the most effective at that time, as it accomplished three economic miracles at once: the evacuation of industrial enterprises from the European part of the country to the Urals and Siberia, rebuilding new industrial regions in half a year; the achievement of productivity and productivity rates in war conditions that exceeded those of Fascist-allied Europe by an order of magnitude; the rapid restoration of cities and production facilities completely destroyed by the invaders.

Roosevelt's new course significantly boosted the mobilization capacity of the US economy, enabling the US to defeat Japan in the Pacific. In post-war Western Europe, the US had no rivals: having fenced off the USSR with the NATO bloc, the US ruling elite virtually privatized the Western European countries, including the remnants of their gold reserves. In the Third World, former colonies of European states became an area of rivalry between American corporations and Soviet ministries. Further world development took place in the Cold War format of two world empires, the Soviet and American, which had similar technocratic and diametrically opposed political models for managing socio-economic development. Each of them had its advantages and disadvantages but was radically superior to the colonial system of family capitalism with its ruthless exploitation of wage workers and slaves in terms of the efficiency of mass production organization and resource mobilization capabilities.

11.4 Possible Political Forms of the New World Order

A similar picture is emerging at the present time. The emerging new world economic order also has three possible varieties. The first of these has already been formed in China under the leadership of the CPC. It is characterized by a combination of institutions of state planning and market self-organization, state control over the main parameters of economic reproduction and free enterprise, the ideology of the common good and private initiative, and demonstrates a stunning efficiency of economic development management, surpassing the American system by an order of magnitude. This is evident in the manifold higher rate of development of advanced industrial sectors in the last three decades and was again confirmed by the epidemic's performance indicators.

The second type of integrated world economy is taking shape in India, which is the largest real functioning democracy in the world. The foundations of the Indian kind of integral system were laid by Mahatma Gandhi and Jawaharlal Nehru on the basis of Indian culture. The post-independence Constitution of India defines its economy as socialist. This norm is practically implemented in the system of strategic planning, social policy norms, and financial regulation. The monetary issue guidelines are set by a special commission, which, based on the planned priorities of socio-economic policy, determines the parameters of refinancing of development institutions and banks in the areas of lending to small businesses, agriculture, industry, etc.

The nationalization of the banking system by the Indira Gandhi government made it possible to align the management of financial flows with indicative economic development plans. The right priorities gave impetus to the development of key areas of the new technological paradigm, and just before the coronavirus pandemic, India emerged as the world's fastest-growing economy. As in China, the state in India regulates the market process to improve public welfare by encouraging investment in manufacturing and new technology. In doing so, financial and monetary restrictions keep capital within the country, while government planning directs entrepreneurial activity toward the production of material goods.

The third kind of new world order is described in the first chapter as an image of the future in the eyes of an American-centric financial oligarchy that aspires to world domination. Bids for the formation of a new world order are initiated from the depths of the "deep state" of the US. On the wave of the pandemic, institutions are being created that purport to govern humanity. The B. Gates Foundation establishes control over WHO activities in terms of vaccination of the population. Vaccination is used to promote the long-developed technology of biological programming to reduce fertility and total control over the behavior of vaccinated people. This technology combines bioengineering and computer science: vaccination is accompanied by chipping, enabling the creation of any restrictions on human performance.[6]

In other words, the third variety of the new world economic order envisages, in fact, the formation of a world government led by the American ruling elite in the interests of the financial oligarchy, which controls the emission of world currency, transnational banks, and corporations, and the global financial market. It is a continuation of the trend of liberal globalization, augmented by authoritarian technologies to control the populations of countries deprived of national sovereignty. It has been described in many anti-utopias, from Orwell's famous "1984" to contemporary religious imagery of the coming of the Antichrist—an "electronic concentration camp" that precedes the end of the world.

Each of the varieties of the new world order described above involves the use of advanced information technologies, which are a key factor in the new technological order. All of them are based on methods of big data processing and artificial intelligence systems, necessary not only for managing unmanned production processes but also for controlling people in systems to regulate economy and social behavior. The goals of this regulation are set by the ruling elite, whose way of formation predetermines the essential characteristics of each of the above-mentioned varieties of the new world economic order.

Power is vested in the leadership of the CPC, which organizes the regulation of the economy to enhance the people's welfare and directs social behavior toward the political goals of building socialism with Chinese characteristics. Market mechanisms are regulated so that the most efficient production and technological structures win the competition, and the profit is proportional to their contribution to the public welfare. At the same time, medium and large corporations, including non-governmental corporations, have party organizations that monitor the conformity of their management's behavior with the moral values of communist ideology. Higher labor productivity and efficiency of production, modesty and productivity of managers and owners are encouraged on the one hand, and abuse of a dominant market position and speculative manipulation thereof, wastefulness, and parasitic consumption on the other are punished. A system of social credit is developed to regulate the social behavior of the individual. According to the intention behind it, each citizen's social opportunities will depend on his or her rating, which is constantly adjusted based on the balance of good and bad deeds. The higher the rating, the greater the credibility of the individual in getting a job, promotion, credit, or delegation of authority. This peculiar modernization of the familiar Soviet system of keeping personal records, which accompanied a person throughout his working life, has its positive and negative sides, an assessment of which is beyond the scope of this book. Its main problem area is the dependence of the mechanism for the formation of a productive elite of society on the artificial intelligence that manages the system of social credit.

The second kind of new economic order is determined by a democratic political system, which can vary greatly from country to country. It is most developed in Switzerland, where major political decisions are taken by popular referendums. Its most important incarnation for the world economy is India and, traditionally, the European social democracies. In most countries, it is severely afflicted by corruption and subject to manipulation by big business, which may be patriotic or comprador. The introduction of today's widely known distributed ledger information technology (blockchain) into the system of popular representative elections could significantly improve the efficiency of this political system, eliminating voter fraud and ensuring that candidates have equal access to the media. The growing popularity of authoring media in the blogosphere creates competition for information sources, facilitating candidates' access to voters. With proper legal provision for the use of modern information technologies in the electoral process, an automatic mechanism of responsibility of public authorities for the results of their activities in the public interest is formed. The more educated and active citizens are, the more effectively a democratic political system works. Its main problem area is the dependence of the ruling elite on clan-corporate structures that are not interested in the transparency and honesty of elections.

Finally, the third variety of the new world order is determined by the interests of a financial oligarchy that aspires to world domination. It is achieved by means of liberal globalization, consisting of the blurring of national institutions of economic regulation and the subordination of its reproduction to the interests of international capital. The dominant position in the structure of the latter is occupied by several dozen intertwined American-European family clans, controlling the largest financial holdings, power structures, intelligence services, media, political parties, and the apparatus of executive power.[7] This core of the US ruling elite is waging a hybrid war with all the countries it does not control, using a wide arsenal of financial, information, cognitive, and even biological technologies to destabilize and chaotize them. The purpose of this war is the formation of a global system of institutions under his control, which regulate the reproduction of not only the global economy but also all of humanity through modern information, financial, and bio-engineering technologies. The main problem of such a political system is its total irresponsibility and amorality, the commitment of its hereditary ruling elite to the Malthusian, racist, and partly misanthropic views.

The formation of a new world order will take place in competition between these three varieties of the new world order. In doing so, the latter excludes the first two, which can coexist peacefully. Just as the victory of Nazi Germany and Japan in the war against the USSR and the US, the Soviet and the American model of the new world economic order were both excluded at that time. After the overall victory, the USSR and the US created competing political systems, dividing the world into zones of influence and avoiding direct confrontation.

Thus, there are three forecast scenarios for the formation of a new world economic order. Their common material basis is a new technological mode, the core of which consists of a set of digital, information, bioengineering, cognitive, additive, and nanotechnologies. Today, they are used to create unmanned, fully automated production facilities; artificial intelligence systems controlling limitless databases; transgenic micro-organisms, plants, and animals; cloning of living beings and regeneration of human tissues. On this technological basis, the institutions of an integrated world economic order are being formed, ensuring the conscious management of the socio-economic development of both sovereign states and, potentially, of humanity as a whole. This is achieved through a combination of state strategic planning and market competition based on public-private partnerships. Depending on in whose interests the regulation of autonomous economic entities is implemented, one of the above-described varieties of the new world economic order is formed. The first two—communist and democratic— can coexist peacefully, competing and cooperating on the basis of international law. The third—oligarchic—is antagonistic to the first two since it involves the establishment of inherited world domination by a few dozen American-European family clans, incompatible with either democratic or communist values.

Which of the three predicted scenarios the evolution of humanity will follow depends on the outcome of the hybrid war unleashed by the US ruling elite against sovereign states. The goal of the American ruling elite, which launched this world war, is to maintain global dominance and strengthen it to world domination. The US strategy is imperialist in nature and conforms to the logic of governance characteristic of imperial IHU. The collapse of the USSR was interpreted by the US ruling elite as its victory in the Cold War, and it immediately brought the post-Soviet space under its control, bringing to power in the Baltics and Ukraine neo-Nazi and Russophobe puppet governments designed to serve the interests of US capital.

American imperialism is a reflection of the interests of the US ruling financial oligarchy and its affiliated transnational corporations seeking control over planetary resources for the sake of an infinite increase in their wealth and power. This is the logic of the imperial IHU, within which the American ruling elite was formed, and the current generation of its constituent politicians, businessmen, generals, and opinion leaders grew up. They are convinced of their right to world domination and even their obligation to impose their ideas about the world order on other countries. At the same time, the motivation of the financial oligarchy that controls the United States does not coincide, and on many issues, is the opposite of the interests of the American people.

Creating "controlled chaos" by the organization of armed conflicts in the zone of natural interests of the leading countries of the world, the US intelligence services first provoke these countries to be drawn into the conflict and then conduct campaigns to stitch together coalitions of states against them in order to consolidate their leadership and legitimize the results of the conflict. This is how the wars against Iraq and Serbia were organized, and provocations continued in order to draw Russia, Turkey, and China into the war. In doing so, the US gains an unfair competitive advantage by cutting off uncontrolled countries from promising markets, creates for itself an opportunity to ease the burden of public debt by freezing the dollar assets of losers, and justifies a multiple increase in its public spending on the development and promotion of new technologies needed to grow the US economy. The overriding objective of this strategy is to orchestrate conflicts between states that the US has no control over and that have the potential to challenge US dominance.

A conflict between Russia and China would be most desirable for the US. Therefore, US agents in Russia have spared no effort to foment Sinophobia, intimidating ordinary people with the Chinese threat through controlled media, provoking business conflicts, and imposing the view that the cultures and worldviews of the two peoples are incompatible. Similarly, in China, US agents of influence foment anti-Russian sentiment by stimulating territorial claims against Russia, discrediting the Russian government, and distorting the history of relations between the two peoples. Fortunately, the mutual understanding between the leaders of the two countries, who are well aware of the American threat and the commonality of interests of Russia and China, and the fundamental importance of the strategic partnership they have established to maintain peace in the world, neutralize the American intrigues.

Having missed an opportunity to drag Russia into conflict with the PRC under Yeltsin and to create a "Chimerica" (a US-led strategic alliance with the PRC) before Xi Jinping came to power, the US has proceeded to weaken its potential rivals one by one. In this, they have had considerable success on the anti-Russian front, occupying Ukraine and turning the millions of Russians living there into Russophobic Nazis. Another successful operation against Russia was provoking the Central Bank to let the ruble exchange rate float freely and to sharply increase the key interest rate, which caused macroeconomic destabilization and paralyzed investment activity and innovation activity. This has multiplied the effectiveness of US financial sanctions.

The Americans have so far failed to weaken the PRC. Xi Jinping has managed to purge the state apparatus and business elite of obvious American agents of influence. Chinese programmers have built the Great Wall of China in cyberspace, protecting their internet from information sabotage. Attempts by US intelligence agencies to stage a riot in Hong Kong were neutralized by the Chinese authorities. US sanctions against Huawei and a number of other Chinese information and communications equipment companies have had little effect. Trump's trade war against the PRC also failed to achieve its results, weakening his position rather than that of the Chinese leadership.

It is interesting to note that Trump actually missed out on a victory in the trade war against China by sacrificing prohibitive concessions from Chinese negotiators to personify himself as a defender of American interests. In 2017, US exports to China stood at around $155 billion, which fell to $120 billion in 2019. Based on the trade agreement, China, according to Professor Wang Wen, would need to increase its imports from the US to at least $230 billion over the next two years.[8] This goal is objectively at the limit of China's capabilities. To achieve it, the PRC would have to phase out imports from other states, including members of the B&R. In this case, the US administration would kill two birds with one stone: it would double US exports to the PRC at the expense of diminishing China's influence in the BRI. Trump's excessive ambition to humiliate China demonstrates the loss of the sense of rationality and pragmatism that has always been a strength of US policy.

The US strategy in the Middle East was relatively successful. Here its main tool has been the chaotization of countries whose leadership it did not control. There is no need to describe all the crimes against the people of Libya, Egypt, Syria, Iraq, and other Middle Eastern countries that the US intelligence services have committed and continue to commit. They are well known, as are the technologies they use for "color" revolutions, "humanitarian" interventions, and civil wars. The meaning of these operations is to remove unwanted US government, to impose a puppet regime, and to establish control over natural resources and competitive industries of the invaded country. World war, organized by the capitalist oligarchy, must, by its logic, be self-sustaining. Government spending on the operations of the Pentagon and the CIA is more than covered by the super-profits of American corporations and PMCs at the expense of the looting of cultural and natural resources of the occupied countries and appropriation of the assets of their deposed governments.

The operation of American intelligence resulted in a successful pseudo-legitimate coup in Brazil, where a BRICS country and a potentially powerful member of the anti-war coalition came under the control of the American oligarchy. Another recent US victory in the Latin American theatre of global hybrid warfare was the coup d'état in Bolivia, which overthrew the Morales government that was not under its control and installed a puppet regime of corrupt security forces.

However, attempts to overthrow the legitimate government in Syria and Venezuela failed. In Bolivia, too, the people returned power to their representatives in recent elections. That leads one to the banal conclusion that when US intelligence agencies are faced with the collective defense of potential anti-war coalition members, they will retreat. They only succeed in defeating known weak victims one at a time. Iran's recent missile response to yet another US administration crime of killing an Iranian general on Iraqi soil was evidence of this. Realizing that it would be impossible to achieve Russia's passive neutrality in anti-Iranian military aggression, the US leadership backed down. The American attack on North Korea also stalled.

The main targets of the American aggression are China, which has become a world leader in the forming of a new world economic order, and Russia, leveling the US advantages in the military and political field with its nuclear-missile shield. The conclusion from this experience of American geopolitical strategy is clear: only a sufficiently strong anti-war coalition involving Russia and China can protect sovereign countries with non-aligned status from American aggression. The sooner this coalition is formed and the broader it is, the fewer opportunities there will be for an escalation of global hybrid warfare.

The strategic partnership between Russia and China is an insurmountable obstacle to the establishment of world domination by the financial oligarchy of the US ruling elite. The power of the latter is based on the emission of world money, the possibilities of which are limited by the political will of sovereign states capable of creating and using their national currencies in international cooperation. If China and Russia can form a monetary and financial system independent of the dollar, at least for the SCO, the outcome of the global hybrid war will be predetermined. Without feeding its balance of payments and state budget deficits with endless world currency issuance, the American empire will quickly lose its military and political power.

So far, however, on the monetary and financial front, the US financial oligarchy is firmly in control of global dominance. The dollar continues to perform the function of world currency. The yuan's conquest of IMF reserve currency status has not led to an increase in its share of global finance, which remains negligible. The US and the EU succeeded in diluting the announced reform of the IMF at the G20. The G20 itself is kept on a short leash by the G7: American and European experts practically control its decisions. The collapse of the rouble due to the IMF-imposed decision of the Bank of Russia to let the rouble float freely has discredited the Russian currency and prevented it from becoming the regional reserve currency of the EAEU. The unjustified increase in interest rates allowed the Russian financial authorities to be dragged into a ruinous carry trade trap, making Russia a cash cow for American speculators. US regulators are effectively manipulating the global financial market, arbitrarily blocking uncontrolled segments through sanctions and seizing assets.

It has to be said that so far, there has been a complete lack of any initiative on the part of the states that have been victims of American financial sanctions. Only China responds to American acts of aggression by symmetrically imposing customs duties on goods imported to the US. Russian monetary authorities, on the other hand, have dutifully swallowed the US government's seizure of control over Rusal. They have not responded in any way to the financial embargo imposed by the US. On the contrary, they exacerbated its negative consequences by means of suicide for the national economy monetary policy based on raising the interest rates and plunging the ruble exchange rate into free float. Corporations and banks around the world are dutifully paying fines to the US for violations of the anti-Russian sanctions regime. Even many Chinese participants in foreign economic activities are afraid of being hit by US sanctions, refraining from stepping up cooperation with Russia.

Meanwhile, the US position on the monetary and financial front is highly vulnerable. Collective action by potential members of an anti-war coalition against the use of US currency could act as a trigger for the annihilation of the US dollar financial system. The bulk of it is, in fact, a collection of gigantic financial bubbles, whose inflation has long ago and repeatedly exceeded the limits of sustainability. Even with the relatively small weight of the dollar reserves of potential anti-war coalition participants in the total dollar liabilities, the very fact that the dollar is no longer used in a significant sector of global trade and economic turnover could undermine confidence in it and trigger an avalanche of flight from the dollar with the collapse of the US financial system.

The US monetary authorities have no effective defense against such a blow. They can default on their obligations to countries they do not control by freezing their dollar assets. They can freeze accounts in Anglo-Saxon offshore jurisdictions and even confiscate money on deposit, as they did with the deposits of Russian entities and individuals in Cypriot banks. By doing so, they would inflict corresponding damage on certain countries. However, if these countries dump the dollars and stop using them, they would be invulnerable to sanctions by US regulators, creating critical risks for the US.

Prior to the US administration's trade war, the Chinese leadership did not set out to build an alternative monetary and financial system, using the dollar as the main currency of payments, settlements, and reserves. The global hybrid war unleashed by the US ruling elite, one of the main objectives of which is to curb China's development, has made the Chinese leadership anxious to develop its payment and settlement channels in yuan and national currencies of partner countries.

Through the creation of bilateral currency swaps, China formulated its international payments system. As the new global economic order emerges, the room for maneuver of the US Federal Reserve is inexorably shrinking: The US economy has to bear the brunt of the depreciation of capital concentrated in the redundant industries of the old technological order, the financial pyramids and the liabilities of distressed countries.

In order to sovereignize and expand its monetary and financial space, China established its national payment card system (UnionPay) and the international segment of its electronic interbank information exchange system. This secured the Chinese financial system from dependence on the Western-based VISA, Mastercard, and SWIFT banking messaging systems.

China's actions to create its own currency and financial instruments are a forced measure in response to the hybrid war launched by the US against both China and a number of its key trading partners: Russia, Iran, Venezuela, Cuba, and North Korea. As this war escalates, these forced measures become part of China's foreign economic security system and are incorporated into its strategy. It is complemented by the establishment of international banks and development institutions beyond US control (AIIB, Silk Road Fund, BRICS Development Bank), the internationalization of the yuan, and the creation of an international segment of the Chinese financial market supported by one of the largest financial center in the world in Hong Kong.

While the monetary authorities in the Russian Federation, despite the escalation of US sanctions, are still following IMF recommendations and are hesitant to move to sovereign monetary policy, the PRC's strategy evolves according to the changing global situation. The more aggressively the US behaves, the more the Chinese leadership is building a system of international payments and settlement that is independent of it. This appears to be an irreversible process determined by the logic of the new world order. If the US stops a trade war with China in time, the dollar-based financial system that maintains its power can continue to dominate the world for quite some time. An escalation of this war could lead to an accelerated dedollarization of Chinese foreign economic activity and accelerate the transition to a new monetary and financial system, consistent with the principles of an integrated world economic order.

From many indications, the Chinese leadership has already decided in its foreign economic strategy to cut itself off from the dollar financial and monetary system. As well as retaining currency restrictions on capital transactions to prevent unauthorized exports, the PBC has announced the introduction of a digital yuan, the circulation of which will be controlled by the central bank. This will allow payment transactions, including cross-border ones, without the involvement of commercial banks, which have proved highly vulnerable to US sanctions.

The PRC has already accumulated experience in effectively ensuring its information security. Having used its extensive technology imports to develop the electronics industry, the PRC leadership has taken timely care to build the Great Wall of Information Security, which is shaped by the PRC's cyber security law that came into force in 2017. It provides the necessary legal framework for "ensuring network security, protecting cyberspace sovereignty and national security, upholding social and public interests, protecting the legitimate rights and interests of citizens, legal persons, and other organizations to promote the healthy development of informatization of economy and society." The law has served as a legal platform for state regulation of information technology (IT), integrating it into the overall design of modern Chinese society. As stressed in the document, the law "applies to the creation, operation, maintenance, and use of the Internet, as well as the operation of (social) networks," with an important role for standardization and control under the dominant role of the government.

Experts consider the key part of the law to be stricter controls and security requirements, which they believe large companies are interested in. China has developed a group of Internet companies that dominate the national segment of the Internet: Alibaba, Baidu, Shanda Group, NetEase, Tencent, Sina, Tom, Sohu, and 360. In the event of a cyber-attack or control over the infrastructure of these companies, the PRC believes there is a danger of controlling the Chinese segment of the Internet and the financial flows through Chinanet through their resources. The tools provided by the law avoid external influence on the Internet trading infrastructure and financial market.

Overall, the PRC is building a comprehensive strategy for its foreign economic space based on the interests of its own socio-economic development. In the context of global hybrid warfare, it is defensive rather than offensive. Nevertheless, it is being created on a systemic basis with a view to self-sufficiency and may well become the basis for the construction of the monetary and financial architecture of the new world economic order.

As in the previous historical cycle, the ruling elite of the dominant country that initiated the world war soon faces the crushing force of more effective institutions of resource mobilization in the countries of the emerging core of the new world order. Two years after the Munich Treaty, the British felt its consequences in the form of the massive bombing of London and the defeat of their troops in France. And it turned out that its most expensive healthcare system in the world was an order of magnitude less efficient than China's. The same is true of the financial system: Despite the fact that the American financial market collapsed by half of its value, China remains resilient and is getting stronger. There is no doubt that on the information and cognitive front, the Chinese leadership is also far more effective than the American and European ones: the cohesion of the Chinese people is admirable against a background of panic, confusion, and growing social unrest and protests in Western countries.

Of the three scenarios described above for the formation of a new world economic order, the option of domination by a global capitalist oligarchy looks the least likely. Although a global hybrid war is currently unfolding under this scenario, the US ruling elite is doomed to defeat due to the qualitatively higher efficiency of China's mobilization capabilities and the lack of interest of all countries in the world in this war.

11.5 The Logic of the PRC's Victory in the US-Led Global Hybrid War

In any scenario of a further unfolding of the global economic crisis, the reproduction mechanisms of the American capital accumulation cycle are eroded, and consequently, the economic power of the United States is weakened. There is no doubt that the American ruling elite will use any means to maintain its global dominance. It will seek to steer the course of events toward the formation of a world government, as former British Prime Minister G. Brown spoke recently.[9] The pandemic of fear of a coronavirus, global warming, and ecological catastrophe fanned by the media under its control is preparing public opinion for this scenario. However, the interest of the US financial oligarchy in consolidating its hegemony in the global financial system and preserving the latter leaves no chance for independent development for the rest of the countries. The Anglo-

Saxon geopolitical tradition has such tools as pitting rival countries against each other, provoking social and political conflicts, organizing coups, and encouraging separatists to chaotize uncontrolled countries and regions to keep them in a dependent position. To minimize the resulting risks for Russia, the EAEU, Eurasia, and humanity as a whole, it is necessary to immediately form an anti-war coalition capable of inflicting unacceptable damage on the aggressor.

Under present conditions, the mechanism of overcoming structural crises through the militarization of the economy and military-political confrontation that has been in effect so far is fraught with a lethal outcome for all mankind. It should be replaced by a mechanism open to all countries for the development of global mutually beneficial projects, the joint implementation of which would allow the leading countries to realize their advantages in the formation of a new technological pattern, while others would receive tangible benefits from participation in its development. Such a mechanism should ensure the setting of global sustainable development goals, including neutralizing threats to human security, developing and adopting global development programs, and establishing a funding mechanism for their implementation.

The creation of such a mechanism requires global institutions to coordinate interests and design and implement mutually beneficial development programs. These could be launched within the UN, whose credibility is currently being seriously undermined by the US's flouting of international law and its pressure on dependent countries. The G20, which brings together the leaders of the world's major economies, might be such an institution.

So far, the countries in the core of the outgoing IHU, led by the US, are not ready to discuss world problems whose resolution is in everyone's interest. Thus, the discussion in the G20 about reforming the global financial system revolves around secondary issues that do not touch on the root causes of the global economic and structural-technological crisis. The G7 countries are blocking fundamental issues of regulating global currency issuance, cross-border capital flows, and assessment of financial risks. They are interested in preserving their monopoly position as emitters of world currencies, which allows them to get out of the crisis at the expense of unlimited emission of money that is exchanged for the real assets of other countries. For the latter, the preservation of the resulting non-equivalent foreign economic exchange is unacceptable; they expect the G20 to take initiatives for radical reform of the global financial system on more equitable and transparent principles.

The opposing interests of global currency issuers and other G20 countries can be resolved by initiating large-scale global innovation projects capable of linking the excessive emission of global reserve currencies with investments aimed at achieving sustainable development conditions in the interests of all humanity. These conditions should include a transition to a new technological paradigm and a genuine balancing of the interests of the leading countries of the world. So far, this has not been achieved, with the result that global economic crises such as the current one have been overcome by the catastrophes of world wars.

One of the fundamental reasons for the intransigence of the leading actors in world politics is their mutual mistrust. Its consequence is the current dominant approach to the formation of global sustainable development mechanisms on the basis of mutual restrictions. The reluctance of some major countries to abide by them has doomed many overdue initiatives to failure. For example, attempts to establish global mechanisms for limiting greenhouse gas emissions, which are considered the main threat of climate change, have so far failed due to the positions of the US and China. International conferences on climate change and sustainable development have proved fruitless in terms of achieving practical results. And even the Cold War-era restrictions on non-proliferation of biological and nuclear weapons, missile technology, and strategic weapons, which seemed immutable, have eroded in recent years.

The logic of mutual restrictions is based on zero-sum game theory. It was characteristic of imperial IHU, with two centers of power confronting each other, each of which could not concede anything to the other. It was believed that a win for one meant a loss for the other. Therefore, they tried to find a balance of interests by making mutual concessions on a parity basis. In order to protect themselves from attempts to win, global international conventions were drawn up by third parties involving all important countries. The new ICC is based on a logic of cooperation based on synergies. Countries come together on a mutually beneficial voluntary basis, each benefiting from international cooperation. International relations cease to be antagonistic, and zero-sum game theory gives way to a strategy of cooperation.

11.6 Possible Plans for an Anti-war International Coalition Based on Repelling Planetary Threats to the Existence of Humanity

Russia and China, with their experience of global leadership, could give impetus to pooling resources to achieve the goals of survival and development of mankind on a mutually beneficial basis with fair distribution of benefits and costs among the participants. To begin with, the goals could be to address the obvious threats to human security, which are easy to reach a consensus on and which require large-scale investment in R&D and the creation of new technological mode industries.

An example of such an approach to defusing international tensions and eliminating threats of world war in the transition to a new technological and world economic paradigm could be a joint development of a global system of protection against asteroid-space danger (ASD) by G20 countries. At the end of the twentieth century, the threat of catastrophic collisions of asteroids or comet nuclei with enormous kinetic energy with the Earth was scientifically proven. As a result of such collisions, humanity could be destroyed instantly or be set back in its development by centuries. Consequently, ASD must be seen as a challenge to humanity as a whole, as well as to the state and international security structures.

The Tunguska meteorite of June 1908 and the "Brazilian Tunguska" in September 1930, both accompanied by explosions of megatons of TNT equivalent, are examples of the reality of this threat. In 2009 and 2012, asteroids with diameters of 50 and 40 m flew near Earth and were discovered less than a week before a possible impact. Apophis is predicted to come close to Earth in 2029. In 2048, an asteroid with a diameter of 130 m will crash into Earth with a probability of 0.0005. This impact would have lethal consequences for today's Earth's bio- and noosphere. Although the probabilities of these events are estimated to be in the hundredths of a percent, the frequency of asteroid impacts near Earth is very high and often unexpected.

An international Planetary Defence System (PDS) could be the answer to the threat of ASD. During the Cold War, practically all the basic components of an EPP—rocket and space technology, nuclear weapons, communications, etc.—were created. In the US and Western Europe, systematic scientific research has been conducted to detect dangerous celestial bodies. Following the fall of the Chelyabinsk meteorite and the recent close flyby of the Halloween asteroid in 2016, NASA created the Planetary Defence Coordination Division. Following the fall of the Chelyabinsk meteorite and the recent close flyby of the Halloween asteroid in 2016, NASA created the Planetary Defence Coordination Unit. The basis for the creation of the PDS could be the conceptual design for an international PDS "Citadel" developed in Russia."[10] It envisages large-scale exploratory and applied research in promising areas of science and technology development, which will give a powerful impetus to the formation of a new technological paradigm. The high-tech industry will receive large orders for the development and mastering of new technologies, which will reduce incentives for militarization as a means of transition to a new technological paradigm.

The scale of this task requires a concentration of global intellectual, scientific, technical, and information resources. It can be solved only by uniting the scientific and technological potentials of Russia, the United States, and other leading countries on the basis of a relevant international program. Deployment of wide international cooperation on the basis of such a large-scale program will promote confidence-building between countries and restrain confrontational tendencies. The implementation of such a program, much better than mutual restrictions, would contribute to the security of mankind by creating a world anti-missile defense system against unauthorized launches.

Financial instruments that contribute to macroeconomic stability could be used to implement this program. The non-commercial part of the program could be financed not by contributions from parties, as was done in the outgoing WEO, but by the introduction of a global tax on financial speculation. The commercially realizable components of the program could be financed by long-term loans and by the World Bank and other international financial institutions, placed against the guarantees of the participating states for 20–30 years.

An appropriate international organization should be established to manage the program, with responsibility for the planning and implementation of the program, to which the funds raised should be transferred. Such an organization may be established on a parity basis by the G20 countries concerned. It can spend the funds in accordance with the procurement procedures adopted by the World Bank. However, the results of the R&D generated by the program should be publicly available, and their developers should be granted the rights to exploit them commercially.

The initiative simultaneously achieves the objectives of developing a new technological order, which is critical to overcoming the structural crisis in advanced countries; tying up excess money issued by their monetary authorities, which is necessary to stabilize the global financial system; access to the latest technology for developing countries, which they need to catch up; and reducing incentives for militarisation and an arms race, which makes it possible to defuse rising politico-military tensions; and probably creating a system to neutralize space, as well as other threats to the existence of humanity.

Another global initiative that could unite countries in the formation of a new world economic order could be the creation of a global system of food security. The aforementioned is an estimate of the agricultural potential of the planet based on a set of modern technologies, which shows the possibility of a full-fledged feeding of 25 billion people.[11] It follows that the problem of hunger is a consequence of the current system of production and distribution relations rather than a consequence of fertility depletion and limited cultivation. The introduction of new technological advances in agriculture removes these limitations, once again refuting the Malthusians' arguments.

The introduction of a global tax on currency and financial speculation would fund the measures proposed below to ensure global food security:

(1)   Averting price spikes and falls in the supply of foodstuffs as well as a significant deterioration in the economic conditions of their production and supply
(2)   The elimination of mass hunger and systematic malnutrition in any region of the world
(3)   Avoidance of mass consumption of unhealthy foodstuffs

The following is a list of measures to meet food security challenges.
(1)   Prevent sharp spikes in food prices. The deployment of a network of food commodity exchanges located in different regions of the world and independent of each other; the establishment of term limits on food commodity futures contracts; the establishment, under the auspices of the International Food Organization, of a system for monitoring the condition of food stocks by States and commercial organizations; establishment of global food commodity reserve funds administered by designated international organizations
(2)   Prevent a sharp decline in food supply. Establishing a global system to monitor threats to agricultural commodity production from natural disasters and the spread of infections and pests, with a mechanism for relaxing WTO restrictions on agricultural subsidies in affected countries; establishment of a global system of operational assistance to countries in need to prevent and neutralize threats of infections and pests of crops and livestock by supplying appropriate vaccines, pesticides, and machinery; developing a system of international land reserves that can be made available for temporary free use by agricultural organizations with an obligation to cultivate the relevant agricultural commodities
(3)   Combat mass hunger and malnutrition of the population. Establishing, under the aegis of the UN, a global system for the procurement and compensatory supply of foodstuffs to regions affected by natural disasters, man-made disasters, and armed conflicts; exclusion of food supplies from international sanctions

(4) Prevent mass consumption of dangerous food products, in addition to existing certification, sanitary, veterinary, and phytosanitary controls, new food products made from GMOs, as well as new technological options for control expanding with the development of a new technological order, a global program of action, with the assistance of the World Bank, should be developed and implemented. Adoption of a system of international standards for genetically engineered and cellular technologies; development and adoption of technical regulations for the production of food products using GMOs and the raw materials derived from them; metrological support for food quality certification and control systems for compliance with the above technical regulations, as well as the development and production of the necessary equipment and its widespread use

(5) Ensure normal conditions for the expanded reproduction of agricultural commodities using highly efficient new technological mode technologies and establish the following limitations on the possibility of abuse of the monopoly position by their rightful owners. Do not protect intellectual property rights over the use of GMOs or limit the protection granted to three years; require genetically modified seed-producing companies to guarantee multi-year (at least a decade) sales at fixed prices to buyers; prohibit the imposition of any restrictions on the circulation of seed; introduce mandatory requirements for producers and sellers of seed material of GMOs to publish information on the technologies used in their production

A shift from the principle of mutual restraint to one of international cooperation is also making progress in tackling climate change. The new technological paradigm and economic modernization based on it can drastically reduce the energy, material, and resource intensity of production. In particular, the use of nanotechnology in the manufacture and coating of construction materials can increase their durability and extend their life cycle by an order of magnitude; in solar energy, it makes it possible to stop burning hydrocarbons, to reduce electricity consumption for lighting, nanopowders increase the efficiency of construction materials and fuel, and cellular technology in medicine eliminates many chemical agents.[12] Modern technology increases the efficiency of waste recycling and disposal many times over and makes it possible to close many technological production processes, making them waste-free. The structural reorganization, modernization, and economic development based on a new technological order make it possible to increase the volume of production and popular consumption without increasing the consumption of natural resources while reducing environmental pollution.

To promote sustainable development and green growth and to combat climate change, it is advisable to take the following measures:

(1) To stimulate wide dissemination of energy- and resource-saving technologies, establish a list of recommended energy and resource-saving technologies for wide application, including their dissemination in the objectives of the United Nations Conference on Trade and Development (UNCTAD); develop and implement a mechanism to transfer these technologies free of charge by subsidizing licensing costs and intellectual property rights; drastically expand the use of advanced energy and resource-saving technologies, using the World Bank's instruments for financing relevant investment projects recommended by UNCTAD; develop model laws to promote energy and resource efficiency with a view to their adoption by the G-20 national authorities and other interested countries

(2) To share equitably the costs of reducing pollution, improve and revitalize the Kyoto Protocol mechanisms by providing for their extension to the emission of all reportable pollutants; participation of multinational corporations; introducing an environmental tax on imports of goods from countries not party to the agreement

(3) Recommend that the G20 countries harmonize their environmental legislation by seeking to unify pollution charges and fines for excess emissions, as well as mechanisms for financing environmental measures through the targeted use of these charges and fines. Appropriate recommendations should be developed based on an economic assessment of the costs of cleaning up pollution that exceeds the environment's assimilative potential

(4) Exclude from the list of WTO-banned subsidies state expenditures and tax benefits provided to stimulate environmental protection activities of enterprises, including waste utilization, installation of treatment facilities, the introduction of energy- and resource-saving technologies

(5) To stimulate the expansion of solar and wind energy, encourage national authorities to exempt solar and wind power facilities from property and real estate taxes and the sale of electricity generated from them from indirect taxes within the framework of the Kyoto Protocol mechanisms to be restored, consider providing subsidies for investments in solar and wind power generation capacity in proportion to the emissions from equivalent thermal power capacity; recommend to the WTO not to consider the above incentives and subsidies as prohibited

(6) To stimulate the electrification of road transport, recommend national authorities to exempt the sale of electric vehicles from indirect taxes and to consistently increase excise taxes on motor fuels. Take similar measures to stimulate demand for hydrogen-powered vehicles

(7) To ensure monitoring of climate processes, objective analysis of factors influencing them, forecasting of climate change processes and their modeling; to stimulate the creation of a global research network with the involvement of global and national environmental funds, taking into account the consequences for the vital activity of mankind

(8) Recommend the introduction of a global tax on military expenditures, to be collected for environmental needs, under the supervision of authorized UN agencies, in order to broaden sources of financial support for the dissemination of environmentally friendly technologies and environmental expenditures and to limit military conflicts. Allow countries that evade such measures to apply a corresponding tax on the imports of their products

The proposed system of measures to reform the global monetary and financial system and international financial institutions and deployment of large-scale international programs to secure humanity aims at ensuring stable, fair, and mutually beneficial conditions for the movement of money and technology. Their implementation will make it possible to move the global financial market from a turbulent to a stable mode, to avoid catastrophic scenarios of escalation of military and political tension or uncontrolled collapse of the existing global monetary and financial system, to create necessary conditions for transition to sustainable economic growth based on the development of a new technological pattern and joint formation of institutions of the new world economic order.

Even in the midst of a world war, it is possible and necessary to think of peaceful solutions to the problems objectively resulting from the change of the IHU. The success of the initiatives proposed above depends mainly on the prudence of the American ruling elite. Probably, under the pressure of growing chaos and social and political tension inside the US, common sense will prevail, and the US leadership will refuse its pretensions for global hegemony and will meet the objective necessity of the world order restructuring on the principles of integral MHI. But, most likely, this will not happen by itself. The image of a superpower is too ingrained in the minds of the power and financial oligarchy. To sober it up, serious arguments will be needed to explain the futility of growing American aggression and the unacceptable damage from its continuation.

NOTES

1. For example, the influential Iraqi electronic newspaper Alefiyah named three high-ranking Iraqi military officials it believes were bribed by the US and ensured the fall of Baghdad and the collapse of Saddam Hussein's regime. Among them was Hussein's relative Abdurrahman al-Tikriti, who even before the war began informing the Americans about the movements of Baghdad regime leaders, including the president and his eldest son Uday Hussein, who commanded Saddam's "fidayeen"; Hussein's personal security officer, whose name was not disclosed, passed information to the United States about a leadership meeting at the presidential compound on the night of 19 to 20 March, and at a house in the Al-Mansour area on the night of 7 April (the Americans carried out massive strikes on both sites); The nephew of the former president, Lieutenant General Maher Sufyan Al-Tikriti, who, as commander of the 100,000-strong Republican Guard defending Baghdad, struck a deal with the US that the Republican Guard would not engage in combat.
2. W. F. Engdahl, *Seeds of Destruction* (Moscow: Celado, 2015).
3. A. Frolov, "US Private Military Companies," War and Peace, October 9, 2008.
4. D. Chiesa, What Instead of Disaster (Moscow: Tribuna Publishing House, 2014).
5. Charles Higham, Trading With The Enemy: An Expose of The Nazi-American Money Plot 1933–1949 (New York, 1983).
6. "Bill Gates Talks about 'Vaccines to Reduce Population,'" URL: https://www.warandpeace.ru/en/exclusive/view/44942/ 4 марта 2010 г.
7. D. Coleman, The Committee of 300: Secrets of the World Government (Moscow: Vityaz, 2005).
8. Wang Wen, "How Can the US Sell More Goods to China?," The Global Times, January 23, 2020.
9. "UK Saviour Proposes World Interim Government," RIA Novosti, URL: https://ria.ru/20200328/1569257083.html, 28 марта 2020 г.
10. A. Zaytsev, "Earth Needs 'Citadel,'" Military-industrial courier, August 15, 2007, accessed July 13, 2020, URL: https://www.vpk-news.ru/articles/3205.
11. N. Y. Klukin, and V. A. Gutnikov, "Evaluation of Biological Capacity of Agrosphere in Order to Determine the Population Limit of Land," *Public Administration*, Electronic Bulletin, no. 69 (2018): 482–497.
12. Nanotechnology as a key factor of the new technological order in the economy.

CHAPTER 12

Shaping a GEP as the Basis for a New World Order

12.1 General Approaches

Theoretical knowledge, general recommendations, and good wishes are not enough to end global hybrid warfare. It is crucially a question of political will and practical action by interested states, major economic players, and social organizations. The need for a sufficiently powerful and broad international coalition capable of inflicting unacceptable damage on the aggressor has already been mentioned above. This coalition is primarily interested in successfully developing countries, forming the core of the new world economy, and rising to the growth of the new technological order, as well as Russia and other countries of the post-Soviet space, with no prospects for development on the periphery of the old WEO. Altogether, relying on their established regional organizations— the SCO and the EAEU, they can start forming the foundations of the integrated WEO, creating corresponding new monetary, financial, trade and economic, transport and energy, and information infrastructures, formalizing them in the norms of international law, as well as developing a common ideology of the future world order.

Potential participants of the anti-war coalition include all countries that are not interested in a new world war and the vast majority of humanity living in them. First of all, these are the countries against which the main blow of American aggression is directed: Russia and China. They are the countries of the new world economic order that are successfully growing on the wave of growth of the new technological mode: China, India, and Indo-China, forming a new center of development of the world economy. They include Japan, South Korea, and all the post-Soviet states that retained their sovereignty and were forerunners in shaping its constituent institutions. And, of course, the beneficiary countries of cooperation with the Asian Development Centre, which benefit from its growth through participation in the B&R and other Eurasian integration processes.

It should be noted that the people of the US and its satellite countries are also not interested in a war, even a hybrid one. In this opposition to their own people's interests lies the weakness of the American and European ruling elites, which entails the destruction of their unity, as manifested in the US election campaign and in Brexit. Nevertheless, the military and political power of US imperialism is consistently directed by the interests of the capitalist oligarchy, and so far, there is no sign of a change in the consciousness of the US ruling elite oriented toward the establishment of world domination.

China's above-mentioned strategy of international economic cooperation is organically combined with the strategic line of Russian President Vladimir V. Putin. Putin's strategy of building equal and mutually beneficial relations between the states in the process of Eurasian economic integration. However, the Russian power and financial elite's adherence to the Washington Consensus doctrine, which focuses on serving the interests of international capital, blocks real strategic partnerships with the PRC and undermines trust in Russia. The dominant power and economic position of the comprador oligarchy and the corrupt bankocracy make it difficult for Russia to form the institutions of the new world economic order and to participate consistently in the anti-war coalition.

The hybrid nature of modern world warfare is manifested, among other features, in the absence of front lines between countries. Fighting in the political, informational, and monetary dimensions takes place within countries torn by antagonistic contradictions between the ruling elite and the people. In Russia, for example, the front line is between an informal alliance of the comprador oligarchy and corrupt officialdom on the one hand and the people's patriotic forces on the other. The former controls the "commanding heights" in the financial, information, and raw materials sectors, while the latter has the support of the majority population and the productive elite of society. And so it is in every country devoid of ideological integrity and concentration of political will. Including in the US and other NATO countries, there are forces resisting the deployment of global hybrid warfare.

It means that the formation of an anti-war coalition should not be confined to political leaders, who often find it difficult to take a clear-cut position without risking political and economic destabilization in their countries. The hybrid aggression of the global capitalist oligarchy, although based on the military and political power of the US, pervades all countries of the world, seeking to paralyze their national security systems. To neutralize it, the anti-war coalition should include not only states but also social organizations, corporations, media, and intellectual centers in all countries of the world, including those who have unleashed the world hybrid war. In other words, the anti-war coalition should be networked and have an infrastructure capable of giving its participants freedom of action. This infrastructure should include all the elements necessary for the reproduction of the modern economy: centers of issue of global and national currencies, exchanges and pricing mechanisms, payment and settlement systems, rating agencies, law and auditing companies, media, scientific and educational centers, etc.

The formation of an anti-war coalition is a necessary but not a sufficient condition for ending global hybrid warfare. The coalition must demonstrate to the aggressor the inevitability of unacceptable damage if the aggression continues. The unacceptable damage to the capitalist oligarchy is the loss of its revenues and wealth. Since the main source of these revenues is the issue of world currencies, above all the dollar, it will suffice to refuse its use in international accounts and reserves in order to cause unacceptable damage.

In response to the rejection of the use of the dollar in international accounting, the US financial oligarchy has so far responded with military aggression. This was the case in the Balkans after the introduction of the euro by European countries. As a result of the military aggression against Yugoslavia, the European currency has severely depreciated, and the dollar has shown its advantage. After Iraq switched to paying for oil in euros, a military invasion and occupation by American troops followed. Similarly, the US ruling elite and its satellites did the same to Libya after Gaddafi abandoned the use of the dollar and embraced rapprochement with the EU.

The anti-war coalition must be strong enough to block the use of military force by the US. The participation of Russia, which has nuclear missile parity with the US, is sufficient to meet this condition. However, Russia does not have enough influence on the global financial system to have a critical impact on it. It is also vulnerable to the use of information technology, a market in which the US has global dominance. To end global hybrid warfare, an anti-war coalition must have sufficient weight in the global financial system, the capacity for independent development of information and communication technology, and indestructible military power. The combined potential of the SCO countries meets these requirements. It could form the basis for a sufficiently powerful anti-war coalition that would be able to inflict unacceptable damage on the US financial oligarchy through its actions.

Another fundamental basis for the formation of an anti-war coalition should be an international convention on cybersecurity that would oblige parties not to use information technology for unlawful purposes, including the use of computer viruses embedded in programs and electronic devices, covert surveillance, eavesdropping and the impact on electronic systems, and to combat these offenses in accordance with national legislation. This treaty could include the creation of filters that protect member states' information systems from external cyberattacks and cut off the segments of global information networks from which these threats emanate. It should also include the possibility of imposing collective sanctions on parties that refuse to join the agreement and abuse their advantages in operating systems, social networks, and telecommunications markets through electronic espionage, hacking, and sabotage on the territory of parties to the agreement. These sanctions could include embargoes on the supply of electronic equipment, telecommunications services, the use of information systems, including social media, as well as the creation of advantages for the development and use of member states' own information technology.

An open international investigation into the origins of the coronavirus could kick-start an anti-war coalition. It could lead to charges that the countries that are parties to the 1975 Convention on the Prohibition of the Development, Production, and Stockpiling of Bacteriological (Biological) and Toxin Weapons and on their destruction could charge the US with violating the Convention, which in 2001 refused to accept its protocol, which provides a mutual control mechanism. The charge could demand the disclosure of data on the network of clandestine bioengineering laboratories set up by US intelligence agencies in various countries on all continents. As a result of the investigation, the protocol could also be supplemented with sanctions against countries that conceal their activities in this area.

The need for an international control system for bioengineering research has been proven by known experts. Even if we exclude the deliberate development of the coronavirus as a biological weapon, based on the available data on its origin, the next most likely theory is that a virus synthesized by US, Australian, and Chinese scientists leaked from a secret laboratory into the environment. According to Klotz,[1] in each of the 14 known laboratories, there is research on airborne viruses, and there is a 0.246% chance that a pathogenic virus similar to the 1918 Spanish pandemic could cause an epidemic of 50–100 million casualties. According to a study of virus leaks in US laboratories, 67%–80% of them are due to human error. The goals of harmonious development based on the growth of people's well-being, which are characteristic of an integrated world economic order, may be interpreted differently in different countries and do not imply international solidarity per se. The existing regional associations of countries trusting each other and building mutually beneficial cooperation on the principles of the new world economic order could be used as a basis for the creation of a global anti-war coalition.

The goals of harmonious development based on the growth of people's well-being, which are characteristic of an integrated world economic order, may be interpreted differently in different countries and do not imply international solidarity per se. The existing regional associations of countries trusting each other and building mutually advantageous cooperation on the principles of the new world economic order may be used as a basis for a global anti-war coalition.

Regional economic alliances of countries seeking to combine national competitive advantages and achieve synergistic effects of accelerated economic development could be an important asset in building up such a coalition. They would contribute to the formation of an integrated world economic order by elaborating common norms of regulation and programs of economic development. Such "integration of integrations," as conceived by Russian President Vladimir Putin, could be the basis for such a coalition. Putin envisaged that this "integration of integrations" could form the basis of the GEP. The EU should not be discounted in this context. At present, the EU strategy is subordinated to the common interests of US-European big capital, which receives unlimited refinancing from the ECB. It is, however, subordinate to the US strategy. EU regulators implicitly follow Washington's lead in the global hybrid war unleashed by the US. Although many European states and corporations suffer losses from US sanctions, they have no means of influencing the European Commission's policies.

In this context, the EU should not be discounted. These days, the EU strategy is subordinated to the common interests of US-European big capital, which receives unlimited refinancing from the ECB. It is, however, subordinate to the US strategy. EU regulators implicitly comply with Washington's directives within the framework of the US global hybrid warfare. Although many European states and corporations suffer losses from US sanctions, they have no means of influencing the European Commission's policies.

The EU's governance structure conforms to the principles of the outgoing imperial world order. It is too centralized, bureaucratic, and formalized, the decision-making system complicated by cumbersome approvals and subject to manipulation by both external and internal power lines of the capitalist oligarchy. A prime example of such manipulation was the forcing of all EU leaders to sign the illegitimate association agreement with Ukraine, led by Nazi criminals who carried out a violent coup d'état in Kyiv under the leadership of US special services.

There is, however, the potential for the EU to acquire an independent strategy in line with the national interests of its constituent countries. This, however, would require extraordinary efforts on the part of their political elites, who are clearly not yet ready for it. Perhaps after Brexit, US pressure on European political elites will lessen. But it will likely take a generational shift for them to regain their national identity. Or perhaps, as a result of the humanitarian catastrophe that the collapse of European multiculturalism has led to, the EU will sink into ideological prostration and lose the opportunity to form a common strategy.

12.2 The Transition to a New World Monetary System

The primary tasks of the anti-war coalition should be to end US aggression and create an economic security zone in Eurasia. The easiest way to do this is through the dedollarization of mutual trade, and the dumping of US debt and joint investments, which will lead to the collapse of the dollar financial pyramid and the global money issue-based US military and political power. This process is already underway. According to SWIFT, the share of US dollars in the international payments market was 40.9% in May 2020, down from 44.1% in March.[2] A couple of years ago, the share was 60%, and decades ago, it was as high as 80%. The share of the US dollar in total foreign exchange reserves of IMF member countries has fallen from 72% in 2000 to 60% today. The share of non-residents holding US Treasuries is also falling to 44% in 2020, down from 49% in 2010.

Thus, the process of fleeing from the dollar is in full swing. It has already acquired steadily increasing trends, which makes it possible to predict the imminent establishment of a new international monetary and financial architecture based on the principles of international law, mutual benefit, fairness, and respect for national sovereignty.

The swelling of the existing global financial system since the 2008 global financial crisis by transferring private risks to the global (system-wide) level through the exponential increase in the issuance of the US dollar and other world reserve currencies and government debt of issuing countries, as well as delaying long-overdue changes makes the transition from a crisis and instability in the world economy into a sustainable growth regime increasingly difficult. It needs to be addressed as a combination of the macroeconomic, geopolitical, technological, and institutional dimensions, taking into account the feedback loops between different areas of regulation and the patterns of long-term economic development.

The futility and danger of the persistence of existing global imbalances and the accumulation of latent systemic risks require a new approach to the formation of a system of requirements for international cooperation based on a system of transparent, equitable, and interrelated principles. It has been shown above that the ongoing global economic crisis is the result of the exhaustion of opportunities for balanced growth of the world economy within the existing technological and world economic patterns. This is manifested in a combination of monetary and financial imbalances, disorderly financial markets and institutions, structural imbalances, growing international tensions, escalating regional military conflicts, the chaotization of vast territories, and the erosion of international law. The exit from the crisis to a new wave of sustainable economic growth is possible if financial stabilization measures are taken simultaneously, regulation of the financial market, banking, financial, and investment institutions are increased, growth of a new technological pattern, and progressive structural changes are stimulated, and institutions of a new world economic pattern are formed. At the same time, the fundamental causes of the global crisis must be addressed, of which the following are the most important ones:

(1) The impossibility of conflict-free resolution of contradictions generated by liberal globalization within the framework of the existing world economic order (economic, social, political, etc.)

(2) The uncontrolled emission of the world's reserve currencies by the monetary authorities of the G7 countries leading to the abuse of the monopoly position by the emitters in their own interests at the cost of growing imbalances and destructive trends in the global financial and economic system

(3) Inability of the existing mechanisms to regulate operations of banking and financial institutions to provide protection against excessive risks and the emergence of financial bubbles

(4) Exhaustion of the limits of growth of the dominating technological model and inadequate conditions for the emergence of a new model, including a lack of investment for the widespread implementation of the clusters of basic technologies that make it up

Large-scale investments in the development of production facilities of the new technological pattern and fundamental changes in the institutional system of economic reproduction with the transition to the new world economic pattern are required in order to get out of the state of crisis turbulence into a sustainable economic growth mode.

Preventing a catastrophic scenario of the global crisis requires eliminating its causes and creating stable conditions for the functioning of the global financial market and the movement of long-term investment, international monetary and financial exchange on a mutually beneficial basis, the development of international industrial cooperation, global trade in goods and technology. These conditions should enable national monetary authorities to arrange credit for the development of production of a new technological pattern and modernization of the economy on its basis, stimulating innovation and business activity in promising areas of economic growth. For this purpose, countries-issuers of world reserve currencies should guarantee their sustainability by keeping certain limits on the size of public debt, balance of payments, and trade deficits. They must also comply with relevant requirements to ensure transparency in the issuance mechanisms of their currencies, to permit their smooth exchange for all assets traded in their territory, including new technologies, and to provide a domestic refinancing regime for foreign banks that meet the established criteria of soundness and transparency. In order to increase the responsibility of issuers of reserve currencies, they could commit themselves to allow other countries to conduct currency swaps with them. This would enable issuers of the other currencies to have access to the amount of "cheap liquidity" they need, leveling the cost of capital and eliminating the adverse effects of credit dumping by global reserve currency issuers that have long maintained quasi-zero or even negative real interest rates.

It is also necessary to link the right to issue world trade and reserve currencies with the obligations of the issuer to ensure the openness of its market for goods, services, labor, and capital, a free regime of technology, and capital transfer. In this case, there will be a long-term mutual interest of countries-issuers of global currencies and countries-providers of global raw materials and labor, which will contribute to the stabilization of the world monetary and financial system and sustainable economic growth.

An important requirement for issuers of global reserve currencies should be to comply with the rules of fair competition and non-discriminatory access to their financial markets. Meanwhile, other countries that comply with similar restrictions should be allowed to use their national currencies as a tool for foreign trade and monetary and financial exchange, including their use as reserve currencies by other partner countries. It would be appropriate to classify national currencies that claim to be world or regional reserve currencies into categories according to the compliance of their issuers with certain requirements.

The "polycentric" architecture of the global financial system will create a more competitive environment for market infrastructure organizations (exchanges, clearing houses, auditing and rating agencies, etc.). It is also relevant for the EAEU to create its own infrastructure organizations, including a rating agency, auditing and consulting companies, an insurance union, etc. The cooperation of several centers will increase the reliability of the entire global architecture.

A necessary element of this polycentric architecture should be the variability of international information exchange systems between banks and financial institutions, as well as payment systems. The current monopoly of global interbank telecommunications (SWIFT) is controlled by US intelligence services and used by them for political purposes. In 2015, China launched its cross-border interbank payment system, and a little later, the Bank of Russia announced its electronic messaging system between banks. However, these systems are still poorly used for international payments. Centralized efforts are needed to translate cross-border settlements into national currencies through these national systems.

At the same time as introducing requirements for issuers of global reserve currencies, there is a need for stricter controls on their movement to prevent speculative attacks that destabilize global and national monetary and financial systems. For this purpose, the G20 countries should introduce a ban on transactions of their residents with offshore zones, as well as prevent banks and corporations established with the participation of residents of offshore zones from participating in refinancing schemes. It is also advisable to impose restrictions on the use in international settlements of currencies whose issuers do not comply with the minimum requirements.

In order to determine requirements for issuers of global reserve currencies and monitor their compliance, rating by categories of their global acceptance, it is necessary to deeply reform international financial institutions, including IMF, World Bank, and Basel Committee, to ensure fair representation of member countries by an objective criterion of the relative weight of each of them in global production, trade, finance, natural potential, and population. A basket of currencies for the IMF's SDR[3] could also be formed according to this criterion, against which all national currencies, including the world's reserve currencies, could be determined. Initially, this basket could include the currencies of those G20 countries that agree to commit themselves to the above-mentioned requirements.

In accordance with the principles of forming an integral IHU, the creation of a new monetary and financial system, including the rules of issue and circulation of the global reserve currency, should be based on the norms of international law. There are many theoretical proposals for the introduction of such a currency, starting with Keynes's "banker" project. There is also a precedent for a supranational currency issued and circulating by international agreement, the euro. There have been many suggestions to use the IMF SDR as such. The theoretical groundwork and practical experience created so far suggest the following approach for the introduction of an international reserve currency consistent with the principles of the new WEO.

There are several options for introducing a legitimate global supranational currency. The most prepared instrument for creating a single world currency is the SDRs mentioned above. They are already used in international settlements and are quoted against the national currencies of all IMF member countries.

The SDRs are defined as an average exchange rate for a particular national currency relative to a basket of four freely convertible currencies (the dollar, the euro, the pound sterling, and the Japanese yen). In order to use the SDR as a supranational currency in today's environment, the range of currencies making up the currency basket on the basis of which the SDR exchange rate is calculated must be expanded. In the first stage, it should include currencies of G20 countries with weights corresponding to the average arithmetic share of the respective country in the global volume of banking system capital, GDP, territory, and population.

Implementation of international settlements in a single currency will sharply reduce the currency risks of exporters and importers, reduce currency speculation, and limit exchange rate fluctuations. At the same time, all SDR-denominated claims on borrowers (including bonds placed on international financial markets) should be accounted for in regulatory systems with lower risk ratios and belong to asset groups with a higher degree of reliability than assets denominated in national currencies.

The introduction of SDRs as a full-fledged currency should be on a voluntary basis and subject to the principles of equality of all IMF member countries and the full liquid asset coverage of SDRs. Oil and other commodity-exporting countries, whose economies have been hit hard by exchange rate swings, are most interested in such a transition.

Other approaches to the construction of a world currency could also be implemented. For example, it could be linked to a set of major exchange-traded commodities.[4] Several global currencies may also function in parallel, including so-called stablecoins," digital currency surrogates (tokens) denominated in grams of gold or other commodities. With the disruption of the global monetary system, manifested in the rapid appreciation of gold[5] (Figure 39), they could be in demand for both international trade settlement and capital accumulation.

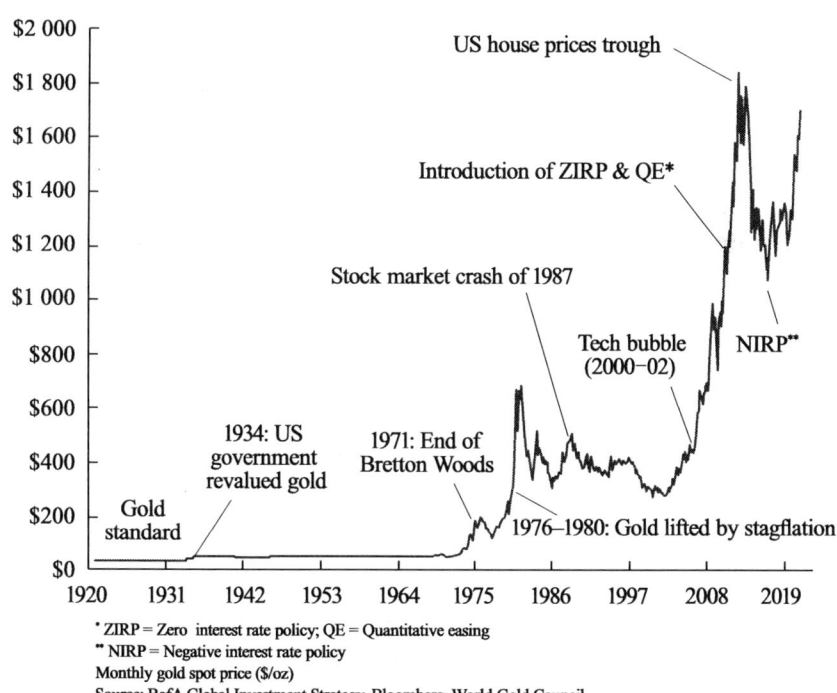

Figure 39   Dynamics of the Spot Gold Price per Ounce since 1920

The foundation of the financial architecture of the new IHU should be an international treaty based on a fair order of formation of the world financial market's regulatory system. The shares of national representation in international financial regulators and in the formation of reserves for the emission of the future world currency should be established according to the following criteria:

(1) A country's share of world GDP at purchasing power parity (PPP), taken as an average over a certain number of years
(2) The country's share in world trade
(3) A country's share of territory (as an integrated measure of natural, resource, and climate weight or potential) in the world's total
(4) The share of a country's population in the world population
(5) A country's weight in the current global financial system, measured through the parameters of both the country's reserves and the use of its currency in international settlements and reserves

In the process of establishing mutually beneficial cooperation between the EAEU and international partners in Greater Eurasia, attention should be paid to the transition to national currencies in mutual trade, dedollarization of economies, import substitution, and formation of full cycle value-added chains in the EAEU, as well as new logistical chains, unlocking transit potential and strengthening the EAEU system of joint financial institutions. Among other things, it is necessary to create a unified financial and trade and payment and settlement architecture for Greater Eurasia in the face of systemic problems and "denial of service" from the global financial and trade system, including the next:

(1) Forming a pool of currency reserves of the SCO countries (following the example of BRICS) as a basis for trade in national currencies
(2) Working out the concept of an international treaty to form a Eurasian payment and settlement unit based on the demographic, spatial, and resource potential of the Greater Eurasian countries
(3) The principles and roadmap for forming a single Eurasian exchange commodity space with pricing of basic (strategic) commodities without reference to exchanges and currencies of third countries

Nowadays, the IMF SDR basket partly takes into account only the latter criterion, which leads to unfairness and inefficiency in the global financial system.

Alongside the introduction of a world currency to prevent the catastrophic self-destruction of the global financial system, the following measures are proposed to restructure it based on the need for a transition to a just world economic order and the formation of the reproductive contours of the new world economic order.

(1) In order to reduce systemic mispricing of market riskiness of quoted assets in favor of one or another country, international standards of rating and credit rating agencies should be developed, and internationally harmonized regulation of rating agencies should be provided. Following the necessary reform of the IMF to ensure fair representation, it may be entrusted with the certification and licensing of credit rating agencies, whose ratings have to be internationally recognized. The same applies to the Big Four audit firms.

(2) Sharp reduction of speculative currency risks. By analogy with banks, all economic entities should be required to take an open currency position and limit it to a percentage of equity. It would be reasonable to introduce uniform financial accounting and auditing rules (based on IFRS and Basel III) for all market participants, not just banks.

(3) Recommend to national monetary authorities that they protect their monetary and financial systems from speculative attacks and suppress related turbulence, a system of financial and capital flow defensive retarders. In particular, such a "retarder" could be a) a capital allowance institution for foreign exchange transactions, b) a tax on gains from the sale of assets by non-residents, the rate of which depends on the period of holding the asset, and c) a tax on currency exchange transactions. For all three instruments, rates (norms) can be temporarily reduced to a minimum when the situation is favorable and increased when financial turbulence increases in order to slow down the inflow (or outflow) of speculative capital.

Narrowly understood (as purely financial) stabilization and the often proposed technical reforms of the financial system cannot ensure long-term sustainability and systemic global economic growth. This requires a whole series of interrelated changes in the world order at the micro, macro, and global levels: from changing the corporate governance paradigm to reforming the WTO, IMF, ILO, and other global organizations in terms of common rules of the game on global markets of goods, labor, capital, resources and technology and preventing any country from monopolizing these markets and procedures for developing and establishing the rules of the game (quality standards; stock exchange, insurance, auditing standards; intellectual property regulations).

An equally important component of the restructuring of the global financial, currency, and economic system is the establishment of international legal regulation of the use of telecommunications channels that ensure its connectivity. In particular, due to the growing share of e-commerce in foreign trade turnover, the share of payment applications on mobile phones in cross-border settlements, and the rapid growth of cryptocurrency turnover, transparent legal regulation of the Internet is of critical importance. Given the global importance of the Internet and other means of communication for the world order, it would be right to remove the issues of their administration from national jurisdiction and adopt (as is the case with other important global issues of international communications—sea and air transport, telecommunications, mail) international agreements and rules that exclude discriminatory access to these global infrastructures.

The transition to supranational regulation of the international monetary and financial system, the extension of international law to the circulation of world currencies, and the use of the global information infrastructure are necessary to keep the world economy connected: international production cooperation, global supply and value-added chains, mutual trade and joint investments by the countries concerned and their associations. They need to be safeguarded against the negative consequences of the hybrid war unleashed by the US. Iran, Russia, and China are already suffering significant losses due to the US's abuse of its dominance in the global financial market.

The financial embargo imposed by Washington has resulted in an outflow of about $200 billion of loans and investments from the Russian economy. In addition, the forced severance of economic ties with Ukraine has caused about $100 billion in losses from the disruption of industrial cooperation and depreciation of investments.[6] Even more damaging—more than 25 trillion rubles of underproduced GDP and 10 trillion rubles of unproduced investment—was the implementation of IMF recommendations by the Bank of Russia, which effectively played along with the aggressor by letting the ruble float and sharply raising its key interest rate in 2014.[7] This allowed financial speculators to crash the rouble, causing an inflationary wave and destabilizing the Russian economy, which plunged into prolonged stagnation. The Bank of Russia has effectively ceded control over the Russian currency and financial market to international speculators, resulting in a complete defenselessness of the Russian system of economic management against American financial aggression.

The US is also creating tangible problems in trade and economic relations between the countries of a potential anti-war coalition. For example, the threat of US sanctions has forced major Chinese banks to stop serving Russian clients, which has damaged mutual trade and investment cooperation. Banking services for trade and economic relations with Iran, which has a preferential mutual trade regime with the EAEU, have been blocked.

Washington's increasingly intrusive abuse of its ability to influence international monetary and financial relations and banks has forced us to consider the design of a payments and settlement system that is impervious to US sanctions and consistent with the principles of an integrated world economic order. The first steps in this direction have been made: political decisions have been made on the transition to settlements in national currencies, Russia and China have created their own payment systems and secure channels for the exchange of interbank information, and the countries have exchanged currency and credit swaps. However, the dollar still occupies a central position in pricing, currency clearing systems, and foreign exchange reserves.

Apart from Russia and China, all countries that are at risk of a hybrid war by the US and issuers of other world currencies, as well as those wishing to get rid of colonial dependence and non-equivalence of foreign economic exchange, are objectively interested in the formation of a new architecture of international monetary and financial relations. An anti-war international coalition for the transition to a new world economic order could unite the SCO, CIS, and ASEAN countries as well as the Latin American countries of the Bolivarian Alliance and the sovereignty-preserving countries of the Near and Middle East.

12.3 Approaches to the GEP

Russian President Vladimir Putin formulated his initiative to establish the CPA based on the regional integration contours emerging in Eurasia as follows.

"They complement each other in a flexible way and allow projects to be implemented on the principles of mutual benefit. We could rely on a whole network of bilateral and multilateral trade agreements with different depths, speeds, and levels of interaction, market openness, depending on the readiness of a particular national economy for such joint work, on agreements on joint projects in science, education, and high technology. All these agreements should be focused on the future, creating a basis for joint harmonious development on the basis of efficient and equal cooperation."[8]

"... We believe that this integration network, a system of multilateral and bilateral agreements, including on free trade zones, can form the basis for a greater Eurasian partnership."[9]

Through the practical implementation of the Russian President's initiative to create a GEP, the global institutionalization of the "integral order" model, embodied in a new integrated world economic order, can be carried out.

Based on the above characterization of the Integral WEO, the following main provisions and principal approaches to the creation of the GEP can be formulated.

12.3.1 Aims and conditions of the GEP

The goal of the GEP is to transform Eurasia into a zone of peace, cooperation, and prosperity. The aim is to create preferential regimes for trade and economic cooperation, develop mainland transport, information, and energy infrastructure, combine national development plans and harmonize international production and technological cooperation, move toward a fair system of monetary and financial relations, and end existing armed conflicts and prevent new ones.

In determining the means to address these challenges, the specific socio-economic and political structures of the Eurasian states must be taken into account. The GEP does not imply their unification. It is based on unconditional respect for the national sovereignty of the states participating in integration, non-interference in their internal affairs, preservation of the diversity of their economic and political culture as a necessary condition for fair competition of national jurisdictions, and joint development based on a combination of competitive advantages.

The GEP should be formed on the basis of a flexible system of legal norms, joint projects, and institutions, taking into account the diversity of interests of the participants and the purely voluntary nature of cooperation. Integration into the partnership can only be multi-speed and multi-tiered, giving each participant the freedom to choose a package of obligations.

Broad Eurasian integration is natural and objective. There is hardly a single state in Eurasia that is not involved in this or that regional association. It is based on centuries of historical experience of cooperation and joint creative activities of the peoples of Eurasia. The formula "peoples of one historical destiny of mankind" proposed by the PRC leadership confirms the idea of Eurasian integration based on the common historical experience of the Eurasian peoples, which was expressed a century ago by Russian philosophers.

The Russian philosopher Trubetskoy, discussing the prospects for post-Soviet Russia as early as 1927, wrote that the basis for the new unification of peoples would be an understanding of common interests based on centuries of history and experience of living together within a single statehood. At the same time, he stressed the need for equality of all reuniting peoples in the new entity and pointed to the threats of nationalism. Neutralizing the latter requires considerable effort to develop a correct understanding of history, a positive interpretation of shared historical experience as the basis for an optimistic image of a common future and its co-creation.

12.3.2 Prerequisites for the formation of the GEP

There are currently a dozen and a half regional economic associations in Eurasia with varying degrees of depth of integration and breadth of areas covered by the regulation. At the same time, only the EU and the EAEU have supranational regulatory bodies, while the others function as interstate ones. Most regional associations are aimed at eliminating trade barriers, creating free trade zones, and harmonizing technical, customs, tariff, and non-tariff regulations. Since almost all Eurasian states are members of the WTO, the norms of this organization serve as a natural basis for regional economic associations.

In addition to the standard regional associations (customs unions and free trade zones) established to form common markets for goods, services, labor, and capital, there are a number of regional initiatives aimed at stimulating investment activity and implementing joint investment projects, including large-scale programs to develop transport and energy infrastructure.[10] International banks and development institutions, both within the respective regional associations and across the Eurasian continent, play an important role in supporting such regional integration initiatives.

The pairing of the EAEU as a classic regional association focused on the formation of a full-fledged common market of its member states, with the BRI, focused on encouraging joint investments in large infrastructure projects, could serve as a model for the assembly of the GEP. Such a model combines the principles of free trade and the pooling of competitive advantages based on joint investments to achieve synergies and mutual benefits for all integration participants.

The single economic space model is currently operating in two regional unions, the EU and the EAEU, which have a common market of $17 trillion and $1.8 trillion, respectively, bringing together economic activity in countries with populations of 512 million and 182 million, respectively. The CIS, ASEAN, ECO, SAARC, GCC, and EFTA countries operate in a free trade environment.[11] Countries such as China, Japan, Vietnam, India, South Korea, Singapore, and Israel have free trade agreements with many countries in Eurasia. The EU forms associations with neighboring countries, providing for free trade relations, and has a common economic space with the EFTA, which, in turn, has an extensive network of free trade relations with many states and their economic associations, both in Eurasia and on other continents. The EAEU has free trade relations with Vietnam, Singapore, Iran, Serbia, and Montenegro, and talks are underway with Egypt, India, and Syria. More than 40 states and international organizations have already expressed their desire to establish a free trade zone with the EAEU.

A promising form of regional integration is China's BRI mentioned above, which aims to implement large-scale joint investment projects, including the modernization of existing transport corridors and the creation of new ones, uniting the economic space of Eurasian countries and facilitating trade and economic cooperation between them. One way or another, this initiative has already been supported by about a hundred states and international organizations.

Subcontinental free trade zones are gradually forming. ASEAN, comprising ten Southeast Asian states[12] with a combined GDP of $2.6 trillion and foreign trade turnover of $2.5 trillion, has concluded negotiations to establish a free trade area with China, Japan, and South Korea. A mega-zone of preferential trade and economic cooperation has emerged in Southeast Asia, with 30% of the world's population, 24% of global GDP, 25% of world trade, and 47% of global exports of high-tech products.

In addition to regional associations with preferential trade regimes, there are many agreements on dozens of international economic cooperation items, including trade in goods and services, removal of non-tariff barriers, simplification and harmonization of customs procedures, liberalization of access to financial markets, convergence of different norms and standards, intellectual property rights, development of international transport infrastructure (road and rail corridors), mutual access to public procurement, the development of international transport infrastructure, the creation of a common electricity market, harmonization of competition rules, mutual recognition of vocational diplomas, and the development of joint initiatives and mechanisms to neutralize regional and global conflicts. They all create the fabric of a new world economic order, of which international law becomes the fundamental basis. Its institutions were formed mainly during the imperial WEO period but acted mainly to regulate relations between superpowers and peripheral countries. The USSR and the US, occupying a central position in the world political-economic system, often did not consider it necessary to comply with it if their international obligations conflicted with imperial interests. The global hybrid warfare being waged by the US ruling elite is accompanied by a widespread violation of international law by the US. In integral WEO, such a situation, if not ruled out altogether, is limited both by the general interest of nation-states in cooperating and maintaining international cooperation and by sanctions, which should be automatic and binding on all, in contrast to the double standard policy characteristic of imperial IHU.

While Europe and Central Asia have already formed coherent regional groupings with supranational governing bodies in Brussels and Moscow, in the rest of Asia, the processes of regional integration are far from complete. The regional superpowers are forming their own centers of Eurasian integration. The combination of already existing preferential trade regimes, international development institutions, joint investment projects, transnational corporations, and consortia form the structure of the GEP, which needs to be given harmony, strength, and attractiveness.

12.4 Principles of the GEP

The principles of the GEP are voluntariness, mutual benefit, equality, transparency, and strict compliance with international law and commitments.

Voluntariness implies non-interference in the internal affairs of nation-states, as the EU and the US did in Ukraine by staging a coup d'état to force Ukraine's unequal association with the EU. Each state should independently and voluntarily determine its participation in these or those associations and commit itself to comply with the decisions it takes based on its national interests and the procedures established by national legislation. Forcing integration by organizing coups d'état, revolutions, and external sponsorship of partisan political forces in order to bring to power political regimes that please the customers of integration should be considered a crime against humanity, and the obligations imposed on the country concerned—as illegitimate, not recognized by the GEP participants.

"... We are convinced that effective integration can only be built on the basis of equality of all participants, respect, and consideration for mutual interests, without any political or economic diktat or the imposition of unilateral solutions. In our understanding, integration is about predictable, long-term rules, and it is about openness to cooperation with other countries and associations both in the East and in the West ..."[13]

Mutual benefit means that all participants in the integration process should receive tangible economic benefits from it, consisting of additional opportunities for socio-economic development, including increased public production, consumption, and living standards, increased employment, and improved competitiveness of the national economy. In the case of asymmetric distribution of the integration effect, when, as in the EU, some countries take advantage of the common market to the detriment of other countries, measures should be taken to adjust integration agreements and create mechanisms to equalize integration conditions.

Equality of integration participants means the right of each state participating in integration to choose the format of decision-making that ensures that its national interests are fully considered. At the same time, on a critical list of issues related to the delegation of sovereign functions to a supranational body, decisions can be taken by consensus, as stipulated by the EAEU treaty legal framework. The principle of equality concerns not only decision-making procedures but also economic exchange between integration participants, which should not be of a non-equivalent nature. Integration mechanisms should dampen the processes of non-equivalent distribution of incomes, including the distribution of intellectual, monopoly, administrative rents, or the shadow age from the issue of an international reserve currency, which is typical for trade between countries of different levels of development.

Transparency concerns all regulatory functions transferred to the supranational level, as well as those affecting the conditions of revenue distribution and efficiency of economic activity: customs control, currency, banking, technical, antimonopoly and tax regulation, and customs duty allocation in a customs union. Participating countries should see and understand how common functions of regulation and control are implemented by the national authorities of other states. Procedures for inter-state coordination and supranational administration should be fully transparent. In order to ensure this principle, a single information system of integrated regulatory processes, including national subsystems and integration segments, should work.

Compliance with international law and the obligations that each state undertakes in the integration process is an obvious condition for its effectiveness and for the fulfillment of all the integration principles listed above. While this is obvious in the actual activities of international organizations, this principle is only partially respected. A number of countries, referring to the primacy of their national legislation over international commitments, consider it possible not to fulfill both their commitments and the general norms of international treaties. For example, the US and the EU allow themselves to fail to comply with WTO norms by arbitrarily imposing economic sanctions against other countries.

12.4.1 Areas of GEP integration

Almost all Eurasian countries are members of the WTO and WCO, ISO, UNCTAD, and other UN sectoral and regional organizations, whose norms, procedures, and recommendations are a natural part of Eurasian integration. Many Eurasian countries are parties to international agreements on the formation of transoceanic partnerships and free trade zones, thereby linking the GEP to other parts of the world. Each of the states and regional groupings in Eurasia has its own network of treaties with other countries and regional groupings, including those located on other continents. Thus, the GEP cannot but be a multi-layered and complex association of countries, each of which has its own specific relations with other states and the resulting international obligations and limitations on its national sovereignty.

The GEP covers economic cooperation, including its trade, sectoral, invest-ment, innovation, science, and technology components. It does not deal with the politico-military, religious, and ethnic aspects of integration. Each of these areas has its own regional associations and international organizations, the specifics of which should not interfere with the formation of the GEP.

The priority areas where the establishment of a GEP can bring additional integration effects are "to make the movement of goods in the Eurasian space the fastest, most convenient, unencumbered"[14] and "customs, sanitary and phy-tosanitary control, sectoral cooperation and investment, protection of intellectual property rights.[15] This could start with simplification and unification of sectoral cooperation and investment regulations, as well as non-tariff measures in the field of technical and phytosanitary regulation, customs administration, and protection of intellectual property rights, moving gradually toward the reduction and then elimination of tariff restrictions …"[16]

In the area of customs regulations, harmonization of customs clearance and control standards could be proposed on the basis of the Automated System for

Customs Data Processing (ASYCUDA) program, the introduction of which in over 90 UNCTAD member countries has helped to simplify customs clearance processes. This system would allow most of the cargo traffic carried out by bona fide traders in the Eurasian landmass to be conducted in a "green corridor" mode.

Norms of sanitary, veterinary, and phytosanitary control are unified in the EAEU on a modern scientific basis and can be offered as a basis for harmonization to all states and regional associations in Eurasia.

Sectoral cooperation has many components, among which transport, telecommunications, fuel and energy, and agro-industrial complexes have the greatest integration effect. ... Comprehensive development of infrastructure, including transport, telecommunications, and energy, should be the basis for effective integration …"[17]

The transport sector and transport infrastructure development traditionally occupy a key position in Eurasian integration projects, including the conjunction of the EAEU and the B&R concept. Efforts are being made to modernize and further develop the main Eurasian transport corridors (road and rail). A promising form of large-scale joint investment projects in this area is the creation of interstate consortia, whose participants could include both public and private corporations, banks and other development institutions, and national, regional, and local authorities. By pooling capital, technology, land, and production facilities, such consortia with supranational management structures could create development corridors on a concessionary basis, connecting production and technological potentials of Eurasian countries.

This approach will open up new opportunities for regional development, increase their investment attractiveness, intensify interregional cooperation, and accelerate the growth of economic sectors. At the same time, the task of optimizing organizational schemes for the distribution of revenues from the integrated use of the transport and logistics infrastructure of the GEP member states should be solved in accordance with their national interests.

The work in this area should be started within the framework of the EAEU and China's BRI. The implementation of the Trans-Eurasian Development Belt project, which is being developed by the Russian Academy of Sciences, could provide a sufficiently strong impetus for this.[18] It links projects to create trans-Eurasian high-speed highways with the construction of "smart cities," the development of natural resource deposits, and the modernization of the economies of the integrated countries on the basis of a new technological paradigm. The creation of common electricity markets and transcontinental fiber-optic communication lines could be part of this work. It should include the harmonization of technical and economic regulations, safety standards, and guarantees for the protection of capital investments.

Cooperation in telecommunications could also include cyber security issues. Modern information technology not only connects countries and continents, forming a single information space, but is also used for illicit purposes by both criminal networks and individual states. To counter this, it would be advisable, as argued above, to sign an international treaty on cyber security. Given the US opposition to its conclusion, such an agreement could first be concluded within the SCO-EAEC-ASEAN framework, with the involvement of Japan, South Korea, and other interested Eurasian states.

An important element of this agreement should be the legal regulation of the functioning of the Eurasian segment of the Internet and other global information systems, taking matters of their administration out of national jurisdiction into the international legal arena and establishing rules to rule out any discrimination against consumers on national grounds. It would also be advisable to introduce a common system for the certification and testing of equipment operated in the signatory countries.

Other issues of regulating Eurasian cyberspace can also be addressed in the framework of the GEP. This includes the tasks of identifying persons working in Eurasian information and communication networks, combating tax evasion and illegal export of capital, as well as illegal business activities on the Internet, including e-commerce and financial services.

The fuel and energy sector has traditionally been an area of competitive advantage for Russia. The EAEU is consistently working on the formation of a Eurasian energy market, including its gas, oil, and electricity components, which should be operational within the common economic space from 2025. An important part of this work should be the development of the Eurasian pipeline network for the modernization and development of which interstate consortia could be created.

In the agro-industrial sector, the main task is to harmonize national and regional markets with an optimal combination of the competitive advantages of Eurasian countries. One should strive to eliminate tariff and non-tariff barriers, harmonize national food standards, and create food exchanges and regional pricing and wholesale distribution centers in the countries that have competitive advantages in the production of relevant products. An important area for the population is the development of the Eurasian Food Security System, which guarantees a sustainable supply of food products and provides, if necessary, food aid to all member states of the GEP. The development of agricultural science is a priority, including the creation of a Eurasian system for the development and circulation of transgenic seeds and pedigree material.

12.4.2 Implementation of large-scale investment projects

Compiling a pool of priority investment projects could be a key focus for the GEP. Russia is ready to take initiatives in this area, including the construction of an "energy super-ring" linking Russia, China, Japan, and South Korea or a transport crossing between Sakhalin and Hokkaido.[19]

Other investment projects proposed by Russia include the following:

(1) The construction of transcontinental high-speed rail and road transport routes within the EAEU, which could form the basis for filling the joint initiative with the PRC Chairman to interconnect the EAEU and the Single B&R

(2) Create a Eurasian aircraft construction consortium to produce aircraft of all types (using the full potential of the engineering schools of Ilyushin, Tupolev, and Antonov)

(3) Construction of a network of pipelines forming the framework of the Eurasian hydrocarbon market

A key component of the Pool of Priority Investment Projects could be the implementation of the aforementioned Trans-Eurasian Development Belt program, which was originally proposed by the Long-Term Investors Club, an informal international association of development banks. The program should integrate plans to create a new generation of integrated infrastructure, territorial and production planning schemes, and instruments to finance long-term direct investments in order to create a viable transport and communications framework for Eurasian integration. For its implementation, it is proposed to form an international consortium comprising interested corporations, investment institutions, and regional administrations. The creation of this consortium involves the allocation by national governments and regional administrations of land and rights to use natural resources, as well as the issuing of bonds and the formation of targeted unit investment funds whose participants will include national and international Eurasian development institutions, regional administrations and public and private corporations from interested Eurasian countries. Approval of the program and the establishment of the Trans-Eurasian Development Belt international consortium will require the adoption of an international agreement.

The pool of investment projects should be formalized through public-private partnership mechanisms using special investment contracts, the network of which will form the fabric of indicative planning for the GEP. The most significant investment projects in terms of integration effect should be financed jointly with international development institutions, including the AIIB, the BRICS Development Bank, the EDB, the IIB, and others. The most ambitious of them should provide for the establishment of interstate governing bodies, as well as an extraterritorial status, which requires the conclusion of relevant international treaties.

Currency regulation and the formation of a common monetary circulation system, not yet covered by regional integration processes, could become a crucial area of regulation of the GEP, in which almost all of the potential members are interested.

Eurasia is deprived of its own international currency, the role of which is played by the American dollar, the euro, and the yen. The consequence of this is a non-equivalent economic exchange due to the unilateral appropriation by the issuers of the world's reserve currencies of the amount of their use by other countries. Another problem that has recently intensified is the threat of destabilization of international economic relations due to the political arbitrariness of the authorities of the states-issuers of world reserve currencies. The application of economic sanctions against Iran, Russia, North Korea, and other Eurasian states by the US, the EU, and Japan outside of international law is now causing significant damage to Eurasian integration, and the states forced to use the currencies of these countries as reserve and settlement currencies. Their issuers abuse their dominant position in the sphere of international monetary and financial relations, irresponsibly applying financial embargoes, seizing accounts and assets, and paralyzing settlements against unwanted countries, their leaders, and enterprises.

Unless the formation of an integral global WEO can be launched on the basis of the goodwill of the leading G20 states, all the transformations of the global monetary and financial architecture described in the previous paragraph will need to be implemented within the GEP. The currently increasing global instability and the high risk, due to the absence of any rules for the circulation of global currencies, of their misuse by their issuers require consolidated measures from the GEP states to curb threats to the stability of international economic relations. This requires the creation of an autonomous digital currency environment in which payment and settlement, financial and investment, and currency exchange transactions necessary to serve mutual trade and international economic cooperation can be conducted in a user-friendly and profitable way for the member states of the GEP.

The infrastructure of the digital currency partnership environment should include the following:

(1) A digital supranational reserve currency of the GEP, pegged to a basket of currencies of the GEP countries with weights proportional to their turnover in mutual trade

(2) An issuing and clearing center operating on the basis of an international treaty of the Member States of the digital currency environment of the GEP, which provides rules for the issue of supranational currency, secured by the respective contributions of the Member States in national currencies, and their obligations to maintain stable exchange rates for their currencies in relation to it

(3) A currency exchange for the operation of the currency of the CPLP and regulatory measures to ensure the stability of its exchange rate, including by blocking its use for speculative transactions unrelated to the servicing of trade transactions and direct investments

The principles of reform of the global monetary system outlined in the previous paragraph can be fully applied to the GEP to create a Eurasian reserve currency. Its implementation could become a pilot project for the subsequent deployment of a new global monetary and financial system.

An international agreement defining the procedure for the issue and circulation of the GEP's supranational currency should also provide for a mechanism of credit distribution in this currency through the funding of international and authorized national development institutions recognized by the GEP. The currency of each country wishing to join would be included in the Pool of Foreign Exchange Reserves and participate in the basket of the GEP's supranational currency, and its interests would be considered in the distribution of credit resources issued in that currency according to an established algorithm. International settlements in a single currency would sharply reduce currency risks for exporters and importers, reduce currency speculation, and limit exchange rate fluctuations.

The issuance and circulation of the GEP supranational currency can be conducted using blockchain technology, which includes a registry of the complete transaction history of each unit of that currency. It allows for easy monitoring of its circulation, as well as the exchange of banking information and transfers, bypassing the politically vulnerable SWIFT while ensuring the highest level of reliability and trustworthiness. This is also important for countering corruption, money laundering, and terrorist financing, as well as preventing attempts at financial market manipulation and speculative attacks.

The advantage of the proposed approach is the ability to operate simultaneously in the new and existing monetary and financial systems. Gradually, the new financial platform as a more technological, legitimate, transparent, and secure form of payment will replace the existing opaque and unfair dollar-centric system. Improving the latter in the framework of the GEP is hardly feasible, as it implies serious international commitments by issuers.

As part of the work to form a common monetary circulation system, the transition to settlements in national currencies in mutual trade and joint investments of the GEP countries should be made as soon as possible. It would be expedient to stimulate every effort to replace the dollar, euro, and pound, which have become toxic in international payments and settlement relations, with national currencies of Eurasian countries that agree to accept the international obligations proposed above.

The development and implementation of a system of measures to create a fair and efficient system of international financial and economic relations, providing the necessary conditions for sustainable economic growth, employment, and welfare of the population, should be an important task of the GEP, whose solution cannot be postponed until the long-awaited reform of the global monetary and financial system, a system of measures to create a regional monetary and financial system and international financial institutions in order to ensure stable, fair and mutually beneficial conditions for the movement of money, while deploying mechanisms for long-term lending for the development of a new technological mode of production, stimulating investment and innovation activity, can be implemented within the framework of the GEP.

12.4.3 Planning the establishment of the GEP

To harmonize and fully realize the scientific and production potential of Eurasia and stimulate the spread of socially significant achievements of the new technological paradigm, a system of strategic planning for Eurasian socio-economic development should be deployed. It should include the elaboration of long-term forecasts of scientific and technological development; identification of prospects for development of the region's economy, regional economic associations, and large national economies; identification and elimination of imbalances in trade and bottlenecks that hinder full use of available resources; identification of opportunities for overcoming existing imbalances, including gaps in the level of development of the GEP countries; selection of priority development areas. In order to implement the latter, the GEP planning system should include indicative plans developed by the expert and business communities of the participating countries together with authorized international organizations.

A Programme should be developed in order to establish the GEP, its sources of financing identified, a Pool of priority investment projects in a public-private partnership format with financing mechanisms, a List of international treaties and joint projects, and a Road Map drawn up.

The program should define targets, objectives, resolution mechanisms, and implementation stages for building the GEP. In the future, it will include strategic plans for the development of the GEP. It is proposed to build on the successful experience of the GEP countries in long-term planning of scientific, technological, and socio-economic development.

The largest and most influential Eurasian states have powerful development institutions and make extensive use of economic planning and state regulation tools in the public' interest. Combining their scientific and analytical resources to elaborate forecasts of Eurasian development in the context of structural changes taking place in the world, strategic and indicative development plans of the GEP will enhance the capacity of member states to develop their scientific, technological, and production potentials, and help concentrate resources to solve partnership tasks.

In order to be realistic, the program for establishing the GEP should include sources of financing for the activities included in it, as well as for the interstate and supranational regulatory institutions to be established. For this purpose, it would be advisable to introduce a globally justified currency exchange transaction tax of 0.001 per transaction volume, levied in accordance with the national laws of the GEP member states and remitted to the authorized bodies of the GEP. This will also contribute to reducing turbulence in the Eurasian financial market. The funds collected from this tax could be used under the supervision of international organizations authorized by the partnership countries for the maintenance of its bodies and the implementation of Eurasian social programs.

The introduction of this tax at the Eurasian level would provide a powerful impetus not only for regional economic integration but also for the formation of a new global WEO. Given the centrality of Southeast Asian and EAEU countries in the Asian century capital accumulation cycle, this tax would actually be levied on most international transactions and spent for the benefit of the GEP. This would create incentives for other countries to adopt it and form the integral WEO system described in the first section. Until then, all of its elements could be established within the GEP.

In particular, in the context of the structural reorganization of the world economy on the basis of a new technological mode, the creation of an international educational network of leading Eurasian universities to train citizens of developing and underdeveloped countries, as well as the implementation of retraining programs for the unemployed in developed countries with new qualification requirements, will be of particular importance for employment and the realization of the human potential of the GEP countries. This will make it possible to reinforce the economical functionality of the GEP with the provisions of humanitarian cooperation necessary for the harmonious development of the economy, to update the common cultural, historical, and spiritual heritage, and contribute to the development of an ideological platform for harmonious coexistence of the peoples of Eurasia in the 21st century.

The creation of the GEP can become a prototype of the Integral World Economy, the establishment of which corresponds to the interests of the overwhelming majority of mankind. It opens up new opportunities for socio-economic development by combining STP with the harmonization of the interests of various social groups on the basis of the rise of social welfare. At the same time, it does not infringe on anyone's interests, including the ruling elite of capitalist countries. It only puts a limit to its global dominance by subordinating the movement of global capital to the aims of socio-economic development by stimulating direct investment and stopping speculative attacks that threaten macroeconomic stability.

The global assembly of an anti-war coalition also requires an ideology capable of resisting the anti-human doctrines of trans- and post-humanism as implemented by the global capitalist oligarchy.

NOTES

1. L. Klotz, "The Pandemic Risk of an Accidental Lab Leak of Enhanced Flu Virus: Unacceptably High," *Bulletin of the Atomic Studies*, June 26, 2020.
2. Wang Wen, "China Confident 'De-dollarization' Is Fast Underway Amid Tense Times," *The Global Times*, July, 20, 2020.

3. Special Drawing Rights (SDR) or SDRs are an artificial reserve and payment instrument issued by the IMF. It is in non-cash form only in the form of bank account entries. Banknotes have not been issued.

4. M. Gelvanovsky, "The Convertibility of the Russian Ruble as a Factor Enhancing the Competitiveness of the National Economy in the Context of Globalisation" (Moscow: Vestnik of the Russian State University for the Humanities, 2007).

5. The current gold price is at just above $1,700 per troy ounce; the record high for gold was 2011 ($1,900); BofA Research predicts that the gold price will rise to $3,000 over the next year and a half as central banks and governments double their balance sheets and budget deficits.

6. L. Kosikova, "The Newest Ukrainian Shocks to the Russian Economy (on the Impact of the "Post-Maidan" Crisis in RU on Reproduction Processes in Russia)," *Russian Economic Journal*, no. 4 (2017).

7. S. Glazyev., "Sanctions of the US and the Policy of Bank of Russia: Double Blow to the National Economy," *Voprosy Economiki*, no. 9.

8. From a speech by Russian President Vladimir Putin at the Plenary Session of the St. Petersburg Economic Forum (St. Petersburg, June 17, 2016).

9. From a speech by Russian President Vladimir Putin at the Plenary Session of the Eastern Economic Forum (Vladivostok, September 3, 2016). Putin at the Plenary Session of the Eastern Economic Forum (Vladivostok, September 3, 2016).

10. Tkachuk S., "EAEU and the All-In-One (The External Contour of Eurasian Integration)," *Russia in Global Affairs*, no. 3 (2016), 94–110.

11. ECO: Economic Cooperation Organization (Afghanistan, Azerbaijan, Iran, Kazakhstan, Kyrgyzstan, Pakistan, Tajikistan, Turkey, Turkmenistan, Uzbekistan); SAARC: South Asian Association for Regional Cooperation (Afghanistan, Bangladesh, Bhutan, Maldives, Nepal, Pakistan, India, Sri Lanka); GCC: Gulf Cooperation Council (Bahrain, Kuwait, Oman, Qatar, Saudi Arabia, UAE); EFTA: European Free Trade Association (Iceland, Liechtenstein, Norway, Switzerland).

12. Indonesia, Malaysia, Singapore, Thailand, the Philippines, Brunei, Vietnam, Laos, Myanmar, and Cambodia.

13. From a speech by Russian President Vladimir Putin at the Plenary Session of the Eastern Economic Forum (Vladivostok, September 3, 2016). Putin at the Plenary Session of the Eastern Economic Forum (Vladivostok, September 3, 2016).

14. "Putin's Speech at the B&R International Forum" (Beijing, May 14, 2017).

15. "Putin's Speech at the Roundtable Meeting of the Leaders of the One Belt and One Road Forum" (Beijing, May 15, 2017).

16. "Putin's Speech at the Plenary Session of the St. Petersburg Economic Forum" (St. Petersburg, June 17, 2016).

17. Putin's article "The XXV APEC Summit in Da Nang: Together Toward Prosperity and Harmonious Development" (November 8, 2017).

18. Integrated development of the Russian Federation territory on the basis of transport spatial-logistic corridors. Topical problems of the implementation of the megaproject "United Eurasia: TEPr - IETS" Ed. by Acad. V. V. KOZLOV, CORRESPONDING MEMBER OF RAS. Kozlov, RAS Corresponding Member A.A. Makosko; Russian Academy of Sciences. Moscow: Nauka, 2019.

19. Putin's article "The XXV APEC Summit in Da Nang: Together Toward Prosperity and Harmonious Development" (November 8, 2017).

GLAZIEV SERGEY YURIEVICH, Academician of the Russian Academy of Sciences (2008). He is the author of more than 400 scientific papers, among them monographs *Economic Theory of Technological Development* (1990), *Theory of Long-Term Technical and Economic Development* (1993), *Genocide* (1997), *Economics and Politics: Episodes of Struggle, Economic Theory of Technical Development, Market Training* (2004), *Nanotechnology as a Key Factor of a New Technological Order in the Economy* (2009 G), *The Strategy of Advanced Development of Russia in the Context of the Global Crisis* (2010), *Lessons of the Next Russian Revolution: The Collapse of a Liberal Utopia and a Chance for an "Economic Miracle"* (2011), *Ukrainian Catastrophe* (2015), *The Economy of the Future* (2016), *The Last World War* (2016), *The Battle for Leadership in the XXI Century* (2017), *Leaping into the Future* (2019), *Economic Development Management* (2019), *The Plague of the XXI Century: How to Avoid Disaster and Overcome the Crisis* (2020), *Beyond the Horizon of the End of History* (2021).

ABOUT THE TRANSLATOR

ZHANG ZHEN, Ph.D., Associate Professor at Zhengzhou University of
Light Industry.